Americans

From the Colonial Wars to Vietnam

at War

William J. Koenig

G. P. Putman's Sons, New York

A Bison Book

Contents

First Published in the US in 1980 by
G.P. Putnam's Sons
200 Madison Avenue
New York, New York 10016
USA

Copyright © 1980 Bison Books Limited

Produced by
Bison Books Limited
4 Cromwell Place
London SW7

Library of Congress Catalog Card Number 79 51034
ISBN 399 12401 2

Printed in Hong Kong

Author: William J. Koenig
Editor: Catherine Bradley
Designer: Michael Wade
Cartographer: Richard Natkiel
Indexer: Jim Farned

Introduction

War has been one of the important forces shaping American history and the way in which Americans have characteristically viewed themselves and their relations with other peoples. The century and a half spanned by the colonial experience was a time of constant threat of total and savage war which caused the military experience and perceptions of the colonists to diverge increasingly and sharply from those of Britain and continental Europe. The colonial period thus saw the genesis of a distinctive American military tradition and particular perception of war as it relates to Americans. This early development was reinforced by subsequent American experiences with war and gave rise to a set of historic American attitudes concerning war and national security which are still largely operant today.

Of the many facets of their military tradition, surely one of the most important to Americans is that it has been a tradition of victory. Americans are proud of the fact that they have never lost a war, at least not until Vietnam. This pride has been an important constituent in their sense of themselves as Americans. The victorious martial tradition in turn has been but one part of an overall legend of 'irresistible success, progress and victory' which holds that varying combinations of luck, technological and organizational ingenuity, abundance of material resources, and military prowess have enabled Americans to weather every major political, economic, and military crisis in their history. The deep impression that this legend has made on the American mind helps to explain its optimistic faith in unbounded progress, the efficacy of material solutions, and the superiority of American arms.

Related to and supporting the legend have been illusions of American political innocence and national virtue preserved from the colonial period. These illusions, which still animate contemporary policies and politics, stemmed not only from the Calvinism of Puritan New England but also from the later deism of the Jeffersonians, each of which believed that 'God's American Israel' had been plucked from the corrupt world of Europe to create a regenerate humanity and restore its lost innocence. Many of the early Americans believed themselves to be God's chosen people, a role which accorded well with the legend of success and victory.

These beliefs evolved early in the nineteenth century into a sense of the unique American mission and role in the world. This mission became an important part of the national spirit – idealistic, self-denying, blessed with divine favor, and dedicated to the enduring values of American society. There were many specific expressions of the mission in the nineteenth and twentieth centuries both military and non-military. The latter tended to focus on service and philanthropy on the personal, corporate, and national levels both domestically and abroad. In their international applications, these expressions all involved the extension of American wealth and political values to other peoples and have often been centerpieces of American foreign policy. The Fourteen Points of Woodrow Wilson, the Good Neighbor Policy and the Four Freedoms of Franklin Roosevelt, the Marshall Plan and subsequent programs of foreign aid, the Peace Corps, and most recently, the Carter human rights campaign all fall under this

of a people. Our suggestion in the following pages is that the experiences Americans have had in their wars shaped a distinctive American approach and attitude to war, military policy, and national security and then perpetuated these. We shall thus examine the main wars Americans have fought to see why they took up arms, their notions of how wars should be fought, their conceptions of strategy and tactics, and the evolution of their military policy and institutions. We shall also follow the changing nature of warfare, largely the result of the technological innovation which was important from the Civil War on and which has come to dictate the nature of warfare today. We shall however ignore the sporadic conflicts with the Indians after 1815 because these became the 'small change' of American warfare. If the Army seems to have been favored at the expense of the Navy, it is only because the latter service traditionally played a peripheral role until it reached the Pacific Theater in World War II. It has since resumed its secondary role with the exception of its nuclear submarines, one leg of our current strategic triad. The American military tradition has been far more focused on land than on sea.

Above:
Howard Chandler Christy's poster for recruiting women was put into practice on 19 March 1917 when the Navy authorized the enlistment of women, and some 11,275 saw service in non-combat duties in World War I.

Left:
The frigate *United States* was decked out with the flags of all nations for her launching ceremony in the Delaware River in 1797.

Above right:
A World War I recruiting poster inspired by the new and exciting prospect of air warfare.

rubric. Their sense of special mission and destiny has also been one of the two main motivations for Americans to take up arms, the other being of course national security. Up through the War of 1812, Americans fought in the main for survival, but from the distorted conception of national destiny bound up with the Mexican War to the mixed ideological underpinnings of the military effort in Vietnam, ideology has played an important if not primary role in American motivations for war.

Usually considered by historians mainly in terms of their causes and results, wars are in fact discrete historical events and as such are important vehicles in the political education

Americans have recently emerged from eight years of large-scale military involvement in Vietnam, involvement which has exacted a high price morally, militarily, strategically, and economically. The war came to be highly controversial during its long course and left most Americans puzzled and perplexed with a minority actively questioning the values of American society. Americans have fought many other wars, most of which were also controversial and engendered considerable internal opposition. Our expectation is that the examination of these preceding wars will place the military experience in Vietnam and its relation to our military tradition in better perspective.

Chapter 1

The Colonial Wars – Genesis

Before delving into the formative military experiences of the American colonists, it is useful to remember that they brought with them the military organization and technology of early seventeenth-century Europe and continued to be influenced by European models almost to the end of the nineteenth century. Europe itself was at that time undergoing profound changes in governmental and military organization. The feudal monarchies of Spain, France, Portugal, and England had begun their transformation into embryonic nation-states, a transformation closely related to the military changes occurring in the previous century. The continual and widespread warfare over national and religious antagonisms had made the sixteenth century an important period of military experimentation which had brought about the rapid development of military organization, tactics, and weapons technology. The significant innovations of the period were the appearance of the forerunners of the modern regimental chain of command and rank structure, a nascent officer corps through crown commissions to captains, and the gradual displacement of the pike and arquebus by the musket. At the same time, a trend toward the centralization of power in the hands of kings gave them increasing albeit still very modest control over the growing wealth of the new middle classes as well as that of the old landowners.

It was the early seventeenth century which saw the emergence of what is usually considered the first modern army, that of Sweden under Gustavus Adolphus. Having only won its freedom from Denmark in 1523, the newly Protestantized Swedes were gaining economically from the declining control of the Hanseatic League over the Baltic trade. Himself a pioneer in the development of military technology and a tactical innovator, Gustavus Adolphus drew on the new economic strength and national and religious fervor of his people to replace the traditional collection of mercenaries and palace guards with a disciplined long-service

Left:
A nineteenth-century lithograph depicting the arrival of the *Mayflower* off Massachusetts. The 102 Pilgrims sailed from Plymouth, England and landed in America on 11 December 1620.

Below:
Well aware of their military needs in the hostile environment of North America, the first Puritan settlers provided themselves with an experienced military consultant in the person of Miles Standish.

standing army. It drew long-service recruits from the local militia and required each district to support its own recruits, thus giving the Army popular foundations and local roots completely lacking in its contemporaries. The field appurtenances of the Army and the equipment of the individual soldier were reduced to increase mobility while a higher rate of fire was achieved through standard issue of muskets and paper cartridges. The increased fire power of the musket in turn resulted in a new battle drill as the troops were deployed in three parallel lines and taught to fire simultaneous volleys. It was the Swedish Army of Gustavus Adolphus which developed the technique of linear deployment and volley firing that subsequently became the central feature of battle in the eighteenth century. He also revised the roles of cavalry and artillery but most importantly devised co-ordinated tactics between all three branches of the Army.

Gustavus Adolphus and his successors used his creation to turn the Baltic into a Swedish lake for more than a century, while his military innovations were carried to England by English and Scottish soldiers of fortune and employed in the English Civil War of the mid-seventeenth century. The wealth of the London merchants and the sheep-farming gentry of the eastern counties provided Parliament with the finances for a professional long-service army, significantly called the New Model Army, whose greater morale and military efficiency was used by its New Model leader, the Puritan Oliver Cromwell, to defeat the more traditionally oriented Royalists and Scots. It was indeed the Puritan armies of the New Model which first wore the traditional scarlet of the British soldier and enabled Cromwell as Protector to become the first British ruler to conquer the whole of the British Isles. Founded under Henry VIII, the Royal Navy was also professionalized by Cromwell.

Whatever its military efficiency, however, the New Model Army was fiscally unsound. Its unpaid troops allowed the Commonwealth to fall when the harsh reality of military dictatorship and the fanatic policies forced upon the British public by the Puritan minority resulted in the restoration of Charles II in 1660. Regiments of horse and foot were established to protect the person of the new king but when his brother and successor James II brought Irish battalions to England to bolster his power and his Catholic policy, the resulting crisis led to the Glorious Revolution of 1688 and the accession of the Dutch Protestant William of Orange to the throne. Their experience with Cromwell had left the English with an abiding fear that a standing professional army could be used as well for internal coercion by an autocratic ruler as for external defense. The army was thus early identified in the English mind as the primary instrument of state oppression, hence the terms of 1688 led to the establishment of the principle of parliamentary control of military power. The power of the parliamentary purse provided an army for de-

fense as necessary but no standing army was permitted in peacetime without parliamentary consent. Further insurance was added by the Mutiny Act which made the wartime disciplinary authority of the Army, without which it could not exist, subject to annual renewal by Parliament. The threat which peacetime standing armies were supposed to pose to the liberty of the people was in this way reconciled with the real military needs of the state. The Royal Navy was not viewed as part of the threat and continued to develop as a unified professionalized organization whose peacetime funding limits were mostly the result of parliamentary parsimony.

England weathered the seventeenth-century challenge of royal absolutism and devised a constitutional limit on the military base of royal power. The other leading states of Europe, however, developed into absolutist monarchies legitimized by theories of the divine right of kings and the indivisibility

of sovereignty. The actual basis of absolutism was in fact military power. In a circular process, the slow centralization of power around the rulers which began in the sixteenth century enabled them to tap the resources of the country to pay for more military forces, which in turn made possible further inroads on the national wealth. The growing capacity of government to use the wealth of the community to create a state mechanism of bureaucracies, fiscal systems and national armies which were used further to enhance control over the community, represents one of the central developments in modern Western history, a development which was retarded in the United States but which still continues today. As the English writer Charles Davenant pithily summed it up in 1695: 'Nowadays the whole art of war is reduced to money: and nowadays, that prince who can best find money to feed, cloathe and pay his army, not he that had

the most valiant troops, is surest of success and conquest.'

France was the pioneer in this development. At the end of the Thirty Years' War in 1648, it had neither bureaucracy nor fiscal system but was near bankruptcy, with a motley army composed of a congeries of private regiments, and had little control over its constituent provinces. In 1700 royal control was exercised through a disciplined and articulated army controlled by a centralized administration able to field upwards of 300,000 men and maintain them there almost indefinitely. This transformation was primarily the result of the development of civil bureaucracies to administer not only the army but the finances of the state. The latter were further strengthened by the philosophy of mercantilism which saw the connection between a full treasury and military capability and between the revenues from trade and colonies to a full treasury. Mercantilist

Above:
The first Americans lived in constant insecurity. This picture shows a family of Puritans under attack. The Puritan migration lifted the population of New England to over 30,000 but the English Civil War meant the Puritans had less reason to leave England.

policies were deliberately intended to increase the wealth of the country in order to pay for its military and to use the military to protect and increase the wealth. It was at this time that colonial and commercial rivalry began to take the place of religion as one of the primary causes of international conflict. The French Army was the most remarkable instrument of state power yet seen in Europe and was copied by other countries even more than they aped other aspects of France under Louis XIV.

Equipped with increasingly effective military and bureaucratic apparatuses, the European monarchs of the eighteenth century did not hesitate to resort to war to strengthen their positions through the acquisition of territory, population and commerce. Though frequent, however, wars were limited in their scope and conduct. The dynastic and commercial motivations of these conflicts lacked the emotional appeal to move the general population which was by now wholly or largely disarmed. Peasants had no need of firearms nor did rulers wish to see these in the hands of bandits and potential mobs. With the loss of its arms, the general public also lost its sense of military responsibility and participation. The limited wars of the eighteenth century involved only a minute part of the population and scarcely touched the lives of the remainder. Mercantilist ministers shrewdly left the people to carry on their normal economic pursuits so as not to harm the fiscal base of the state.

The limited mode of warfare stemmed partly from the pragmatic requirements of mercantilism and partly from the development of rationalism during that remarkable period of innovative thought known as the Enlightenment. The rationalism of the early Enlightenment realistically saw force as the ultimate and perhaps indispensable sanction in human affairs and so accepted war as inevitable since some issues of national import could only be decided by that means. The genius of the Enlightenment was to reduce the devastation and effects of war through reason and law so that there was a minimum of disruption to the normal life of the community. It was further held that all men were entitled to equal rights under natural law and therefore abuse of civilians in war was a barbarous breach of the rights of humanity. Thus was born the humanitarian ideal, one of the important children of the Enlightenment, which for the first time isolated and specialized the military function in society.

In this restricted conception, war was fought not by enlightened citizens defending their rights and interests but by the dregs of society. The military had to be drawn from the unproductive classes of society such as peasants, the urban unemployed, and mercenaries since mercantilism did not permit the military to deplete the wealth of the state in any way. Recruits to the British Army, for example, were the sweepings of jailhouses, poorhouses and ginmills, vagrants, those forcibly seized by press gangs, and country bumpkins persuaded to 'take the King's shilling.' Rather than stalwart defenders of the community, soldiers were hired or purchased instruments of war in much the same category as ships, artillery, and horses. They were viewed with contempt by the civilian population and with extreme suspicion by their officers. The unreliability of the soldiers was controlled by harsh discipline, frequent and extreme corporal punishment, and strict and continuous supervision by noncommissioned officers. The armies of the day lacked patriotic spirit and élan and suffered from endemic desertion. By the mid-eighteenth century, most European states were forced to resort to conscription.

The officer corps of these armies tended to be manned by the younger sons of the nobility and the sons of the social-climbing commercial and technical classes. As one student of the British Army has noted, 'To pitchfork the knave or fool of the family into the army was the whole duty of a thoughtful parent.' The motivation of officers was most often social or business. Commissions were normally bought and sold while investment in the colonelcy of a regiment was considered an attractive business proposition offering a good return from malfeasance in feeding, clothing, equipping, and recruiting the ranks. Other than experience, there was virtually no professional expertise in the officer corps except among the engineers and artillerists who needed mathematic and mechanical knowledge.

Further refining the infantry tactics developed by Gustavus Adolphus, limited warfare raised massed formations of infantry to primacy on the field of battle. Armed with flintlock muskets fitted with ring or socket bayonets, soldiers were deployed in long dressed lines to exploit the murderous firepower of simultaneous unaimed volleys fired on word of command. The key was the line which depended on rigid drill and discipline since the smallest deviation could cause the volley to inflict more damage on neighboring comrades than on the enemy. Indeed, modern close order drill is directly descended from the linear battle drill of the eighteenth century. So important was the symmetry of the line that it was not uncommon for troops advancing under fire to halt in order to re-form their line. The volley had to be withheld as long as possible because of the limited range of the musket and then followed by a bayonet charge. Iron discipline was required to force troops to advance against musket and cannon fire at the standard cadence of eighty steps to the minute. The untrustworthy nature of the troops and the exigencies of 'linear' tactics made the generals of eighteenth-century Europe subscribe wholeheartedly to the dictum of Frederick the Great of Prussia that the purpose of discipline was to teach the soldier to fear his officers more than he did the enemy.

Above:
The British were not the only ones to settle in North America. The Dutch settled on Manhattan Island and founded the province of the New Netherlands. The Swedes ventured to Pennsylvania and Delaware. Above, the Swedes negotiate the purchase of land from Indians.

Deploying into line required time and a considerable expanse of level ground to accommodate the broad frontage of the opposing lines, thus battle could only be joined with the consent of both sides since one had only to withdraw to inappropriate terrain to decline. When battle did occur, the volleys discharged into massed ranks caused casualty rates of 30–50 percent. Since the line was not really adaptable to pursuit, which was officially forbidden in many armies owing to the fear of desertion in the confusion, a complete victory was a rare occurrence. Recruits were scarce and required at least two years to train in the exactitudes of linear warfare, hence generals were not anxious to waste these expensive commodities nor did the limited objectives of war justify bloody encounters. Apart from the scarcity of military manpower, armies remained small owing to the difficulties of maneuvering large forces, the problems of supply in the field, and the generally undeveloped road system of the time. The French marshal Maurice de Saxe held the view that to have in excess of 45,000 men in a field army was only an embarrassment to its general. The conduct of war was also dictated by the seasons as the roads had to be passable, the weather dry enough for flintlock muskets to be usable, and green forage available for the horses.

The result of these factors was that war acquired the character of a great game of maneuver and counter-maneuver, march and counter-march, diversion and deception. The essence of generalship was to menace the enemy's lines of communication and maneuver him into an inferior position so that he would have to fight at a disadvantage or concede defeat. Battle became the last resort. 'I do not favor pitched battles, especially at the beginning of a war,' wrote de Saxe in 1732, 'and I am convinced that a skillful general could make war all his life without being forced into one.' However low the general quality of their men, the European armies of the eighteenth century demanded good generalship as the chess-like approach to campaigning required a reasonable intellectual caliber. Apart from generalship, the armies were virtually identical in weapons, tactics and logistics. Among the great artists of this style of war were de Saxe and his countryman Turenne who had a long and successful career. Only two generals transcended the norm of their times. Marlborough of England and Frederick the Great of Prussia were agile tacticians who retained a firm belief in battle as the decisive factor in any campaign in war.

This tidy mode of warfare and the attitudes underlying it remained dominant in Europe until the advent of the French Revolutionary Wars in 1793. It is generally thought to have had little relevance to the American colonists in the New World but in fact the two decisive wars of the colonial period – the so-called French and Indian War and the American Revolution – were in essence limited wars of the European style, only somewhat modified to American cir-

cumstances. The colonists in America had large and very imperative objectives in their wars but they remained to a surprising extent within the European military tradition of the eighteenth century.

The first English settlement in North America appeared at Jamestown in Virginia in 1607 and was followed shortly by the Puritan ventures of Plymouth, Massachusetts Bay, and their subsequent breakaway Rhode Island. Other colonies were founded as the century progressed until the establishment of Georgia in 1732 made the thirteenth and last colony. That North America would be a hostile environment for the English colonists was evident from the outset. The Indians were initially an unknown quantity whom the English had high hopes of converting to Christianity, but suspicion and overt hostility occurred almost immediately as the Indians attacked Jamestown within a month of its founding. 'There came the Savages creeping upon all foures, from the Hills, like Beares, with their Bowes in the Mouthes, charged us very desperately in the faces . . .' wrote a colonist of this first attack. Thus was inaugurated the long and savage struggle between white man and red man, a struggle which continued militarily until the beginning of this century and is now being waged judicially.

But the Indians were only the most immediate threat to the English settlements. To the south lay the weak Spanish colony of Florida centered on Saint Augustine while to the north was developing a thin band of French settlement reaching from Acadia

(Nova Scotia) up the Saint Lawrence valley into the Great Lakes region. Making concessions only to Portugal, Spain had claimed the right to the entire New World since 1493 but by 1670 had been forced by reality to accept formally the English occupation of the east coast as far south as the Savannah River. Although the disputed territory south of the river would later become a source of conflict, the Spanish presence in Florida represented no real threat to the English colonies in the seventeenth century. With a European population of less than 10,000, French Canada was also little threat until almost the end of the century since it was separated from the English settlements by vast stretches of wilderness. Locked in a mortal struggle for survival with the Indians, the English colonists only had to confront their European rivals in the New World in the succeeding century.

Separated from the mother country by an expanse of ocean which took months to traverse, the early settlements could expect little protection from home and were therefore granted full powers to conduct their own defense. The charter of Massachusetts Bay, for example, required its inhabitants to 'incounter, expulse, repell, & resist by force of armes, as well by sea as by land' any threat to the colony. The case was put more fully in the charter of Maryland granted to Lord Baltimore in 1632: 'in so remote a region, placed among so many barbarous nations, the incursions as well of the barbarians themselves, as of other enemies, pirates and ravagers probably will be feared; therefore we have given . . . as full and unrestrained power as

Left:
Virginians defend themselves from Indian attack. The growth of settlements in North America was slow. By 1619 Virginia had no more than 2000 people. The real influx came after the English Civil War when immigration raised the population of Virginia by 1670 to almost 40,000.

Below:
This engraving commemorated the first day in Jamestown, Virginia in May 1607. The first settlement was laid out with a fort, a church, a storehouse, and a row of little huts.

any captain-general of an army ever had . . . to summon to their standards, and to array all men . . . in the said province of Maryland, to wage war, and to pursue, even beyond the limits of their province, the enemies and ravagers aforesaid. . . .'

Defense required obligation, organization, weapons and training, hence the colonial charters included the power to raise troops and impose martial law. The colonists brought with them the system of compulsory military training through citizen militia developed in England under the Tudors and continued under the Stuarts, an institution which was not popular but accepted by the English people as normal and with which many of the early colonists must have had experience. The principle of universal compulsory military service was immediately established in Virginia which during its first decade was subjected to repeated Indian attacks 'and barely survived under the 'iron rule' of three successive soldier-governors who organized it as a complete military colony. After it had nearly been destroyed by Indians in 1622, the colony came under royal control and a militia system was formally instituted requiring all males between 17 and 60 to belong to a unit. The Puritan colony of Plymouth had also foreseen the security problem and arrived equipped with a supply of arms, some small cannon and a professional military consultant in the person of Captain

Miles Standish who was to train the Pilgrims in the martial arts, lead them in battle if necessary, and build the militia system. By 1636 fines were levied for missed training sessions and no man was permitted to establish a household unless he had the arms and ammunition required of a head of household. With their main settlement at Boston, the Puritans of Massachusetts Bay had a similar system. So manifest were the perils of the New World that other colonies followed suit and most colonists honestly discharged their military obligations.

The militia obligation required every freeman to possess a serviceable musket, powder, shot, spare flints, a sword, bayonet or hatchet, and other modest accouterments. Taxes paid for further stockpiles of military supplies in various public depositories against time of need. Militia companies varied in size and often subdivided into new companies as the population grew. Officers were appointed by the royal governors in colonies where the aristocratic tradition was strong and were locally elected or appointed by the colonial assemblies elsewhere. Whatever the mode, it made little difference since men of the better sort tended to hold these positions. Except as drummers, trumpeters and laborers, most colonies soon came to bar the enrollment of tame Indians and blacks, the latter having been first introduced to North America in 1619, the year that representative

Dessins de Sauvages de Plusieurs Nations, N. Orleans 1735

government also came with the convening of the first Virginia assembly.

Only in a local emergency was a militia company called out and sent into action as a unit. It normally met to drill a specified number of days annually and several times joined other companies for larger maneuvers. Training included marksmanship and rigorous and exact drilling, especially musket drills, on the evolving European model to teach the men order and discipline. The officers studied contemporary European military manuals such as the *Treatise of Military Discipline* published in 1727 by Humphrey Bland of London, a work especially favored by Colonel George Washington of the Virginia militia, and Richard Elton's *The Compleat Body of the Art Military* which gave instructions on duties, formations and the various musket postures. There was a necessary emphasis on control and discipline as unauthorized absence, disorderliness, and insubordination were punished by fines or corporal abuse. More personal means were also employed as a Virginia commander of the early 1700s recorded of a man who 'was drunk and rude to his captain . . . I broke his head in two places.'

When men were required for service in a major expedition against a distant objective, each local company was assigned a quota of recruits which was filled by volunteers or men selected by lottery, their local officers or sometimes the select men of the community.

These men were formed into new companies under new officers and given additional training. It was fairly common for a man selected for this duty to pay a substitute to take his place. This system left the local militia company intact and pursuing its routine functions which to modern eyes would appear as a combination training command and draft board. The Americans also adopted the old English custom that militia men could not be sent outside the borders of their home jurisdiction except in the event of actual invasion. This early colonial practice became the basis of the American tradition that compulsory military service cannot be imposed on the people solely at the will of the executive power.

The governor was generally the chief of the militia which also answered to the colonial assemblies and local town councils, thus civilian authority dominated the military structure at every level. The subordination of defense and the military to civil power was one of the key legacies left by the colonials to their posterity. As the Virginia Bill of Rights later expressed this legacy in 1775: '. . . in all cases the military should be under strict subordination to, and governed by, the civil power.'

Most of the seventeenth-century settlers were Christians and as such held some awareness of the pacifism within the teachings of Jesus but had little compunction about forcibly defending their families and lands. The people were well able to accept the common argument concerning the lawfulness of defensive and offensive war in a just cause. 'Self-preservation is a fundamental Law of humane Nature, and Christianity does not overthrow any such Laws but establishes them,' wrote the Puritan preacher William Williams. While the Reverend Ebenezer Gay of Boston warned his flock that there was no exemption from military service 'for Men, nor Women; for the Righteous, nor the Wicked; for the High, nor the Low; for the Rich, nor the Poor; for the Strong, nor the Weak; for the Old, nor the Young; for the most buisy; the new-married, nor the fainthearted.' The training days of the local militia companies provided the occasions for pastors to indoctrinate the men with what were known as 'training day' or 'artillery' sermons filled with Old Testament platitudes about the just war and casting the colonists as David against their enemies (the Indians, French, and ultimately the British) as Goliath. It was commonly accepted that the justness of a given war should not be questioned by the individual who should as-

sume that the government had good reasons, but blind faith in the wisdom of government proved less than satisfactory even in colonial times. Some preachers thus stated that the dictates of conscience should be followed if the injustice of a particular war was 'notoriously evident,' to quote the Puritan divine Cotton Mather.

There was no colonial consensus about the place of war, however, as the mid-seventeenth century witnessed the appearance of settlers who opposed all war and war-related activities. These new arrivals – Anabaptists, Mennonites, Moravians, and Quakers – posed a real and divisive problem for a society which existed under almost constant and immediate threat of attack. Despite the strictures and punishments meted out to them, the conscientious objectors steadfastly and consistently eschewed the military obligation and in fact the 'peace testimony' of the Quakers was the official policy of Pennsylvania from its founding in 1682. To the distress of its non-Quaker inhabitants, that colony had no defense at all until Benjamin Franklin organized a voluntary militia to

ward off attacks by French privateers in 1748. The situation became so serious that even the Quakers in control of the government finally questioned their own pacifism and stepped down. 'I have clearly seen that Government without arms is an inconsistency,' wrote one Quaker official. The American tradition of conscientious objection thus also had its roots firmly planted in colonial history.

Troubles with the Indians had begun almost immediately after the first colonists came ashore at Jamestown while similar problems quickly beset the Puritan colonies to the north. The division of the Indians into many warring tribes was noticed early by the colonists and became the starting point of their relationships with the Indians. To aid them in their internecine squabbles, most of the tribes near European colonies became loosely attached to the English, French, or Spanish which tended to accentuate the belligerent Balkanization of the tribes. Treaty relations with the Indians were a major responsibility of colonial governors who, in view of the fact that Indians initially

outnumbered Europeans, felt it necessary to impress upon the natives that the newcomers were in command. Troubles with the Indians were frequent and made a profound and permanent impression on the colonists, especially the apparently unprovoked attack which almost annihilated Virginia in 1622. Fear of secret Indian plots became obsessional and all Indians were seen as untrustworthy at best but basically hostile. God too was surely on the side of good Christians struggling against the pagans 'of the cursed race of Ham.'

The Indian style of war consisted of disorganized individualism. Decorated with war paint and armed with clubs, tomahawks and bows and arrows, war parties gathered by a chief or distinguished warrior bent on vengeance or plunder were endowed with great mobility and range by subsisting on parched corn carried in individual leather pouches. Once contact was made with the foe, a favorable position was established from which to launch or await attack. A shower of arrows was followed by savage hand-to-hand combat. Beyond the highly developed art of ambush, no tactics were employed. Accustomed to organized combat with well-developed tactics and still retaining remnants of the feudal concept of honor, the colonists found the stealthy, elusive, and no-holds-barred mode of Indian warfare fearful and abhorrent. A common view of the Indians may be found in the words of the Reverend Solomon

Stoddard of Massachusetts who complained: 'They are to be looked upon as thieves and murderers. They do acts of hostility, without proclaiming war. They don't appear openly in the field to bid us battle, they use those cruelly that fall into their hands. They act like wolves and are to be dealt with all as wolves.'

Although the colonies grew rapidly in military potential as their population increased, they had a low capacity for defense because of the rapid spread and dispersed nature of settlement. The problem of raising and concentrating military force in emergencies was never solved but only alleviated somewhat through the old English system of hilltop beacons, signals by musket shots, and heralds. The initial colonial advantage of firearms disappeared in the 1630s when the Indians obtained muskets. The Indian war of movement and sudden attack led to the erection of wooden forts, blockhouses, and garrison houses, rudimentary versions of the medieval castle or manor house. Since Indian attacks on fortified positions were neither skillful nor persistent, these provided a minimal solution to the problem of defense. The New England colonies with their more condensed pattern of settlement and larger communities had a greater capacity to resist Indian raids than did the colonies to the south, which had a much more dispersed and isolated settlement pattern.

Denied victory through offensive use of

their superior weapons and military organization by the hit-and-run nature of Indian warfare, the colonists found other ways of dealing with their Indian problem. After the murder of a European fur trader touched off the Pequot War in New England in 1637, the colonists virtually annihilated the entire Pequot tribe through destruction of its two main villages and the massacre of their inhabitants. As the Puritan chronicler Nathaniel Morton described the second attack: 'At this time is (sic) a fearful sight to see them thus frying in the Fire, and the streams of Blood quenching the same; and horrible was the stink and scent thereof; but the Victory seemed sweet Sacrifice, and we gave praise thereof to God. . . .' A savage war in Virginia in 1644 set another precedent with the systematic destruction of Indian crops as well as villages. But the climax of the early Indian wars came in 1675–76 in both New England and Virginia. King Philip's War involved an attack on the colonies of Plymouth, Massachusetts Bay, and Connecticut by a coalition of Indians centered on the Wampanoag tribe and its chief King Philip who hoped to roll back the tide of European expansion. After a number of initial disasters, the New Englanders coped by attacking and massacring Indian villages, destroying Indian food caches and crops, the use of Indian auxiliaries, recruitment of captured Indians, and adoption of different marching formations for rapid deployment. The foremost figure of

Left:
The American security problem was compounded by the presence of pacifist groups such as the Quakers and the Moravians, seen here negotiating the Delaware. They also settled in Georgia.

Below:
A representation of a Susquehannock Village. The American settlers finally resorted to destroying these villages as the only way of eliminating the Indian threat.

this war was Captain Benjamin Church of
Plymouth whose independent company of
colonial volunteers and Indian auxiliaries employed the new tactics with great success and
eventually trapped and killed King Philip. A
concomitant war broke out in Virginia in
1676 when frontiersmen embittered by Indian atrocities not only attacked the Indians
but also the inept rule of Governor William
Berkeley in what is known as Bacon's Rebellion. Under the audacious leadership of
an opportunistic young planter named
Nathaniel Bacon, the Virginians nearly ex-
terminated the Susquehannock tribe and
drove the governor from the capital.

These and other nameless wars served to
clear most of the northern Atlantic seaboard
of the bulk of its Indian population by the
1680s. Only the Delawares, the last substantial coastal group, remained to be forced
across the Alleghenies in the 1740s. The
other major Indian group, the five nations

of the Iroquois Confederacy, had early on
found a community of interest with the English settlers against the French. With their
large population, more advanced political
organization, and strategic position athwart
the Hudson-Mohawk corridor, the Iroquois
bargained with the English on nearly equal
terms and were to be an important factor in
the coming struggle with the French.

The English colonists thus gained the
upper hand, first by striking at the Indian as
the Indian struck at them through raid and
massacre and then by adapting their tactics
to meet the Indian in the forest on his own
terms. The colonial incapacity to defend
against Indian raids had thus led to a strategy
of retaliation and annihilation and to a growing desire for a definitive solution to the
problem of relations with the Indians. The
cost was high, however, as the exigencies of
the Indian wars brutalized the colonists.
Both sides killed indiscriminately, tortured
and enslaved prisoners, received and returned treachery. Once victory had been attained, there was a strong emphasis on complete submission and strict control to prevent

the tribe from regaining strength. As early as
1646, Virginia and Massachusetts experimented with confining tribes to specified reservation areas but then, as later, expanding
settlement made the integrity of such reservations difficult to maintain. After 1676,
however, reservations were increasingly seen
as a long-term solution to the Indian problem. By the end of the seventeenth century,
the superior and expanding population,
economy, organization, and technology of
the colonists had pushed the declining Indians from center stage to the wings and in
the process tested and proved the militia system, the only military instrument available to
the colonies.

The English colonies in America had been
little affected by European events until the
reign of James II. In furtherance of his absolutist ambitions, that monarch had combined
New York, New Jersey, and New England
into one super-colony called the Dominion
of New England for greater administrative
efficiency and subordination to his power.
Harboring the same Protestant suspicions of
the Catholic James as did their fellow Englishmen, the colonists in a popular uprising
had swept his autocratic and arbitrary governor Edmund Andros from power even before
news of the Glorious Revolution in England
reached the colonies in 1689. The English

constitutional crisis was deeply felt in America and, in an important portent for the future, the colonists had shown themselves ready to repulse by force of arms any intrusion on what they saw as their rights as Englishmen. But the events of 1688 in England had another more immediate effect on the colonies. Replacing James on the English throne, Prince William of Orange quickly opened hostilities with France and thus launched the War of the League of Augsburg (1689–97) in Europe. For the first time, a European conflict was projected to North America in a war between the British and French colonies. Known to the English settlers simply as King William's War, this was but the first of four struggles which in North America were undertaken to determine if that continent was to be 'French and Catholic or British and Protestant.'

Waged more or less independently of that in Europe with no military investment by either of the metropolitan powers, King William's war set the pattern for future conflicts in America. The English colonies had at least ten times the population of their French opponents but the problems of resources, mobilization, logistics, and distances for each side led to much of the fighting being carried on by Indian allies with only sporadic clashes between Europeans. The French were supported by many of the Algonquin tribes while the Iroquois, strongly oriented toward the English, aggressively attacked the French and their allies. Lacking any real offensive or defensive capacity against the superior English, the French quickly developed what was to remain their basic strategy in future wars, a campaign of surprise raids on the New York/New England frontier by Indians under French leadership aimed specifically at civilian lives and property. The campaign of terror demonstrated yet again the great military vulnerability of the colonial frontier and drew English military resources into ineffectual attempts at defense. This tactic not only led the English colonies to see the war as an intensification of their long-standing conflict with the Indians but to identify Canada as the basic threat to their security since, in the words of the Puritan Increase Mather, 'It was Canada that was the chief Source of New-England's miseries . . . thence Issued Parties of Men, who uniting with the Savages, barbarously murdered many Innocent New-Englanders. . . .' The perennial English war objective thus became the conquest of Canada with King William's War producing a plan of campaign that became standard in

Below:
King Philip, also known as Metacomet, was killed during the war named after him. His head was publicly exhibited at Plymouth for 20 years as a warning to Indians.

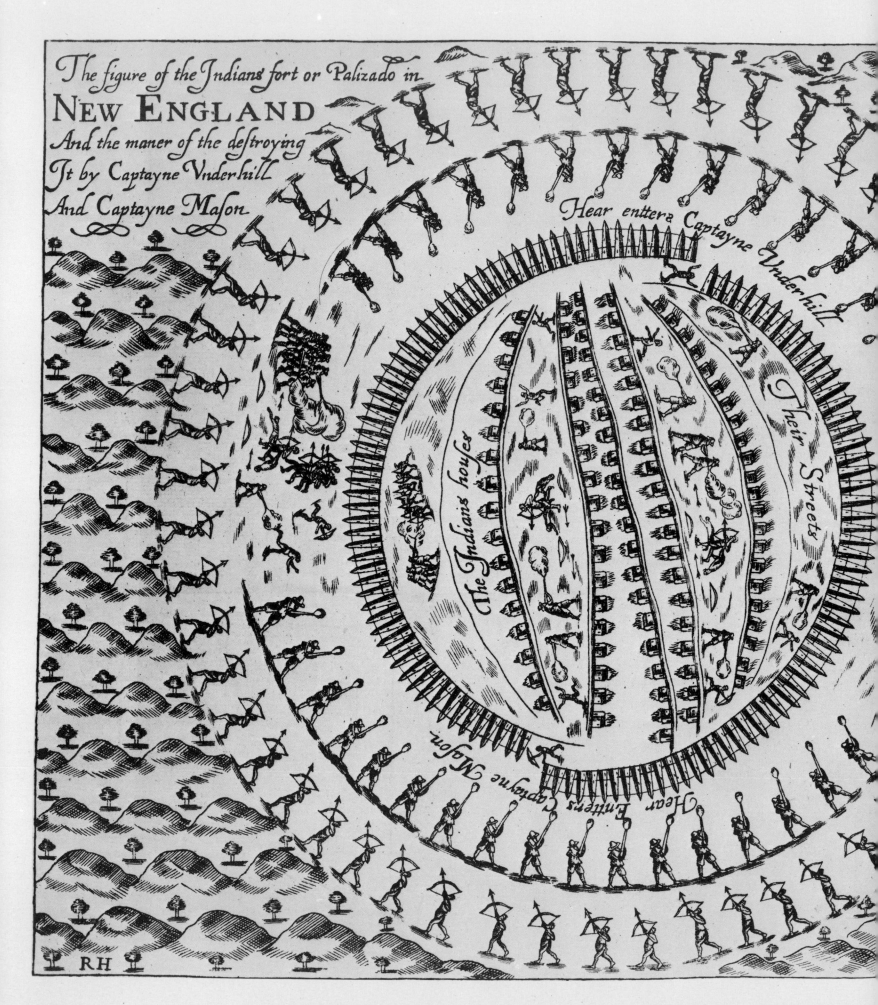

The figure of the Indians fort or Palizado in
NEW ENGLAND
And the maner of the destroying
It by Captayne Underhill
And Captayne Mason

Hear enters Captayne Underhill

Their Streets

The Indians houses

Hear Enters Captayne Mason

RH

20

future wars. One force moved up the Champlain valley from Albany against Montreal while a seaborne force was launched from Boston to strike at Quebec via the Saint Lawrence, thus forcing the French to divide their meager defenses. Led by Sir William Phips, the first such attempt on Canada foundered far short of its goals not because of French resistance but from the difficult problems of organization, terrain, weather, disease, Indians, and logistics in the wilderness, a fate which was to befall future expeditions as well. The barbarity of the French and Indian method of war, which the English colonists quickly imitated, and the perception of Canada as the source of threat combined with the fervent anti-Catholicism of the English to imbue these attacks on Canada with the zeal of crusades.

King William's War was followed by Queen Anne's War and then King George's War. The former was the War of the Spanish Succession fought by England, Holland and Austria against France and Spain to prevent Louis XIV of France from gaining effective control of Spain with its empire and the concomitant capacity to dominate Europe and the Atlantic commerce. The latter began in 1739 with a war between England and Spain over commercial rivalry in the Caribbean, colorfully known in English history as the War of Jenkins' Ear, which merged with the War of the Austrian Succession in 1744 when England belatedly joined Holland and Austria against Prussia, Spain, and France. Spanning the first half of the eighteenth century, these conflicts and the intervening period of 'cold war' in North America represent an intensification and broadening of the Anglo-Franco-Spanish rivalry for commerce and empire.

In America, the basic patterns of King William's War were repeated by each side. The French inflicted their war of terror on the northern frontier while the English launched further crusades against Canada. Gaining in appreciation of the imperial significance of North America and of the nature of the struggle there as a result of some effective colonial lobbying in London, the British crown now proved willing to commit modest land and naval forces to the attacks on Canada while the increasingly cosmopolitan colonials contributed some forces to British operations elsewhere. Thus 3600 Americans under Governor William Gooch of Virginia joined Admiral Edward Vernon's 1740 expedition against Spanish Cartagena in the Caribbean, a disaster of the first magnitude from which only a fraction of the Americans returned. Those who did, however, entered colonial myth as heroes. The great triumph of colonial arms came in 1745 with the capture of the great French fortress of Louisbourg on Cape Breton Island by 3000 colonial soldiers from Massachusetts, New Hampshire, and Connecticut under the amateur but competent leadership of William Pepperell, the 48-year-old commander of the Maine militia, supported by four British warships under Commander Peter Warren,

senior British naval officer in the West Indies. The progress of the little expedition was watched with intense interest by all the colonies where news of the victory touched off delirious rejoicing and even in distant London was celebrated with 'bonfires and an excess of all the usual concomitants.'

King George's War has further significance as it was in this period that a mutual antagonism between Americans and the British military establishment took firm root. The colonial soldiers in the Cartagena expedition experienced condescension and contempt from British officers and sarcasm and abuse from British NCOs. Justly proud of their military triumph at strategic Louisbourg which they viewed as an important gain in their quest for security, the colonists were further frustrated and resentful when that fortress was handed back to the French in the Treaty of Aix-la-Chapelle in one of the intricacies of eighteenth-century European diplomatic maneuver. As one student has noted, here began the emergence of 'an increasingly articulate distrust between the Englishmen of Europe and the Englishmen of continental America' accompanied by the growth of a conscious if nascent feeling of 'Americanism,' a development whose significance can hardly be overstated.

With France now established in Louisiana and Spain involved in the ongoing conflict, the southeast became a second theater of war and intense rivalry. The modest French moves in Louisiana and the Mississippi valley were misperceived by Americans as a grand design to block their westward movement and confine them to the eastern seaboard. A more immediate concern was the possibility of a combined attack by the Spanish in Florida, the French in Louisiana, and their Indian allies on the exposed flanks of the Carolinas and southern Virginia. A triangular struggle similar to that in the north emerged in the south as the English and French vied for the support of the six main tribes of that region – the Catawbas, Yamassees, Creeks, Cherokees, Choctaws, and Chickasaws. Local tensions exploded into the fierce Yamassee War in 1715 which galvanized the English crown into founding Georgia in 1732 as a military colony to protect the vulnerable Carolinas.

The English were gradually gaining the upper hand in the contest for the Indians throughout this period. The French came as traders rather than as settlers and thus presented little threat to Indian lands. They were also willing to fraternize with the natives at a level rejected by the English. One English observer wrote that the French 'live and marry among them, in short are as one people which last is not Commendable but gains their affection . . . but our Nation is quite the reverse Notion, and will be baffled out of this trade.' Far from being 'baffled out,' the English used their superior industry and transport system to meet the Indian need for a large and steady volume of trade goods at reasonable prices whereas all French goods had to be sent from France and transported long distances through the wilderness. The Indian dependence on the English fur trade for guns, ammunition, liquor, knives, blankets and other goods somewhat offset their well-founded fear of the pressure of English expansion. Caught between the rival imperialisms of the French and British, the Indians' attempts to attain some measure of security and trade with one or the other side only made them seem capricious and treacherous to their European patrons who made cynical use of their Indian clients. 'We only bring them in the Wars to leave them in the Lurch . . .' observed one Englishman.

King George's War had finally come to an end in 1748 with the Treaty of Aix-la-Chapelle which returned North America to the territorial *status quo ante bellum*. Britain and France were both exhausted and wished to avoid any further contest but the local struggle for empire in North America determined otherwise. The focus of rivalry now became the rich Ohio valley region claimed

Above:
Dashing General William Pepperell, a rich landowner from Maine, at the siege of Louisbourg, Nova Scotia in 1745, which was considered to be 'impregnable.'

Below:
The 1745 siege of Louisbourg was a great triumph for the American colonists. The French fort was handed back in 1748 at the treaty of Aix-la-Chapelle. In 1758 the fort was again besieged by Anglo-American forces and taken.

by Pennsylvania, Virginia, and Canada. Alarmed by English inroads on this strategic area, the French launched a successful campaign to drive out their rivals and intimidate the pro-English Indians. Governor Robert Dinwiddie of Virginia responded by sending a weak force under George Washington to establish itself at the confluence of the Allegheny and Monongahela Rivers (Pittsburgh), but the 21-year-old major and his men were quickly beaten and English power restricted to the eastern side of the Appalachians. This sad little defeat might have had little importance in an earlier day but the modern concept of empire had by then taken firm root. States and their colonies were seen as systems whose economies were increasingly interdependent. Conflict between rival imperial systems was no longer just territorial and commercial but a struggle between alien modes of life. Every advance or seeming advantage gained by a rival now called for a countermove in the strategic game.

The Ohio valley seemed to London distant and safe enough that a highly provocative response to the expulsion of the Virginians would not lead to the war which neither Britain nor France wanted. Deciding that the colonials were unable to cope with the trans-Appalachian threat of the French, London took a further momentous decision that not only led to one of the great wars of the eighteenth century but altered the nature of warfare in North America as well. Under the command of Major General Edward Braddock, a stolid veteran of more than 40 years experience, a major force of regular British troops was sent to America to fight the colonists' battles for them. Braddock's instructions were to move west to capture Fort Duquesne established by the French at the Forks of the Ohio and then turn north to reduce the other French forts such as Presque Isle, Leboeuf, and Venango recently erected along the northern frontier. This campaign would restore the vast western

Left:
Another episode from the French Wars. The brave Edward Braddock died in 1755 when his forces were ambushed short of Fort Duquesne.

Above:
Braddock's intention had been to drive the French from the Forks of the Ohio but he failed.

Right:
George Washington served as an aide-de-camp in this ignominious engagement. The myth of his early military leadership was built on this incident and it was claimed that had Braddock listened to Washington's advice on fighting Indians the defeat would have been averted.

territory partly occupied by the French and sever their lines of communication and trade with Louisiana. The London ministry was clearly gambling that such a massive counterthrust at the vitals of the French empire in North America would not lead to war but lead to war it did. Paris knew Braddock's instructions even before he departed England and imitated the British move by dispatching a force of French regular troops to Canada.

A rude frontier fortification garrisoned by only 300 French regulars and Canadian militia supported by Indians, the reduction of Fort Duquesne should have been a minor military exercise for the forces at the command of Braddock. The real problem lay in moving his troops, artillery, and supplies over 110 miles of densely wooded Pennsylvania hills. The standard military procedure of that time was to construct a road to the objective with periodic fortified supply depots but such an endeavor would probably have consumed the entire campaigning season. In a remarkable feat, Braddock pushed straight through and arrived near Fort Duquesne on 9 July 1755. On that fateful day, his advance guard under Colonel Thomas Gage neglected to secure some high ground on the right flank of the column and

then encountered and was overwhelmed by a superior force of French and Indians sent to block the advance. Another officer tried to reach the strategic hill with his troops but could not get through the press of Gage's retreating men on the narrow forest road. The entire column fell into confusion before Braddock could come up to retrieve the situation and he himself was mortally wounded. The colonial auxiliaries fought from the woods but were ineffectual and took heavy casualties. When the day was out, British losses stood at 63 of 86 officers and 914 of 1373 ranks. 'Braddock's Defeat' as this encounter has come to be known was stereotyped by Americans as an outstanding example of the inappropriateness of European methods of war in America and Braddock as an arrogant drillbook commander who refused the sagacious advice of his colonial officers. The real cause of the disaster, however, was the lack of Indian scouts with the column, the tactical mistakes of subordinate officers, and the competence with which the French and Indians fought that day. Braddock himself was on good terms with his colonial officers who numbered among them the newly promoted Colonel George Washington as an aide-de-camp.

The war officially began in Europe the following year when, in a major reversal of traditional alliances known as the 'diplomatic revolution of 1756,' France, Austria, and Russia came to oppose Britain and Prussia, while Spain remained neutral. Britain sent the Earl of Loudoun to direct the war in America that same year while the Marquis de Montcalm arrived to take charge of French fortunes. Never self-sufficient, Canada was in the throes of a near famine due to the British blockade of the Saint Lawrence and again lacked the capability to do more than launch its traditional campaign of terror on the northern frontier since, as the Canadian Governor Vaudreuil wrote, 'nothing is more calculated to disgust the people of those Colonies and make them desire the return of peace.'

Montcalm had some important successes against English forward bases in New York and loosened the allegiance of the Indians to the British, but Loudoun accomplished little and was replaced the following year when the dynamic William Pitt became Secretary of State in London. At odds with his fellow politicians and even the King, the 48-year-old Pitt drew his political strength from his immense popularity with the people. While the Hanoverian King George II and his ministers remained focused on British concerns in Germany and the European balance of power, Pitt was a complete mercantile imperialist who saw the war as a panoramic struggle for empire. His general goal was to dismember the French and Spanish empires to make the world safe for English commercial expansion and his intended first step was to deprive the French of Canada. He

Below:
The second capture of Louisbourg by the British in 1758.

Bottom:
Another episode from the war with France and perhaps one of the most famous victories of the Seven Years' War. General James Wolfe leads his men up the redoubt to attack Quebec on 13 September 1759.

Below right:
George Washington raises the British flag over Fort Duquesne, which finally fell in 1758 without a shot being fired.

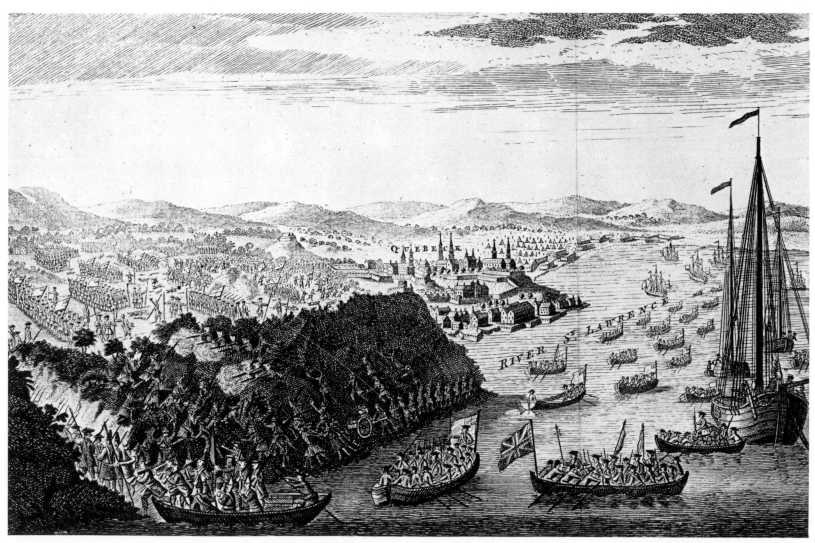

revived the traditional colonial strategy of the pincer attack on Quebec and Montreal. To ensure success, he sent John Forbes and Jeffrey Amherst, talented officers in their 40s, as subordinates to the pedestrian Scot James Abernathy upon whom the King had insisted as Commander in Chief. Great care was taken to provide sufficient numbers of regular troops, naval support, and supplies while colonial participation was bought with generous subsidies from the crown coffers.

Abandoned by the French in the face of overwhelming opposition, Fort Duquesne was occupied by Forbes without a shot fired in the summer of 1758 while Amherst captured Louisbourg with a classically conducted European siege. Abernathy's campaign in the Hudson valley came to a bloody and futile end when in a remarkably shoddy piece of generalship he shredded his forces in a frontal assault on French defensive redoubts without reconnoitering, using his artillery, or attempting to turn a weak flank. Amherst assumed overall command of the campaign of 1759 but became mired in the Lake Champlain area and failed to take Montreal until 1760. His subordinate James Wolfe led the expedition from Louisbourg against heavily defended Quebec in 1759 and won that city in a standard European linear battle on the Plains of Abraham, a battle in which both he and Montcalm were killed. The scattered French posts in the west now lost all Indian support and all of Canada was soon under British military administration.

The final conquest of Canada came in the same year that George III ascended the throne of England. The new king was suspicious of Pitt who was also under pressure from his war-weary constituency to bring the hostilities to an end. The war on the continent collapsed in 1762 but Spain joined France in that year in a war of imperialism against Britain. When the Peace of Paris was finally concluded in 1763, France ceded all of North America east of the Mississippi to Britain, except New Orleans which went to Spain and the two tiny islands of Saint Pierre and Miquelon off Newfoundland which were retained as fishing bases. Spain made Florida over to Britain as well. Greatly weakened by the protracted maritime and imperial war, France seemed almost relieved to be no longer burdened with Canadian defense. As the savant Voltaire wrote to the foreign minister Choiseul, 'I like peace better than Canada and I think that France can be happy without Quebec.'

The British and the Americans had hoped that the removal of the French would leave the Indians docile but the latter remained restive in the wake of the victory of 1760. Land-hungry settlers began to stream over the Appalachians and new British forts were erected while Amherst foolishly forbade the giving of gifts in dealings with the Indians and restricted the amount of gunpowder which could be traded. The result was a massive rising in 1763 led by the Ottawa chief Pontiac who was joined by many other tribes. In an effort to placate the Indians and restore the lucrative fur trade, London decreed that the area between the Appalachians and the Mississippi was an immense Indian reservation barred to new white settlers and accessible only to traders licensed by the British authorities. The grand design of the French, which the Americans had feared so long, had come to pass at the hand of their own king.

The Seven Years' War in America was fought and won primarily by British regulars under British officers with Colonial American troops usually relegated to auxiliary and often ignoble roles. The arrival of the British Army in force in America was an important event in Anglo-American relations because it exacerbated the antagonism already existing between the colonials and the British Army. It further gave rise to quite erroneous American and British stereotypes of each other, stereotypes which played no little role in the willingness of each side to resort to arms in 1775. Braddock's defeat had led many Americans to see a contrast between the stiff and stupid redcoat adhering to drillbook formations and the new style of war developed by Americans as an amalgam of Indian tactics, colonial responses, and the more useful of the European formations. This stereotype was certainly one component in the growing

The Taking
of
Port Mahone.

dispersed these to his regular regiments as training officers. He subsequently raised the 80th Light Infantry Regiment under Thomas Gage in 1758 in an attempt to combine traditional discipline with ranger warfare. By 1770 all the British regiments in America had received some training in forest or irregular warfare. The measure of the adaptation of the British Army to American conditions can be seen in the battle of Bushy Run in which a small force of Scottish Highlanders on its way to relieve Fort Pitt during Pontiac's rebellion encountered a larger force of Indians in wooded terrain not far from the site of Braddock's defeat, maneuvered the enemy warriors into open ground and annihilated them with a bayonet charge. The secret of the success of the British Army in America, however, was not these minor tactical adjustments but its rigorous discipline and training which gave its soldiers a tough competence and steady persistence to carry them through unexpected circumstances and often force battle on their own

the community, while the militia of the southern colonies tended to view the apprehension of fugitive slaves and suppression of slave revolts as its main duty. Recent research suggests that the actual fighting was done increasingly by those who did not have full status in the community – white servants and apprentices, white vagrants and drifters, free blacks, and tame Indians – who were either paid or drafted. To fill its contingent of men for Braddock's expedition, for example, Virginia in 1755 drafted 'such able bodied men, as do not follow or exercize any lawful calling or employment, or have not some other lawful and sufficient maintenance' while exempting men with the vote who by definition were property owners. These then were Forbes' 'scum of the worst people,' the very same pool of manpower from which the British recruited for their American regiments and who indeed largely came from the same 'unproductive classes' as did the soldiery of the European armies. Their stereotype of the colonial militia and the

Left:
The British capture Port Mahon(e) in Nova Scotia.

Top:
Major Robert Rogers, a Scotch-Irish frontiersman, led his rangers against the Indian chief Pontiac.

Above:
An early call for colonial unity. The segments of the snake representing the colonies must be joined together under a constitution.

self-esteem and confidence of Americans after 1763, confidence which caused some Americans to assert in the early 1770s that King George's troops would suffer the same fate at the hands of Americans as had Braddock's at those of the French and Indians.

Braddock's defeat had in fact inspired considerable interest in the problems of colonial warfare on the part of British officers and induced some changes in traditional thinking. This new attitude was well expressed by John Forbes who wrote: 'And I must confess in this country, wee must comply and learn the Art of Warr, from Ennemy Indians or anything else who have seen the Country and War carried on in it.' As early as 1756, Parliament had authorized the formation of the Royal American Regiment with mostly American personnel to be trained in forest warfare while the New Hampshire frontiersman Robert Rogers had begun training a corps of rangers to specialize in bush fighting and Indian tactics. Loudoun sent 55 British volunteers to serve with Rogers and then

terms. The skill and discipline of the professional soldier had been proved as valuable in America as in Europe.

The professional British soldier had in turn acquired a low opinion of the colonial militia and indeed of the American as a fighting man from his experience in the war with provincials who deserted or mutinied in droves. Forbes again expressed a common British opinion when he wrote that the American troops were 'an extream bad Collection of broken Innkeepers, Horse Jockeys, and Indian traders . . . a gathering from the scum of the worst people. . . .' What most British officers failed to realize, however, was that there were two types of colonial militia, those who served on the basis of their military obligation as free men and those who were recruited for money or drafted for long service expeditions. As the immediate Indian threat had waned at the end of the seventeenth century, the militia in most places had become more social than military, with membership representing full citizenship in

American fighting man led the British to overestimate greatly their ability to effect a quick military solution to the American crisis of the early 1770s.

By the end of the Seven Years' War, colonial Americans had been conditioned by more than a century and a half of military experience in the new world. They had fought and won a long and brutalizing struggle for their very survival with the Indians in the seventeenth century and had seen the French and Spanish eliminated as threats to their security by the middle of the following century. Native Americans constituted nearly a quarter of the British force which defeated the French in Quebec. Their basic ideas about the military function in their society had been articulated, their belief in their special aptitude as warriors firmly implanted, and their basic military institution had become a living tradition. But it remained for two more colonial wars to be fought, each against Britain, before they were to achieve a lengthy period of security.

Chapter 2

The Revolutionary War – Independence Won

Below:
The first shots were fired at the Battle of Lexington, April 1775, a skirmish which grew out of a symbolic gesture by the local militia against the British advance on Lexington in April 1775.

With the dull and corpulent figure of Lieutenant Colonel Francis Smith at their head 700 grenadiers and light infantry, the elite troops of the British Army, marched out of Boston late on the night of 18 April 1775. Equipped with detailed intelligence and maps by the hand of Dr Benjamin Church, the first American traitor, their mission was the destruction of the gunpowder and other stores cached by the Massachusetts Provincial Congress in the town of Concord sixteen miles from Boston. Roused by the colonial agents Paul Revere and William Dawes with the chance assistance of Dr Samuel Prescott, some seventy-odd colonial militia drew up in two straggling ranks on the edge of Lexington Green at sunrise to make a moral protest at the passage of the British advance guard. As the overexcited British troops moved in to disarm the Americans, a scuffle and scattered shots were followed by a volley from a British platoon. The British officer in charge only regained control of his men 'who were so

31

wild they cou'd hear no orders' some minutes later when eight Americans lay dead and ten wounded. The main British force arrived in Concord several hours later to discover that the forewarned colonials had removed most of the supplies and gathered a large force of hostile militia. The second battle of the American Revolution then occurred as heavy sniper fire and skirmishing harassed the British return march to Boston and cost the beleaguered column 22 percent of its men. As the first day of the American Revolution drew to its end, the Massachusetts militia were mobilizing to begin a siege of Boston, unaware that they were embarking on eight long and weary years of war, longer by far than any other American war until the eight-year involvement in Vietnam 190 years later.

It is not known which side fired the first shot at Lexington but the conflict which led to that confrontation had been in the making since the end of the Seven Years' War in 1763. With the exclusion of France from North America in the Peace of Paris, Britain had acquired a vast trans-Appalachian region extending from Canada to the Gulf of Mexico and west to the Mississippi. Peopled mainly by Indians and eyed hungrily by white settlers, especially English, Scotch-Irish, and Germans in the heavily populated back country of Pennsylvania and Virginia, this area awaited agricultural exploitation and further development of the fur trade. Pontiac's rebellion in 1763 had demonstrated

the immediate need for the organization and regulation of this region to stem white land pressure and abuses of the Indian population and led to the Proclamation of 1763 banning further settlement and strictly controlling the Indian trade to avoid future conflict. This immensely unpopular act with Americans became even more hated when the instrument chosen for its enforcement was the British Army. Comprising over a hundred regiments at the end of the war, the Army normally would have been reduced by half but due in part to the pressure of the numerous regimental colonels holding parliamentary seats and in part to the need to police the new transmontane, the military establishment was maintained at 75 regiments. About fifteen regiments totaling 6000 troops were stationed in the American West, so the London ministry told the colonies, for their protection. Since Britain had in part fought the war for America and incurred an enormous national debt in the process, it seemed only fitting to London that Americans should be taxed to pay for the troops in the West. Thus the Sugar Act of 1764 and the Stamp Act of 1765 were adopted by Parliament without regard to the 150 years of Anglo-American constitutional development and experience.

The presence of the British Army in peacetime and the novelty of taxation by Parliament, issues which were closely linked in the American mind, roused strong opposition in

the colonies. Variant views of the political structure of the British Empire lay at the heart of the conflict. Parliament had passed legislation taxing the American colonies on the assumption that the Empire was unitary with legal authority centered in London. Americans opposed such legislation in the belief that the Empire was a federal system in which the colonies were autonomous and their legislatures co-ordinate with Parliament under the king. Disbelieving the explanation of defense needs to justify the presence of the troops, Americans asked what other purpose the soldiers could have but to enforce the illegal acts of Parliament and expressed their opposition in noncompliance, riots, and the formation of armed associations called the Sons of Liberty to oppose the Stamp Act 'to the last extremity, even to take the field.' The London ministry backed down in this first contest and at the same time was forced to recognize the failure of its western policy as the Army had proved to be ineffective in enforcing the Proclamation of 1763. Softening its restrictive policy in the West, London now became preoccupied with the colonial challenge to Parliamentary authority and passed the revenue acts proposed by the quixotic Chancellor of the Exchequer Charles 'Champagne Charlie' Townshend in 1767. The violent American response to this second attempt at parliamentary taxation, including a boycott of British goods, led London to shift the Army eastward since, as

Above:
This early piece of propaganda was engraved, printed and sold by Paul Revere. Its message was 'Remember the Boston Massacre' of March 1770, which became a slogan of Revolutionary America.

Below left:
Captain Abraham Whipple leads a party of Americans aboard HM Revenue Schooner *Gaspee* on 9 June 1772.

Above:
The Boston Tea Party was triggered off when the British government allowed the British East India Company to import tea virtually free of duty, thus granting it a monopoly at the expense of American merchants and smugglers. On the night of 16 December 1773 a party of 50 men disguised as Indians climbed aboard the tea-laden ships and poured 343 chests of tea into the harbor.

Below:
General George Washington taking command of the newly formed Continental Army at Boston on 3 July 1775. As the only man in Congress with any significant military experience, Washington was called on to build a standing army from scratch.

In the illustration: *Boston cannonaded* · *Boston port Bill* · *BOSTON petition* · *Military Law*

Left:
This anti-American cartoon was published in London in 1774. It shows the Bostonians tarring and feathering an Excise Man.

Above:
Paul Revere produced another cartoon showing America being ministered by evil George III and the Duke of Grafton and forced to swallow a bitter draft, the so-called Coercion Act. The Massachusetts Assembly was suspended, and the port of Boston closed.

Viscount Barrington wrote to General Thomas Gage, Commander in Chief in North America, 'Nothing can make Great Britain obey'd and respected in North America, but a proper force collected together.' Three regiments were stationed in the middle colonies and two in Massachusetts where opposition to the various revenue acts was most strongly expressed.

Although most English politicians at this time favored a hard line with the recalcitrant colonies, the use of British troops was, in the words of Lord George Sackville, 'a point of such delicacy in our constitution that I doubt much of its being properly executed.' George III was also a strict constitutionalist opposed to the use of force but the troops were not withdrawn and remained a focal point in the growing Anglo-American tension, tension which finally exploded in the Boston Massacre of 5 March 1770. While the anti-military tradition had waned in Britain as a result of parliamentary safeguards, the Jacobite

threats, periodic war with France, and the needs of defending and enlarging the empire, it remained very much alive in America from the popular militia experience and dislike of the British Army stemming from earlier experiences in the colonial wars. The genuine American concern over the presence of British troops was expressed by the schoolteacher James Lovell after the Boston Massacre who wrote 'what check have *we* upon a British Army? can *we* disband it? can *we* stop its pay?' and was blown up to extremes in the rantings of radicals such as Samuel Adams and John Hancock. A concurrent campaign from press and pulpit advocated military preparedness.

Colonial opposition to parliamentary tariffs was again dramatized in the Boston Tea Party of 1773 which caused an infuriated Parliament to pass punitive legislation against the port of Boston and the colony of Massachusetts. American unity in the rapidly escalating crisis was expressed in

the First Continental Congress the following year which urged military preparations and support of Massachusetts. Led by the King, the hawks in London brushed aside constitutional restraints and the criticism of such eminent figures as William Pitt, Edmund Burke, David Hume, and Charles James Fox by ordering Gage to restore royal authority by force in unruly Massachusetts with the 3500 troops under his command in Boston. Since the provincials were very short of munitions and could not resist without these, Gage decided the best way to retain military control of the situation was to destroy the colonial stores at Concord.

The debacle of 19 April was a shock to the pride of the British Army and to London while royal authority had collapsed in its aftermath as royal governors fled from American mobs. Besieging Gage in Boston, Massachusetts asked Congress to take control of the operations to muster greater support and direction while London sent Generals William Howe, John Burgoyne, and Henry Clinton to spur the inert Gage to action. These energetic commanders moved quickly to restore the prestige of the British Army by attacking some Americans entrenched on Breed's Hill on the Charlestown peninsula on 17 June. As Burgoyne, who watched the action from a Boston rooftop, explained the purpose of the attack: 'I believe in most states of the world as well as in our own, that respect, and control, and subordination of government . . . depend in a great measure upon the idea that trained troops are invincible against any numbers or any position of undisciplined rabble; and this idea was a little in suspense since the 19th of April.' Howe elected to demonstrate the invincibility of the British soldier through repeated frontal assaults on the exposed American position and did ultimately dislodge the defenders at a cost of 42 percent of the attackers. It was Gage who perceived the real point made at the misnamed battle of Bunker Hill: 'These People shew a Spirit and Conduct against us, they never shewed against the French, and every body had judged of them from their former Appearance, and Behaviour . . . which has led many into great mistakes.'

Believing that the outbreak of fighting would shock Britain into negotiations, Congress in August 1775 sent its 'Olive Branch Petition' to George III begging him to protect American rights against Parliament but the King declared the colonies to be in rebellion only two days after its arrival. Having

already renounced Parliament, the colonies had to renounce the crown now but it took almost another year for the idea of independence to become widely enough accepted for Congress to pass unanimously the Declaratation of Independence on 4 July 1776. That act resolved a dilemma for many Americans since, as Joseph Barton of Delaware wrote, 'I could hardly own the king and fight against him at the same time, but now these matters are cleared up. Heart and hand shall move together.' Even before the resolution of the dilemma, the Continental Army had forced a British evacuation of Boston in March 1776 and an ill-advised invasion of Canada had failed to make that province the fourteenth colony.

By the summer of 1776 the protagonists were fully committed to a war in which European professional warfare would dominate both sides but in which citizen soldiers would also find an important role. Anticipating a change which only came to Europe with the French Revolutionary Wars of the 1790s, the American Revolution reintro-duced ideological content into warfare and thus weakened the restraints under which the opposing armies fought. Even so, the American Revolution was a conservative event characterized politically by a remarkable stability of institutions and continuity of leadership and militarily by a conventional strategy which served as a buffer for American society and politics. Even as Americans hesitated over the question of independence in the winter of 1775–76, King George and his Colonial Secretary George Germain planned to smash the rebellion with overwhelming force in the summer of 1776. In so doing they were asking the British Army, in the words of the British historian Piers Mackesy, to undertake a task of pacification 'never paralleled in the past, and in relative terms never attempted again by any power until the twentieth century.' The military task was magnified by the fact that the war roused little enthusiasm in the British public and quickly spawned a vocal anti-war effort while the Whigs in Parliament consistently favored some form of conciliation. The

domestic base of the war was thus shaky from the outset in Britain. But British policy dictated that the issue of American independence was to be decided by armed force mobilized on a large scale.

The Army which was to be employed in the American pacification comprised in 1775 48,000 men serving in the infantry, cavalry, and artillery. The British infantry regiment at this time was made up of eight companies of infantry and one company each of light infantry and grenadiers although the 'grenades' pitched by the latter had gone out of fashion some years before. Due to chronic shortages of recruits, it is thought that the average number of effectives in a regiment was about 292 rather than the decreed paper strength of 477 of all ranks. The standard weapon was still the smoothbore flintlock musket commonly called the Brown Bess after the first matchlocks with browned barrels and fittings introduced during the reign of Elizabeth I. Now with a steel bright barrel, this four-and-a-half foot long weapon weighing ten pounds fired a .71 caliber slug from a .75 caliber barrel. That it was accurate at hardly more than 50 yards mattered little since the soldier was taught not to aim but 'to point his weapon horizontally, brace himself for a vicious recoil and pull a ten-pound trigger till his gun went off: if, indeed, it did go off when the hammer fell.' Even with the use of standard paper cartridges, two or three shots per minute was thought a very good rate of fire but misfires were common. The musket was in fact more useful as a delivery system for it had a 21-inch bayonet in whose use the British soldier was highly skilled. The most successful mode of British attack was charges with the 'white weapon,' dreaded by Americans, and thus the bayonet proved to be the most effective British weapon throughout the war.

The British Army was typical of the professional armies of the eighteenth century in that it employed linear tactics in a limited style of warfare and was always pressed for manpower. The Army had to resort to pardoning criminals and deserters and impressing beggars, former jailbirds, vagrants, and others without a fixed place in society. Since this was an age when few if any fought for patriotism, the nationality of a nation's soldiers mattered little, Britain having already turned to hiring German troops in the War of the Austrian Succession in the 1740s and again during the Seven Years' War. At the outbreak of hostilities in 1775, therefore, the ministry in London first tried to lease 20,000 Russians from Catherine the Great of Russia, then to buy a Scottish brigade in Dutch service, but finally made contracts for a total of 17,000 men from the small German state of Hesse-Kassel and another 12,800 from Brunswick, Hesse-Hanau, Anspach-Bayreuth, Waldeck, and Anhalt-Zerbst. Because the majority came from Hesse-Kassel, the German troops were all termed Hessians by Americans. While the Germans were well-disciplined, theirs was a hard life and American service was not popular. Con-

gress and the individual states offered inducements such as land, livestock and liberty to deserters, many of whom found refuge in the German settlements. In the end, it has been estimated that only 58 percent of the 30,000 Germans finally returned to their homelands as a result of disease, desertion, and combat.

The generals of the British Army were drawn in the main from the aristocracy and more often than not held seats in Parliament. Those who served in America – Gage, Howe, Clinton, Cornwallis and Burgoyne – all fell into this category except that Gage was not a Member of Parliament as were the others. There was no rush to secure appointments to

the force being readied in 1776, however, since there was little glory to be gained from suppressing a tedious provincial rebellion but much potential for disaster. Generals such as Jeffrey Amherst, Henry Conway, and Lord Cavendish refused appointments for political or career reasons while the Earl of Effingham resigned from the Army, saying 'I cannot, without reproach from my conscience, consent to bear arms against my fellow subjects in America in what, to my weak discernment, is not a clear cause.' Even William Howe had hesitated before accepting a posting to America. 'This is an unpopular War,' wrote one British colonel, 'and men of ability do not chose to risk their reputation

by taking an active part in it.' Thus some of Britain's best officers declined to serve while the officer corps in general was less than enthusiastic.

To fight the war in America, Britain had to rely on the Royal Navy for transport, supply, and blockade duties, yet the Navy, like the Army, was only mobilized to a limited extent. The Navy in the Seven Years' War had been the largest in British history but had decayed to a great extent owing to the parliamentary practice of 'judicious economy' in naval affairs and the unseaworthiness of many ships hastily constructed of green timber. The rupture with America cost the Navy access to American raw materials, seamen, and merchant ships which had all made an important contribution during the Seven Years' War while naval demands had to compete with commercial needs for seamen, shipwrights, and shipyards in an economy highly oriented toward the merchant marine. The Navy had to resort to press-gangs and bounties resulting from a high attrition of manpower from disease and desertion. The naval officer corps was more professional than that of the Army and boasted first-class fighting admirals in Richard Howe, Rodney, Jervis, Parker, and Kempenfelt who, like their Army counterparts, were politicians as well as sailors. Poor transport and a thin and hostile population made America a limited source of supply, so their ships would be required to carry not only the military stores but virtually all the food for the British forces. The administrative machinery of the British government, fragmented and unsystematic as well as riddled with inefficiency and corruption, would have difficulty meeting the supply requirements of the forces in America.

King George, the Colonial Secretary George Germain, and General William Howe who had replaced Gage as Commander in Chief in America, all believed a major military defeat was the best means to end the rebellion since, as Germain said, 'nothing is more to be desired or sought after

Left:
A Virginia rifleman in 1775. Until 1778 the acute shortage of clothing in the Continental Army prevented any conception of uniformity. On Washington's advice the men sported the hunting shirt of the rifleman. The rifle was more accurate than the musket but it was slow to load and did not have a bayonet.

Above:
An original line engraving taken from a contemporary painting by John Trumbull of the Battle of Bunker Hill.

by us, as the most effectual means to terminate this expensive war.' Germain and the Admiralty thus made a monumental effort to provide Howe with 32,000 well-equipped British and German troops supported by 73 warships under his brother, Admiral Sir Richard 'Black Dick' Howe, to strike at New York and maneuver the Continental Army into a decisive battle, while a force under Governor Guy Carleton pushed southward from Canada down the Lake Champlain/Hudson River axis to truncate the rebellion. In the hope of a speedy military victory, Britain put its largest effort of the war into the campaign of 1776. While Germain was an enthusiastic hardliner, the Prime Minister Lord North continued to press for an attempt at political reconciliation, hence a peace mission headed by Admiral Howe accompanied the expedition as a sop to the domestic opposition and a vehicle for accepting American surrender.

As the Howe brothers sailed toward New York with their mighty force, Congress tried to come to grips with the reality of war with the mother country. Congress itself was only a committee representing what amounted to thirteen semi-sovereign entities. Until the ratification in 1781 of the Articles of Confederation as the first American constitution, Congress was an extralegal body and even after the ratification, it still had no coercive or legislative power in that it could not levy taxes, regulate commerce, compel the states to honor its requisitions, or deal directly with the citizens. The direction of the war effort was further hampered by the lack of congressional machinery to administer and finance the Continental Army and the strong anti-military tradition in America. Given that Americans had rebelled over the issue of taxation to support a standing army and that standing armies were equated with tyranny in the minds of most Americans, the states

Right:
John Trumbull's painting 'The signing of the Declaration of Independence.'

Below left:
Soldiers of the American Revolution raise their flag over Charlestown, which was occupied following the British victory at Bunker Hill.

Below right:
Thomas Gage decided to attack the American forces on Bunker Hill in a front-on attack. The carnage that followed resulted in 1054 British and 441 American losses.

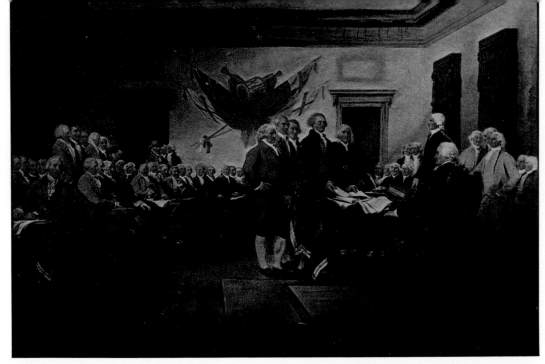

jealously guarded their power to tax and forced Congress to resort to the printing press. Over 200 million dollars' worth of bills of credit were issued and led to a rampant inflation, yet Congress had no choice but to continue because 'to stop would have been political suicide.' After 1778 gifts and loans from France, Spain, and Holland as well as domestic borrowing helped ease the situation, but the end of the conflict found Congress with a massive war debt. The administrative machinery and authority of the state governments was also weak, hence the congressional levies of money and supplies on these bodies often went unheeded as they struggled with their own fiscal needs and defenses.

The anti-militarism which had played a role in bringing on the Revolution remained very much alive in Congress and in the minds of the people throughout the war and led to Congress investing much of its time and

LE GENERAL WASHINGTON

COMMANDANT EN CHEF DES ARMEES AMERICAINES

né en Virginie, en 1732.

Above:
Esek Hopkins, Commander in Chief of the American Navy during the War of Independence.

Left:
George Washington (1732–1799) was born in Virginia, descending from a family originally from Northamptonshire, England. As a military commander his notable successes were Trenton, Princeton, and Yorktown. He became the first President of the United States and served from 1789-1797.

Right:
The Continental Army had few officers of real ability and could hardly afford the loss of the talented Montgomery in the ill-conceived attack on Canada.

Below:
A drawing depicting Dr. Benjamin Franklin on the USS *Repulse* en route for France where he was to serve as the diplomatic representative who masterminded the French alliance of 1778.

energy in watching and worrying whether its Army might turn on it. As Samuel Adams wrote, 'a standing army, however necessary it may be at some times, is always dangerous to the liberties of the people. . . . Such a power should be watched with a jealous eye.' Thus John Adams felt it necessary to write to his constituents that there was 'no design to New Model your army' in a direct allusion to the New Model Army of Oliver Cromwell and its political consequences. Fear of an army coup quickly led to the growth of machinery to administer military affairs, first ad hoc committees, and then a Board of War and Ordnance in 1776, the latter never being very effective and falling into limbo after 1778. With the strongest fear of what was then called 'executism,' the radicals in Congress had transferred their fear of the British government to any government and retarded the growth of the administrative base of Congress. The various crises of the war, however, created a counter-belief that the war effort required better management and finally led to the ratification of the Articles of Confederation. It was only in 1781 that Congress formed a War Department which actually took over the routine administration of the Army and military affairs but by then the operational side of the war had already come to an end.

Congress accepted sponsorship of the motley horde of New England militia besieging Boston on 14 June 1775 and appointed a general of the Army the following day. A tall 43-year-old colonel in the Virginia militia who had seen no active duty since 1758, George Washington at the head of the Continental Army, the first national institution, quickly became the first meaningful symbol of American unity. Endowed with a large fortune and aristocratic background, he brought a needed respectability to the Revolution yet even the Boston radicals never questioned his 'full intention to devote my Life and Fortune in the cause we are engaged in, if need be.' Despite the respect he had already earned from his congressional colleagues, Washington's was a political appointment. It was generally recognized that the naming of a non-New Englander was necessary to demonstrate that the war was not just New England's but America's. Coming from rich and populous Virginia, Washington would raise support from the Middle States and, more importantly, from the lukewarm Deep South. Washington himself was brave, possessed great physical stamina, and was a methodical administrator. He accepted no pay and gained the confidence of Congress with his strong and sincere deference to civilian authority. He was to make many

tactical and strategic mistakes but most were in the first half of the war. Most of the time he had to proceed by trial and error due to the vaguely worded authority of his commission from Congress, that extralegal body claiming to represent a nation which did not yet exist.

Washington was not atypical of the senior officers appointed by Congress to the four major generalships and eight brigadier generalships of the Army. They too came from the upper or middle class, possessed little command experience, and were not familiar with the handling of large bodies of troops or the employment of cavalry and artillery. They had, like Washington, been selected on the basis of sectional politics, Philip Schuyler of New York being appointed Major General 'to Sweeten and to keep up the spirit in that Province.' Washington could make brevet appointments beneath this level while the state legislatures made permanent appointments and promotions in their regiments. In addition to the thirteen general officers of the Army, Congress also appointed an Adjutant General, Commissary General, Quartermaster General, and Paymaster General.

The members of Congress in 1775 envisaged an infantry army modeled on the conventional European armies of the day and in particular on the British Army with which they were most familiar. Congress first authorized an army of 38 regiments of between 500–1000 men which Washington then organized into six brigades of six regiments each and two divisions of three brigades each. The tactical employment of brigades and divisions did not occur in Europe until the French Revolutionary Wars, hence the Continental Army, like its European counterparts, fought as a whole using battalions as the units of maneuver while divisions, brigades, and regiments functioned as administrative headquarters. The following year Congress remade the Army into a more efficient and compact force of 28 regiments, each with 728 officers and ranks, to be officered and organized by the states. An establishment of 88 regiments totaling 76,000 men was later authorized but the Army never approached this paper figure, reaching its peak on 1 October 1778 with 18,472 effectives. The discipline of the Army was also drawn from the British Articles of War and relied on the lash. The maximum penalty for absences without leave, violations of camp rules, and other misconduct was 100 strokes inflicted in two lots of 50 each. Since the Revolution was in part a struggle to preserve property rights, looting was usually a capital offense.

The direction of the Army was somewhat diffuse as Congress retained control and emphasized Washington's subordination and duty to report regularly and in detail as well as to consult with the other general officers on every decision. Nor did a well-structured command system ever develop since Washington was always leading a field army and hence unable to direct the operations of all the American forces. Washington's field force operated for the most part in southern New York, New Jersey, and Pennsylvania, so this area was designated the Middle Department while the Northern and Southern Departments became virtually independent commands.

With only their militia tradition and experience on which to build, it was inevitable that the Army created by Congress would face many severe problems, foremost among which were officers, manpower, and supply. Appointed for political reasons, most officers were drawn from the militia and lacked real experience in training and leading men in combat or in running the supply and administrative services. Washington's personal staff was composed of earnest but inexperienced young men which meant that he simply did most of the work himself. The problem of inexperience extended from Washington down to the level of noncommissioned officer as there were failures of leadership at every level. Varying success was had with foreign officers such as von Steuben, Duportail, Pulaski, de Kalb, and the 20-year-old Marquis de Lafayette who quickly distinguished himself in combat and became an important element in Franco-American relations. Most of the French officers recruited by the American agent in Paris, Silas Deane, proved a nuisance to

Congress and Washington and were discharged. Largely because of the officer problem, the Army was always erratic in its battlefield performance, a sad fact which tempered all of Washington's tactical and strategic moves. 'We want nothing but good officers to constitute as good an army as ever marched into the field' wrote Nathanael Greene. 'Our men are better than the officers.'

Keeping the Army in existence was a constant problem which expanded to major crises at crucial moments for Washington. The Massachusetts Provincial Congress had

called for an army of 8000 New Englanders, on the day after Lexington and Concord, to blockade the British in Boston. In the face of the immediate threat, over 24,000 turned out but enthusiasm flagged as the siege wore on and only 16,000 greeted Washington on his arrival to take command. The men were only enlisted to the end of the year since most Americans believed a negotiated peace would bring the hostilities to a speedy end. Had the idea of a longer war been broached, it would probably have seriously damaged the already tender American cause. As it became apparent that the war was to continue, Washington hoped to recruit 21,000 soldiers from the militia and train them out

of their tradition of part-time amateur soldiering to as near as possible the level of the British professional soldier. This arrangement would leave the traditional militia system intact for local defense and able to render reinforcements and support to the regular Army in specific situations.

As 1775 drew to a close, Washington watched in dismay as his Army disbanded in the face of the enemy at Boston but fortunately Sir William Howe was not disposed to fight. When the American force had dwindled to 4000, New England provided an additional 5000 short-term militia enlistees to

maintain some semblance of strength. American enthusiasm was rekindled by the signing of the Declaration of Independence and Washington was able to muster 19,000 Continentals and militia to counter Howe's descent on New York in that same month. Further recruitment was stifled by the disaster of the New York campaign and the Army again shrank drastically. Nor did the militia come forward once more to save the day in the face of the military foundering of the American cause. On 25 December 1776 Washington had only 2500 demoralized effectives which he employed in an audacious attack on the German post at Trenton to boost American morale and spur recruiting. Enough of his troops were persuaded to remain to make a follow-up attack on Princeton possible a few days later. These two minor victories forced a British retrenchment in northern New Jersey and reversed the momentum of the war enough to keep the Continental Army in existence as a fighting force.

Even though the Revolution survived the early manpower crises, maintaining the strength of the Continental regiments was a constant and major struggle to the end of the war. Members of an already affluent society, most Americans had much to lose in economic terms from being in service for more

Right:
Major General Marie Joseph Paul Yves Roch Gilbert du Motier Marquis de Lafayette (1757–1834). He fought enthusiastically for the American Revolution and had a share in the English defeat at Yorktown.

Below:
The famous painting by Emanuel Leutze of Washington crossing the Delaware. After the summer of 1776 Washington was in retreat. Having been deserted by the New Jersey and Maryland militia he crossed the Delaware on 7 December 1776 intending to take up winter quarters. He then went on to two victories at Trenton and Princeton which restored the morale of his tattered army.

than a brief period. Many were further reluctant to serve long periods when so many of their neighbors did not serve at all. Congress was therefore forced to turn to conscription to meet the minimal manpower requirements of its army. Conscription meant a quota levied on the states which they in turn apportioned among their militia regiments. Conscripts from local regiments were selected by lottery or by the officers but could avoid service by paying a fine or hiring a substitute, which many did. Entire communities sometimes avoided sending any men by payment or the hiring of men from neighboring locales. The states employed a similar mode of conscription as early as 1776 to meet their

local defense needs. Congress offered bounties of land and money to men enlisting for the duration and money only to three-year enlistees, but often found itself outbid in the contest for manpower by the higher bounties of the states.

Both Congress and the States also returned to earlier practices such as the impressment of felons and the 'idle, vagrant or dissolute.' It was also not uncommon, particularly in Pennsylvania and later in the Carolinas, to recruit British prisoners of war and deserters while the British, equally pressed for men, reciprocated with Americans. Free blacks, black slaves, and white bond servants were tapped as another important pool of

manpower. Congress had not recommended the recruitment of blacks but the scarcity of manpower brought New England to this practice by 1777 through normal enlistment and conscription while Virginia recruited free blacks and Maryland slaves. The military crisis in the South in 1779 brought congressional calls to arm the black population but Georgia and the Carolinas refused. Many blacks were hired as substitutes for whites. Away from the South where blacks were relegated in the main to roles as spies and laborers, most blacks served in the Continental Army in integrated units. Many Americans quickly saw the inconsistency between the ideals of their revolution and the institution of slavery, leading Pennsylvania and Massachusetts, followed by the other non-Southern States, to abolish slavery; New York in 1799 being the most tardy in this respect. The Revolution set the pattern for black participation in America's wars, as Benjamin Quarles has observed, by ignoring the pool of black manpower until the need became too acute.

Desertion contributed to the manpower problem but there are no statistics to describe it. The reports of Washington and other officers, however, show that it was high. Some men joined the British in return for pardons and land, while others left for personal and family reasons or weariness of the material hardship of life in the Continental Army. The use of bounties for enlistment created a group of men who repeatedly deserted and re-enlisted in other regiments, making it 'a kind of business' as Washington noted. The number of men in the regular regiments thus fluctuated radically and forced Washington to keep making calls for short-term militia to keep up his strength.

It is not really certain how many Americans bore arms during the war nor is it even known what the general population was at

Below:
Despondent and puzzled by the poor performance of his troops at the battle of Long Island, 27 August 1776, Washington is rowed to the mainland.

Bottom:
Lord Howe organizes the evacuation of Boston on 17 March 1776. He took with him to Nova Scotia many of the leading families who knew it was in their interests to support the British military establishment.

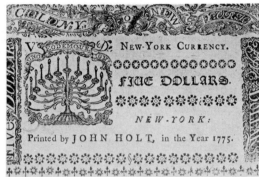

that time. Congress estimated three million while the British ministry thought 2.5 million, including 600,000 blacks. There may have been 250,000 males of fighting age but a modern scholar, Howard Peckham, has suggested that no more than 100,000 different men actually served. Revolutionary America was a middle-class society but contained a large and growing number of poor people. The better-off citizens tended to serve relatively brief periods in the militia in response to specific crises while those who accepted enlistment in the Continental Army and bore the brunt of the long-term military burden tended to be paupers, laborers, and blacks who as a group were poorer and less rooted sociologically. As John Adams remarked of the 1775 enlistment crisis with reference to Massachusetts, no more than a regiment 'of the meanest, idlest, most intemperate and worthless' citizens would have enlisted for more than a year. A large proportion of the white male population and a significant portion of the black male popu-

Above:
The American forces made a poor showing at Long Island. Howe landed on Long Island with a force of 20,000 and had no trouble in wiping out the local patriots.

Above right:
The first paper currency issued by New York.

lation went on active service, concludes John Shy, but only a relative few gave extended service and these largely came from the lower socio-economic level of society. The soldiers of the Continental Army thus tended to have a certain sociological similarity to their counterparts in the professional armies of Europe.

Although Congress had early created the offices of Quartermaster General and Commissary General, the Army lived on the brink

Much of the Army was unfit for duty at Valley Forge because the soldiers were literally naked and unable to leave their quarters. The problems were so critical that Washington received near dictatorial powers from Congress to commandeer supplies from civilians and lodge sick and wounded soldiers in private homes without the consent of the householder. Although the succeeding winter was bad, the winter at Morristown was acknowledged by all as the worst. 'Those

of starvation and nakedness and periodically slipped over. The delivery of food and clothing to the troops was hindered by a combination of the problems of developing a transport and purchase system and the rapid movement of the Army during the campaigning season which wore out shoes and uniforms at a rapid rate. The Commissary in particular broke down under incompetent and corrupt management. The winters were the worst times – Valley Forge in 1777, Middlebrook in 1778, and Morristown in 1779. At Valley Forge the soldiers sometimes received no rations for days and survived the remainder of the time on fried flour paste known as 'fire cakes.' At one point, a group of soldiers tried to barbecue and eat their shoes while several officers dined on a pet dog.

who have only been in Valley Forge or Middlebrook the last two winters know not what it is to suffer,' wrote Baron de Kalb. While Washington reported, 'We have never experienced a like calamity in any period of the war.'

Officers also had a difficult time as they were required to clothe and feed themselves. All found the war an economic hardship which left many impoverished and embittered. Many resigned their commissions while some defected to the enemy, the best known of these defectors being Benedict Arnold. Mutinies broke out among the starving and unpaid ranks in 1780 and 1781 while the officers lobbied and threatened Congress over pensions. The mutinies and agitation reflected the fact that the supply services

Below left:
Major General Benedict Arnold (1741–1801) was a prominent commander of the Continental Army and took part in the capture of Ticonderoga. He was in command of forces at Quebec on 31 December 1775. After 1779 he started to pass on information to the British and defected to them in 1780.

Below:
'The foraging party at Valley Forge,' painted by Harrington Fitzgerald. After the grueling winter there in 1777 the Continental Army emerged as a viable fighting unit.

Bottom:
Baron von Steuben, a staff officer of Frederick the Great, arrived in 1778 as a volunteer. In this painting by Edwin Abbey he drills Washington's army at Valley Forge.

never overcame their problems, that Congress and the states remained parsimonious to the end and that Congress was, as Russell Weigley has written, always more interested in investigating and regulating the Army than assisting it.

However pressed for food and clothing, the Army generally possessed sufficient muskets and artillery. The exigencies of the frontier and the earlier colonial wars had created a relatively widespread gunmaking industry while clandestine shipments of munitions and Charleville muskets soon began to arrive from France, and the only serious shortage of muskets occurred on the eve of the New York campaign in 1776. An initial critical shortage of powder and shot was overcome by the output of small mills and foreign imports which together maintained a generally adequate supply. There was never a real shortage of artillery either, due to cannon owned by the militia and removed from ships. The chief of artillery was Henry Knox, a 25-year-old Boston bookstore owner and military dilettante, who trained his gunners well, encouraged the development of the American cannon founding industry, and laid the tradition of artillery excellence.

Above:
General Howe moved south to wrest control of Philadelphia. He defeated Washington's Army at the Battle of Germantown on 4 October 1777, forcing Washington to spend a discouraging winter at Valley Forge.

The training of the Continental Army was haphazard until Friedrich Wilhelm, Baron von Steuben, was appointed Inspector General in the spring of 1778. A former staff officer in the Army of Frederick the Great, who was the acknowledged master of conventional warfare, the Prussian drillmaster tried to adjust his training to American circumstances and conditions. His main improvements were to train officers to train their men, to consolidate the understrength regiments into training battalions of 200 men, and to increase the speed of march and deployment into battle line by introducing the column of fours. His 1779 publication of *Steuben's Regulations for the Order and Discipline of the troops of the United States* remained the official military manual of the Army for 33 years. Steuben helped form the Continental Army but though improved, it was never a reliable battlefield instrument.

Both Congress and Washington envisaged a conventional American Army which would fight a limited war against the conventional British Army but the manifold defects in his Army – officership, manpower, supply, training – made it impossible for Washington to employ conventional strategy and tactics. The troops were too poorly trained and officered for linear attack or outflanking the enemy on the battlefield. To engage the main British Army in open battle might well have brought about the destruction of the Continental Army and with it the end of the political revolution. The American cause depended on the existence of an army in the field, and Washington found himself forced into a defensive strategy of attrition, explaining that 'on our side the War should be defensive . . . we should on all occasions avoid a general Action, or put anything to the Risque, unless compelled by necessity, into

Above right:
Shortly before the Wyoming massacre American and British forces clashed at the Battle of Monmouth in June 1778. Washington's troops attacked Sir Henry Clinton's rearguard as they withdrew from Philadelphia to New York.

Right:
The massacre of Wyoming took place on 3-4 July 1778 in the Wyoming Valley, Pennsylvania. The British used 300 Indians to gain control of the valley thus alienating the population.

which we ought never to be drawn.' The only military objective compatible with political independence was to force a complete British withdrawal but Washington's dilemma was that his Army was not an adequate instrument to achieve this objective. He therefore developed a defensive strategy based on the hope that a protracted and unwinnable war would eventually force an enemy withdrawal. However unpopular the war may have been in Britain, only a minority of people in America were actively supporting the revolutionary cause, while the political coalition represented by Congress lacked the material and moral resources to endure a lengthy contest. Washington's gamble was that a long war would cause the British to give up before his countrymen. The outcome depended on Washington's army.

badly bungled the assault on Bunker Hill that Washington had developed quite unrealistic hopes of defeating the British offensive entirely from defensive positions. In the event it was a disaster for Washington as he was badly outgeneraled and outmaneuvered by Howe. Even in their prepared positions, the green Americans often fled before the advancing British and German bayonets, causing Washington to storm 'Are these the men with whom I am to defend America? Good God, have I got such troops as these!' The New York experience taught Washington that American troops, even when entrenched and supported by artillery, could not stand up to a strong British attack.

Withdrawing from New York, Washington's actions were dominated by the strategic defensive in which he sought to

Washington had little idea of what to expect from his troops when he took command at Boston in July 1775. Lexington and Concord had shown that American militia could skirmish with British regulars while the former had fought adequately from well-prepared positions at Bunker Hill. With only these two engagements from which to generalize, Washington tried to fend off Howe's opening attack on Long Island in July 1776 by repeating the Bunker Hill strategy of fortifying important places. Howe had so

Above:
In an attempt to prevent the British gaining control of the South, Horatio Gates's 300-strong army met Lord Cornwallis's army at Camden. The American troops were soundly defeated at this engagement on 16 August 1780.

Top:
By 1779 the infantry of the Continental Army was equipped with blue coats and white breeches.

Right:
Anthony Wayne led an American force which recaptured Stony Point, New York on 16 July 1779.

avoid direct confrontations with Howe to preserve what remained of his Army and only attacked inferior parts of the enemy as at Trenton and Princeton. The remainder of the campaigning season of 1776 and the season of 1777 were spent maneuvering across New Jersey and Pennsylvania to avoid a potentially fatal encounter with Howe while constantly seeking to erode British strength and sustain American morale with minor jabs. After two futile summers of leisurely following Washington and sustaining an unacceptable casualty rate from the minor encounters with the American, Howe appears to have concluded that his task was hopeless both in terms of military victory and negotiations. Only once had he been able to bring Washington to a major battle at Brandywine in September of 1777 when politics had dictated that Philadelphia should not be given up to the enemy without a fight. Here was the only time that Washington chanced his Army against the main British force and largely caused his own defeat by failing to protect an open flank, but remained in the field as a fighting force by drawing on the pool of militia manpower. Howe was replaced in early 1778 by his subordinate Henry Clinton who marched overland from Philadelphia to New York and thus gave Washington the opportunity to attack the British rearguard at Monmouth Courthouse on 28 June 1778. Here the more experienced and better trained Continental regiments exchanged repeated volleys and bayonet charges with the redcoats in a standard and indecisive linear battle. By dint of bitter experience and hard work, Washington and his Continentals were becoming professional enough to stand up to the British in conventional battle. The irony of the situation is that Clinton withdrew to New York while his opponent took up position at White Plains, causing Washington to note 'that after two years Manoeuvring . . . both Armies are brought back to the very point they are set out from.'

From the summer of 1778 to the fall of 1781, the war in the Middle Department was stalemated. Holding only New York City and Newport with the support of the British fleet, the cautious Clinton undertook no real initiatives and thus gave Washington no openings for minor strokes. Washington's achievement at this point was to have kept his Army in being and in the process to have frustrated completely the British plan to extinguish the rebellion militarily. But while the existence of the Continental Army and the possibility of defeating it at the level of conventional warfare distracted the attention of the London ministry and its generals in America, an unconventional war of revolution and counter-revolution was being fought at another level between the Revolutionary militia and the loyalists.

The American Revolution was a civil war not only in the external sense that the English of America fought the English of England but also in the internal sense that Americans fought among themselves both fiercely and extensively. In the early 1770s few if any Americans were prepared to carry their grievances against Britain to the extreme of political disengagement but many supported the various forms taken by resistance to parliamentary taxation. The American response to the draconian measures enacted by Parliament in the wake of the Boston Tea Party was a Congress-sponsored boycott of British goods known as the Continental Association. The Association was enforced by local committees whose coercive power lay in groups of armed volunteers drawn from the local militia. The local militia was in many cases the military arm of the local association committee while in other cases heavy opposition to the boycott prevented its enforcement by any means. In either case, however, the old colonial militia structure tended to be dissolved as unsympathetic officers were ousted and unco-operative intermediate levels of state government by-passed by an alternate line of authority from Congress to the committees. What tended to emerge from the Association and the conflict surrounding it locally was a new Revolutionary militia structure purged of officers and men opposed to the developing aims of the American patriot cause. In addition to its traditional role of local draft board and emergency local defense force, the new militia took on the functions of a local police force and instrument of political surveillance.

From this beginning, the Revolutionary militia developed into the infrastructure of the political revolution by controlling local communities through a combination of coercion and political persuasion. By whatever means the local militia produced enough recruits annually to keep the Continental Army in existence and turned out large numbers of men for service in emergencies. Membership in the militia became a test of loyalty as non-performance of military service brought trial, imprisonment, and occasionally execution. When dismantled by British or loyalist attack, the militia was reconstituted by intervention from other districts as occurred when Connecticut units intervened in the New York City area and forces from Reading and Lancaster came to the assistance of Bucks County, Pennsylvania.

The militia represented the activist element in the population with rebel sympathies but fully a fifth of all Americans are thought to have remained actively loyal to King George. The concentration of loyalists was highest among the religious and cultural minorities, excepting generally Jews and Whig-oriented Catholics, and may have included as much as 50 percent of the people in the more heterogenous middle colonies, 25 percent elsewhere but only 10 percent in New England. The rebellion was by no means unanimous but the royal governors and Howe grossly misled London on the strength of loyalism and caused policies to be formulated which placed undue reliance on the American Tories. New York City, Philadelphia, and the Deep South in particular were seen as strongholds of loyalism whose manpower could be tapped to reduce the need for British troops (and thus the cost of the war) and reverse political opinion in the general populace. Such was the inspiration behind an abortive expedition to Charleston in 1776 by Clinton and Admiral Peter Parker and Howe's otherwise pointless decision to take Philadelphia in 1777. But loyalism in the Quaker state proved a mirage, forcing Howe to inform Germain that the people 'excepting a few individuals are strongly against us.'

British relations with the Tories were never easy since each carried the baggage of past history with them. Like the rebels, the loyalists had an erroneous stereotype of the British Army, wanted short enlistments, and were disinclined to fight outside their own colonies. With their own stereotype of the

Below:
On 7 October 1780 1400 Virginians and Green Mountain Men, all sharp-shooting frontiersmen, slaughtered a force of 1000 Tories at King's Mountain. This redressed the balance of forces in the South and marked the beginning of the successful campaign in the South conducted by Nathanael Greene.

American fighting man reinforced by the poor showing of the Continental Army, the British in addition had a traditional contempt for colonials and the professional's dislike for amateurs. Loyalist officers were denied the benefits accorded British officers while Tory units tended to be assigned to menial and labor tasks, giving rise to the contemporary doggerel: 'Come, gentlemen Tories, firm, loyal and true. Here are axes and shovels and something to do. For the sake of our King, come labor and sing.' Many loyalists indeed came and went out of their dissatisfaction with their second-class status.

The clash of organized loyalism and the Revolutionary militia led to a 'dirty little war of terror and murder' on the local level, a war which often served as a cover for criminal activities and the settling of private scores. The two most extreme examples of such conflict were Westchester, New York and Bergen County, New Jersey where many atrocities and much looting occurred. The loyalists were particularly to the fore in this respect, orders for one raid in New Jersey reading: 'Seize Kill or Apprehend the Rebel Guards in that or any other part of the Country you may march through also every other disaffected person that is known to be aiding the rebellion.' There were various British proposals to unleash the Tories in a campaign of counterinsurgent terrorism but Howe and Clinton, well aware of the nature of the conflict being waged, declined to do so,

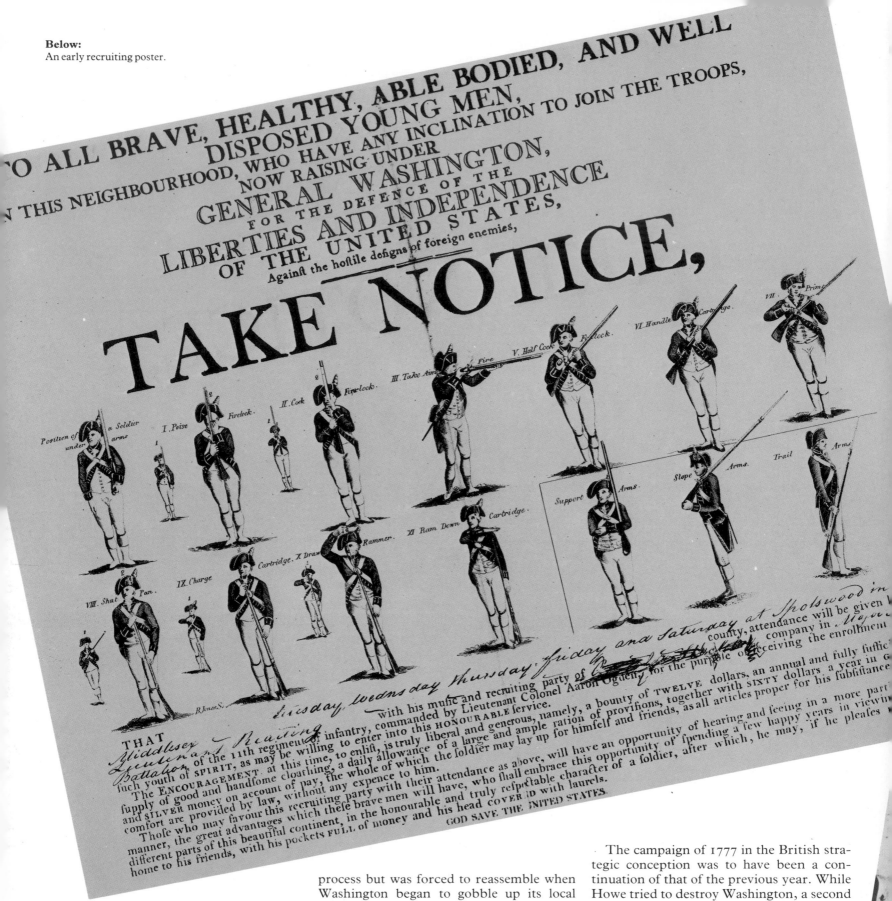

TO ALL BRAVE, HEALTHY, ABLE BODIED, AND WELL DISPOSED YOUNG MEN, IN THIS NEIGHBOURHOOD, WHO HAVE ANY INCLINATION TO JOIN THE TROOPS, NOW RAISING UNDER GENERAL WASHINGTON, FOR THE DEFENCE OF THE LIBERTIES AND INDEPENDENCE OF THE UNITED STATES, Against the hostile defigns of foreign enemies,

TAKE NOTICE,

partly from their sense of decency as British officers but more from a fear of allowing the war to degenerate into senseless and indiscriminate violence which might well have destroyed American society.

Had the British Army been able to disperse, it could have destroyed the Revolutionary infrastructure and paved the way for a loyalist counterrevolution. The Army did disperse in the winter of 1776 and early 1777 in northern New Jersey and virtually extinguished the Revolution there in the process but was forced to reassemble when Washington began to gobble up its local detachments as he did at Trenton and Princeton. The existence of the Continental Army thus also served the function of protecting the militia against direct British attack. The following year, however, the militia of New York and New England displayed a capacity for partisan operations against the British Army which added a new military dimension to the war. This gave the British a foretaste of what they were to experience in the South, at the hands of Nathanael Greene, Daniel Morgan, and Francis Marion.

The campaign of 1777 in the British strategic conception was to have been a continuation of that of the previous year. While Howe tried to destroy Washington, a second army of 8000 British, Germans, Canadians, loyalists, and Indians under John Burgoyne was to strike down the Lake Champlain route at Albany and then down the Hudson to isolate the hotbed of rebellion in New England. Ignoring its manifest strategic defects, the plan to march an army overland from Canada made the assumption that the population, if not loyal, was at least not actively hostile. On his leisurely march to the South, at one point covering 23 miles in 24 days, Burgoyne passed his nights 'singing and drinking and amusing himself in the company of the wife of a commissary, who was his mistress, and, like him, loved champagne,' recorded a German with the expedition. His opponent Philip Schuyler obstructed the roads, removed or destroyed all food and raised the countryside in arms. Augmented by large numbers of New England militia, his successor Horatio Gates annihilated Burgoyne's foraging detachments and harassed his lines of communication and outposts. By September, Gates had cornered the exhausted and hungry British, already reduced by 50 percent, at Saratoga and accepted the surrender of 'Gentleman Johnny' Burgoyne on 17 October.

The strategic folly of the British in 1777 demonstrated on a large scale what had occurred many times since Lexington. Able to mobilize large numbers quickly, the militia greatly limited the ability of the British Army to move except in great force and made any such movement costly. Another important aspect of the relation of the militia to intrusions by the British Army has been established by John Shy. The mobilization of the militia in response to the appearance of a British force was the factor which politicized communities and individuals by forcing them to make a definite choice between King George and Congress. As the war progressed, the majority of dubious, frightened, or apathetic Americans in the middle were sooner or later pushed off the fence by the combination of the appearance of a British force and the demands of the revolutionary militia. In the end, it was the militia which by force if necessary kept the American people at the wearisome task of war for so many years and caused the failure of every British pacification program and attempt to reimpose royal authority short of massive armed force.

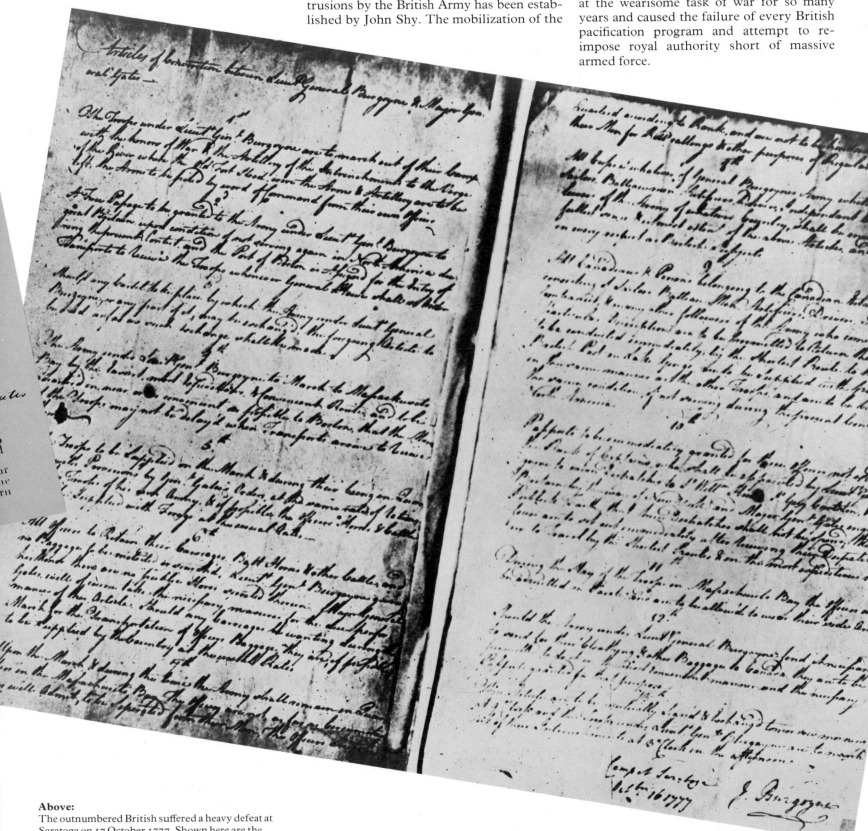

Above:
The outnumbered British suffered a heavy defeat at Saratoga on 17 October 1777. Shown here are the Articles of Capitulation signed by General Johnny Burgoyne who surrendered to General Horatio Gates.

As the London ministry reassessed its strategy in the winter of 1778, it had to face not only the failure of its military approach to the American problem but also a completely changed war situation. The Americans had demonstrated a quite unexpected capacity to thwart and in one case even destroy British field armies while Britain's old enemy, France, had signed a treaty with Congress and entered the war. Partly moved by American offers of commerce but far more by a desire to regain its lost prestige in Europe at the expense of Britain, France had been rendering clandestine assistance to the rebels since 1775 while closely monitoring the situation through secret agents in America. Britain on the other hand had after 1763 completely isolated herself from the power politics of the continent through an unwilling-

away from the numerous, well-armed and hostile population of the north to the thinly populated colonies of Georgia and South Carolina which were relatively inaccessible by land routes from the North, dependent on outside markets and fearful of slave revolts. It was believed with some reason that the area contained numerous loyalists who needed only the protection of the British Army to start the long sought-after counter-revolution. It was finally realized that the military resilience of the rebels in the North lay in their ability to control and tap civilian manpower and that the loyal and neutral citizens of the South had to be protected and organized for a similar phenomenon to occur. In what amounted to a real program of political pacification to counter a revolutionary war, the Army was to regain mili-

Below:
General Francis Marion, 'the Swamp Fox,' inviting British officers to share his meal. Marion was one of the best guerrilla fighters of the Revolutionary War. This engraving was taken from an oil painting by John Blake White which hangs in the Capitol of the United States in Washington.

ness to bear the financial burden of the old alliance with Prussia and a mercantilist belief that America was the important factor in the European balance of power. Even Germain now admitted the unlikelihood of successful pacification since Congress was irrevocably committed to independence and had a new ally. Within the British Army in America disenchantment was so widespread, wrote one officer, that almost every general officer and many field officers wished to be relieved of their postings.

The Prime Minister Lord North now suggested that 'this damned war' was not worth the cost but George III, in an eighteenth-century version of the domino theory, held that relinquishing the American colonies would lead to the piecemeal loss of the remainder of the empire and refused to bow to the swelling chorus of opposition. In a major realignment of strategy, the king and Germain decided to shift the focus of the war

Above:
Colonel William Washington at the Battle of Cowpens, 17 January 1781. Lieutenant Colonel Banastre Tarleton had been dispatched by Cornwallis to drive General Morgan's force against the main force of the British Army. Morgan decided to make a stand at Cowpens and soundly defeated Tarleton.

tary control of Georgia, restore civilian government and then expand this government northward behind further conquests by the Army. The southern strategy further enabled the King to answer the opposition's criticism with the argument that he was fulfilling his duty to protect the loyal citizens of the South and at the same time reducing the cost of the war through greater reliance on Tory manpower, a kind of 'Americanization.'

The plan began well enough as British forces took Georgia in late 1778 and early 1779, while Charleston and the entire rebel army in the South were captured by Clinton in May 1780. Organized resistance south of Virginia collapsed when shortly thereafter Lieutenant Colonel Banastre Tarleton and his British and Loyalist Legion wiped out an American cavalry command at the Waxhaws settlements near the border of the two Carolinas. With no organized American force in the field, British forces were enabled to establish a series of forts in the interior and disperse for local pacification.

Despite its auspicious start and the exploitation of the strong loyalist factions in the highlands which traditionally opposed the Revolutionary politicians of the Tidewater, however, the pacification soon fell into serious difficulties. The Tories capitalized on their reversal of fortune to settle old scores with rebels while looting by British and loyalist forces was widespread. Some prominent former rebels were thus driven back into opposition, the most important being Thomas Sumter who was soon elected Brigadier General of the South Carolina militia. Clinton foolishly ended the system of parole for former rebels and punished all who refused loyalty to the British crown, thus forcing the neutral majority into a hard political choice. The British policy of hostility to the Presbyterian Church, based on the dubious assumption that religious dissenters ipso facto must be rebels, also drove the heretofore largely indifferent Scotch-Irish population into the rebel camp. There was much general irritation over the fact that British troops tended to see any person not in arms for the crown as a probable rebel. Overoptimistic about pacification, British commanders tended to withdraw in favor of new conquests while the new loyalist militia was still vulnerable to the revolutionaries, thus overextending themselves and leaving the loyalists exposed.

Below:
General Daniel Morgan's forces decimated Banastre
Tarleton's British force at Cowpens on 17 January 1781.

Below:
George Washington fires the first shot at the siege of
Yorktown. The group on the left are Rochambeau,
de Lauzun, Montmorency, and General Knox.

Bottom:
Storming the British positions at Yorktown. Although
Cornwallis's troops fought valiantly they were heavily
outnumbered, and since their escape route had been
sealed off they had no option but to surrender.

Right:
Rochambeau, Washington, and Lafayette (left to right)
leave their command tent as Rochambeau gives the final
orders prior to the attack on Yorktown.

brought unacceptable destruction and political alienation. In the South too, the militia
still had call on Indian fighting skills long
since lost in the North. Congress thus sent
Horatio Gates, the victor of Saratoga, to try
to retrieve the situation but Gates lost
another army by prematurely challenging
Cornwallis, now commanding in the South,
to battle at Camden in August 1780. With the
situation so bleak that even the French suggested the permanent loss of the South as
part of a peace treaty, Washington sent one of
his ablest field commanders, a young former
Quaker from Rhode Island, who developed
more fully the irregular warfare which had
destroyed Burgoyne at Saratoga and maneuvered the war to its military conclusion in
America.

Nathanael Greene possessed a fine sense of
strategy and was further blessed with a talented crew of guerrilla commanders for what

As rebel bands coalesced in the hills and
swamps to raid loyalist settlements and attack British detachments and lines of communication, a bloody civil war of attack and
reprisal sprang up to spell the doom of the
British pacification program even before
Washington and Congress were able to intervene in the situation. The French alliance
of 1778 with its prospect of French troops
and seapower had raised Washington's hope
that he could abandon his strategy of attrition and win a major battle to force a
resolution of the war. French seapower in
particular could neutralize Britain's most
important asset in the war – control of the
sea – and make possible assaults on the coastal
enclaves. Such was not to be the case, however, as British admirals skillfully fended
off the generally superior French fleet off
North America while several joint Franco-
American sea and land attacks were fiascos.
The Comte de Rochambeau only arrived
with 5000 French regulars in 1780 by which
time the unfolding campaign in the South
had created the very situation awaited by
Washington.

It was immediately obvious to Congress
that a field force, however weak, must be
organized in the South to assist the partisans,
in a situation which bore some parallel with
that of the North where Washington's Army
provided some shield for the revolutionary
militia. The thinly populated hills and
swamps of the South offered a possibility of
broader guerrilla war lacking in the more
heavily populated colonies from Virginia
north, a region where such a war might have

has been called the 'most impressive campaign of the war.' Greene lacked the strength to engage Cornwallis in main battle and thus adopted the tactic of using the numerous partisan bands to harass the enemy while he divided the 1000 men under his command into three divisions. One was to operate along the coast under Francis 'the Swamp Fox' Marion and Henry 'Light Horse Harry' Lee while 600 under the frontiersman Daniel Morgan, another of Washington's ablest leaders in the field, harassed the British in western South Carolina. Keeping only a few hundred men with him, Greene confounded orthodox military thought by dividing his forces in the face of a superior enemy, yet such a move seemed warranted in view of the scarcity of provisions and the possibility that Cornwallis would also divide his army to chase the three divisions, thus becoming more vulnerable to the partisan bands and Greene's inferior divisions. This modification of Washington's strategy of attacking detachments rather than armies further placed Cornwallis in a strategic bind. If he marched west to subdue Morgan, the other two divisions would sever his lines of com-

munication and menace Charleston, but if he did not deal with Morgan, that bold spirit would raise the west in rebellion and capture the important British forts in that area.

In the end Cornwallis sent Tarleton to deal with the western threat and gave Morgan the opportunity to win the 'clearest American battlefield victory of the war in a contest involving regular British forces' at Cowpens on 17 January 1781 where Tarleton suffered 90 percent casualties. The infuriated Cornwallis then pursued the combined forces of Greene and Morgan in an exhausting chase from western South Carolina across North Carolina to the Dan River on the Virginia border, harassed all the way by swarms of partisans. Greene then exchanged a tactical victory at Guilford Courthouse in return for 500 British casualties, a loss which forced the frustrated Cornwallis to withdraw to the coast. Here again Greene emulated Washington's tactic of losing minor battles in order to bleed his enemy of irreplaceable regular troops. Indeed, Howe had refused to accept another engagement with Washington after the battle of Germantown in October 1777 as the price of his string of tactical victories had been too high. Totally frustrated in the Carolinas, the aggressive Cornwallis decided to take his offensive energy into Virginia in search of greener pastures and more loyalists, leaving Francis Rawdon to win another debilitating and meaningless victory over Greene at Hobkirk's Hill which ironically forced the depleted British to retire to the environs of Charleston while Greene, Morgan, Marion and company systematically knocked off the British forts of the interior. Faring little better in Virginia than in the Deep South, Cornwallis soon positioned himself on the Yorktown peninsula where he expected the support of the British Fleet. After four years of waiting, Washington was finally able to strike the decisive blow that ended the war. Employing the standard geometric siegecraft of the times, Washington and Rochambeau squeezed the hapless Cornwallis into surrender on 19 October 1781. After Yorktown, Clinton maintained the coastal enclaves of New York and Charleston and undertook no further operations until peace became official in 1783.

The war from its inception had almost entirely consisted of land operations in the coastal areas. The colonies did launch a navy never expecting it to challenge the British Fleet but, in keeping with the thought of the times, to attack British trade and colonies. Congress voted to build thirteen frigates in 1775 but only a few actually put to sea. Captains such as John Barry, Lambert Wickes, Nicholas Biddle, Seth Hardy, John Young, and the Scot John Paul who later added Jones to his name took around 200 prizes and fought occasional single ship combats with British frigates, the most famous of which was Jones' captaining of the old French East Indiaman, *Bonhomme Richard*, to victory over the *Serapis* in 1779. Colonial privateers to the number of 2000 took an additional 600 British merchant ships. While the victories of the Navy helped American morale, they had no discernible effect on the outcome of the war.

Above:
Nathanael Greene (1742–86), one of the finest military commanders to emerge from the Continental Army. His great successes were the last campaigns waged in the South.

Left:
Daniel Morgan fought the British under Tarleton at Cowpens and with Greene in the South.

Right:
Captain John Paul Jones in the *Bonhomme Richard* challenged the frigate *Serapis* on 23 September 1779 and took her, although his own ship was so badly damaged she sank two days later.

Nor did the trans-Appalachian west or the Indians influence the course of the war. The British maintained small garrisons at Detroit, Niagara, and Michilimackinac in the north, Kaskaskia in the Illinois country, and Mobile and Pensacola in the south. Although both sides initially hoped that the Indians would remain neutral, Indian resentment of American abuse and settlement made such a prospect unlikely. Much of the frontier was in flames by 1777 as many Indians went on the warpath with no encouragement from either side. The state militias in response raided Indian villages, destroyed food supplies, and massacred women and children as Americans resorted to the only tactic they knew to make the Indian stand and fight. Although a 25-year-old surveyor named George Rogers Clark fought the British-led Indians in the Illinois country and General John Sullavan fought a campaign in western New York, neither side had the capacity to wage a serious war in the west. The Indian raids did drive many Americans into the rebel camp and provide many others with the opportunity to seize yet more Indian land.

Failing to realize the depth of feeling and ideological nature of the conflict on the American side, Britain had initially tried to treat the problem as a police action and, after Lexington and Concord, came to see it as a political problem requiring a military approach. This approach failed because the Howe brothers knew that a determined naval blockade and pursuit of the Continental Army to destruction would probably have left the colonies unpacifiable and ungovernable while the negotiations of Richard Howe came to naught because he had little to offer beyond surrender and Congress was never that desperate. Britain then found itself fighting a global war in 1778 with the entry of France, followed by Spain in 1779, and Holland the following year while the other powers of Europe were loosely aligned against her in the Russian-inspired League of Armed Neutrality. Preoccupied with protecting the home islands, the West Indies, and other parts of the empire, Britain sharply downgraded the North American theater in its overall strategy. The inception of the southern campaign owed more to internal political considerations than to the sound dictates of strategy. As the third and last stage of Britain's attempt to retain America, the southern campaign as a pacification program had failed even before Greene arrived on the scene to force Cornwallis back to more conventional military operations.

After their initial enthusiasm and aggressiveness at Boston and in Canada, the Revolutionary minority in America struggled hard to keep their cause alive in the face of apathy, hardship, Tory opposition, and British military pressure. They too faced a major crisis in 1778 when many disillusioned officers deserted to the enemy and Washington's leadership came under no little criticism. But the Continental Army emerged from its early ordeal at Valley Forge almost as the kind of fighting force desired by Washington and began to give a better account of itself on the battlefield. Washington also grew with the Revolution and ultimately triumphed by sheer tenacity in the field. His defensive strategy made Howe and Clinton pay for their tactical victories and inland penetrations in 1776–77 with unacceptable casualties and finally demonstrated the bankruptcy of British strategy. Greene and the partisans defeated the initiative of the British in the south with a co-ordinated pattern of guerrilla operations related to the presence of a field army too weak to operate alone.

Although in a passage reminiscent of the modern guerrilla strategy exemplified by Mao Tse-tung, Greene wrote, 'We fight, get beat, rise and fight again,' the American Revolution never came close to approximating a true guerrilla war in which revolutionary violence is aimed at destroying popular responsiveness to the state and replacing the old authority with new without resort to conventional warfare. In the American case, the local and intermediate levels of government were taken over with relative ease early in the conflict, no explicit doctrine of revolutionary warfare ever emerged, and military strategy as envisaged by Congress and Washington relied almost completely on conventional warfare. Already an affluent society by the standards of the time, Americans were fighting to preserve not only their institutions but also their property, and guerrilla warfare was not compatible with these aims. Congress never considered, in the words of Walter Millis, 'immolating men, women, and children alike on the altars of patriotism.' The rebels and the British Army did contend for the support and control of the civilian population, but the British Army could not occupy all places at all times and the loyalists were too few to make a critical difference, hence the American cause triumphed at this level through the pervasiveness and tenacity of the revolutionary militia.

In spite of its manifold problems, the Revolution did triumph and the sovereignty of the United States of America was recognized, albeit grudgingly, by the powers of Europe with the signing of the Treaty of Versailles on 20 January 1783. That treaty did not, however, resolve all outstanding problems between the United States and Britain. Indeed, many Americans in future years came to wonder if independence had truly been attained in 1783. When Clinton's regiments embarked on transports at New York for evacuation later that year, it was not the last time that the scarlet coat of the British soldier was to be seen on the soil of America in wartime.

Left:
The return of Cornwallis's defeated army. Despite his reputation in America as the loser at Yorktown Cornwallis went on to a distinguished career in India.

Below:
John Paul Jones.

Left:
Burgoyne's surrender at Saratoga.

Far left below:
Soldiers at Vincennes in February 1779.

Below:
A musketman of the Pennsylvania State Regiment.

Above:
Captain Abraham Whipple.

Above:
Captain John Barry.

Chapter 3

The War of 1812 – Independence Affirmed

'I verily believe that the militia of Kentucky are alone competent to place Montreal and Upper Canada at your feet,' opined Henry Clay of Kentucky to his fellow Congressmen in 1811, while a substantial segment of popular opinion agreed that the conquest of Canada would only be a matter of marching. Propelled by such bellicose if erroneous sentiments, the United States in 1812 declared war on Britain, one of the two great powers of Europe. Politically disunited and militarily unprepared, Americans were in little better position to wage war than they had been 37 years earlier at the outset of the American Revolution. The military contest itself was again to reflect the eighteenth-century style in terms of armies, weapons, and tactics. Earlier patterns were also repeated in the cause of the war in that

Americans had again become enmeshed in a conflict between Britain and France and again perceived themselves victims of British oppression. 'If we submit to the pretensions of England now openly avowed, the independence of this nation is lost . . .' was how John Calhoun of South Carolina framed the issue for Congress on the eve of war. 'This is the second struggle for our liberty.'

The conflict in Europe which ultimately drove the United States to arms was 23 years of almost uninterrupted war from 1792 to 1815 between revolutionary and Napoleonic France and her neighbors. Freed from the restrictions of the British Navigation Acts after the peace of 1783, American maritime commerce had expanded rapidly and was further enhanced by the opportunities presented by the European war, opportunities

which left American bottoms with the largest share of the neutral carrying trade. The prominent American commercial position led to a host of maritime disputes with Britain and France as a result of their respective efforts to weaken each other through commercial warfare. The successive administrations of George Washington and John Adams avoided war by negotiating some settlements abroad and soothing rising passions at home, but the fledgling American Navy was still forced to fight a quasi-war with Revolutionary France in 1798 as a result of French attacks on American commerce. The revolution in France had virtually destroyed the French Fleet as an effective fighting force and the Royal Navy soon completed the task, hence the main maritime disputes – definitions of blockade and contraband, search

Below:
On the morning of 22 June 1807 the frigate USS *Chesapeake* headed out for the open sea. She was followed by the British frigate *Leopard*. The British asked the American ship to surrender deserters. When the officer in charge refused there was a communications problem and the *Leopard* attacked the defenseless American frigate killing three and wounding eighteen sailors. The *Chesapeake* limped home and Commodore James Barron was found guilty of negligence.

Above:
American privateersmen board a British letter-of-marque during the war of 1812.

and seizure on the high seas, American trade with French colonies, and impressment – lay with Britain. Often without allies, that country was fighting for its life for what in the eyes of its citizens was the freedom of Europe from the terror and disruption of the French Revolution and later the tyranny of Napoleon. Britain's war effort in this mortal struggle demanded control of the high seas, control which was threatened by American trade with France and her colonies and by the wholesale desertion of British sailors to the better conditions and wages offered by American captains. Restrictions thus began to be placed on American trade while the naval manpower drain became so intolerable that British captains forcibly impressed British sailors from American vessels. There were over 2000 cases of impressment between 1797 and 1801 while the total had risen to over 6000 by 1812.

The maritime issues could be and were negotiated to varying extents with the exception of impressment on which each side remained immovable. The crux of this complex issue was the British claim to the service of any British-born sailor under the concept of 'indefeasible nationality' even though many British seamen had become naturalized Americans. Such a claim struck at the very heart of American nationhood since Britain was grossly violating American sovereignty by seizing American citizens and also denying the American right to trade freely. If the United States could not defend its citizens and its commercial rights, it was not in fact an independent country. As President James Madison summed up the basic issue, 'Americans can never submit to wrongs . . . which are avowed and justified on principles degrading the United States from the rank of a sovereign and independent power.' France also continued to abuse American commerce in various ways, giving rise to demands for war with that country, but the indisputable fact to Americans was that Britain was the major abuser of their sovereignty. Between 1803 and 1812 Jefferson and Madison tried both diplomatic and economic suasion to secure relief from British and French harassment but Madison was finally forced to admit that American sovereignty would have to be maintained by force. The national honor demanded war.

The maritime issues stemming from the triangular relationship in which the United States was caught between Britain and France were not wholly one-sided, as Britain also had genuine grievances against the United States. Nor did the war arise solely from maritime causes as the steady American push to the west continued old conflicts with the Indians and the British in Canada. Relations between Americans and Indians still centered on expansion, broken treaties, and trade abuses. The 1780s and early 1790s had seen considerable fighting in the Northwest Territory which only came to an end with the victory of General Anthony Wayne at Fallen Timbers in 1794 and the cession of a large amount of Indian land in the Ohio area.

The Indians after 1783 found the British in Canada to be a natural ally as the British, also opposed to American expansion with the Indian wars it tended to provoke, avoided surrendering all their northwest posts after 1783. The Indians relied on the British alliance but were wary, as they had been betrayed in 1783 and again in 1794 when Britain agreed at last to evacuate the territory. An attempt at a pan-Indian movement was begun in 1805 by the Shawnee chief Tecumseh and his brother the Prophet whose goal was to drive Americans from the Northwest Territory. As conflict over the maritime issues led to naval incidents and intensified after 1807, the British administration in Canada renewed its ties with the receptive Indians to strengthen its hand against the possibility of war. Paradoxically the British had to restrain their aroused allies from actually provoking the war.

The increasing bellicosity of American relations with the Indians culminated in the pre-emptive attack on the Shawnees at Tippecanoe in 1811 by William Henry Harrison, Governor of the Indiana Territory. It was widely believed that the British were inciting the Indians but even those making this charge had to admit a lack of proof in their more dispassionate moments. Anti-British feeling was further increased by blaming the maritime restrictions of that country on American trade for an agricultural depression which grew in the Mississippi valley and south Atlantic states in 1808. The elections

of 1810 brought a large turnover in Congress which developed a strong war faction led by younger and more nationalistic men such as Henry Clay, John Calhoun, Peter Porter, and Felix Grundy. A combination of the maritime issues, the British-Indian relationship, the depression, and a new mood in Congress brought a declaration of war on 18 June 1812 even as Britain belatedly began to make significant concessions on the maritime issues. The declaration was far from unanimous, however, as more than 40 percent of Congress voted against going to war with Britain.

The war itself was to be fought largely on eighteenth-century lines as both the United States and Britain had remained largely unaffected by the significant changes in warfare ushered in by the French Revolutionary Wars. The ideology which fueled the French Revolution was also the motivating force for the involvement of the general populace in warfare. Thus the French Revolution and its military exigencies brought a shift from limited to mass warfare. Lacking the time, resources, and inclination to train its citizen armies, Revolutionary France relied on the *levée en masse* leavened with a residue of pro-

fessionalism from the *Ancien Régime*. The mode of attack changed from the line to the column which gave greater offensive shock and better control of undisciplined troops. Free-moving skirmishers widened the arena of combat. Field armies were articulated into independent divisions to endow military movement with greater speed and flexibility, and less rigid battlefield employment of artillery attempted to produce greater superiority at a given point. The new uses of infantry and artillery were intended to create a decisive concentration of force to break the deadlock of linear battle in favor of clear-cut victory. Nationalism, sheer numbers, and good leadership compensated for deficiencies in training and tactical skill in the French armies whose victories forced the rest of the continent to emulate their tactics and organization. Under the subsequent leadership of Napoleon, the mass armies of France overran Europe in a manner not to be repeated until World War II.

Britain alone of the European states refused to enter the nineteenth century militarily because its insular position allowed it to rely mainly on its superb Navy for defense while its Army remained essentially the small long-service professional relic of the age of limited warfare. The purchase of commissions and the regimental system still made money the main factor in the recruitment of officers and insured gentry control of the Army. Recruitment of ranks was strengthened by a system of limited conscription based on the active militia and made possible the small British expeditionary forces on the continent. Linear battle tactics were still employed as the Army fought in two open ranks to increase its firepower and relied ultimately on the bayonets wielded by its thoroughly trained troops. The dominant figure of the Army was Arthur Wellesley, a military and political conservative firmly opposed to tactical and organizational change. The limited nature of the campaigns he was called on to fight and the old-fashioned discipline of his troops gave Wellington his victories over Napoleon. The real strength of Britain lay in its Navy of 600 warships, including 120 ships of the line and 116 frigates. Treated more generously by Parliament than the Army, the Navy had overhauled its administration and tactics and, led by such fighting admirals as Nelson, Howe, and Jervis, had destroyed the French, Spanish, and Dutch fleets to give Britain a global naval dominance after 1805 which lasted through World War I.

While Britain had already been at war for nearly 20 years, the United States was still plagued with a weak central authority, an empty treasury, political disunion, and a chronic inability to raise an effective army. The federal government had obtained more power as a result of the Constitution of 1787 but still had little administrative or financial machinery to exercise its power while Congress was most timid on the issues of taxation and conscription. That body had in fact refused to renew the charter of the First Bank of the United States in 1811 which forced the

Treasury to try to finance the war through the congeries of state banks. With various changes in leadership to weaken further its direction of the finances of the war effort, the Treasury had to borrow over 80 million dollars between 1812 and 1816. Borrowing was in turn made more difficult because the New England and Philadelphia banking and mercantile communities. Federalists staunchly opposed to the war, withheld financial support in the hope of ending what they termed 'Mr Madison's War' while at the same time reaping huge profits from it. Americans were in fact deeply divided over the war and more than two out of five congressmen had voted against the declaration. The main states in support were Kentucky, Ohio, Tennessee, and New York while the political and economic leaders of New England refused to cooperate in any aspect of the war effort, trafficked with the enemy on a grand scale, and in the face of British invasion in 1814, demanded changes in the Constitution under threat of secession at a gathering known as the Hartford Convention. Yet many New Englanders enlisted in the Regular Army.

Although Jefferson and Madison had pursued a progressively stronger foreign policy vis-à-vis Britain and France, American diplomacy lacked credibility because of their weak military policy. Indeed, in the belief that the United States was too weak to risk war, Britain made no concessions until domestic political and economic pressures forced a reconsideration of its maritime policy in 1811–12. Congress had abolished the Continental Army and Navy immediately after the peace of 1783 in the belief that the Atlantic Ocean was adequate defense against European threats. But domestic rebellions in Pennsylvania and Massachusetts, the Indian wars of the Northwest Territory, and the need to protect the expanding maritime commerce soon demonstrated the necessity of a regular army and navy. The Army had grown back to around 4000 men for Anthony Wayne's campaign in the northwest but serious discussion of national defense and military policy only began with the onset of war in Europe. In response to the harassment of Britain and the Barbary pirates of Algiers, the Naval Act of 1794 authorized the construction of six frigates and a number of coastal forts to protect key harbors and ports while the quasi-war with France led to the purchase of more warships and the creation of a small navy department. But even the increasing tension with Britain and France and a small naval campaign against the pirates of Tripoli failed to overcome the deep-rooted anti-militarism which was such an important part of the early American political tradition.

Thomas Jefferson was elected president in 1800 in part due to his anti-military stance. Suspicious of all standing forces and ever mindful of economy, Jefferson's military policy relied on the militia on both land and sea. Accepting realistically that the militia was ill-armed, badly organized, and trained, Jefferson retained the regular Army and

Above:
Units of the fledgling American Navy at sea off the coast of North America.

Left:
William Henry Harrison (1773–1841) was the victor at Tippecanoe. During the War of 1812 he received command in the northwest and eventually routed the British forces at the Battle of the Thames. He was elected President of the United States in 1840 but died only a month after his inauguration.

Below:
Stephen Decatur, was the youngest man to hold the rank of captain in the Navy, at the age of 25. He built up his reputation in action in the Mediterranean in 1805. Stephen Decatur (1779–1820) served in the war against Tripoli with great distinction. He was a flamboyant character and one of the ablest naval commanders of his time. As a result of personal grudges he was challenged by James Barron to a duel and died of his wounds.

gradually increased it as war appeared to draw closer. In the interim, the Army was used to explore the west as in the expeditions of Lieutenant Zebulon Pike and of Captain Meriwether Lewis and Lieutenant William Clark, for roadbuilding, and for negotiating with the Indians. First established in 1794 as a school for engineers and artillerists, West Point was reorganized by Jefferson in 1802 as a military academy to give the Army intellectual direction and doctrine, but the academy suffered teething troubles for many years. Jefferson based his naval policy on a fleet of 50-foot, single-gun boats to be manned by a maritime militia and to be laid up for the most part in time of peace. The overall Jeffersonian military policy thus envisaged a passive defense except in the case of the Indians and condemned the United States to the same situation it had faced in 1775. A lack of military means to achieve its goals and a war effort built on the militia.

The Army entered the war with most of the same problems that had burdened it during the Revolution. Leadership was poor from the office of President Madison down to the level of non-commissioned officer. Madison was neither qualified nor inclined to be a wartime commander in chief nor was he an effective political leader since his control of his party and cabinet was weak. Secretary of War William Eustis was simply incompetent, having ordered General William Hull to hurry from Ohio to Detroit to assume command but neglecting to inform him of the declaration of war. The country was divided into nine military districts with a general officer over each and general coordination by Eustis. The average age of the general officers was 60 as the Army relied on elderly veterans of the Revolution of little talent or energy. The older regiments were commanded by such veterans while command of the newer units formed in the few years before the war had fallen to political appointees. Little concerned with training or military exercises, the officer corps was described by the young Winfield Scott, himself court-martialed for appropriating part of the pay of his troops and slandering his superiors,

Congress could not bring itself to accept any form of conscription and limited itself to increasing the land bounty. Only with the threat of British invasion in 1814 did enlistment creep up enough to give the Army 35,000 men with an additional 35,000 in volunteer militia units on extended duty. As in the Revolution, those who joined the Regular Army tended to be from the less advantaged segments of society. The war effort was further hamstrung by the constitutional issue of whether the militia could be employed outside their home state or on foreign soil, a question which was to cost the United States several battles.

Even in peacetime the Army had been the victim of continual shortages of food, clothing, and quarters as the revolutionary system of supply by private contractors and competitive bidding with no quality control was still employed. After war came, Major General Jacob Brown suggested that the reason five men died of disease for every one killed in battle lay with the policy of the government which appeared to assume that a soldier 'could bear all the vicissitudes of climate and weather without requiring either quarters or covering.' The fact that most of the fighting took place in the west and south meant that logistics and supply remained poor throughout the war and were important factors in the failure or prolonging of many American operations. The American soldier in 1812 did not fare much better than had his predecessor in the Revolution.

The lack of experienced officers and NCOs, leadership cadres which the system inherently failed to produce, was reflected in the poor state of training of the forces. There was little difference between regulars and militia since all were raw recruits. The Army used a ten-company battalion as its tactical unit but had no special units of light infantry or grenadiers and made almost no use of cavalry or mounted infantry. Mainly employed in Indian fighting, the regulars were only familiar with skirmishing tactics. The American soldier in 1812 therefore still fought as an individual, aiming his shots and unfamiliar with the use of the bayonet. Weapons were never in short supply, however, as the Federal Government had encouraged the arms industry since the Revolution. Munitions were produced in government arsenals and foundries as well as by private manufacturers such as Eli Whitney who manufactured 10,000 stands of muskets under government contract.

Neglect by Jefferson and Madison and poor administration of the War Department under first Henry Dearborn and then William Eustis, both devoted to thrift in Army affairs, had left the Army demoralized years before the war occurred. The replacement of Eustis by John Armstrong after the first year brought some change as the latter improved the staff of the War Department and lowered the average age of the general officers to 36 by promoting a group of younger and abler men including Jacob Brown, Andrew Jackson, and Winfield Scott.

as 'swaggerers, dependents, decayed gentlemen and others fit for nothing else . . . totally unfit for any military purpose whatever.'

The Regular Army stood at 6744 men at the outbreak of war and Congress soon authorized a military establishment of 35,000 regulars, 30,000 federal volunteers and 80,000 state militia. New England provided no militia while the response of other states was erratic. The War Department itself emphasized the recruitment of regulars by offering enlistment bounties of $40, three months' pay in advance and 160 acres of land, but sluggish enlistment left the Army with only 15,000 men at the end of the year. The disasters of the early war made necessary periodic recruitment campaigns but the level of enlistment was low throughout the war, a testament to its unpopularity. Even at the worst crisis of the war in 1814,

Above:
Major General Jacob Brown, who was in command at the Battle of Sackett's Harbor in 1813, later became Commander in Chief of the Army.

Right:
Henry Dearborn had been Secretary of War in the Jefferson Administration. At the time of the War of 1812 he was over 60 years old and the senior major general of the Army. He led the Army in the first disastrous campaign against General Brock.

Right:
When war broke out in 1812 Andrew Jackson was major general of the state militia in Tennessee. In September 1813 he led the militia against the Creek Indians in Alabama and decisively defeated them at the Horseshoe Bend of the Tallapoosa in March 1814.

Far right:
In the right foreground stands a sergeant of the Regiment of Light Artillery, an elite horse artillery corps. The horseman is an infantry surgeon in the uniform adopted in January 1812.

Below:
In the left foreground stands a general staff officer wearing the uniform adopted in 1813 and retained for the next 20 years. In the right foreground stands a rifle regiment field grade officer in the dress uniform adopted in 1814.

Once committed to war, the United States was faced with the problem of formulating its war strategy. There were only two means by which the country might attack Britain and hurt it enough to secure redress of American grievances. The tiny American Navy and privateers could attack British commerce and British Canada could be invaded. The former approach offered some possibilities as Britain maintained only one ship of the line and seven frigates in North American waters in 1812 but Canada was obviously the main point of British vulnerability. The most limited view among Americans was that Canada should be captured for use as a hostage to extract concessions from Britain but a stronger argument harked back to the lessons of the colonial wars and demanded the permanent expulsion of British power from North America as necessary for American security. Westerners tended to see the capture of at least western Canada as the solution to the Indian problem. The more extreme end of the spectrum of American opinion is found in the words of Congressman Richard Mentor Johnson: 'I should not wish to extend the boundary of the United States by war if Great Britain would leave us to the quiet enjoyment of independence; but, considering her deadly and implacable enmity, and her continued hostility, I shall never die contented until I see her expulsion from North America, and her territories incorporated with the United States.'

Canada became the primary American war objective and should have been within the American military capability since Americans outnumbered Canadians six million to 500,000, the bulk of the British Army was irrevocably committed to Europe, the frontier to be defended by Canada along the Saint Lawrence River and Great Lakes was also its

Pl.519.   Pub.27 Oct. 1818 by J.Gold. 103 Shoe Lane.   Baily sc.

Sacketts Harbour on Lake Ontaro.

Above:
Sackett's Harbor on Lake Ontario was an American naval base during the War of 1812. This illustration was published in 1818.

Left:
The British general Isaac Brock effected the capture of Detroit without firing a shot against the timorous William Hull.

only line of communication, and the loyalty of the French and American segments of its population was suspect. The Governor of Canada, Sir George Prevost, had only about 4000 regulars, 3000 provincials, and a militia system similar to that of the United States to hold the 900-mile frontier. Well aware of the disunity south of the border, Prevost did not want to provoke the enemy to concerted attack and decided to defend Lower Canada (Montreal and Quebec) as strongly as possible, leaving Upper Canada (Ontario) to fend for itself under Major General Isaac Brock with one regiment of regulars, such militia as could be raised, and the Indians. Prevost and Brock were both experienced soldiers, the former having been informed by London that he was only expected to hold his own defensively and the latter wishing to harness the Indians and militia for limited offensives. To Brock, the war was the opportunity he had been seeking for some years to build his military reputation. Circumstances thus dictated that Canada remain on the defensive while the United States had to launch an offensive.

The strategic imperative for the United States was to strike quickly before Canadian defenses could be reinforced by Britain. The obvious strategy was a thrust up the historic invasion route of Lake Champlain and the Richelieu River against Montreal. Capture of this city would sever the British line of communications and quickly bring control of all the territory to the west. Madison, much maligned as a war leader, at least realized the importance of speed and of Montreal as the objective but circumstances militated against that move. The Regular Army was as yet too small and dispersed along the frontier; consequently the New England militia would have had to be mobilized for the job. Invoking the constitutional limitations on the employment of the militia, however, the New England governors refused to co-operate in this as in other aspects of the war. Stymied in this line of attack, Madison and his Cabinet adopted a plan proposed by Major General Henry Dearborn, a Revolutionary War veteran and recent Secretary of War. A force under Dearborn would move on Montreal via the Lake Champlain route while other attacks were launched from Detroit, Niagara, and Sackett's Harbor. The shift in emphasis toward the west was to no little extent the result of the perceived Indian threat which loomed large in American minds. A further factor influencing the decision was the fact that a third of the 100,000 people in Upper Canada were American in origins and sympathies. The American offensive strategy thus became diffused in its application

largely as a result of non-military factors.

Dearborn set up headquarters in Albany and spent months in fruitless negotiations with the recalcitrant New England governors while Stephen van Rensselaer, commander of the New York militia, began to gather forces at Niagara. Brock shrewdly assessed the feebleness of the American threat from Niagara and shifted the bulk of his meager forces west to face the 2000 regulars and militia under Major General William Hull at Detroit. Dangling at the end of a 200-mile-long supply line which was under attack by Indians and British gunboats on Lake Erie, Hull allowed himself to be bluffed into inactivity by Brock's inferior force and the threat of 600 Indians under Tecumseh. Hull's performance was such that his own officers requested 'the arrest and displacement of the General.' Before Brock even mounted an attack, Hull surrendered Detroit on 16 August and sealed the fate of the subsidiary posts in the west. For his paramount role in one of the most disgraceful episodes in American military annals, he was sentenced to death by a court-martial but reprieved by Madison on the basis of his service in the Revolutionary War. Brock's bloodless triumph influenced the course of the war in important ways. With the whole American northwest open to invasion and Indian depredation, the United States was forced to divert vital military strength away from the east toward its recovery the following year. The initial defeat in the west thus ruled out any possibility of quick victory in the east.

These four pictures show the progressive destruction of the *Java* by the *Constitution*.

Above:
After an hour's fighting the *Java* has lost her foremast and become totally unmanagable.

Below:
The *Java* only has a main mast left.

Above:
With all her masts gone the *Java* was forced to surrender. Survivors on the *Java* were taken onto the *Constitution*.

Below:
The *Java* was damaged beyond repair and was blown up.

These paintings were drawn by Nicholas Pocock from sketches made at the battle by Lieutenant Buchanan.

With the threat in the west removed, Brock hastened to Fort George on the Niagara frontier where he knew the main attack should come. Van Rensselaer had managed to gather about 6000 disease-ridden, undisciplined regulars and militia at Niagara and was forced into action by threats of the militia to decamp if there was no immediate attack. A thrust was planned against Queenston, an objective of little import. On 13 October Brock's well-deployed troops threw back the American attack with heavy losses in the battle of Queenston Heights where Brock himself fell leading a counterattack. The issue was really decided, however, when the bulk of the militia refused to cross the river into Canadian territory to support their hard-pressed comrades. The battle itself had minor military importance but Isaac Brock and Queenston Heights have retained special significance in Canadian history as the man and battle that repelled an American invasion. Van Rensselaer resigned and was succeeded by Major General Alexander Smyth of the Regular Army whose hopeless incompetence not only wasted the remainder of the campaigning season but caused him to be dropped from the rolls of the Army.

By mid-November Dearborn had gathered a force of over 6000 men, most of whom were raw recruits, and advanced from Albany to Plattsburgh. Here again the militia refused to cross the frontier and brought the campaign of 1812 to an ignominious and bloodless end. Faced with major military and logistic problems of their own, the British by virtue of the leadership of Brock had turned back the American attack in the east and won control of the northwest. As its generals and troops in the field compiled an unparalleled record of military disaster and sheer incompetence, the United States was forced to endure a year of helpless humiliation in the war which had been declared to uphold American honor.

The fiascoes of 1812 led to the resignation under fire of Eustis of whom Treasury Secretary Albert Gallatin was moved to remark, 'His incapacity and total want of confidence in him were felt through every ramification of the service.' The politically weak Madison found himself forced to name as the new secretary the alleged author of the controversial Newburgh Addresses of 1783. John Armstrong had been a colonel in the Revolutionary War, was politically ambitious and unburdened by scruples. His best contribution to the war effort was to promote more able officers to positions of command but he, too, actively courted yet more military reverses. The strategy of 1813 was dictated largely by politics since it was an election year. Madison's survival in office required a new offensive in the west to subdue the Indians and recapture Detroit. The lessons of 1812, on the other hand, were that the war required better military leadership and naval control of the Great Lakes. British policy was in fact based on control of the Indians and naval dominance of the lakes to protect its line of communications. American strategy thus came to include an offensive in the west under William Henry Harrison, 39-year-old governor of the Indiana territory, a naval program on Lakes Erie and Ontario under Commodore Isaac Chauncey, and a renewed attack on the Niagara front by Dearborn.

Plagued by logistic problems, Harrison's campaign developed slowly and was soon bogged down in winter while part of his force was defeated and massacred by British and Indians at the River Raisin. Reduced from 6500 to 1000 men as the enlistments of his militia came to an end, Harrison built Fort Meigs and withstood repeated attacks by Brock's less able successor, Colonel Henry Procter. Chauncey began to construct a flotilla of small warships on Lake Ontario and dispatched Commodore Oliver Hazard Perry to do the same on Lake Erie. Perry's squadron soon came to comprise nine assorted ships in the bay at Presque Isle (Erie) against six British ships commanded by Captain Robert Barclay who had lost an arm at Trafalgar. The fleets clashed off Put-in Bay on 10 September in one of the few engagements that decisively altered the course of the war. In a hard-fought action which cost Barclay his other arm, Perry annihilated his undermanned and out-gunned opponent and then wrote his famous dispatch to Harrison: 'We have met the enemy and they are ours: two ships, two brigs, one schooner and one sloop.' With complete naval control of Lake Erie now resting in American hands, Procter's position to the west was much less tenable as his line of communication had been cut. He was therefore forced to withdraw north to the Thames River from the Detroit area where he had been confronting Harrison. The thoroughly demoralized British and their Indian allies were destroyed and Tecumseh was killed by a superior force under Harrison at the battle of the Thames on 5 October, a British fiasco for which Procter was later court-martialed.

Dearborn's campaign on the Niagara frontier suffered various minor disasters and led to his replacement by James Wilkinson whose deep involvement in the Aaron Burr conspiracy and other dubious activities had made him a most controversial figure in the Army as well as many enemies. With a deficient grasp of tactical and logistic reality, Armstrong sent the reluctant Wilkinson on a campaign east along the Saint Lawrence with Montreal as the ultimate object. The operation was doomed from its inception by the absence of naval control of Lake Ontario and inadequate men and supplies and resulted in yet another American disaster, the court-martial of Wilkinson, and heavy British raids on American towns and settlements all along the central frontier. The second year of the war thus came to a close with the American position in the west recouped and the Indians broken as a result of Perry's victory on Lake Erie, but with the war now carried to American soil farther to the east. In spite of great Canadian inferiority, the vastly superior power of the United States had accomplished less than nothing as a result of politics, disunity, bad leadership and the overwhelming logistic problems which dominated every operation. Having failed to exploit its early military superiority, the United States was now forced on the defensive as the war in Europe reached its final denouement.

That lengthy struggle was entering its final stage at the end of 1813. The British expeditionary force under Wellington had broken the French hold on the Iberian peninsula while the Russian General Kutuzov had taken the measure of Napoleon in Eastern Europe. In the end, it was Russian bayonets which forced Napoleon into capitulation and exile in April 1814 and freed Britain's Army and Navy for her other war. The end of the war in Europe, however, removed the original maritime causes of the American declaration of war. Even before the defeat of France, the two reluctant belligerents had been negotiating to negotiate. Although there were other pressing claims on Britain's attention and resources, peace was delayed because British popular opinion demanded that 'Jonathan should be given a good drubbing' for his perfidy in attacking Britain in her hour of mortal peril. The 15,000 veterans of Wellington's peninsular campaign provided the perfect instrument of retribution and the Iron Duke himself was offered the command in America. But distances and logistics made America a difficult environment for a large field army to operate and, as in the Revolution, there was still no political or economic center of import to be attacked. Wellington thus declined and advised peace, saying, 'I do not know where you could carry on . . . an operation which would be so injurious to the Americans as to force them to sue for peace. . . .' London nevertheless planned an offensive on three fronts to force a quick and favorable peace from the United States. Prevost was to have the bulk of the peninsular veterans to gain control of the frontier waterways in the north, large naval raids were to be directed at the eastern seaboard, and a third force was to strike at New Orleans to cut the Mississippi Valley and back settlements off from the sea and acquire a bargaining chip for the peace negotiations. The aggressor now became the victim as the roles were reversed.

Below and inset:
At the height of the Battle of Lake Erie, Perry was forced to abandon his flagship *Lawrence*. With his flag in hand he had himself rowed to the *Niagara* through the intensive fire. After the battle he sent a dispatch (inset) announcing the victory to General William Henry Harrison.

As Britain prepared to take the offensive, the United States reached its nadir. The Treasury was bankrupt from the failure of prewar Republican administrations to provide an adequate system of taxation and the refusal of New England, the richest section of the country, to participate in the war. The tiny American Navy had made a brave showing in 1812 but by the following year was bottled up in its harbors, along with the American merchant fleet, by a British blockade from New Orleans to New York, New England having been exempted because of its pro-British attitude and the important role it played in supplying Canada. Elsewhere the economy was on the verge of collapse as a result of no exports, soaring prices, and the inability to move goods internally from one section of the country to another. Such popular support as the war had initially enjoyed had been dissipated by the virtually unblemished record of military ineptitude and disaster, hence recruitment for the Regular Army sank to a new low. Unable to recruit or employ an effective army, Washington had essentially lost control of the management of the war and had to rely on the sections of the country threatened with invasion to defend themselves.

Except for minor raiding, the war in the west had come to an end with Harrison's victory at the Thames and continued to be deadlocked on the central front. Even before reinforcements began to arrive from England, the American forces had lost the abil-

ity, however seldom realized, to overpower the inferior Canadian defenses despite better training and leadership in the army. Wishing to undertake one last offensive before being forced completely on the defensive, Armstrong ordered the crack troops under Jacob Brown and his subordinates Winfield Scott and Eleazar Ripley to attack York (Toronto). After two fiercely fought stand-up battles against British regulars at Chippewa and Lundy's Lane, the Americans were forced to withdraw. Isaac Chauncey and Captain Sir James Yeo, British naval commander in the Great Lakes area, were at the same time engaged in a naval arms race for control of Lake Ontario. Furiously building ever larger

Above:
The *Constitution* takes the British frigate *Guerrière* on
19 August 1812.

Below:
Seamen on the USS *Constitution* cheer as they engage
the British frigate *Guerrière*.

Below:
Captain Isaac Hull, commander of the USS
Constitution, an expert in maneuvering and gunnery.

Below:
The HMS *Shannon* commences battle with the American frigate *Chesapeake* on 1 June 1813.

Bottom:
Captain Broke of the *Shannon* leading a boarding party on to the USS *Chesapeake*.

Below:
Thomas MacDonough in command of naval forces at Lake Champlain.

ships until each side was laying down three-deck battleships of over 100 guns, neither Chauncey nor Yeo dared risk battle and defeat because naval control of the lake was so crucial to the military contest on the northern frontier. Lacking such control, neither antagonist could follow up local successes or mount a major offensive. It was for this reason that Prevost decided to mount his major move against the American base at Plattsburgh on Lake Champlain. The success of the move again depended on naval control of that lake but when Captain Thomas MacDonough's little American flotilla defeated a similar British squadron in Plattsburgh harbor on 11 September, Prevost withdrew out of fear for his line of communications. Wellington's veterans (their attack on Plattsburgh recalled before it was barely underway) were scarcely tested in battle against such inferior American forces. The war on the northern frontier thus came to an end with the British having made no better use of their time of superiority than had their opponents.

While the war in the north wound down to its anti-climax, Vice-Admiral Alexander Cochrane with a powerful naval force and Major General Robert Ross with 4000 veterans fell on the defenseless east coast. The blockade had earlier been accompanied by raids on coastal towns but Cochrane now

Above:
Commodore Thomas MacDonough directing the fire of his ship during the Battle of Lake Champlain.

Below:
American troops trained by young Winfield Scott fought well in a last ill-conceived invasion of Canada.

Above:
Letter commissioning an officer of the state of New York issued during the War of 1812.

Below:
Winfield Scott ordering the charge of McNeil's battalion at the Battle of Chippewa.

extended the embargo to New England to worsen the American financial crisis, sent out raiding parties against New England ports, and occupied part of Maine. Launching hit-and-run raids aimed at destruction, demoralization and loot, the British had learned a lesson from their experience in the American Revolution as they no longer tried to hold coastal enclaves and conduct inland penetrations. The culmination of this strategy came in August when Ross defeated a totally disorganized rabble of Americans at Bladensburg, Maryland, marched into the abandoned capital of Washington and burned the public buildings because he could find no one with whom to bargain for their ransom. His next objective was the privateering base of Baltimore but a stout defense led by Samuel Smith, a tough veteran of the Revolution, the ability of Fort McHenry to withstand a barrage of 1800 cannon balls, shells and bombs, and the death of Ross in a skirmish led to a British withdrawal. Watching the bombardment of Fort McHenry from a British ship where he had gone to arrange the release of a friend, the lawyer Francis Scott Key was moved to compose the first draft of 'The Star-Spangled Banner,' published a week later in a Baltimore newspaper and later set to the tune of the old British drinking song 'To Anacreon in Heaven.' For his failure to or-

ganize any defense for the capital, Armstrong was drummed out of the cabinet and replaced by James Monroe, young and capable but unable to effect any change in the management of the war effort and strategy before hostilities ended a few months later.

The death of Ross brought Major General Sir Edward Pakenham, a brother-in-law of the Duke of Wellington, to command the third phase of the British offensive. The war thus came to its denouement in the south, a region which had already seen considerable fighting and mobilization. There had been strong regional sentiment in 1812 for seizing all of Florida from Spain, an ally of Britain but a country with which the United States was not at war. A force of militia had been mobilized for this purpose by Andrew Jackson, a martial lawyer and politician from Tennessee, but the agreeable Madison had been unable to get the necessary legislation through Congress. Incited by the wide-ranging Tecumseh, part of the Creek nation had gone on the warpath the following year in a campaign against American expansion. The ensuing war saw large numbers of Indians killed and major cessions of Indian land in a long and hard fought campaign by Jackson's Tennessee militia. Appointed Major General and assigned command of the Tennessee, Louisiana and Mississippi military district, Jackson and a motley assortment of militia, Indians and pirates from Barataria defeated a frontal assault by Pakenham's 10,000 blooded troops in a Bunker Hill style battle on 8 January 1815 at New Orleans. The war thus ended on a high note for Americans as news of this victory became current at the same time as word reached America of the signing of a peace treaty on 24 December 1814. Derived from negotiations underway at Ghent since the summer, the treaty simply recorded the agreement of each belligerent to cease hostilities and return to the territorial *status quo ante bellum* because the military operations in the war had been so indecisive.

Above left:
MacDonough's squadron overcomes a British force under Captain George Downie on Lake Champlain.

Below:
Ignorant of the official end of the war, Andrew Jackson defeated the British at New Orleans on 8 January 1815.

Above:
Lord Gambier and John Quincy Adams shake hands over the Treaty of Ghent, Christmas Eve, 1814. The British had relinquished all territorial demands and the other reasons for war – neutral rights and the impressment of seamen – had already been settled.

The Anglo-American clash of 1812 was a footnote to the general European war in which Britain had invested all her resources. With comparatively few troops, Canada simply defended itself in spite of financial woes, the many American sympathizers within its population, staggering logistic problems and a difficult defensive situation. In spite of its large military potential, the United States was unable to mobilize much force or apply effectively such force as it had.

As most operations occurred in the west and south with their long and trackless distances, much of the effort of commanders in the field on each side was focused more on trying to feed their men than on fighting. The military operations were thus indecisive because neither side possessed the capacity to launch a serious offensive.

The formative period of the American military experience was brought to an end by the Treaty of Ghent in 1814. The military threats and turbulence of the period from 1607 to 1815 had made military and political survival an important issue for American society and led to a conception and conduct of war in sharp contrast to that of Europe. While Europeans were evolving a system of war and diplomacy which protected society from the worst effects of warfare, Americans found themselves involved in a series of wars with the Indians characterized by incredible barbarity. The low capacity of the colonies for self-defense led to the emergence of a strategy of retaliation and annihilation, the goal of which was a definitive solution to the problem of military security. As the colonies began to master the Indian problem in the late seventeenth century, Britain entered a long period of war with France and Spain which perpetuated the horrors and anxieties of the early Indian wars. Wars which were fought in limited fashion in Europe became savage conflicts in their North American extensions as both France and Spain used

the Indians to compensate for their inferior military capacity. Powerless to prevent the military projection of European conflicts to North America, the definitive solution for American security came to be seen as the total elimination of France and Spain from the continent.

There was increasing perception of Britain as a threat to American security after 1760, a perception which led to the Revolutionary War and the War of 1812. Britain was not

Top:
Andrew Jackson seen directing operations at the Battle of New Orleans. His army was an unconventional combination of frontiersmen and Indians (not shown in picture) and faced veteran British forces under one of Wellington's lieutenants. The victory was as stunning as it was futile and made Jackson a national hero, as well as restoring some of America's lost pride.

Above:
Original copy of The Star-Spangled Banner. It was written by Francis Scott Key, a young Washington lawyer. He was aboard a British warship attempting to arrange an exchange of prisoners in the wake of the rout at Bladensburg and the destruction of Washington. While on board he watched the unsuccessful British bombardment of Fort McHenry. The sight of the American flag waving over the unscathed fort as a symbol of American endurance prompted him to write what was to become the National Anthem.

A Scene on the FRONTIERS as Practiced by the HUMANE BRITISH and their WORTHY ALLIES___

Bring me the Scalps and the King our master will reward you___

Reward for Sixteen Scalps

W. Charles del et sculp

Arise Columbia's Sons and forward press,
Your Country's wrongs call loudly for redress;
The Savage Indian with his Scalping knife,
Or Tomahawk may seek to take your life,

By bravery aw'd they'll in a dreadful Fright,
Shrink back for Refuge to the Woods in Flight;
Their British leaders then will quickly shake,
And for those wrongs shall restitution make.

evicted from Canada in either conflict but the two countries did develop a peaceful and successful means of settling disputes and demilitarized the American-Canadian border. The War of 1812 also saw the complete defeat of the last major Indian attempt to retain significant land east of the Mississippi, an attempt which had begun half a century earlier with Pontiac. In addition to these significant advances in national security, the conflict of 1812 marked the beginning of American independence of the European system. No longer were European wars to involve America nor European affairs to determine American foreign relations. Independence from European interference was expanded rhetorically to include South America as well in the Monroe Doctrine of 1823 and ironically was enforced by the Royal Navy as British economic influence became predominant in Latin America in the aftermath of the destruction of the Spanish and Portuguese colonial systems. The United States did not become involved in European affairs again until 1898. Americans had thus virtually achieved their concept of absolute security by 1815 and in the process transformed their notion of definitive solutions into a traditional demand for total military answers to national security problems.

During the formative period, Americans developed an identifiable perception of the pattern of war. In the Indian and French Wars, the Revolution and War of 1812, invasion and early defeats were followed by recovery, endurance, and final victory. In all cases, the very survival of society was seen to be at stake, and war occurred mainly in the context of mortal peril and widespread anxiety. Often surprised and always unprepared, Americans had become confident of their ability to overcome adversity and persevere to victory. 'Prowess in arms became an integral part of patriotic pride' as Marcus Cunliffe has observed, a fact reinforced by the frequency of wars, campaigns and skirmishes with the Indians. The origins and early expression of American national character were mainly military in form, the most conspicuous and enduring expression of the early American martial spirit being 'The Star-Spangled Banner,' composed at the height of battle and standing as both anthem and battle cry. In the early American creed, freedom had been won and maintained by war, hence the free man must be a martial man. It was George Washington who wrote in 1783 that 'every Citizen who enjoys the protection of a free Government owes . . . his personal services to the defense of it.'

Through the end of the War of 1812, the militia was the basis of the American military system not only in myth but in reality. The amateur general was exemplified in the career of Washington, often compared with the Roman Cincinnatus, and the virtue of the citizen soldier demonstrated in such battles as Concord, Bunker Hill, and Saratoga; the southern partisans under Marion, Greene, and Lee; Harrison at the Thames; and most of all, Jackson's astounding victory at New Orleans where Pakenham lost not only his own life but over a quarter of his force against a mere handful of American casualties. The citizen soldier embodying the somehow 'American' virtues of spontaneity, robustness, and innate military skill dominated the public imagination in contrast to the professional soldier, somehow un-American, slightly sinister and politically suspect. Yet in spite of the popular esteem of the militia concept, so much an expression of American political ideals, Congress and the states were never able to create a well-organized and efficient militia system because such a system paradoxically was politically unacceptable to most Americans who resisted its inherent notion of compulsion and infringement of the states' sovereignty. In keeping with their long-standing opposition to permanent

armies and professional soldiers, Americans were reluctant to let their militia become too efficient or too much under federal control. The War of 1812 had been mostly fought by the militia but the humiliating train of defeats failed to alter the national myth that the militia was the best defense in time of national danger.

Yet the military tradition which raised the citizen soldier to primacy also had a place for the regular soldier. The Continental Army of George Washington had differed from its European counterparts in standard rather than concept. Both the Army and the Navy had slowly been accepted as necessities, however dubious, since the complete demobilization after the Revolution and emerged from the War of 1812 with considerable popularity. In the case of the Army, it was the showing of regular troops trained by Winfield Scott at the battles of Chippewa and Lundy's Lane in 1814 that won public favor. After extensive study of the corpus of classical European texts on warfare, Scott had become a talented practitioner of the limited warfare of the eighteenth century. Following the example of von Steuben in the Revolution, he trained the officers of 3000 raw recruits under the command of Jacob Brown, to train their own men in attack and

Below:
Capture of the *Essex* by HMS *Phoebe* and *Cherub* off
Chile, March 1814. Under the command of Captain
David Porter, the *Essex* cruised the South Pacific
throughout 1813, raiding British merchant ships and
whalers, and pirates of other nations. He took many
prizes including one English ship carrying £11,000
worth of specie.

defense with the bayonet and musket, unit maneuver, and tactical deployment. Ten hours of daily drill for several months produced troops which supposedly caused the British commander at Chippewa to exclaim 'These are regulars, by God!' The troops trained by Scott were the only units of the regular Army or militia able to meet British regulars in open battle on equal terms. The remainder of the men of the Regular Army differed little from the militia since neither received much training. Later advocates of the Regular Army and disciples of the late nineteenth-century historian of military policy Emory Upton seized on Chippewa and Lundy's Lane as proof of the superiority of the regulars over militia when in fact the battles of the war demonstrated only that well-led soldiers, whether regulars or militia, perform better than poorly-led troops of whatever status. Largely due to the efforts of Winfield Scott, the Regular Army thus emerged from the war with new popular esteem and enabled succeeding presidents and secretaries of war to encourage an increasing trend toward professionalization and reliance on the regulars for national defense.

The Navy had comprised only six frigates, a corvette and nine assorted sloops and brigs when hostilities commenced in 1812 and compiled a very creditable record at a time when the war on land was a national disgrace. Well-trained, efficient and blooded by recent operations against France, Tripoli, and Algeria, the Navy already had a high standard of professionalism as well as frigates which were larger and heavier gunned than their British counterparts. Victory in single ship combats was won by Isaac Hull in the *Constitution* over the *Guerrière* and *Java* and by Stephen Decatur in the *United States* over the *Macedonian* but the motto of the United States Navy was originated by James Lawrence of the *Chesapeake* as he lay mortally wounded and in defeat by the *Shannon*: 'Don't give up the ship. Fight her till she sinks.' The *Essex* under David Porter had a colorful and destructive cruise among British shipping in the Pacific before being overpowered by two British frigates. The Navy also won seven of eight sloop and brig single combats. These glamorous successes made the sailors visible and popular, hence the Navy also emerged from the war in a stronger position.

Americans thus emerged from the War of 1812 and their formative period with firm beliefs in war as a serious business, in military security as an absolute value, and in their own military prowess, but with a not quite complete belief in the efficacy of the amateur over the professional soldier. The war itself was an important event in the development of American nationhood. Because the war had been a fumbling draw, it became a moral victory in American eyes as it seemed that once again the United States had held off the might of Britain. 'The War renewed and reinstated the national feelings and character which the Revolution had given, and which were daily lessened' wrote former Secretary of the Treasury Albert Gallatin. 'The people now . . . are more American: they feel and act more as a nation. . . .' Despite a divided Congress and citizenry, the United States had met the test of war as a nation and, at least in American eyes, had vindicated the national honor by the triumph of its arms. A new sense of national identity and purpose was the result. Victories such as New Orleans, the Thames, Lake Erie, and Baltimore tended to blind Americans to the true nature of the military contest and its lessons and only reinforced that evolving blend of national pride, confidence and chauvinism which would soon receive the label of 'manifest destiny.'

Chapter 4

The Mexican War and Manifest Destiny

It was not a popular war, no more so than was the War of 1812, 34 years earlier. The Whigs of 1846 echoed the charge of their political ancestors, the Federalists of 1812, crying, in the words of a congressman from Kentucky, 'It is our own President who began this war.' Brought on by the clash of American westward expansion and Mexican nationalism, the United States entered its third war in a frankly imperialist mood, a war which was to have important consequences for its political and military development. Itself a curious mixture of eighteenth century and Napoleonic warfare in Mexico with a sideshow of opera bouffe in California, the military contest produced an unbroken train of victories to nourish Americans in their legend of success and military prowess. Although large numbers of citizen volunteers served and fought well on the whole, the Mexican War belonged to the regulars who emerged in the public eye as a successful professional force. The everpresent interplay of war and politics ballooned to such an extent that restraints were placed on overt politicking by the military. By adding vast tracts of new territory to the country, the most important result of the war, however, was to bring to a boil the simmering sectional crisis which erupted thirteen years later in the Civil War while at the same time training an entire generation of military leadership for the conduct of that conflict.

Americans had been expanding steadily since their first arrival in North America but in the surge of nationalism after 1815, many began to envision a country encompassing the entire continent. John Quincy Adams, the imperialistically-minded Secretary of War under President James Monroe, spoke of 'our natural dominion in North America' while extracting Florida from Spain by treaty in 1819 and negotiating a joint occupation of the large Oregon territory with Britain. The subsequent Monroe Doctrine of 1823 relating to the non-colonization of the western hemisphere by European states was in effect reserving it for American expansion. The public fever for territorial expansion eased after 1820 but revived in the 1840s to become a dominant issue in American politics over the question of the annexation of Texas, a question whose resolution led directly to the war with Mexico.

The drive for continental expansion became incorporated into the notion of the American uniqueness and mission. As first expressed in seventeenth-century religious terms, the mission was to create a regenerate society dissociated from the decadence of the old world. The idea of regeneracy received a political dimension in the later eighteenth century with the American ideals of repub-

lican government and absence of hereditary privilege and was further refined by the Jeffersonian support of state sovereignty as well as the later Jacksonian concept of broader democracy. By the 1840s the idea of the unique American mission was a vague amalgam of political, agrarian, and business democracy. A free confederated republic on a continental (and occasionally hemispheric) scale was to have a classless society, freedom of religion and political democracy expressed in wide suffrage, frequent elections, and one-term presidents. Agrarian democracy meant the availability of land to all and business democracy meant free trade and the absence of legalized monopolies. The natural resources of the continent were to be developed for the benefit of mankind while its backward peoples, excluding the heathen Indians who were 'rightfully' dispossessed by Christians, were to be regenerated and room made through expansion for those fleeing the oppression of monarchical Europe.

The mission of the American people was therefore a rather idealistic sense of heaven preordained expansion over a vaguely defined region. As the scholarly Secretary of the Navy, George Bancroft wrote, democracy and republicanism were the will of God who had assigned the task of their dissemination especially to the United States. Journalist John Sullivan coined the term 'manifest destiny' for this complex of attitudes in an editorial in the *Democratic Review* in 1845. Indeed, the progress of American expansion already attested to the veracity and historical reality of manifest destiny. Utilizing the concept of the political compact or covenant derived from the compact made by the Plymouth Pilgrims aboard the *Mayflower* in 1620 to form a 'civil body politic' in the absence of any legal authority, settlers migrated into new areas, organized themselves politically by compact, and applied for admission to the American Union, a process which had already given the United States 20 million people and 28 states by 1844. As Americans defined the Western hemisphere as the arena of their manifest destiny, they extended the notion of the compact to the Latin American states emerging from Spanish rule and modeling their political institutions on those of the United States.

It was the duty of Americans to admit neighboring peoples who had achieved self-government by compact or revolution to the 'temple of American freedom and institutions' but it was also evident that the hispanic peoples just emerging from colonial rule would require a lengthy period of education and preparation before admission.

Manifest destiny had its proponents in all parts of the country in the 1840s but its real strength lay in the northwest and northeast and particularly in Illinois and New York. Northwesterners tended to be more aggressive about expansion, advocating war with Britain over Oregon (54–40 or fight!) and a hard-line toward Mexico long before relations with that country had reached the problem stage, while northeasterns tended to be opposed to obtaining territory by force. The whole issue of expansion was weakened by two factors – the question of the further spread of slavery and racism. The addition of more territory to the country raised the question of whether new States would be admitted to the Union as slave-holding or free. In either case, the precarious sectional balance between North and South, free and slave-holding states, would be upset. Many Northerners favoring manifest destiny in principle opposed it in practice for fear of the spread of slavery. Southerners recognized that the West was not really suited to plantation agriculture and a slave-oriented economy and would eventually be part of the free state bloc. Southerners in general and many Northerners as well were not sanguine about the possibility of regenerating black and hispanic peoples as this was the period of growth in the North of legislated segregation and racial discrimination. While a strong force in American politics, manifest destiny never had the strength to become a crusade.

Mexico was one of the newly independent Latin American countries which the supporters of manifest destiny thought would eventually join the American Union. Achieving independence from Spain in 1821, that country had adopted a constitution modeled on that of the United States three years later, but was dominated by a small aristocratic land-owning and professional class which continued to control the mass of illiterate Indian and mestizo peasants. Mexican politics were quickly split by conflict between the Centralists, conservative aristocrats favoring authoritarian government whether monarchy or military dictatorship, and the Federalists who supported the republicanism of the constitution of 1824. With its northern provinces largely unsettled and ungoverned, the Mexican government offered liberal land grants to colonizers and attracted a surge of Americans to the fertile

JAMES K. POLK.
FREEDOMS CHAMPION.

MATTY MEETING THE TEXAS QUESTION.

soil and good climate of Texas. Further immigration by Americans was banned in 1830, however, as the government had come under the domination of a succession of Centralist-backed political generals who were unable to tolerate the importation of American political ideals into Texas and by extension into Mexico proper. General Antonio de Santa Anna, a fantastic figure who became military dictator on four separate occasions in Mexican history, abrogated the constitution in 1835 and became dictator. Texans joined in a general but futile Federalist rising against Santa Anna while remote California refused to recognize his authority as well. When a substantial army led by Santa Anna invaded Texas in early 1836, Texans declared their independence, formed the Lone Star Republic and, under the leadership of Sam Houston, defeated and captured Santa Anna at the battle of San Jacinto. The subsequent application of Texas for statehood made manifest destiny and the related issue of the spread of slavery the major issue in American politics. The desire to preserve the existing sectional balance postponed the annexation of Texas until 1845 while the election of 1844 brought James Knox Polk, a strong advocate of expansion, to the White House as the first 'dark horse' presidential candidate in American history.

While the controversy surrounding the admission of Texas to the Union had a strong impact on American politics, the American annexation of Texas became the dominant issue in Mexican politics in the summer of 1845. With Santa Anna in exile in Cuba, the Centralists seized on the moderate and realistic policies toward the United States of the weak Federalist government of José Herrera to whip up a nationalist fervor over the loss of Texas, which was pictured as an American attack on Mexico. Facing imminent overthrow, Herrera tried to strengthen his domestic position by refusing to negotiate the outstanding issues – recognition of the Texas annexation, payment of Mexican debts to American citizens, and Polk's offer to purchase the southwest and part of California – between the two countries but fell to the even more intransigent Centralist general Mariano Paredes in December 1845. Believing that the United States was on the verge of war with Britain over Oregon and even indulging itself in fantasies of French aid, the Centralist faction of Paredes announced its intention to recover Texas by war, mobilized the Army, and sent a strong force to the Rio Grande. War came in April when Paredes proclaimed a state of 'defensive war' and Mexican cavalry attacked a detachment of dragoons from a force of 4000 regulars under Major General

Zachary Taylor encamped at the mouth of the Rio Grande on ostensibly American soil. The Texas border had in fact never been defined. Americans claimed the Rio Grande while at the outbreak of war, the Mexicans for the first time claimed it was the Nueces River several hundred miles to the north. The American declaration of war came on 13 May after Polk told Congress that Mexico had 'shed American blood on American soil' and that war 'existed by act of Mexico.'

The nearly unanimous war vote by Congress, however, actually concealed much opposition as the Whigs and anti-slavery Democrats saw the war only as a device to add more slave states to the Union, a view widely held in New England and voiced by intellectuals such as James Russell Lowell, Ralph Waldo Emerson, and Henry David Thoreau. With Southern support also lukewarm, it was in fact the population of the Mississippi valley which was most enthusiastic and supplied the largest number of volunteers for the Army. Remembering the fate of the Federalists who had destroyed their party by their steadfast opposition to the War of 1812, however, the Whigs feared the same fate and never were effective in opposition. Once having voted for the war, they were trapped in their support as they did not wish to be accused of impeding the war effort and endangering the troops in the

field. Making cynical political capital, they thus denounced the war and Polk in general terms while praising the generals and troops in combat. Seizing on the question of the disputed Texas border, the Whigs charged Polk with occupying Mexican territory and launching the war on false premises. For the first but not the last time, the character of a president became a political issue as charges of 'duplicity, equivocation and mendacity' flew in both the press and Congress.

For the first time in American history, the Army entered the war in a well-prepared and effective state. Years of fighting the western Indians and two difficult wars with the Seminoles in Florida had left the regulars tough and blooded. The Army in 1846 consisted of eight seasoned regiments of infantry, two of dragoons, and four of artillery, comprising a total of 734 officers and 7885 ranks. The military was also abreast of technological innovation as production of flintlock muskets by United States arsenals had ceased in 1842 after the invention of the fulminate of mercury percussion cap by a Scots clergyman.

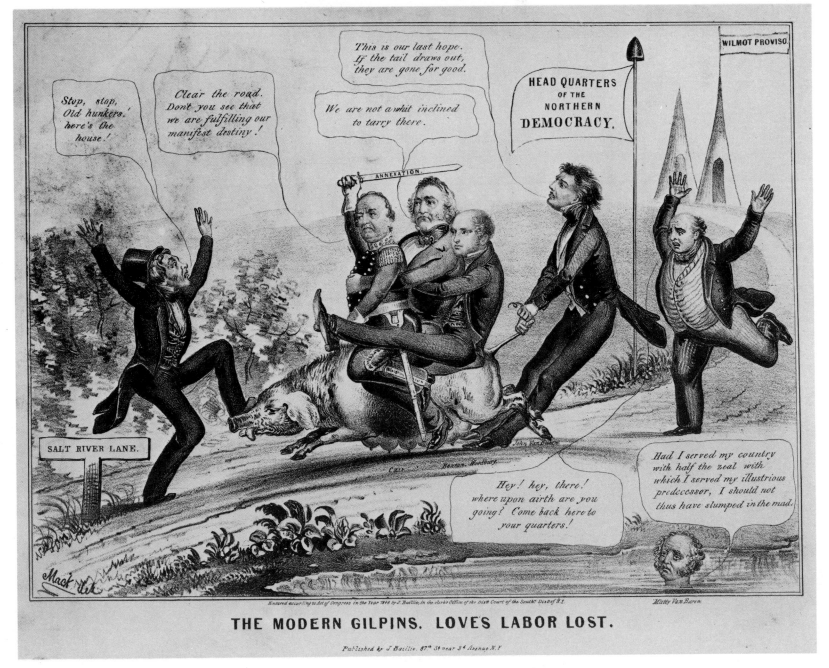

VOLUNTEERS!

Men of the Granite State!

Men of Old Rockingham!! the

strawberry-bed of patriotism, renowned for bravery and devotion to Country, rally at this call. Santa Anna, reeking with the generous confidence and magnanimity of your countrymen, is in arms, eager to plunge his traitor-dagger in their bosoms. To arms, then, and rush to the standard of the fearless and gallant CUSHING----put to the blush the dastardly meanness and rank toryism of Massachusetts. Let the half civilized Mexicans hear the crack of the unerring New Hampshire rifleman, and illustrate on the plains of San Luis Potosi, the fierce, determined, and undaunted bravery that has always characterized her sons.

Col. THEODORE F. ROWE, at No. 31 Daniel-street, is authorized and will enlist men this week for the Massachusetts Regiment of Volunteers. The compensation is $10 per month---$30 in advance. Congress will grant a handsome bounty in money and ONE HUNDRED AND SIXTY ACRES OF LAND.

Portsmouth, Feb. 2. 1847.

The standard shoulder arm was now the Model 1841 Springfield caplock, still a smoothbore as the problem of rapid loading for rifled arms had yet to be solved. General in Chief Winfield Scott however felt the new caplocks were too complicated, thus most of the guns in service during the war were still flintlocks. The artillery had also undergone a significant change in 1838 when horse-drawn light guns for mobile use on the battlefield were adopted after study of the Napoleonic style of war. The importance of this innovation was to be demonstrated in every engagement fought by Zachary Taylor during the war. War Department management of supplies, equipment, and logistics was also much improved by the reforms of various secretaries of war after 1815. Although profiteering and a waste of time, effort, and money characterized the attempt to upply and equip the 50,000 volunteers that Polk immediately called for, uniforms, supplies, and equipment in adequate quantities reached the theaters of operations. The genuine privations suffered by the soldiers in the field resulted not from War Department ineptitude but from the mismanagement and poor planning of field officers, Zachary Taylor being the most notorious offender.

The most significant change in the Army was the increasing professionalization of the officer corps. The impact of Napoleon on the nineteenth-century European and American minds was profound, and Presidents Madison and Monroe and their secretaries of war emerged from the turmoils of the Napoleonic period strongly impressed by military professionalism and in particular the French model. This impact was translated into the support given to West Point and the appointment of Sylvanus Thayer as Superintendent in 1817. The mission of West Point was now to produce professional officers for a professional army, a modification of the earlier mission which included service to the militia as well. Comprising academics, military studies, and engineering, the revamped four-year curriculum provided the best technical and scientific training available in the country before the Civil War. The most influential teacher to emerge at West Point was Denis Hart Mahan, himself an academy graduate in 1824, who not only wrote important early texts for American engineering but was the first American to write texts for the study of military theory and policy based on a broad historical approach. His student Henry Wager Halleck, later to play an important role in the Civil War, published in 1846 what became the standard text on the history and theory of war from an American perspective in which he also derived a military policy for the United States. Emphasizing a passive defense, he envisioned a per-

manent cadre of experienced professional soldiers under trained professional officers rapidly expansible in wartime by the absorption of civilian manpower. West Point, Mahan, and Halleck were advocating a professional approach to war in the United States which received further support with the establishment of the postgraduate Artillery School of Practice in 1824 and the Infantry School of Practice three years later. Selected officers were also sent to the continent to study the European practice of war.

The dominant influence on American military thought was the writing of the Swiss Antoine Henri, Baron de Jomini, a former staff officer of Napoleon, who became the premier interpreter of Napoleonic warfare. The work of his Prussian contemporary Karl von Clausewitz did not become well known outside Prussia until the 1870s. Jomini's interpretation of Napoleon emphasized continuities with the limited warfare of the eighteenth century in that he abhorred indiscriminate bloodshed and devastation, advocated superior concentration against inferior parts of the enemy achieved through maneuver against the enemy lines of communication and careful preservation of one's own, and capture of strategic places to dominate the theater of operations. He did, however, emphasize the offensive which was the

heart of Napoleonic warfare. The work of Mahan and Halleck was largely a restatement and paraphrase of Jomini, hence successive classes of cadets from the 1820s to the Civil War received large doses of Jominian strategic and tactical concepts. Yet, as Clausewitz and other students of Napoleon have shown, the overriding goal of Napoleonic strategy was to annihilate the enemy physically in climactic battle and, by precipitately and radically altering the military balance, achieve psychological annihilation as well. The reality of Napoleonic warfare was lavish expenditure of manpower to inflict even greater losses on the enemy, expenditure which ultimately was Napoleon's undoing as the cumulative losses of his climactic battles so reduced his overall strength that he was inferior to the combinations of the enemy. As will be seen in the Civil War, it was not the Jominian war of precise rules, maneuver, and places which had captured the imaginations of the West Point cadets but the Napoleonic war of glorious and bloody battle aimed at annihilation.

The Army thus could draw on a large cadre of West-Point-trained professional officers who tended to be proud of their membership of the professional military elite. Professionalization, however, had only improved the lower and middle ranks, leaving the upper echelons still dominated by elderly non-professionals in the absence of a retired list. Winfield Scott, a contentious

Above:
Henry Halleck was America's foremost military intellectual prior to the Civil War. He was a devoted student of Jomini, whom he often plagiarized.

Right:
Recruiting poster for volunteer company raised for the Mexican War.

Below:
An 1829 cartoon lampooning the state of the common militia and America's military preparedness.

figure of large proportions at 6 foot 5 inches and 230 pounds, had been made General in Chief in 1841 after having been passed over in 1828 because of his rancorous public feuds with other officers. The Army was so small and opportunities so limited that officers lived in an atmosphere of constant intrigue which erupted into frequent and violent quarrels over rank and jurisdiction. In spite of his feuds, Scott had become the country's foremost soldier and strategist through experience, study, and discipline. The other major figure of the war, Zachary Taylor, had spent much of his life in the Regular Army but was not really a professional soldier even though a tough and determined battlefield commander and fair tactician. The other senior officers were largely political appointees of Polk and barely managed to hold their own in a small war. American troops in Mexico were for the first time organized into divisions but it was difficult even to find able divisional commanders. Scott said of his divisional commander David Twiggs that he was not really qualified to command 'in the presence or in the absence of an enemy' while one of Taylor's own subordinates complained that Taylor himself could not choose gun positions properly, manage his supply lines or, in common with the other senior officers of his command, properly form a brigade into line.

The enlisted personnel of the Regular Army had traditionally been drawn from

Pub. for the Proprietors by R.H.Hobson. Chesnut S.ᵗ Philad.ᵃ 1829.

THE NATIONS BULWARK.

A well disciplined Militia.

LINCOLN CAVALRY

Col. ANDREW T. McREYNOLDS, Commanding.

WANTED
A FEW GOOD MEN!

To be in the field by 4th of July, if possible, who can furnish their own horses and equipments.

"EXTRACT FROM OFFICIAL ORDERS."

The allowances for Clothing for Cavalry, shall be $3 50 per month. Each Officer, Non-commisioned Officer, Private. and Musician, shall furnish his own Horse and Horse Equipments. [Equipments and Clothing can be furnished for $50] In case the Horse is lost in action, the Government pays for same 50 Cents a day is allowed for use of Horse.

Some good FARRIERS and BLACKSMITHS, wanted for the above Regiment, PAY EXTRA.

This is the only Cavalry Regiment accepted by the United States Government for immediate Service, and to serve during the War.

☞ Apply immediately to Head Quarters,

403 Walnut Street, Phila.. or to William H. Boyd, Box 661 Post Office.

☞ The person receiving this bill will please post it in a Conspicuous Place

DUROSS BROS., Printers, Black Horse Alley, Philadelphia

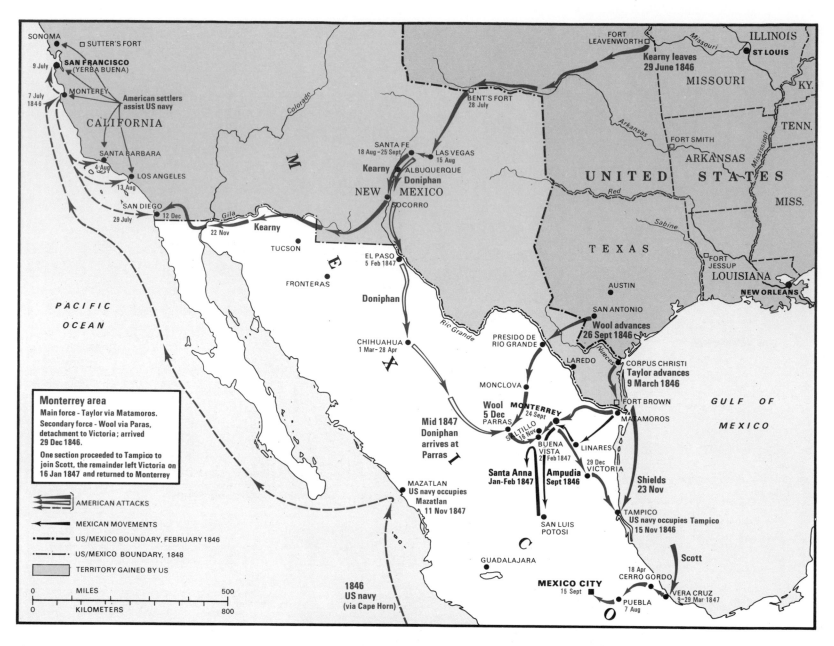

the sociologically disadvantaged elements in society but the expanding economic opportunities after 1815 brought a marked diminution in the quantity and quality of recruits. One commander wrote of his 55-man company: 'It appeared that nine-tenths enlisted on account of female difficulty; thirteen . . . had changed their names, and 43 were either drunk, or partially so, at the time of their enlistment.' Officers often referred to low intelligence, loose morals and habitual drunkenness while the troops were low in the public esteem as two soldiers lamented in 1836: 'The respectable portion of the community will not employ us . . . a few will pity us, but we will . . . only . . . confirm them in the belief that the army is a school of iniquity.' Faced with declining enlistments, the Army came to rely heavily on immigrants, the largest group being English and Irish deserters from the British Army, which further lowered the status of the soldier in the public eye. About 50 percent of the regular troops during the Mexican War were European born, thus disadvantaged immigrants were beginning to replace disadvantaged Americans as the mainstay of the Regular Army.

Above:
The siege of the Alamo, during the Texan war of independence against Mexico, became a national symbol and legend. All its defenders died and were remembered as martyrs to freedom.

DEUTSCHES BÜRGER MILITAIR VON PHILADELPHIA   THE GERMAN VOLUNTEERS OF PHILADELPHIA

Above:
General Winfield Scott conducted a spectacular campaign in which he took Vera Cruz and proceeded inland to capture Mexico City. However, he was overshadowed in the public eye by Taylor and was embroiled in feuds for much of his career.

Top:
As illustrated by this 1841 lithograph, the Volunteer Movement embraced all ethnic groups except the blacks.

The one pool of manpower which the Army did not tap either before or during the Mexican War was the black population whose social, political, and economic position had been progressively deteriorating in the North and South since the Revolution. Blacks were early barred from the regular forces and state militias due to low manpower requirements and the anxiety caused by the Haitian revolution, the greatest slave rebellion of modern history. Largely excluded from the Army and militia forces in the War of 1812, blacks constituted 10–20 percent of the Navy which had a severe and continuing manpower problem and remained the least segregated part of American society through the Civil War. While up to 30 percent of the Navy was black during the Mexican War, the Army General Regulations of 1821 limited enlistment to 'all free white male persons,' thus blacks served in the land forces only as body servants.

The main problem faced by the Army was desertion resulting from the isolation, tedium, and hard work of army life on the frontier. Up to a third of the Army deserted in some years before the Mexican War, and the Mexicans were able to form an entire battalion out of some 200 American deserters. Flogging had been abolished in 1812 but was reinstated between 1833 and 1861 expressly to deal with the problem of desertion. The Army, however, was never able to cope with high rate of abscondment.

While the Regular Army was being altered by the professionalization of the officer corps and the influx of immigrants, the other arm of the American military was also being radically transformed. The traditional standing militia of the states had fallen into extreme decay by 1846. The Indian threat was far removed and no foreign danger was evident. Militia duty was seen by many as pointless, needlessly compulsory, and undemocratic as the burden fell on the middle and lower classes who could not afford to pay the fines for noncompliance. Efforts to correct the manifest defects of the system after 1815 failed because the people objected to the compulsion and federal control necessary for an efficient system and also because the permanency of the Regular Army was guaranteed after the War of 1812. By 1840 it was generally accepted that the Regular Army was the core of the armed forces with the militia serving as inferior auxiliary troops rendering assistance in emergencies. With few exceptions, the States neglected their armories and militia structures and abolished fines for non-attendance.

The decline of the militia was not related to any decline of martial spirit, however, as a large number of paramilitary volunteer companies and organizations grew up in most communities over the country. The same American ideal of the spontaneous military effort of the citizens which condemned the Regular Army as effete and both the Regular Army and common militia as inegalitarian provided the impetus for the volunteer movement. Independent volunteer companies grew rapidly in the eighteenth century, more often than not in response to some local crisis. These companies were invariably militarily elite units such as rifles, lancers, dragoons, or light infantry and togged out in the gaudy uniforms of high military fashion. Since the cost of uniforms, equipment, membership dues, and often clubhouse fees was high, the companies were socially as well as militarily elite. Writing of the New England Guards of Boston, the commander observed that his unit had always 'enjoyed a reputation as a military company of gentle-

men.' The volunteer movement underwent two further developments in the 1840s. The older socially elite units were joined by many companies of artisans, clerks, and immigrants – Germans, Irish, and some Jews. At the same time, those states with any remaining pretense to a militia incorporated the volunteer companies first as flank units and then designated them as the entire effective militia. Increasing reliance on the Regular Army and the growth of the volunteer movement thus filled the military vacuum left by the demise of the common militia.

With the declaration of war, Congress authorized 50,000 volunteers for one year at the discretion of the President. One of Polk's major mistakes in the war was to allow the volunteers the option of enlisting for one year or the duration, a policy which deprived Winfield Scott of seven volunteer regiments whose enlistments ran out at a crucial point in his campaign. In a departure from the manpower policy of 1812, large numbers of new units were not authorized for the Regular Army to give it an illusory paper strength but reliance placed on the volunteer companies which were already partly recruited and officered. Thus many of the independent volunteer companies such as Jefferson Davis' Mississippi Rifles were federalized and compiled respectable records in Mexico. The strength of the Regular Army eventually grew to over 30,000 by increasing the size of the existing companies and author-

izing only ten new regular regiments, some 15,000 of the new regulars were recruited from volunteers already serving in Mexico.

High command and strategy making was still a problem as it had been in the Revolution and War of 1812 since the relation between the President, Secretary of War, and the General in Chief remained vague. Polk, the youngest President yet elected at 49, minimized this problem by aggressively managing the war himself, the first in which civilian control and effective military management were combined. Narrow-minded, unimaginative, and suspicious, Polk was a hard worker who paid diligent attention to the details of planning and management, chose his commanders, and planned the grand strategy and the attendant campaigns. His remarkable performance completely overshadowed Secretary of War William Marcy whose duties Polk sometimes assumed.

Grand strategy was a problem in itself. Taylor had already fought two major battles even before war was declared. His original orders had been to occupy and defend Texas as far south as the Rio Grande but he was challenged by the 8000 men of the Mexican Army of the North under General Mariano Arista. Although including a number of crack veteran units, this force was largely made up of raw conscripts and convicts, underfed, ill-trained, and ever ready to desert. Taylor and Arista clashed on 6 May at

Above:
An 1847 lithograph of the storming of the Bishop's Palace during the capture of Monterrey by Taylor's forces, 24 September 1846.

Left:
Contemporary engraving of the death of Major Ringgold at the battle of Palo Alto, 1846. Ringgold devised the close support artillery tactics which played such an important role in Taylor's victories.

Palo Alto on the northern side of the Rio Grande in a battle dominated by the Napoleonic use of artillery on the American side. The mobile batteries of Major Samuel Ringgold and Captain James Duncan fired over 3000 rounds to tear gaping holes in the Mexican line and demolish every enemy attack before it gained momentum. With casualties ten times greater than Taylor's five dead and 43 wounded, Arista's demoralized troops retreated over the river and suffered a second defeat the following day at Resaca de la Palma.

The question was what next? The national mood was bellicose but a setback could swing opinion against the war (and Polk). Mexico had to be persuaded to halt the war and accede to American demands. The capital of Mexico was too far from Texas to be considered seriously as a war objective, and so for want of a better alternative Polk ordered Taylor to occupy the northern states of Mexico and particularly the city of Monterrey to punish Mexico into peace. Polk also wanted California which contained about 700 American settlers and where government had disintegrated the year before. Colonel Stephen Kearney with a small force grandly termed the Army of the West was dispatched from Fort Leavenworth in Kansas on an arduous and lengthy march through the southwest to southern California. The Pacific squadron of the American Navy was also ordered to assist in the conquest of that territory.

The Mexican nationalists had been encouraged to embark on the war because of the widely held belief in their military superiority over the United States. Over four times the size of its American adversary, the Mexican Army was thought by European observers to be one of the strongest in the world. It was well armed with used British equipment, disciplined, and experienced since the country had been in a state of internal war since 1821. In the face of Taylor's modest force and the long American line of communications by land or sea, the Mexican

military envisaged a strong offensive into Texas and a sweep along the Gulf coast against New Orleans and Mobile. Stunned by the back to back defeats and the near loss of the Army of the North, now reduced by 50 percent from casualties and desertion, the Mexican government quickly replaced Arista with Francisco Mejía whose failure to halt Taylor's advance on Monterrey led to the appointment of Pedro de Ampudía. But Ampudía was forced to surrender the supposedly impregnable city in the face of a two-pronged assault by Taylor in September.

Taylor's victories had made him the man of the hour in the United States and caused the Whig-dominated Congress to award him several gold medals for his service 'in a war unnecessarily and unconstitutionally begun by the President of the United States.' Taylor, a Whig, had satisfied the craving of the American public for swift and spectacular victories but his campaign in the remote and sparsely populated provinces of northern Mexico put no pressure on the Mexican government to make peace. The strategic irrelevance of Taylor's occupation of northeastern Mexico combined with the blatant Whig promotion of him as a presidential candidate to bring Polk to a new strategy in October 1846. Finally overcoming his extreme distaste for Winfield Scott, twice before a Whig possibility for the presidential nomination, Polk ordered Taylor to hold a defensive position around Monterrey and withdrew 80 percent of his troops for a campaign to be conducted by Scott against Mexico City. Believing himself a victim of Polk's notorious penchant for partisan politics, the piqued Taylor chose to misinterpret his orders and moved south about 70 miles to Saltillo in search of the last glorious victory which he hoped would propel him into the White House. At the hacienda of Buena Vista on February 22–23, he achieved that strategically pointless victory against a hastily gathered force of 20,000 Mexicans under Santa Anna, now returned from his Cuban exile. With only 4700 men, 90 percent of

conducted a perfectly executed amphibious landing, the first in American military history, and then forced the surrender of Vera Cruz with a classic eighteenth-century siege. The objective of Scott's campaign was to force the Mexican government to formally recognize American possession of Texas, the Southwest and California, territory which was already under American military occupation. Scott's plan was to follow the route of Hernán Cortés, the sixteenth-century Spanish conqueror of the Aztecs, direct from Vera Cruz to Mexico City. Capture of Mexico's capital and center of political life would, it

Santa Anna, fresh from his disaster at Buena Vista and now leading a shaky centralist government, out of successive positions at Cerro Gordo and Puebla. Using the tough Texas rangers of John Coffee Hays to keep his lines of communication to Vera Cruz free of bandits and irregulars, Scott moved inland and, after a futile attempt at armistice and negotiation, closed in on the capital.

Racked by confusion and intrigue, Mexico City stood alone as the provinces refused to heed appeals for men and money. The defense of the city was bungled by Santa Anna who concentrated such forces as he had in the

whom were volunteers rather than regulars, Taylor negated the numerical superiority of the enemy with his own inspired leadership and the skillful use of his artillery. Buena Vista was an artillery victory par excellence which sent Santa Anna into disorderly retreat. With Scott's campaign already underway and with his politically motivated victory in hand, Taylor returned to Monterrey to await the next presidential election.

Launched by the capture of Tampico, Scott's campaign got underway a few weeks before Taylor's victory at Buena Vista. In March Scott and the United States Navy

was thought, paralyze the country and force peace on any Mexican government which wished to remain in power. As the Mexicans had already demonstrated their ability to raise new armies from the ashes of disaster, Scott with his 11,000 men could not afford the casualties necessary to destroy the Mexican capacity and will to fight nor was such a strategy of annihilation necessary. In keeping with his own predilections and previous experience, Scott opted for an eighteenth-century strategy of maneuver and low-cost warfare. Artfully using his divisions to flank the enemy, he maneuvered his opponent

east against a final assault which came from the west. After a seventeen-minute battle at Contreras and heavy fighting at Churubusco and Chapultepec, the defenses of the city collapsed and American forces began their occupation on 14 September. Scott's bold thrust into the heart of Mexico, which many foreign observers had predicted would be a disaster, achieved its objective as the Mexicans opened negotiations. The Treaty of Guadaloupe Hidalgo of February 1848 ceded Texas with the Rio Grande as the boundary as well as New Mexico, California, and the rest of the western territories. Polk

Left:
The American fleet under Matthew Perry bombarded and finally took the fort at Vera Cruz on 29 March 1847. It took over a week of sea- and land-based shelling. Several weeks earlier, the fleet had engaged in a major and innovative amphibious landing of 8600 troops under Winfield Scott, just north of Vera Cruz.

Above:
The Texas Rangers were brought in to solve the problem of Mexican and guerrilla attacks on Scott's lines of communication. Under the leadership of John Coffee Hays, they effected a thorough if brutal pacification of the countryside.

Below:
An 1847 lithograph of the battle of Buena Vista, 23 February 1847, a major victory for Zachary Taylor against a numerically superior enemy force.

had withstood the many demands in the United States for the annexation of all Mexico. Thus the continental boundaries of the United States were completed in 1848 with the exception of the Gadsden Purchase from Mexico in 1853 which added the Gila Valley in southern Arizona six years later.

The American military had accomplished a remarkable feat in the defeat of Mexico, a feat which many European observers, including the Duke of Wellington, had believed impossible. Such assessments had been based on the fumbling American performance in the Revolution and the War of 1812, the fact that the American Army was primarily an Indian-fighting and frontier police force dependent in wartime on unreliable volunteers and militia, and the great distance of Mexico from the centers of American power. Yet relatively small numbers of American troops – Taylor never had more than 6000 and Scott less than 11,000 – had confounded these pessimistic predictions. True, the deep split in Mexican politics between centralists and federalists and the near-feudal nature of Mexican society had left that country with a shaky base on which to build a war effort. The northern provinces had rebelled and co-operated openly with Taylor while the southernmost province of Yucatan had been in rebellion since 1839 and declared its neutrality in the war, a neutrality respected by the United States. Nor had the expected Anglo-American war over Oregon occurred as Polk had settled that issue with Britain by treaty in 1846. The hidden weaknesses of Mexico notwithstanding, however, the exceptional field performance of the American Army had been the decisive factor.

Left:
Amphibious assault by troops under Commodore Matthew Perry on the fortified town of San Juan Bautista, an important supply center. This was the culmination of a successful 74-mile naval expedition up the Tabasco River.

Far left:
American troops under Winfield Scott defeated the Mexicans at the battle of Cerro Gordo, 18 April 1847. This was one of Scott's six victories with inferior numbers and lengthening lines of communications on his march from Vera Cruz to Mexico City.

Below:
Mexican guerrilleros in 1848. Guerrilla bands caused much damage during the Mexican War and were to play an important part in Mexican history well into the twentieth century.

This exceptional performance is attributable to two factors. It was again demonstrated that American civilians with good basic training fight well. As a result of serving beside well-officered and trained regulars, the volunteers in Mexico, in the words of Lieutenant Ulysses Simpson Grant, 'became soldiers themselves almost at once.' Both Scott and Taylor required six hours of daily training for the volunteers in their commands. The volunteers thus generally fought well and deported themselves acceptably but a number of companies did break and run in battle while the treatment of the local population by the volunteers was often reprehensible. There was also more than a little tension between regulars and volunteers; the former disliking the enthusiastic and more loosely disciplined amateurs who in return reflected the traditional American attitude of disdain for the 'effete' professionals. The departure of seven regiments of volunteers, whose enlistments were up, forced Scott to halt his campaign halfway to Mexico City pending replacements but thousands of volunteers enlisted as regulars in the field.

Winfield Scott had proved during the War of 1812 that training could quickly make decent soldiers of Americans but his had remained an isolated instance because officers able to train had never been available. The Mexican War was the first time that an adequate supply of professional officers was available to train the troops. The second factor and the real strength of the Army lay in the existence of a corps of professionally trained junior officers who displayed a high level of skill and battlefield performance. Virtually every officer later holding high command in the Civil War had a distinguished battle record in Mexico, a factor directly attributable to West Point. After the War of 1812, the majority of officers were West Point graduates who vindicated their training in the Mexican War. Many of the volunteer regiments were also commanded by former cadets such as Jefferson Davis. A member of the West Point Board of Visitors said that the academy had 'fought itself into favor' while the anti-war, Whig editor of *The National Intelligencer* wrote 'How nobly training at West Point has vindicated itself! This war has settled the wisdom and value of that institution.' One important result of the war was thus to establish firmly the principle of the professionally trained officer and endow the Regular Army with enhanced but still modest respectability. And the Mexican War was the last in which the senior commands were not held by West Point graduates.

Although the Army dominated the military operations and headlines, the Navy also played a role in the war. The Home Squadron operating in the Gulf under Commodore David Conner maintained a tight blockade of the Mexican coast, captured several Mexican ports, prevented a privateering campaign against American shipping, and assisted the forces of both Taylor and Scott. It was Commodore Robert Stockton of the Pacific Squadron who federalized the rebellious Americans of California under John Fremont and declared that state as American territory. Without the decisive presence of Stockton and his eight ships, California would have remained in anarchy as Mexicans and Americans fought each other in an almost comic war of minute proportions but high passions.

Perhaps the most remarkable feature of the war, however, was the extent to which military operations and domestic politicking became entwined. Polk was a keen politician who well knew the political appeal of military heroes to the American public. Heroism in warfare, or at least meritorious service in the militia, was an important credential for public office to the American electorate whose fondness for military presidents was attested to by Washington, Monroe, Jackson, and Harrison, not to mention the soldiers who ran unsuccessfully. Politics had been the essence of the old militia system while the volunteer companies, as Marcus Cunliffe has observed, were as much parapolitical as paramilitary and were often associated with political parties. Nor was the Regular Army immune from politics as nomination to West Point, direct appointment to army commissions, and choice assignments were dictated by intense lobbying and favor trading in the Congress and administration, causing one disgruntled officer to remark, 'In the Army, merit is no recommendation and political influence is everything.' Indeed, one standard objection to a standing army was the power of patronage it offered to the party in power in an age when the federal bureaucracy was still minute. Charges were laid in both 1812 and 1846 that some of the efforts to increase the size of the Army were inspired by the need for additional patronage to bolster the political position of the administration.

Both Taylor and Scott were politically ambitious, the latter having been considered for the Whig nomination in 1839 and again in 1844. Polk had originally chosen Taylor to lead the initial operations of the war because he represented less potential political danger than Scott. But as Taylor rolled up a succession of victories and was lionized by the press, public and Whig king-makers, Polk decided that he could not be allowed the crowning victory of capturing Mexico City and ending the war and reluctantly turned to Scott. Taylor was fond of comparing himself to Washington and after Buena Vista thought that he would be nominated by both parties and elected by acclamation. His dream was realized when the Whigs did nominate him in 1847 and he won the ensuing election.

The cynical political use made by Whig politicians of Taylor as a war hero stimulated Polk to unleash his own natural partisanship. As one senator noted, Polk had 'wanted a small war, just large enough to require a treaty of peace and not large enough to make military reputations dangerous for the presidency.' He therefore loaded the commands of both Whig generals with democratic appointees which projected domestic party politics into the military operations. Taylor circumvented Polk's attempt to rein in his military-political operations by 'misinterpreting' his orders. As Scott too mounted a successful campaign, Polk began to criticize him publicly, anonymous attacks appeared in the press, and ultimately a pretext was manufactured to recall him. In later wars, the dominance of the West Pointers over High Command inhibited this sort of crass and overt politicking by generals which in turn enabled presidents to curb their own inherent partisanship. The promotion of Taylor, a slave-holding plantation owner, for the presidency had greater ramifications as well because it evoked a strong reaction from the reform faction of the Whig party which later became the nucleus of the modern Republican party.

Although the war had added millions of square miles to the country, manifest destiny was never consummated. Enmeshed in party politics and undercut by the problems of race and slavery, it had failed to become a national drive and receded into the background to lie dormant for 50 years before re-emerging in a different age. In the aftermath of the Mexican War, American politics and society became dominated by the sectional struggle over the governance of the new territories, a controversy which all too soon escalated into the Civil War.

Below:
Commodore John Drake Sloat, US Navy, raises the American flag and takes possession of California at Monterey, 7 July 1846. The American inhabitants had already revolted in San Francisco and set up the independent Bear Flag Republic. In the peace treaty finally arranged in February 1848, America received from Mexico not only California and Texas but all the territories in between, which include what are now Utah and Nevada – a total gain of 918,000 square miles.

Chapter 5

The Civil War – The American Mission Reaffirmed

CHARLESTON

MERCURY

EXTRA:

at 1.15 o'clock, P. M. December 20th, 1860.

ORDINANCE

"State of South Carolina and under the compact entitled "The ...tes of America."

...onvention assembled, do declare and ordain, and ...y, on the twenty-third day of May, in the ...y-eight, whereby the Constitution of the ...ts and parts of Acts of the General ...d Constitution, are hereby repealed; ...d other States, under the name of

Left:
Jefferson Davis, President of the Confederacy throughout the Civil War, photographed by Matthew Brady.

Center:
Announcement of the decision of the General Assembly of South Carolina to secede from the Unìon.

Below:
The election of Abraham Lincoln as President of the United States was the signal for the secession of the Southern States.

In a speech in Baltimore in 1864, the President observed, 'When the war began, three years ago, neither party, nor any man, expected it would last till now. Neither did any anticipate that domestic slavery would be much affected by the war. But here we are; the war has not ended and slavery has been much affected.' And Abraham Lincoln was right. Americans of all persuasions had expected the Civil War to be of brief if epic proportions while all but a minority had tried to cling to the fiction that slavery was not at the root of the conflict between North and South. Fueled by ideological commitment, each side had gone to war to defend its particular version of the American dream, the South for its 'peculiar institution' and the way of life built on it and the North for the democratic hopes of all Americans and its vision of competitive economic opportunity. Begun in the single political objective of maintaining or dividing the Union, the war of itself quickly generated its own purposes and values and painfully taught the American people yet again that war is always a social process from which even the victor emerges transformed. They emerged from the Civil War ambivalent about 'the enemy' and who actually won.

The war itself was a unique event, far more so than other wars. Americans had assumed that it would be fought with the limited political objectives and restrained military style characteristic of previous American wars and indeed of European warfare as well. But the conflict quickly evolved into mass warfare, the first ever experienced by Americans, and subsequently into total warfare of a kind which was taken as a model by the military and political leaders of the twentieth century. The Civil War was indeed the harbinger of modern industrial warfare with its deliberate assault on civilians and its mass armies recruited by patriotic appeal, equipped and maintained by the industrial system, and then decimated by that same system. The horrors of the new warfare were so great that Americans romanticized the grim reality of the Civil War and remembered it as a heroic time.

The long-standing and deeply divisive issue of the extension of slavery to the new States and territories being formed in the West came to a final crisis in December 1860 when South Carolina seceded from the Union, followed by six more States. With Jefferson Davis as their President and Montgomery, Alabama, as their capital (it was

Above:
Harper's Weekly illustration showing training of a volunteer unit before the Civil War. Such companies provided the backbones of both the Union and Confederate armies for the first year of the war.

Top center:
Print from a Northern magazine (13 July 1861) showing the horrors of a slave auction in the South.

Right:
Last meeting between General Scott and the Cabinet. Scott's strategy was unacceptable to the government and he was retired early in the war.

subsequently moved to Richmond), these seven formed the original Confederate States of America. By following a policy of inaction, President James Buchanan tried not to aggravate the situation but his successor Abraham Lincoln, taking office early in 1861, quickly realized that force was the only means of preserving the Union. Opinion in the North was deeply divided, however, and the new President knew that the first overt act of violence would have to come from the South. The Confederates obligingly fired on Fort Sumter in Charleston harbor on 12 April 1861. That act unified the North, not for long but long enough for Lincoln to issue a proclamation declaring a state of insurrection and calling for a volunteer army to re-establish order. Four additional States then parted company with the Union. Correctly interpreting Lincoln's insurrection proclamation to mean that the South was to be invaded, President Davis called for volunteers to defend the Confederacy. The nation rose in arms against itself.

Slavery lay at the root of the conflict between North and South. As Lincoln himself said, the 'only substantial dispute' dividing the country was that 'one section . . . believes slavery is right, and ought to be extended, while the other believes it is *wrong*, and ought not to be extended.' The central paradox of American history is indeed the rise of liberty and equality side by side with slavery in American society, a paradox already recognized at the time of the American Revolution. Yet slavery had remained firmly entrenched after the Revolution because the eighteenth-century conception of republican liberty contained an inherent mistrust of the poor and the landless of whatever color. Elements of anti-slavery ideology were also long present in America as well as adverse sectional stereotypes. A coherent critique of slavery began to emerge in the 1820s and 1830s as the federalist world view of an organic society based on harmonious order and distinctly separate social ranks broke down and was replaced by a new vision which rejected the organicism of society and permanent subordination of any class or group of people. Society was coming to be seen as a collection of individuals, each with the birthright of freedom and the further right to seek personal betterment in competitive society. Slavery then became not a functional institution but a personal sin of master against bondsman. Such a view of society was in keeping with the equalitarian spirit of Jacksonian America and the rapidly expanding market-oriented capitalist economy then evolving.

Arising out of the transformation of Northern society, the anti-slavery movement entered politics through the development of the instruments of mass democracy – the popular press, postal campaigns, propaganda, mass political parties – and provoked a Southern defense of slavery in the same vein. The organizing principle of political conflict gradually became the two sectional ideologies, each of which descended to its simplest formulation to achieve the broadest possible following. The choices came to be defined as free society versus slave society, losing the intermediate alternatives in the clamor. Secession came with the election of a Republican administration in 1860 because Southerners knew that slavery could not survive the debate the Republicans were determined to force. The war was the result of the inability of either side to compromise its position on slavery.

Yet the crux of the issue was expressed in constitutional rather than moral terms. Since the Constitution guaranteed the right of existing States to maintain slavery so the battle focused on the extension of slavery to the territories which would eventually become States. The Republicans were adamantly opposed to the spread of slavery which also conflicted with the aspirations of free white labor in the new territories. Southerners saw in this attitude an indirect attack on their institution which modern studies have shown to have been a highly profitable investment. If denied room to expand, plantation agriculture would exhaust the soil of the South and thereby make slavery unprofitable. Much of the white population would migrate west while those remaining

would be too few to exercise racial control. The war was thus really over the permanence of slavery rather than over the right for slavery to exist.

Since slavery was sanctioned by the Constitution, that document was thought to be undermined by direct attacks on that institution. Lincoln and the North believed that the Union had to be restored with slavery intact. The crime of the South was argued to be secession which violated the most fundamental American right – the peaceful settlement of issues by majority rule within the bounds of the Constitutional Union. As William Barney has noted, the Americans of that time were intensely, even obsessively, proud of their system of self-government and believed that majority rule must prevail to prevent anarchy. The perceived threat to the fundamentals of their democracy was what aroused the people of the North and carried them through four years of war. The sole objective of the war was the perpetuation of the Union in the eyes of the majority of Northerners while a small minority believed that the Union must also be regenerated through the war. Had the freedom of the slaves been a

Above:
The siege of Charleston, South Carolina by Federal Forces. Unlike most of the Carolina coast, Charleston was not captured, largely because the Union Navy was unable to maneuver in the waters around it.

Right:
Recruiting for the New York Zouaves, showing the Flag of Fort Sumter which had been damaged during the first fighting.

Below:
The small Union regiment guarding Fort Sumter were the victims of the first engagement of the Civil War.

FRANK LESLIE'S
ILLUSTRATED
NEWSPAPER

Entered according to the Act of Congress, in the year 1861, by FRANK LESLIE, in the Clerk's Office of the District Court for the Southern District of New York.

No. 285—Vol. XI.]   NEW YORK, MAY 4, 1861.   [PRICE 6 CENTS.

THE NEW YORK ZOUAVES RECRUITING.

THE dashing exploits of the famous French Zouaves, and the report made to the United States Government by the Military Commission, sent to Europe during the Crimean War, attracted the emulative attention of all the light infantry tacticians of America. Instinctively a military people, our young men were fascinated with the stories of the agile, impulsive, effective and somewhat dramatic movements of "The Zouaves," and the tour of the Chicago Zouaves but added zest to a desire which inspired most of the young military aspirants. This feeling found a prompt exhibition in the chief cities in the formation of companies in imitation. When Colonel Ellsworth's corps visited New York last summer the excitement about light infantry tactics arose to fever pitch. Although strict in discipline, still the movements gave a sufficiently free-and-easy margin to the usual military drill, which was especially attractive.

Immediately a number of Zouave companies were organized, one of which, taking their name from the State, appointed Colonel R. C. Hawkins as drill-officer, no regular commander having been appointed. Since the war excitement broke out the company has been recruiting and extending itself into a regiment, at the head of which it has placed its brave and efficient drill-master.

Our artist has given a spirited glimpse of the recruiting process, which has everywhere commanded the cheers of the populace

and attracted a large body of athletic men to the ranks, which now number eight hundred gallant fellows, who are desirous of emulating in the service of the Stars and Stripes the glory of their French prototypes. They are nearly of one height and all under thirty years of age. Some of the principal officers are men fully capable of leading them to renown.

The Colonel, R. C. Hawkins, is an ex-officer of the Mexican War. The Lieutenant-Colonel, George C. Betts, is a son of United States Commissioner Betts, of the Southern District of New York, and has also participated in the glories of the army in Mexico. The Major, E. A. Kimball, likewise, has had experience of grim war against a foreign foe and was brevetted for gallant services in the last war. He was formerly Captain in the Ninth Infantry, and was the dashing soldier who, at the Storming of Chepultepec, it is said, hauled down the Mexican flag and hoisted the inspiring Stars and Stripes over that fortress. Adjutant Evans also distinguished himself as an officer of the Ohio Volunteers in Mexico, and the Quartermaster, W. H. Elliott, has seen active service.

With these men at their head, the New York Zouaves cannot fail to be an efficient adjunct to the military now rushing to the support of the national flag.

The commands, which were temporarily and inadequately stationed at Castle Garden, have been garrisoned in the armories over the Centre Market.

The regiment undergoes a most rigid drilling, and will be on the march in a few days.

THE FLAG OF FORT SUMPTER, AS IT APPEARED AFTER THE BOMBARDMENT.

THE FLAG OF FORT SUMPTER.

THE disastrous measures taken to reduce Fort Sumpter have already thrilled the whole country. Love of the Stars and Stripes is a distinguishing feeling with the people; as a reverence for the national flag typifies and thrills the people of every nation even where they are not so blessed with freedom and happiness as the American. The disaster to the flag is the secret of the great uprising of the North, and the perforations made in it are felt by men of all parties as a national calamity, as, in fact,

stated war aim in 1861, the North probably could not have mustered a war effort since most of its people would have refused to fight. Lincoln based the North's resort to force on the idea that secession was illegal and was the work of a small group of slave holders who did not represent the popular will of the South. This belief, widespread in the North until the end of 1862, resolved the problem of coercing an entire people back into a 'free' government. Thus the Unionist motif was the basis of Northern unity and was formalized by Congress in the Crittenden Resolution of July 1861 which stated that the goal of the North was 'to defend and maintain the supremacy of the Constitution, and to preserve the Union.'

When war finally came in 1861, the United States was still firmly rooted in the dual military tradition of its past. One aspect of the dualism was 'strict and rather lonely professionalism,' as Marcus Cunliffe has observed, while the other was 'amateur and violently anti-professional.' The latter tradition was well exemplified by the words of Congressman Joshua Giddings of Ohio who said during the Mexican War, 'Had we been destitute of an army, the President would have been unable to involve us in hostilities with Mexico. . . . The Army is a cancer upon the body politic.' Indeed, after the Mexican War the volunteers were discharged and the new regular units were disbanded. The Army had a strength of only 17,867 in 1855 and

was used extensively by Secretary of War Jefferson Davis to patrol, explore, and map the Western territories opened up by the Mexican War. The Regular Army was still outside the mainstream of American society and still attracted the disadvantaged. One estimate of 1859 emphasized that over 9000 of the ranks were foreign born, 'the Irish element . . . predominates, and next to it, the Germans.' The heavy reliance on immigrants stemmed from the bleak and undesirable character of army life which kept the desertion rate high. An energetic Secretary of War, Davis won a pay increase for officers and ranks but the Army remained small due to the sectional dispute in national politics. Both North and South preferred a small

military establishment so that neither would acquire a potential military advantage. An early reflection of the sectional awareness of the military factor came in 1843 when Congress decreed that cadets would be appointed to West Point from congressional districts to maintain the sectional balance of the officer corps.

If the Army had not materially changed since the Mexican War, neither had the amateur side of the American military tradition. The common militia was in an even more advanced state of desuetude than it had been in the 1840s while the volunteer movement had been further strengthened by the success of the volunteer regiments in the war. Responding to the tensions of 1859–60, the

Top:
Print from *Harper's Weekly* of a Union encampment near Leesburg, Virginia.

Above:
Scene of the Federal advance on Confederate position on Henry House Hill during First Battle of Bull Run, 21 July 1861.

volunteer companies recruited themselves to full strength and new units were formed. The volunteers still retained the inherent limitations of the old militia, however, because they were materially and psychologically unprepared for more than brief service in the field. Their most important contribution in the coming conflict would be to provide each side with hordes of eager recruits and a cadre of amateur officers with at least some training. It was in fact the volunteer companies of each side which enabled the small engagements of the summer of 1861 to take place before a serious war effort could be mustered and mobilized.

While American capabilities for land warfare remained largely within the historic mold, the Navy by contrast was well abreast of the technological revolution occurring in nautical matters. In the years before the Civil War, the Navy underwent the transition from sail to steam in common with the navies of Europe. At that time, steam was still generally supplemental to sail in sea-going ships since engines were very inefficient and consumed huge quantities of coal. In 1842 the Navy acquired its first steam screw-propeller warship, the *Princeton*, whose engine, armament, and propeller were designed by the Swedish engineer John Ericsson. The Navy in the following decade was well aware of the growing trend toward armored ships or 'ironclads' as they were called. In the Crimean War of 1853–56, France used armored floating batteries with such success that Napoleon III ordered four ironclad warships to be constructed. First to be completed was the *Gloire*, the most powerful warship of the time, while Britain produced shortly thereafter her first ironclad to counter the threat to her naval supremacy. The American Navy had no ironclads at the outbreak of war but did have six new first-class steam frigates, the best known of which was to be the *Merrimack* from its capture and subsequent use by the South, and twelve steam sloops. All told, 42 ships were in commission.

Along with the shift to steam, new ordnance was being produced. After some experimentation with gun barrel pressures, a young lieutenant named John Dahlgren successfully began to design guns of larger caliber after 1847. The 'Dahlgrens' were smoothbores and fired both shot and shell. Guns under eight-inch bore often had rifled barrels, making them more accurate than the smoothbores. Although Dahlgren could produce a thirteen-inch gun, the new steam frigates of the Navy were armed with only nine-, ten- and eleven-inch guns. On the eve of the war, therefore, the Navy was a small, relatively modern force, augmented by a large merchant marine and abundant ship-building resources. Like the Army, it counted a large proportion of foreign-born personnel in the ranks.

Technological advance was most visible in the Navy but it was land warfare that was to be thoroughly altered by three technological innovations of the mid-nineteenth century: the railroad, telegraph, and rifled weapons.

Workable steam locomotives had been built by both British and American inventors in the 1820s while the first American railroads went into service in 1830 and 1831 with trains that traveled about twelve miles an hour. Almost 9000 miles of track had been built by 1850 but most of the lines were in the

Eastern States and ran from the coast inland. The following decade saw a consolidation of the many local railway companies in larger entities and the development of a more rationalized network of track. A fully effective telegraph was produced by Samuel Morse, a painter by vocation and scientist by avocation, in 1837 while the first telegraph became operational between Washington and Baltimore in 1844. By 1861 the numerous early small telegraph companies had been consolidated into the Western Union Telegraph Company and it was possible to send messages to California.

With the advent of the railroad and telegraph, the rapid movement and supply of mass armies became possible along with central direction and co-ordination of operations. The railroad enabled troops to be shifted rapidly over considerable distances and to arrive at full strength in good physical condition. Evacuation of sick and wounded, provision of replacements, and leave for troops during protracted campaigns became possible. More importantly, the entire economy of the country could be oriented to the war effort and mass armies maintained in the field indefinitely. Indeed, once the administrative problems of military use of the railroads had been solved, there was literally no limit on the size of field formations in the Civil War. The size of the armies in the field thus came to be the dominant factor in military power for the first time. These characteristics of the railroad freed strategy from many of its traditional constraints but in turn tied it to the paths of the rail lines themselves.

It was the telegraph which made possible the military use of the railroads. Developed in the Crimean War, the military applications of the telegraph returned with the American observers of that conflict. The South was to make less effective use of the telegraph but all Union forces were linked in a telegraphic network developed by the former head of Western Union and emanating from the office of Secretary of War, Edwin Stanton. The telegraphic network gave instant communications between operations in the field and the political administration of each belligerent. With this communication came control and direction of military operations. The strategic impact of the telegraph was not matched in the tactical sphere, however, because the instrument was too cumbersome for battlefield use. Despite the advent of the Signal Corps and semaphore code, tactical command, and control remained essentially the same as in the Revolution.

The other important effect of the telegraph was to bring the war to the public of both sides in an immediate fashion. The 50,000 miles of telegraph lines in the Eastern States were heavily used for journalistic purposes and turned Americans into a nation of avid newspaper readers. The war created a tremendous demand for news and brought soaring circulations and profits. Of the 500 Northern correspondents covering the war, the *New York Herald* alone had 63 in the field and spent a million dollars on its war reporting. Thirty years behind the times, the Southern press was in the main weeklies with small circulations which tended to use serving officers as ad hoc correspondents or one correspondent to service a pool of papers. What the papers received as news bears little relation to modern journalism, however, since correspondents were inexperienced, untrained, and grossly underpaid. The sustenance of both civilian and military morale was seen to be a central factor of reporting. One correspondent even declared to his readers that 'It is not within the province of your correspondent to criticize what has been done by the Army or Navy; nor will he state occurrences which it may be unpleasant to read,' while another observed that 'Men turned up in the Army more fit to drive cattle than to write for newspapers.'

The importance of the railroad and telegraph notwithstanding, the nature of combat in the Civil War was revolutionized far more by rifled weapons. The Civil War was in fact the first high fire-power war as the old smoothbore musket was replaced by the rifle. With the old muskets, as Lieutenant Ulysses Grant said in the Mexican War, 'At the distance of a few hundred yards, a man might fire at you all day without your finding out.' But the French Captain C. E. Minie had invented in the late 1830s a conical bullet with a hollow base which was expanded by the gases from firing to fit snugly the rifling of the barrel. The flintlock firing mechanism was replaced by the far more reliable per-

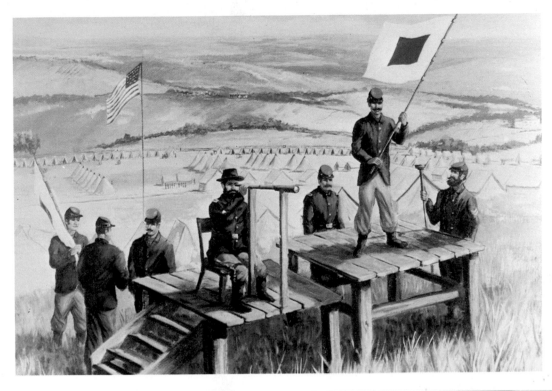

cussion cap. The spiral grooves inside the barrel increased range and accuracy fivefold. The Model 1855 United States Rifle which Jefferson Davis had adopted as the standard infantry weapon fired a .58 caliber Minié bullet at an effective range of 200-250 yards and an extreme range of over 1500 yards. The Model 1861 was even more lethally potent due to an improved firing mechanism and percussion cap. By the fall of 1862, most Union soldiers were equipped with the new rifles or muskets converted to rifles. Southern soldiers were nearly as well supplied through the capture of federal arsenals early in the war, imports from Europe, and manufacture with the equipment captured at the Harpers Ferry Arsenal. Up to 40 percent of Southern arms were scavenged from battlefields. Breechloading rifles were also available but not adopted by either side for various technical reasons.

Rifled cannon were also in existence at the outset of the war but did not have as significant an impact as did the rifle. By 1863 perhaps half of the Union field artillery consisted of three-inch rifles with effective ranges of 2500 yards and extreme ranges of 4000. Despite its great range and accuracy, the rifled gun proved to be not that effective because at the ranges necessary to be safe from rifle fire, its explosive shells did little damage to entrenched troops. This problem was only solved in the Franco-Prussian War with the development of the shrapnel shell which exploded over the trenches. The most favored gun of either side remained the twelve-pound Napoleon smoothbore which fired solid shot for 800–1000 yards and wrought carnage with its case shot at close quarters. The use of artillery was mainly defensive, serving counter battery purposes and supplementing the defensive fire of the entrenched infantry.

Rifled infantry weapons supplemented by

Above:
General Ulysses S. Grant, Commander in Chief of the Federal forces from spring 1864. He had left the Army to enter civilian life, running a rather unsuccessful tannery business, until the beginning of the war when there was a desperate need for trained and experienced officers.

Top:
Battle between the ironclad warships the USS *Monitor* and the CSS *Virginia* (*Merrimack*) at Hampton Roads, Virginia on 9 March 1862. The battle was in fact inconclusive after four hours of firing, and the two ships never met again.

Right:
The capture of Fort Walker by naval forces under the command of Samuel Du Pont on 7 November 1861. Fort Walker and, later the same day, Fort Beauregard were abandoned by their Confederate defenders after heavy naval bombardment, before a single Union soldier was landed. Du Pont's victory was a major boost to Union morale and caused panic in the South.

rifled artillery emphasized the defensive and inflicted casualties of 50–80 percent on the offensive. Rifles were so new that their tactical potential was not yet known, thus infantry tactics varied little from eighteenth-century linear warfare. The line was less tightly drawn and there was more emphasis on skirmishers but the essential element was still to get a controlled mass of troops close to the enemy, loose one volley and engage with the bayonet. The point of these close order tactics was to permit the officers to control the combat and to break the enemy defense position through the weight of the attackers against a critical point already shattered by the Napoleonic tactic of forward artillery fire. The vastly increased range and accuracy of the rifle in the early battles of 1861 decimated the attacking formations long before they came within bayonet range and made

the Napoleonic use of artillery impossible for the same reason. Indeed, the withering rifle fire of both sides forced soldiers to seek natural shelter or dig rifle pits and trenches. Troops on the attack tended to break ranks and move from cover to cover which left them too lightly concentrated to carry the enemy position and also out of control of their officers. Generals on the offensive thus had to prepare carefully controlled mass charges, such as Pickett's famous endeavor at Gettysburg, and accept the high casualty rates.

Decisive battlefield victory in the Napoleonic tradition was impossible under these conditions. The key to success became attrition which meant that the belligerent with superior demographic and economic resources would ultimately win. The immense casualties caused by the disparity between

defender and attacker and the inappropriate infantry tactics of the latter which characterized the Civil War were a direct precursor of the bloody stalemate of World War I caused by similar factors. The Civil War was thus the first of those costly wars of attrition and military indecision, a kind of warfare which changed only when new technology in the form of the tank and airplane again brought some parity between offense and defense after World War I.

The revolution in technology was not paralleled by a similar event in tactics and strategy. Command in the Civil War was largely, as T. Harry Williams has pointed out, in the hands of West Point graduates. The 60 major battles of the war saw command of both sides by West Pointers in 55 cases and of one side in the remaining five. These officers had never seen formations

larger than the small field forces of Taylor and Scott in the Mexican War and few had even been in command of so much as a regiment. None therefore had had any direct experience of management of the massive field forces which were the main feature of the Civil War. On the Union side, the top twelve generals ranged in age from 30 to 45 while the Confederates ranged from 40 to 58. What these officers all had in common was an exposure to the strategic and tactical concepts taught at West Point, a commonality which profoundly influenced the strategic evolution of the war.

As we have seen earlier, the Napoleonic approach to war had made a strong impression on both the European and American mind. A theoretical literature on Napoleonic warfare quickly developed with the Swiss Antoine Henri, Baron de Jomini, as its leading figure. Jomini, whether accidentally or deliberately, missed the essence of Napoleon's ability to force decision out of war through the climactic battle which annihilated the enemy both materially and morally to alter suddenly the balance of power. The emphasis in the writings of the Swiss was more rooted in the limited warfare of the eighteenth century and emphasized control of geographic points and mass concentration against those points. The two most ardent American students of Jomini were Denis Hart Mahan and Henry Wager Halleck who both taught at West Point. Mahan influenced the whole pre-Civil War generation of officers with his emphasis on mass concentration against a decisive point and consideration of war only from the point of view of the battlefield. His writings reflect a view of war waged in a virtual vacuum by professionals with no awareness of technology or of political objectives as factors. Halleck spent years translating Jomini and writing works which were a restatement of the master and in some cases plagiarism. In addition to his unoriginal scholarship, he later proved a total failure as a Union commander but ultimately came into his own as chief staff officer for Lincoln and Grant.

As the first to attempt to develop an American strategy and military policy, Mahan and Halleck were far more in tune with the cautious and limited warfare of George Washington than the panoramic power of Napoleonic conflict. Complementing the teachings of Mahan and Halleck was the dominating figure of Winfield Scott who served as Commanding General of the Army for the two decades prior to 1861. The premier American strategist of the first half of the nineteenth century, Scott was a near-perfect eighteenth-century general who aimed for low casualties, protected the civilian environment, used maneuver skillfully, and avoided costly frontal assaults. In spite of Mahan, Halleck, and Scott, however, the climactic and decisive battle of Napoleonic warfare was what had captured the imaginations of both the public and the younger generation of officers. With the exception of Grant and Sherman, the Civil War commander tended to hold as his goal the one big battlefield victory which would break the enemy and win the war. At the same time, strategic conception was dominated by the Jominian fixation with decisive points and linear and logistic advantages and disadvantages. There were, however, no 'decisive' points for either side while the rifle and the railroad invalidated both Jominian and Napoleonic tactics. The war ultimately was decided only by a strategy of grinding attrition.

Each side was required to mount a massive war effort as the conflict dragged on year after year with no decision in sight. This in turn required a high degree of social and economic mobilization which came to be far greater for the South than for the North. The former had entered the war with a high degree of popular consensus and ideological commitment to its cause. Except for the black population forced to support the war effort, Southerners shared a common sense of persecution by the North and espoused secession as a 'necessary and legal act of self defense.' 'Ours is not a revolution,' said Jefferson Davis. 'We are a free and independent people that had the right to make a better government when they saw fit.' Southerners believed that their Northern antagonist had broken the original constitutional covenant of the founding fathers by abandoning mutual forbearance on sectional differences. They therefore adopted a constitution closely modeled on the original document to show that they were the real conservators of the American tradition of liberty and states' rights. The one anomaly was that slavery was thoroughly protected as an institution. The war thus had a holy aspect, the defense of homes and the right to self-government as enshrined in the Declaration of Independence. The South had a strong ideological underpinning for its war effort as one of its papers stated in 1861, 'The Southern labor system is not only moral, in the highest sense of the word, but it is a holy cause. It is the cause of humanity and civilization.'

Leadership for the war effort came from the planter class which was defending its privileged position and possessed genuine leadership and managerial skills. Poorer

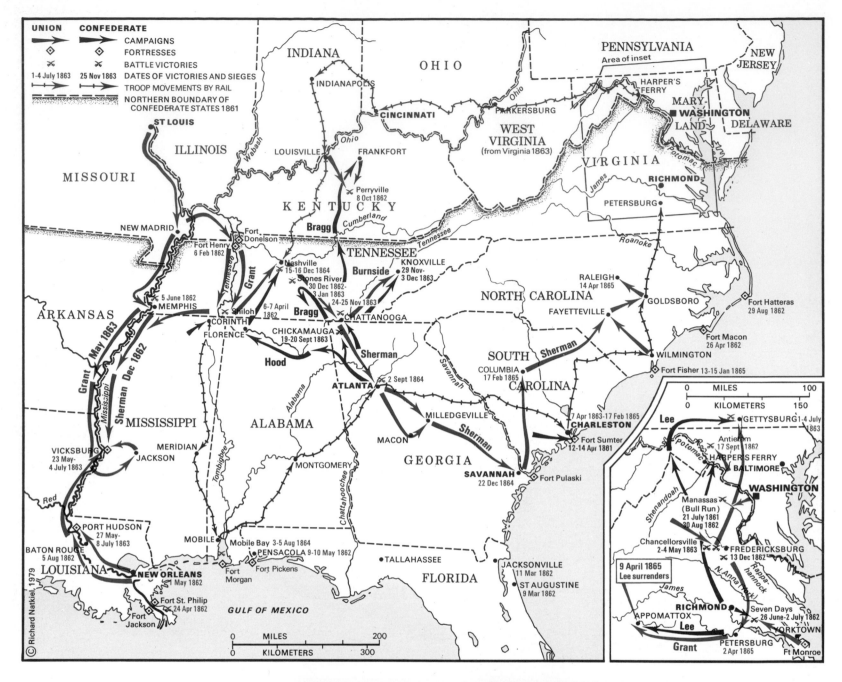

whites were also strongly committed. They identified the Northern objective as the emancipation of the slaves and feared for the deterioration of their position through economic competition and social amalgamation with blacks. The general white dogma was that emancipation meant loss of racial control and debasement of the white race. This high level of white commitment led to intense community involvement and willingness to sacrifice for the cause. Volunteers for the Army came forward in eager droves while women threw themselves into auxiliary activities such as sewing uniforms, packaging rations, and making ammunition. A visiting British correspondent wrote in 1861 that 'All were anxious to do or sacrifice something for the general weal' while a Southern minister said in that same year, 'We have nothing before us but self sacrifice and devotion to a cause which exceeds in character that of our first revolution – and an unshaken trust in the righteousness and goodness of God.' Most Southerners remained intensely loyal to their cause at great personal cost.

Above:
Manassas Junction, Virginia after its evacuation by the Confederates in March 1862. Confederate policy was to destroy everything in the path of the advancing Union armies, thus catching the Southern population between the 'total war policies' of Grant and Sherman and the 'scorched earth' policy of their own government.

Left:
A safe house in Virginia as these slaves try to escape in 1862. The outbreak of the Civil War was the signal for a mass exodus of slaves from the South. They were not really welcomed in the North until their rights were established in the Emancipation Proclamation. Many were encouraged to join the Union Army and fight the South.

Southern dedication was constantly reinforced by the fact that the North was the aggressor and also by the destruction of homes and property and the freeing of slaves. As had the intrusions of British troops during the Revolution, the encroachments and raids by Union troops in Southern territory stiffened resistance and confirmed stereotypes. The worst fears of Southerners were realized on 1 January 1863 with the issuance of the Emancipation Proclamation. 'The people of the Confederacy, then, cannot fail to receive this proclamation,' said Jefferson Davis to the Confederate Congress, 'as the fullest vindication of their own sagacity in foreseeing the uses to which the dominant party in the United States intended from the beginning to apply their power.' A clause of the proclamation urging slaves to remain passive further heightened popular anxiety by touching on the primordial Southern fear of slave rebellion. Southerners were even more horrified when black units in Union uniform began to appear in combat. 'The Yankees know they make it ten times worse

for us for sending Negroes to commit these atrocities' wrote a Southern woman after a raid utilizing black troops in April 1863. The response was an official policy of executing captured black troops and their white officers, the most extreme instance being the Fort Pillow massacre in which 100 surrendered blacks in uniform were summarily dispatched at the command of Nathan Bedford Forrest who was later instrumental in the founding of the Ku Klux Klan. Lincoln quickly halted this practice by announcing that one Confederate prisoner would die for each Union soldier, white or black, so executed and that one Confederate would do hard labor for each captured black soldier returned to slavery. In the end, the majority of captured black troops were placed in prison camps. The net effect of these factors was strongly and continuously to reinforce the popular determination of the South to persevere. The fusion of the slavery issue with the war effort silenced what little opposition there was in the Confederacy and held the loyalty of the people to the bitter end.

Left:
'First at Vicksburg': a painting, used as an army poster, of the Union Army assault on Confederate lines at the Battle of Vicksburg, 19 May 1863. This assault was actually a failure: it would take two more months of hard fighting to capture Vicksburg, thus splitting the Confederacy. The 1st Battalion, 13th Infantry, pictured here, lost 43 percent of its men in the assault but successfully reached the top and were therefore authorized by General Sherman to inscribe on their colors, 'First at Vicksburg.'

Popular determination was a central but not the only factor in the ability of the South to prolong the war for four years in the face of the many innate advantages of the North which was superior in most sources of economic power. The South suffered a 2–5 disadvantage in population, 1–3 in wealth and capacity to produce, 1–4 in capital of incorporated bonds, 1–10 in value of annual manufactures, 1–2 in railroad mileage, and possessed virtually no maritime shipping capacity. But apart from the 'superior animation' of its people fighting for homes, way of life and independence, Southerners saw themselves as having the advantage of terrain in their rivers, swamps, and mountains, as strong in food and livestock, possessed of a commodity highly necessary to France and Britain in cotton, and blessed with the precedents of history. Had not the Americans triumphed over the British in far worse circumstances?

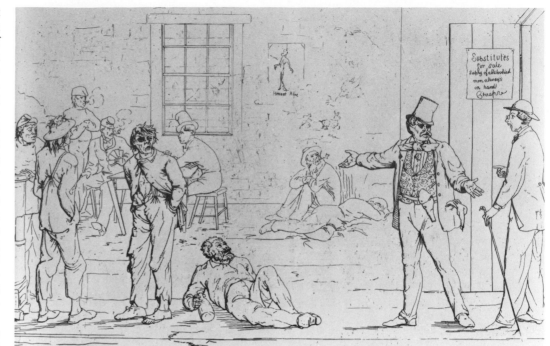

The Confederacy therefore proceeded to mobilize for war to a degree never before seen in American history and not seen again until World War II. For an agrarian society dominated by a landed gentry, the Southern conduct of the war was surprisingly efficient. By passing the first comprehensive conscription act in American history in April 1862, the South put around 80 percent of its white population of military age in the field, some 800,000 men of whom 50 percent were dead, disabled, or captured by 1864. Rigorously enforced, the draft had virtually exhausted the pool of Southern manpower by mid-1863. There was also far less desertion from Confederate than from Union armies. An industrial program was improvised which rather successfully kept the field armies supplied with the necessities of combat. Innovative ability, self-sufficiency, and quasi-nationalization of the private sector were the operative elements in the Southern war effort. Large amounts of goods were imported throughout the war since the success rate for running the Union blockade was 90 percent in 1861 and had only declined to 60 percent three years later. Cotton paid for these imports but even more of this basic Southern commodity was sold to the North in a trade sanctioned by the Union government. Cotton thus made a significant contribution to the Southern war effort but it was never a strong enough motive for the European intervention which so many Southerners believed was imminent in the first years of the war.

The main failure was food production. Although there was a major shift from cotton to food production in the agricultural sector, various other factors combined to offset any benefits. Crop yields dropped as efficiency declined due to lack of manpower, tools, and livestock. Agriculture depended on women, boys, old men, and invalided soldiers while slaveless farms suffered the most. The agricultural base steadily contracted as more regions were lost to Union forces and the remainder became increasingly subject to Union raids. The root of the problem was

that there simply was not enough food for both civilians and soldiers, thus both came to coexist with starvation. One soldier wrote, 'There was . . . no fear in the Confederate ranks of anything that General Grant might do, but there was an appalling and well-founded fear of starvation, which indeed some of us were already suffering.' Food may have been the primary factor sapping civilian morale in the South. For the military, poor management of the supply system compounded the problem.

Another primary weakness of the Confederacy was its failure to devise an adequate financial system. In an age when most taxation was indirect, the Confederacy did use new forms of direct taxation but still derived 60 per cent of its income from printing paper money. A massive inflation resulted and forced the people to pay for the war in a different way. But despite its various failures, the South fought a vigorous and inventive war in the best American tradition and demonstrated that it was far from the moribund society pictured by its contemporary and modern critics.

The Confederate Constitution designated the President as Commander in Chief, a role for which Jefferson Davis felt himself admirably qualified. An 1828 graduate of West Point, he had commanded a brigade for Zachary Taylor in Mexico, served as Secretary of War in the Pierce Administration from 1853 to 1857 and also chaired the Senate Military Affairs Committee. He was a man with clear views on military matters and warfare. He believed that war was justified to protect the honor and security of a nation and that warfare should not involve civilians but be restricted to organized armies. White Americans and especially white Southerners had superior martial qualities in his estimation. Many officers were appointed because Davis had known and liked them at West Point, in the old Army or in the Mexican campaign. His evaluation of military competence, however, tended to reduce itself to whether or not he thought the officer in question had 'character.' Courage, modesty, and experience were qualities he admired and found in Robert Edward Lee, Albert Johnston, and Sam Cooper while he disliked Joseph Johnston and P. G. T. Beauregard because they would not admit that his knowledge of military matters was as great as theirs. He firmly believed that the war would be both just and glorious and that Southerners would acquit themselves superbly. Basically a romantic, Davis tended to ignore unpleasant realities, minimize military disasters, and demand more of his generals than their resources would permit.

Davis was fully determined to be the arbiter of strategy as there were various options open to the Confederacy to achieve its war aims. The primary goal was to prolong the war until the Union grew war weary and recognized Southern independence while the second important goal was to protect as much as possible the people and property of the South. Invasion of the North could not be considered as a serious war-winning strategy since with but one exception the invasion routes were blocked by rivers controlled by Union gunboats. Nor was there a railroad from Virginia to Pennsylvania to supply the invasion. A strategy of guerrilla warfare was also unthinkable because the South was not a suitable environment for guerrillas who must rely on popular support for success. Half of the population of the Deep South was black and therefore of suspect loyalty. Further, retreat into the hills and swamps meant surrendering the very way of life and racial control for which Southerners were in arms. Because of the manifest disparities in strength between the antagonists, it was clear that the South would have to fight a defensive war in the conventional mode of the time.

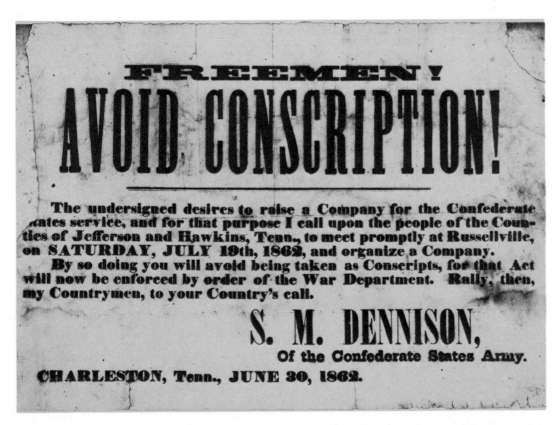

Below:
The Battle of Gettysburg, 1-3 July 1863, was in many ways the decisive battle of the war. In this painting by C.D. Green, Confederate troops under General George Pickett charge a well-defended Union position under intense fire heroically but with disastrous consequences.

The best strategy and the one preferred by
Davis would have been a cautious and selective defense on the lines of that utilized by
George Washington in the Revolution, a
strategy which conserved the manpower
both Washington and Davis lacked. But
Washington's situation had been different
since he was able to keep his force concentrated by ignoring the defense of territory
and people. As with those of the North, the
people of the South, however, were accustomed to a central government which provided for their defense and would not tolerate being exposed. Political realities thus
forced Davis to attempt to defend the entire
perimeter of the South, a strategy for which
the South simply did not have the resources.
As a result, the perimeter was weak at many
points, and it was only a matter of time
before superior concentrations of Federal
troops began to break through. And indeed, serious ruptures came early on. In
late August of 1861, Flag Officer Silas

Stringham's squadron demonstrated that steam warships and shell guns could destroy coastal forts if given enough open water in which to maneuver. Port Royal, South Carolina was seized after Stringham's guns blasted its defensive forts to pieces in the first amphibious operation of the war. That and succeeding operations brought wide stretches of the Carolina coast under Federal control and forced the Confederate defenders to move inland beyond the range of naval guns. Charleston was saved only because its harbor was not spacious enough for Stringham's ships to maneuver. West Virginia also passed into Union hands as Federal forces under George McClellan cleared the Confederates out of the area in the fall of 1861 and an expedition under Lee to regain the territory failed. The third and most serious breakthrough came in the West where Albert Johnston was expected to defend a 300-mile front from the Cumberland Gap in southeast Kentucky to Columbus on the Mississippi River with only 43,000 men and no natural defenses for aid. A superior concentration of Federal forces supported by gunboat fleets operating on the Tennessee, Cumberland, and Mississippi Rivers enabled Brigadier Ulysses Grant to overwhelm the Confederate defenders in the beginning of the campaign which ultimately led Grant to Vicksburg and the severing of the West from the Eastern Confederacy.

Although the North had yet to win a major battle, the fact that it was gaining ground steadily against the Confederate perimeter forced Davis to turn to the strategy pressed on him by most of his general officers. Selectively drawing from Jomini not his concern with decisive points but his emphasis on offensive action, these officers argued that the South had to seize the initiative so that it could determine when and where the military interactions were to occur. Only in such specific cases could it then meet the enemy on equal or better terms in spite of its overall inferiority. This strategy of the 'offensive-

defensive' was of itself opportunistic in that it was basically a series of temporary strategic spoiling operations to thwart the main initiatives of the enemy. Only in this way could the North be prevented from cracking the defensive perimeter through superior concentrations of force. Beyond these strategic expedients, the South did not evolve an overall strategy to realize its war aims.

The leading proponent of the offensive-defensive was the President's military adviser. Robert Edward Lee was the son of the Revolutionary War commander 'Light Horse Harry' Lee who had played a role of some significance in Nathanael Greene's partisan campaign in the South. Lee had graduated from West Point in 1829, served with distinction as a staff engineer under Scott in Mexico and as Commandant of West Point in the 1850s. A Virginian of aristocratic background, Lee resigned from the Army when Virginia joined the Confederacy and became military adviser to Davis. His first field assignment had been the unsuccessful attempt to regain West Virginia while his second was the equally unsuccessful effort to deal with Union naval and amphibious operations against the South Atlantic seaboard. He was given a task of critical scale in May 1862 when Davis placed him in command of the Army of Northern Virginia in the most crucial theater of war for the Confederacy.

Then 55 years old, Lee's broad experience left him with a more realistic view of Southern prospects than many other Southern political and military leaders. Even at the low point of Union relations with Britain over the Trent affair, he did not believe that that country, however sympathetic to the Southern cause, would intervene militarily to save the Confederacy. While many were advancing the 'King Cotton' argument that the British dependence on this commodity alone would suffice for military intervention, Lee said, 'We must make up our minds to fight our battles and win our independence alone. No one will help us.' He also believed that an indefinite war would bring inevitable defeat for the South. The Confederacy must weaken the will of the North, he argued, play on its divided feelings about the war, and work for an armistice before the South was overwhelmed militarily. He therefore urged Davis to encourage the peace movement in the North and himself sought an annihilating battlefield triumph of Napoleonic magnitude to shatter northern morale.

Recognizing the dependence of his theater on the western theater, Lee urged that both theaters be reinforced by reducing the defenses of less important points on the perimeter and pulling the substantial numbers of garrison troops out of the rear areas. But the decentralized nature of Confederate military organization in autonomous departments and popular demand for territorial defense prevented this shift from occurring. Lee further urged that the best means of stemming the Union pressure in the West was the employment of the offensive-defensive in the East to force Union troop transfers and

disrupt the Union plan of operations. The essence of Lee's strategy was the rapid concentration of forces through the use of the railroads and telegraph for surprise spoiling attacks on the exposed points of the various lines of the Union advance to 'alarm and embarass' the enemy in order to 'prevent his undertaking anything of magnitude against us.'

The fact that Union armies were approaching the Confederate capital of Richmond from four different directions to split the defenses in 1862 made it imperative that Lee concentrate his forces and go on the attack. His first implementation of the new strategic approach was the Valley Campaign of General Thomas Jonathan Jackson, popularly known as 'Stonewall' from the resolute stand of his brigade at Bull Run and probably the best corps commander of either side, in April and May 1862. This operation successfully drew several Federal armies away from their original objectives and permitted Lee to attack a weakened Union main force under McClellan on the Peninsula and deflect it from Richmond in the Seven Days' Battles of 25 June-1 July. With McClellan in a disadvantageous position, Lee was then unable to deliver a follow-up blow because his commanders and staff officers were incapable of the close co-ordination of divisions necessary to exploit the opportunity. Lee himself wrote that 'Under ordinary circumstances the Federal Army should have been destroyed' but staff and command was only part of the problem. Confederate troops had gone on the attack in close-order formations which cost Lee 25 percent of his total force of 80,000. His obsession with destroying his opponent in one climactic encounter that would decide the war apparently blinded him to the tremendous advantage the rifle conferred on the defense.

A fresh Federal army under General John Pope then moved into Northern Virginia. With improved intelligence and command, Lee drew Pope into an awkward situation and decisively defeated him at Second Bull Run in a near-classic example of Napoleonic maneuver and attack. Here again casualties of 20 percent were the price of his moral and psychological victory. Lee had now become a hero to the Southern population for his brilliant defense of the Confederate capital. But having suffered casualties of only 10-13 percent, the Union forces were still menacing and growing while the aftermath of Lee's victories found his own men physically and morally exhausted.

Frustrated in his quest for a military solution to the war, Lee next determined to cross the Potomac River for several reasons. His victories to date had failed to weaken the war will of the North nor had they affected the Federal advance in the Mississippi Valley. To remain on the defensive in Virginia was actually detrimental to the strategic position of the South nor could Virginia adequately feed his army. With Washington too well defended to be an objective, he planned a campaign in Maryland in the hope of de-

taching that border state from the Union. Such a blow to Northern morale might at last bring some response to Southern feelers for an armistice. Whatever the case, he knew that the Federals could not allow him to impinge so boldly on their territory without challenging him to battle. But the plan was foolhardy because the opposing force under McClellan numbered 75,000 to his 50,000 while his plan of campaign was already known to McClellan from a set of captured orders. Lee should have withdrawn but he feared to damage further the already slim chances for foreign recognition of the Confederacy and could not bring himself to accept such a moral defeat. He instead found McClellan in a strong defensive position at Antietam and attacked on 17 September 1862 at a cost of 14,000 casualties. Antietam was the first major Northern victory and is arguably the turning point of the war.

Following his retreat back into Virginia, Lee began to recruit and refit his shattered army while pondering how to force a decision in the war. His first victories had rescued Richmond from the converging forces of the Union but the full employment of the offensive-defensive strategy had failed to destroy the Federal forces confronting him. While he was holding his own in the East, the Union drive in the Mississippi Valley was nearing success and the naval blockade was becoming more effective. This train of events left no prospect for an armistice. It now became clear to Lee that this goal would not be accomplished by annihilating a Union army or two. The military pressure had to be increased by victories on Northern soil and even the occupation of Philadelphia or Baltimore. He finally determined to escalate from the offensive-defensive to a full-scale strategic offensive. In the meantime, Federal

armies continued to penetrate into Virginia to do battle. First he turned back a force under Ambrose Burnside at Fredericksburg in the most crushing and humiliating Union defeat of the war and then used his 60,000 men to defeat the 134,000 man force of Joseph Hooker, the largest field army yet to appear in the war, at the battles of the Wilderness and Chancellorsville in the spring of 1863. Then Lee marched his men northward, some 75,000 strong, in search again of the strategic victory that would enable him to occupy a major northern city and thus change the course of the war.

An almost accidental skirmish over a cache of shoes, badly needed by the ill-shod Confederates, at the little town of Gettysburg, Pennsylvania between a southern detachment and a Federal cavalry troop mushroomed into the great battle of the war. From 1–3 July, Lee's army suffered some 23,000 casualties in frontal assaults on well-entrenched Federal troops under George Meade, an able Union general on his best in a defensive role. The high point of the engagement was the charge of George Pickett's brigade of 15,000 across open ground against first artillery and then rifle fire. Pickett's force was wiped out virtually to a man while the overall casualty rate reached 30 per cent for Lee. Lee had finally found his strategically decisive battle and lost it. No longer could he contemplate the salvation of the Confederacy for the offensive capability of the Army of Northern Virginia had been shattered. Therefore he returned to his original war of maneuver in northern Virginia and ultimately was forced into trench warfare around Petersburg and Richmond.

The South had a difficult, perhaps even irresolvable, strategic problem which it had largely entrusted to Lee but an even more complex problem confronted the North in its conduct of the war. Military victory would not be enough as the outcome of the war had to be the acquiescence of the Southerners to the re-establishment of the Constitutional Union, a problem similar to that faced by the British in the American Revolution. The longer the war dragged on, the more difficult the restoration of the Union would become as a result of increasing bitterness and the more brutal policies the North would find necessary to achieve its end. The worst scenario which haunted Northern strategists was a South pushed into guerrilla warfare. 'In considering the policy to be adopted for suppressing the insurrection, I have been anxious and careful that the inevitable conflict for this purpose shall not degenerate into a violent and remorseless revolutionary struggle,' said Lincoln as he expressed his hope to establish a rational control over the war. The initial aim of the North was to conduct the military pacification of the seceded states in as humane and restrained a manner as possible.

The problem of the North was further compounded because, unlike the South where popular opinion was largely unified, much ambivalence and outright doubt existed about the war. The chief locus of doubt lay in the Democratic Party which had as its constituency mainly those who equated good government with local independence and personal rights free of Federal control. Democratic voters were from lower socio-economic levels and included many recent immigrants. In economic competition with free blacks, these people were amenable to racist ideas, fearing an influx of newly freed blacks who would depress wages, compete for jobs, and be a welfare burden. Abolition was a volatile issue in the North where many

saw the war as subverting the Constitution and interpreted it as an attempt to ensure Republican political dominance. Indeed, Democratic politicians charged the Republicans with waging an unconstitutional war for abolition in the congressional elections of 1862. The problem was also reflected in the officer corps where many officers opposed to a hard approach to the war were ultimately rooted out by the notorious Congressional Committee on the Conduct of the War in probably the first major political witch hunt in American history. Even McClellan, the premier Union general of 1861–62, was a Democrat with no anti-slavery feelings and geared his military operations toward reconciliation with the South.

Nor were the material advantages of the North as great as they seemed on the surface. Northern resources were superior to be sure,

but there were problems in their mobilization and in maintaining the popular will to fight. There was also the question of maintaining the border States with their slave populations and divided loyalties in the war. If the North was given the time, it clearly would grind the South down but, given the ambivalent feelings of the Northern public, Lincoln could not be certain of enough time. Like the South, the North too needed a quick military resolution of the conflict.

Yet the North created no more coherent a strategy than did the South. A country lawyer of modest origins, the 52-year-old Lincoln could only bring to the war effort his intelligence and common sense, having no formal military background, while Secretary of War Simon Cameron was 'a machine politician who had received his appointment in exchange for putting Pennsylvania in the

Republican column in 1860.' He was soon replaced by Edwin Stanton, personally difficult but hard working and a good administrator. So gouty and obese that he was barely ambulatory, Winfield Scott at 75 was still Commanding General and proposed a strategy known as the 'Anaconda Policy' in which the North laid siege to the South in all quarters by land and sea and gradually dismembered it in logical approaches. But popular impatience demanded quick action and victory by bringing the military potential of the North to bear in Napoleonic battles. Scott was retired to become Commandant of West Point where he died five years later. His position as Commanding General was assumed by George McClellan, a 34-year-old soldier with impeccable military credentials. Much damage was done to the war effort by the treatment of military command as politi-

INVASION OF PENNSYLVANIA—ACTION AT WRIGHTSVILLE AND DESTRUCTION OF THE COLUMBIA RAILROAD BRIDGE, JUNE 28.—FROM A SKET

cal patronage since many appointments were a function of Republican politics and factional connections. Political considerations also dictated the objectives of a number of campaigns, including several directed by Lincoln into east Tennessee in the face of military reality and the initial impetus to re-open the Mississippi River in response to local political pressures in the Old Northwest (the states between the Great Lakes and the Ohio).

With the same Jominian orientation as their Southern counterparts, the Northern generals tended to see the various theaters as discrete rather than interrelated parts of a whole. Fixated on the Jominian doctrine of concentration, they planned for one major effort in one theater. McClellan, when he became commander of the Army of the Potomac in 1861, planned to mass 270,000 men

Above:
General George G. Meade replaced Hooker as supreme commander of the Federal Army after the debacle at Chancellorsville. Meade won the Battle of Gettysburg (July 1863) but was not prepared to take advantage of the victory and therefore missed his chance to destroy the Confederate Army.

Top:
Four of the Union generals present at the battle of Gettysburg: Hancock, Birney, Barlow, and Gibbons. Gettysburg put a stop to Lee's invasion of the North and decisively threw him back on the defensive for the rest of the war.

Left:
After his major victory at Chancellorsville, Lee decided to invade the North itself. Here, the Confederate Army is seen entering Pennsylvania and destroying the Columbia Railroad Bridge at Wrightsville, 28 June 1863.

OR SPECIAL ARTIST, A. BERGHAUS.

in the Eastern Department. From the doctrinaire conviction that more resources were necessary for the 'big move,' McClellan spent nine months trying to achieve this logistically fantastic goal and did create the largest and finest army ever seen in North America. Lincoln, Stanton, and the retired Scott viewed the war in larger perspective from a desire to exploit the superior overall power of the North and fear of the time constraint. Lincoln was continually frustrated by the inactivity of his generals who complained of never having enough men for a serious campaign. In the winter of 1861–62, he implored McClellan for even a minor operation to bolster sagging morale. Refusing to acknowledge the possibility that Northerners might become so disenchanted as to abandon the struggle, McClellan steadfastly refused because he was not yet ready.

As a war of ideas that neither side could compromise, the conflict was clearly going to be an intense and unconventional struggle. Yet Union generals attempted to wage it with the strategy and tactics of the preceding age of limited warfare and limited objectives. Their emphasis was on the capture of cities and territory rather than the war-making capacity and resolve of the enemy. McClellan was proud of the 'victories' he 'won' at Manassas and Yorktown because there were no casualties – the enemy had decamped and allowed him to occupy the positions unopposed! He in fact suffered considerable emotion when the first blood was shed in his command. Halleck, now in uniform, professorially lectured his subordinates that 'There is no object in bringing about a battle if this object can be obtained without one'; while his former student McClellan stated that he preferred 'maneuvering rather than fighting.'

But McClellan did in fact maneuver his mammoth force close to Richmond with the support of gunboats on the strategic rivers at a low cost in lives. The subsequent stalemate between him and Lee on the Peninsula caused the deeply disappointed Lincoln to turn to Pope, again to McClellan, and then to Burnside, Hooker, and Meade in succession. With some reason Burnside had no personal confidence in his ability while Meade was a good defensive officer but overly cautious on offense. Pope and Hooker cost the North dearly in casualties in their headlong pursuit of a major battle to break Lee and seize Richmond, an objective of no military or strategic importance but possessing great symbolic at-

will, strong character, and his intuitive understanding of the real nature of the war combined to bring ultimate victory to the North and sweep him to the White House. His success in clearing the Mississippi Valley, particularly his victories at Vicksburg and Chattanooga, won him the rank of Lieutenant General (the first since George Washington), and the chance to confront Lee in the East. Grant assumed overall direction of operations with Halleck as Chief of Staff, Meade in tactical command of the army of the Potomac, and his trusted lieutenant William Sherman in charge in the West.

Little acquainted with Jomini, Grant had drawn his own conclusions from the ten-

armies through continuous military pressure. So Grant gathered all available Union forces by stripping defensive functions, tightened the naval blockade and occupied more Southern ports. 'I arranged for a simultaneous movement all along the line,' he said, so that Lee and Johnston would be forced to fight continually and lose men continually. Facing two excellent field generals, Grant accepted the necessity of heavy casualties to maintain the pressure and earned the reputation of a butcher. Never expecting decisive results to come from one encounter, he planned to exhaust the enemy. He made it a question of which side could sustain the highest number of casualties for the longest time.

traction. Halleck was given overall command in mid-1862 in the hope that he would produce a long-range plan to win the war but he too clung to the ideas of concentration, leaving Lincoln in desperate frustration at his lack of leadership.

It was not until March 1864 that Lincoln found a general who understood that mass armies meant mass destruction in a war of the railroad, telegraph, 'minny ball,' and unlimited objectives. Ulysses Grant had compiled a mediocre record at West Point, was a poor academic student of war, and had actually resigned from the Army in 1854 with a severe drinking problem. Many of his fellow officers had doubts about him but his iron

acious resistance of the South and the tactical stalemate produced by technology. Grant's philosophy of war was elementary: 'The art of war is simple enough. Find out where your enemy is. Strike at him as hard as you can and as often as you can, and keep moving on.' He knew he had to destroy the two principal Southern forces still in the field, the Army of Northern Virginia under Lee and the Army of Tennessee under Joseph Johnston. Maneuvering to gain territory was pointless nor were climactic Napoleonic battles the answer since the South was determined not to surrender. Grant instead adopted the larger Napoleonic end of annihilation and set out to attain it by grinding down the enemy

But the skillful delaying actions fought by Lee and Johnston still rendered the contest indecisive so Grant went beyond a strategy of military annihilation to one of total war in which he attacked the social fabric of Southern society to destroy the popular morale. He sent Philip Sheridan into the Shenandoah Valley, a prime source of supplies for Lee, to turn it into a desert. 'I have destroyed over 2000 barns filled with wheat, hay and farming implements; over 70 mills, filled with flour and wheat; have driven in front of the army over 4000 head of stock . . .' reported Sheridan. 'The people here are getting sick of war.' Grant sent Sherman to ravage the Deep South. Johnston was by struggle' was finally realized. Sherman put it well when he said, 'We are not only fighting hostile armies but a hostile people, and must make young and old, rich and poor, feel the hard hand of war, as well as the organized armies.'

But Sherman's devastation of the Deep South was not what brought Lee to Appomatox Courthouse on the morning of 9 April 1865 to surrender his starving force of barely 20,000 men to Grant. The Confederate general finally was enveloped by the huge Union Army under Grant and had no escape. Lee's surrender was an admission that the South had lost the war but the peace was still an open question and already the game was

Military demand had brought recovery by 1863. The civilian staff of the Quartermaster Department expanded from 890 to 130,000 to handle the equipping and feeding of the Union forces. Production of raw materials, manufacturing, textiles, meat packing, and related industries all prospered as did the railroads which were employed to peak capacity. Sweeping economic reforms, including the first paper greenbacks and a system of federally chartered banks, made possible a public debt of 2.6 billion dollars which served to finance further industrial expansion. Agriculture underwent substantial mechanization and produced huge surpluses which not only fed the Union armies but made

then too weak to prevent Sherman from capturing Atlanta and then marching across Georgia to Savannah where he laid waste to the Carolinas. His purpose was to demonstrate to Southerners that the Union was 'in earnest' and that 'if they were sincere in their common popular clamor "to die in the last ditch," that opportunity would soon come.' Only at this point did popular morale begin a serious decline as the people found themselves defenseless and began to perceive their cause as truly lost. Only at this point did Confederate armies suffer a serious desertion problem as men went home to protect their families. Lincoln's fear that the war would descend into 'remorseless revolutionary

changing. Only five days later, Lincoln fell prey to an assassin's bullet in Ford's Theater in Washington.

At the end of the war, dazed refugees huddled amid the smoking ruins of the South. It has been estimated that 43 percent of the wealth of that region was destroyed by the war, a factor which affected the economic development of the South until well after World War II. The North by contrast was strengthened economically by the war. The Northern business community initially opposed the war for fear that loss of the markets and investments in the South would bring depression and social unrest. There were in fact many business and banking failures.

possible the large wheat sales to Britain, a primary factor in British non-intervention. King Wheat triumphed over King Cotton so it was the North which reaped the advantage of British munitions imports rather than the South. Most Northerners prospered or held their own with the exception of industrial workers whose real income declined through inflation. In general, Northern society during the war was characterized by a shift from laissez-faire agrarianism to industrial capitalism and the forging of the long-standing alliance between big business and the Republican Party. The economic revolution and social adjustment were already taking place: the Civil War highlighted the changes.

Gettysburg was not only a decisive battle, but became a symbol of the horrors of this war.
Lincoln's 'Address' after the battle (right) summed up the ideals for which the North fought,
but its significance was not widely recognized at the time.
One paper simply reported, 'The President also spoke.'

officers and men was rudimentary. The ranks learned close-order drill to keep their lines disciplined in battle and to deploy into line of battle from marching column. Most of the officers were amateurs who studied military manuals and learned by experience as had so many of their predecessors in wars gone by. On both sides, the ranks elected their officers who in turn elected the higher officers up to regimental level. Concern over the quality of leadership in the Federal Army led to the first establishment of efficiency boards by the War Department to weed out the incompetent while an act of 1861 created the first military retirement benefits for 40 years service or disability.

If the Northern white population prospered and the Southern white population suffered from the war, what of the black population around which the whole grim exercise revolved? Slavery proved to be an indispensable asset to the Confederacy as the exploitation of black labor permitted the near complete mobilization of the white population. But even at the height of its manpower problems, the South could not bring itself to employ blacks as soldiers. As Gen-

This economic power enabled the North to enroll 2.67 million men for the war and keep about a million in the field in the later stages. The magnitude of this achievement can be appreciated when it is realized that the Regular Army in 1861 numbered around 17,000 scattered in detachments in the West. About a quarter of these troops were lost when Texas seceded while 313 of the 1108 officers also joined the South. The Mass Army that the Union finally fielded was possible only because of the American military tradition and institutions. Volunteers were the basis of the Union war effort with conscription playing a modest role. The old practice of bounties to lure recruits was employed but the Enrollment Act of March 1863 brought the first real conscription in American history by asserting the universal military obligation of the white male population always inherent in the common militia but with the obligation to the federal rather than to the state governments. Conscripts ultimately comprised about six percent of Union manpower. Federal conscription is one of the enduring military legacies of the Civil War to future generations. Although the draft was not very efficient and served mainly to encourage the recruiting of volunteers, it did provoke violent opposition in the form of draft riots, most notably in New York City in the summer of 1863.

Soldiers of both armies were typical Americans of the time, strong individualists disproportionately drawn from the rural population and neither overly concerned with discipline nor overly respectful to their officers. Both sides enforced discipline with harsh punishments such as branding, suspending by the thumbs, and firing squads for deserters while violent attacks (which practice was later known as 'fragging') were often directed at unpopular officers. Training for

Top:
Congress only approved the enlistment of Black soldiers in July 1862 and did not grant them equal pay until January 1865. Black soldiers fought with great enthusiasm and heroism throughout the war, which made a forceful argument for full Constitutional equality after the war.

Above:
Men of the 23rd New York Infantry. The arming of blacks by the North aroused fear and hatred in the South. Many atrocity stories circulated.

Right:
Picket station of black troops in Virginia, November 1864. Toward the end of the war white recruitment faltered, but thousands of black soldiers were still available.

eral Clement Stevens said, 'The justification of slavery in the South is the inferiority of the Negro. If we make him a soldier we concede the whole question.' Then there was the further problem of what would motivate blacks to fight except the promise of freedom. So the black population of the South worked and suffered alongside the white population until freed by advancing Federal troops.

Blacks, although initially enthusiastic, were precluded from service with Northern armies since Lincoln's aim was to restore the Union with slavery intact. Northern racism also militated against black military participation. But as the war dragged on, casualties mounted while volunteering slacked off. Racist arguments against the use of blacks in combat roles were transformed into 'the lives of white men can and ought to be spared by the employment of blacks as soldiers.' Originally fearing to alienate the border states, Lincoln opposed the combat use of blacks but gradually changed his view as the true nature of the war became more apparent. Two of the aims of the Emancipation Proclamation of 1 January 1863 were to deprive the South of black labor in the war effort and to prepare for the enlistment of black soldiers in the North. In the end, the Bureau of Colored Troops recruited and supervised sixteen black regiments totaling 186,000 men, mostly under white officers. The Navy contained a further 30,000 blacks out of a total of 118,000 men.

Blacks were treated badly in several respects, most notably pay, by the army and were used as laborers and garrison troops in the main. But when permitted, they fought well, earning thirteen Congressional Medals of Honor and maintaining a generally high standard of discipline. Indeed, the conduct of black troops in the war did come to alleviate certain aspects of northern racism. Some desegregation measures were passed in various states while a movement developed in support of black suffrage North and South. The right of blacks to live in the country for which they had fought was recognized by the cessation of federally-sponsored initiatives to return blacks to Africa, a pet project of Lincoln among others. As one Union officer noted, 'Till the blacks were armed, there was no guarantee of their freedom. It was their demeanor under arms that shamed the nation in to recognizing them as men.'

The gross disparity between the strength of the North and the South raises the question of why the war lasted so long but a number of reasons can be suggested. In its cordon defense, the South had chosen the worst possible strategy and then switched to one which destroyed its manpower pool. Lee's urgency in seeking a decisive military resolution of the conflict led him to be the tactical agressor in eight of the first twelve major battles so that after Gettysburg he had used up 175,000 men. Federal generals also consumed manpower at a great rate but the North was able to outspend the South in this crucial area. Warfare was also not very efficient in its use of manpower. Disease

ravaged the armies of both sides, taking two soldiers for each lost in battle and reducing armies to one third to one half of their paper strength. Thus armies suffered a continual decline in combat efficiency exclusive of combat.

The obsolescence of infantry tactics against the rifle also led to casualty rates of up to 80 percent on occasion. Remembering that frontal assaults had won the Mexican War, commanders found that only one in eight succeeded in the Civil War. Most were similar to that described by the Confederate General Ambrose Powell Hill in the Peninsular campaign:

> As each brigade emerged from the woods, from 50 to 100 guns opened up on it, tearing great gaps in its ranks; but the heroes reeled on and were shot down by the reserves at the guns, which a few squads reached. . . . It was not war, it was murder.

The cost of battle was high for both victor and defeated not only in casualties but also in the combat readiness of the survivors. McClellan noted that a sizeable battle left 'many thousands unfitted for duty for some

Far left:
General William T. Sherman, personally a humane man, is most famous for the destruction he caused in his march through Georgia in 1864 and the suffering he brought to the civilian population. He provisioned his army through pillage and destroyed all property, public and private, in his path.

Left:
Sherman's march across Georgia officially aimed only at pursuing the Confederate Army under General Johnston and preventing it from linking with Lee in Virginia. However its implications for Southern morale and resources far exceeded these achievements.

Below left:
Sherman was in fact no more than an average tactical commander but he understood what was necessary to break the Southern will to fight.

Below:
Sherman's men destroying a railroad in Atlanta. When Atlanta had been conceded, the way was open to Sherman to cross Georgia to the sea, destroying everything on a 60-mile wide front.

days by illness, demoralization and fatigue' which was an important reason why Civil War generals rarely were able to exploit an immediate tactical advantage arising from a major engagement. The Union was further constrained by the fact that half of its uniformed manpower was employed in the garrison and administration of conquered areas by 1864 and thus not available for combat.

While the South failed to win with an essentially conservative military strategy, the North developed a new approach in total war. Sherman and Sheridan destroyed the moral and economic base of the southern war effort while Grant fixed and ground down the main enemy force. As Sheridan characterized the new warfare, 'the people must be left nothing but their eyes to weep with over the war.' Terror inflicted on the general populace was an important aspect of victory and presaged the total war of the twentieth

157

century. Sherman's destruction of the enemy's rear areas fascinated later generations of Americans and Europeans, which were able to employ the airplane to the same end.

The Civil War was and is the major event in the popular imagination of Americans. There were more lives lost and more impact on the survivors of 'the war' than from any other American war. It was seen as the dividing line between the pastoral innocence of early America and the affluent and materialistic America of the machine age and capitalism. Yet the war had been brought on by the popular nationalism of both sides and had spurred American nationalism generally by superficially defusing the sectional issue. Much of the nationalistic stimulus came from the mass armies of the North and South. The Union Army, for example, was the largest national organization yet to appear in the United States.

America's identity as a nation is far more intimately related to the Civil War than to the Revolution. The republic proclaimed in 1776 was not flexible enough to cope with the increasing socio-economic complexity of the country as it developed and collapsed in 1860. But the Civil War was only a quasi-revolutionary war, as William Barney has argued, and thus wrought only a quasi-revolutionary transformation of the Union. The war did bring to an end the notion of dual sovereignty between the States and the Federal government and brought a transfer of power away from the States to the Federal government and in particular to the Presidency. The war also destroyed slavery as a legal institution but the reassertion of constitutional orthodoxy afterward coupled with the pervasive notions of racism found in both North and South constrained the changes.

The Civil War also brought reassurance to many in their conception of themselves as Americans and of their unique destiny in history. The tensions which escalated into secession came as an appalling shock to most Americans because it confirmed a not-so-secret fear that the American experiment in democratic government was unstable and based on wrong principles. Indeed, one Northerner wrote in his diary in 1858 that 'Our civilization is decaying. We are in our decadence. An explosion and crash must be

Above:
General Grant at Cold Harbor, Virginia, June 1864. Grant suffered devastating losses but continued south.

Below:
Following a ten-month siege, General Lee abandoned Petersburg in April 1865.

at hand.' Perhaps democracy was too self-indulgent and corrupt. Perhaps God was punishing America for its materialism and political corruption. The whole uniqueness and mission of America had been called into question. But what had begun as a manifestation of American incompetence and weakness ended as a demonstration of American strength and reaffirmed virtue. Slavery had been destroyed and the Union restored. The war had purified America and saved the soul of the nation. The sign of God's renewed favor was the restoration of obedience to law which enabled even Southerners to find virtue in their defeat.

The fact of the Civil War created other problems for Americans whose legend was success and victory. How could the South have defied this legend with its failure and defeat? This anomaly was handled by collusion between North and South in the creation of a myth that both sides won. The South had fought valiantly and won a moral victory. 'They never whipped us, Sir, unless they were four to one. If we had had anything like a fair chance, or less disparity of numbers . . .' wrote one contemporary Southerner. The myth thus also endowed the Confederate soldier with enhanced military prowess. Southern heroes such as 'Stonewall' Jackson and James Ewell Brown Stuart were incorporated into the American pantheon but the foremost figure in the myth was Robert E. Lee. Lee in fact is the only cult general in the English-speaking world. His evolving legend made him a symbol of victory for the defeated South and thus for all Americans. Lee was often presented as a Washington-like figure and after 1900 as a Christ-like figure, Appomatox being equated with Gethsemane.

Too horrible and incomprehensible in its reality, the war itself was idealized in popular memory as a humane and uplifting struggle with no emphasis on the human and material cost. One Union general said, 'In the lapse of years, the war recurs to us as a picnic on a large scale. . . .' A Confederate counterpart also observed, 'The war was the mildest and most humane ever fought.' Although Americans had fought other Americans, this fact too was assimilated in the 'legend of the Blue and Gray bound together in uplifting work.' 'Our friends the enemy,' was a motif imputing virtue to both sides but which created ambivalence about the meaning of the war and the nature of the enemy. This motif caused American soldiers to become ambivalent about their enemy and about the justice of the cause for which they fought in later wars, especially the Indian wars and the Spanish-American War, and only disappeared after World War I.

Americans thus created a complex structure of legend and myth to ease their shame and guilt about the war and to assist in healing its wounds. With no major military conflicts over the next three decades, the wounds did largely heal and the military resumed its traditional modest position on the periphery of American society. Only when another national crisis, also related to doubts about American uniqueness and mission, arose in the 1890s would Americans again be moved to war in search of national rejuvenation.

Below:
Union soldiers in front of the courthouse at Appomatox where Lee surrendered on 10 April 1865.

Chapter 6

The Spanish-American War – Manifest Destiny Revisited

Commodore George Dewey was startled around mid-morning on 1 May 1898 to be informed that only fifteen percent of the ammunition for the guns of his main batteries remained. He immediately ordered his four modern cruisers to cease blasting a rusty and ill-positioned Spanish squadron and to withdraw farther out into the blue water of Manila Bay. But he soon learned that the information had been garbled in transmission for in fact only fifteen percent of the ammunition had been expended. The situation clarified, Dewey and his cheering crews returned to their task. The ensuing complete annihilation of the enemy squadron gave an astounded American public its first taste of victory only five days after Congress had declared war on Spain. Dewey, a relatively obscure desk officer until Assistant Secretary of the Navy Theodore Roosevelt tapped him for the Far Eastern command, became overnight the man of the hour for jubilant Americans and began to harbor presidential ambitions. A lust for battle swept the country as his aroused countrymen clamored for the chance to fight and agreed with Teddy Roosevelt who wrote his friend Henry Cabot Lodge, 'I do not think a war with Spain would be serious enough to cause much strain on this country.'

The immediate cause of what future Secretary of State John Hay termed 'a splendid little war' lay not in the Pacific, however, but halfway around the world in the Caribbean. One of the last vestiges of the Spanish empire, Cuba suffered under an oppressive political system, economic domination by the metropolitan power, and repression of all attempts at reform. This situation had brought earlier rebellions against Spanish rule, the longest of which was the Ten Years' War of 1868–78. Lying not a hundred miles off the coast of Florida, Cuba roused intense sympathy among Americans because of their commercial, strategic, and emotional ties with the islands. Demands for American intervention were loud and repeated during the second half of the nineteenth century but one president after another declined in favor of pressing reform on Spain through accepted diplomatic channels.

A new revolt burst forth in 1895, a revolt which Spain was unable to suppress and which quickly descended to bloody barbarism on the part of both sides. The horrors of the war were fully reported in the American press, especially the *New York Journal* of William Randolph Hearst and the *New York World* of Joseph Pulitzer. Engaged in an all-out circulation battle, these papers supplied what little sensationalism the revolt failed to provide of itself through gross exaggeration, distortion, and outright fabrication,

Opposite:
Pulitzer's *The World*'s coverage of the explosion of the USS *Maine* in Havana Harbor, in which 260 lives were lost. William Randolph Hearst's *New York Journal* had already been clamoring for war against Spain and the *Maine* incident gave the newspapers a field day.

reaching 'a depth of irresponsibility never before plumbed' in the words of historian Frederick Merck. The rebellion was disastrous for American commercial and financial interests in the island as exports to the United States, its principal customer, fell by half between 1894 and 1896 while both sides destroyed American property. Incited by the potent Cuban rebel lobby in the United States, American public opinion was further outraged in 1896 when Captain General Valeriano Weyler attempted to deal with the rebellion through his policy of 'reconcentration.' Forerunner of the Briggs plan during the Malayan emergency and the strategic hamlet program in South Vietnam, reconcentration assembled the noncombatant population in fortified cities and towns so that it could not support the rebels. The American press called the inventor of reconcentration 'Butcher Weyler' while even the normally judicious President William McKinley remarked, 'It is not civilized warfare. It is extermination.'

Succeeding Grover Cleveland in office in March 1897, McKinley continued the passive policy of his predecessors by demanding reform and making offers of mediation. But he also insisted that military intervention was a viable policy alternative as he warned Spain that 'The United States is not a nation to which peace is a necessity. . . .' McKinley did not in fact want war because he believed that the country was unprepared nor was it clear that the war would be limited to Spain. He was doggedly resisting a rising tide of jingoist hysteria and war fever when he made his cardinal mistake. In an effort to curb the jingoes, he sent the battleship *Maine* to call at Havana where it mysteriously exploded on the evening of 15 February 1898 with the loss of 260 of the crew. The cause of the explosion has never been ascertained but the event sealed the fate of McKinley's search for a peaceful solution to the Cuban issue. Despite the fact that Spain was making important

concessions in the diplomatic negotiations, the outpouring of public outrage over the *Maine* made McKinley and his Republican cohorts fear that Congress would declare war without him. 'The people want no disgraceful negotiations with Spain' editorialized the *Chicago Tribune*. 'An administration which stains the national honor will never be forgiven.' War preparations began after the *Maine* incident and McKinley sent to Congress in April a war message which stated '. . . the destruction of the *Maine*, by whatever exterior cause, is a patent and impressive proof of a state of things in Cuba that is intolerable.' War was declared on 22 April while the Navy had already put to sea four days earlier to blockade the main ports of Cuba.

War did not come because of the *Maine* or other provocations such as the de Lôme letter (an intercepted Spanish communication which called McKinley a 'spineless weakling'). Nor did it come because of the 'yellow press' which screamed 'Remember the *Maine* and to hell with Spain' and then sent 200 correspondents to cover the ensuing war. In fact a variety of factors converged to create a national mood receptive to and even desirous of war. Among these factors was the worst depression since 1787 which brought widespread hardship and spawned a protest movement of Populists and Free Silverites strong enough to capture the Democratic Party. The defeat of William Jennings Bryan by McKinley in the hotly contested presidential election of 1896 left the former's alienated constituency especially responsive to the appeal to rescue suffering Cuba by force of arms. But a far broader spectrum of American society than just the disadvantaged was feeling restless and discontented at that time. Many saw the youth of the nation fading and with it the unique American national strength and mission. The maturation and bureaucratization of American business seemed to signal the end of the era of competitive economic opportunity which Americans saw as such an important part of their history. Closely associated in the mind of the 1890s was the closing of the western frontier and the apparent end of limitless free land. The historian Frederick Jackson Turner expressed what many felt in his famous essay of 1893, '. . . the frontier has gone, and with its going has closed the first period of American history.' Americans also saw other undesirable developments in their society such as slums, waves of immigrants, outrageous urban corruption, bloody strikes, and the rural agitation over free silver. The aggregate of these widespread popular anxieties and discontents was what Richard Hofstadter has termed the 'psychic crisis of the 1890s.'

863,956
WORLDS CIRCULATED YESTERDAY

"Circulation Books Open to All."

The World.

"Circulation Books Open to All."

863,956
WORLDS CIRCULATED YEERDAY

VOL. XXXVIII. NO. 13,330. {Copyright, 1898, by the Press Publishing Company, New York World.} NEW YORK, THURSDAY, FEBRUARY 17, 1898. PRICE {ONE CENT in Greater New York and Jersey City. TWO CENTS outside of Greater New York and Jersey City and Staten.}

MAINE EXPLOSION CAUSED BY BOMB OR TORPEDO?

Capt. Sigsbee and Consul-General Lee Are in Doubt---The World Has Sent a Special Tug, With Submarine Divers, to Havana to Find Out---Lee Asks for an Immediate Court of Inquiry---260 Men Dead.

IN A SUPPRESSED DESPATCH TO THE STATE DEPARTMENT, THE CAPTAIN SAYS THE ACCIDENT WAS MADE POSSIBLE BY AN ENEMY.

Dr. E. C. Pendleton, Just Arrived from Havana, Says He Overheard Talk There of a Plot to Blow Up the Ship---Capt. Zalinski, the Dynamite Expert, and Other Experts Report to The World that the Wreck Was Not Accidental---Washington Officials Ready for Vigorous Action if Spanish Responsibility Can Be Shown---Divers to Be Sent Down to Make Careful Examinations.

DRAWN FROM A DESCRIPTION BY EYE-WITNESSES ON THE STEAMSHIP CITY OF WASHINGTON WHO SAW THE EXPLOSION, FOLLOWED BY "A VOLCANO OF FIRE AND SHOWERS OF BOATS, BODIES, IRON AND GUNS," CABLED TO THE WORLD BY ITS OWN CORRESPONDENT IN HAVANA, SYLVESTER SCOVEL.

THE WHOLE STORY OF THE DISASTER TOLD IN A FEW WORDS.

Growing Belief that It Was Not Accidental—Visitor from Havana Reports that He Overheard a Plot—Sigsbee and Lee Suspicious.

At the hour of going to press for this edition of The World it is not known whether the explosion which caused the destruction of the

e-ship Maine in the harbor of Havana was an accident or the result bomb or torpedo placed with an intent to blow up the vessel.

he consensus of opinion of the naval officers and experts in this is that the disaster was not accidental. It is believed that the as blown up. This view appears to be borne out by Comm Lee and Capt. Sigsbee, Commander of the Maine.

n official cable to the State Department Lee makes the signif quest that a court of inquiry be held to ascertain the cause of losion.

Capt. Sigsbee officially cabled Secretary Long his conclusion, after a hasty examination, that the disaster was not caused by an accident.

He expressed a belief that whether the explosion originated without or within, it was made possible by an enemy.

Dr. C. E. Pendleton, who has just arrived from Havana, says that he overheard there a conversation in which it was declared that there would shortly come a great sensation; that there were wires all around the Maine and that she could be blown to pieces at a moment's notice.

Capt. ———, perhaps the foremost expert upon explosions

in warfare, declares that he is almost sure that the Maine was destroyed by a dynamite torpedo or bomb.

A despatch from Washington says that Secretary Long and Assistant Secretary Roosevelt called all the chiefs of the Navy Department in consultation yesterday morning to secure expert opinion as to the cause of the Maine's loss and its effect on the navy.

Consul-General Lee cables officially that the number of ... 260. Lieuts. Merritt and Jenkins are still missing.

aggressiveness and a desire to reassert the national power and vitality through war. The Cubans were seen as similar to the Americans of 1776, victims of a brutal colonial oppression. As Ernest May has noted, all the influences and anxieties of the times became translated in some irrational way into a concern for the plight of Cuba. For both people and government, war with 'monarchical, Catholic, Latin Spain' served the primary purpose of relieving emotion. For the Republican administration, war in 1898 was a political necessity without which, said Senator Henry Cabot Lodge, 'we shall go down to the greatest defeat ever known.'

Americans had few military inhibitions against the thought of war with Spain since the latter was militarily as well as economically decrepit. Spanish military weakness and incompetence were graphically demonstrated by the course of the insurrection in Cuba. Spanish forces in Cuba consisted of about 100,000 Iberians and 80,000 Cuban loyalists, both characterized by poor training and leadership and ravaged by disease. At any given time, up to 40 percent were hospitalized. Between 25,000 and 40,000 insurgents were under arms, laborers and plantation workers led by wealthy planters and businessmen. Armed for the most part with

modern rifles, the rebels maintained civil government in areas they controlled, along with farms and crude workshops. Their main tactic was to destroy agriculture, especially the sugar industry, through skillfully conducted guerrilla warfare. Much of their finance and support came from Americans. Spanish strategy was unimaginatively defensive, tying down the majority of troops in forts and outposts with few available for offensive operations. The Spanish scorched-earth policy in tandem with the tactics of the insurgents had reduced much of the island to desert. The Spanish had maintained the upper hand in the west while the main insurgent field force under General Calixto Garcia dominated the thinly populated east.

The Spanish strategic problem in the war lay in the fact that Cuba was an island on America's doorstep, totally dependent on overseas supply and reinforcement. The strategic reality of the war required that the Spanish Navy break the American blockade and keep the island's line of communications open. Defeat was thus certain because the Navy only had four armored cruisers, three destroyers, and four gunboats actually in an operational state. The country was simply too poor even to keep these ships adequately manned, repaired, and supplied. Admiral

Above:
Company K, 9th Massachusetts Volunteers leave
Clinton, Massachusetts for training camps on 4 May
1898. These eager recruits did not see action since the
fighting was over in ten weeks.

Left:
Prospective recruits talk to the corporal at a New York
recruiting station in May 1898.

Pascual Cervera lamented that any war
'would mean a terrible catastrophe for poor
Spain.' But court circles, conservative politicians, and nationalists in Spain preferred
defeat in war to any surrender to American demands. 'They know Cuba is lost,'
Ambassador Stewart Woodford cabled
McKinley from Madrid, 'but they will seek
honorable defeat in war.'

The honorable defeat which Woodford
anticipated for Spain would be inflicted by
American forces which were passing through
a fundamental transformation. Both the
Navy and the Army had had their wartime

missions redefined as the ideas about warfare
and commerce systematized and popularized
by Mahan were translated into national
policy. Mahan's conception of American
power built on expanding mercantile commerce required a fleet of armored, steam-
propelled capital ships to command the
coastline and attack the enemy as necessary,
coaling stations for these ships in the Caribbean and Pacific located on strategic islands
with good harbors, and control of the projected isthmian canal. Thus the mission of
the Navy became not the traditional commerce raiding and harbor defense but squad-

ron and fleet actions far from the coast. In 1898 the Navy had five modern battleships, two armored cruisers, three protected cruisers, nine smaller cruisers, and ten gunboats. Four cruisers and two gunboats made up the Asiatic squadron of which Dewey took command in December 1897. Under Secretary John Long and Assistant Secretary Teddy Roosevelt, the Navy Department was efficiently run and had over two years earlier developed a comprehensive plan of operations against Spain in the Caribbean, Europe, and Far East in case of need.

In view of the new role of the Navy, the Army was charged with the traditional defense of the homeland, garrison and defense of the new colonies, and the provision of small expeditionary forces to assist the Navy in seizing and retaining strategic foreign points. Conceding the central wartime role to the Navy, the Army had a limited auxiliary function. Shortly after retiring as Commanding General in 1897, General John Schofield described the logic of the unequal roles in these words, 'In a country having the strategic situation of the United States, the Navy is the *aggressive* arm of the national military power. Its function is to punish an enemy until he is willing to submit to the national demands.'

As naval combat had been revolutionized by the advances in technology which made possible the shift from wooden sailing ships to armored all-metal steamships, armed with rifled cannon firing high explosive shells long distances, so too was technological advance forcing significant changes in the preparation for and conduct of land warfare. The single-shot muzzle loader had given way first to the single-shot breech loader and then to the magazine repeater firing high velocity steel jacketed bullets with smokeless powder. Muzzle-loading smoothbore iron cannon had been replaced with rifled steel breech loaders firing shrapnel and high explosive shells great distances with improved accuracy. Although tactically undigested, machine guns were also available. The telegraph and railroad promised more decisive campaigns from new strategic combinations made possible by central direction and swift movement and supply of large forces.

New tactics and training were needed as the firepower of small arms and artillery made the traditional close order infantry formation suicidal. The emphasis in training was now placed on physical conditioning, marksmanship, direction of fire, skirmishing, and use of terrain. More intensive and broader training from privates up stressed individual initiative and tactical decision, teaching soldiers to move and fight in small groups. With training more complicated and requiring greater periods of time, it became increasingly clear that the army with the best training in peacetime in the new war of machines and firepower would win. Prussia led the way but all the major powers followed suit by maintaining highly skilled standing armies, creating mass citizen armies trained in peace but rapidly mobilized in war, and

developing general staffs to plan and co-
ordinate in peacetime.

Owing to its geopolitical situation, however, the United States had no need for a
mass army but rather a small, highly professional standing force supplemented by a
large rapidly mobilizable ready reserve.
Since the Army was the victim of repeated
economy drives in Congress, its strength had
hovered at the number of 25,000 men as it
went about its post-Civil War job on policing
the Indians and breaking strikes. There were
no war plans nor any staff to make such plans.
Federal law in fact forbade any formation
larger than a regiment in peacetime and even
regiments were seldom assembled as units at
one post.

Even so, considerable change was taking
place in an era of military innovation and
reform, spurred by a creative minority.

William T. Sherman, serving as Commanding
General from 1869 to 1883, encouraged the
reformers and founded many officers schools
and the Military Service Institution of the
United States. Modeled on the Royal United
Service Institution of Britain, the latter was
a voluntary society for the study and discussion of military affairs. Publishing its own
journal, the Institution was a primary forum
for discussing new ideas and reform. At the
center of the program of the army pro-
gressives were the ideas of Emory Upton, a
West Point graduate, whose revulsion at the
slaughter and incompetent leadership he
witnessed as a Union officer in the Civil War
led him to devote his career to army reform.
His idea of a rapidly expansible army built
around a small highly professional standing
force was espoused by army reformers but
clashed in practice with the other long-
standing facet of the American military
tradition.

The plans for a federal military reserve to
fill out the army in wartime came to naught
as a result of the rejuvenation of the state
militias. Paralleling the army reforms of the
1880s and 1890s was the reform and expansion of these moribund organizations. These
had languished until the great railroad strike
of 1877 when the States became acutely
aware of the police value of the militia. By the
mid-1890s, all States had reformed volunteer
militias with the governors as commanders in
chief for the maintenance of law and order
and defense against invasion. These militias
were already termed the National Guard in
38 States and aggregated about 114,000 men
in 1897. Training, support units and armament were generally poor as was discipline.
The United States National Guard Association was formed in 1879 and was politically
powerful in the state legislatures and Congress as it represented large blocs of votes. By
the 1890s, the army reformers and the National Guard had worked out a compromise
whereby the federal government assumed
the burden of National Guard expenditure
from the States in return for the imposition
of army standards and training, in order to
achieve a uniformity.

Below:
Rear Admiral George Dewey aboard his flagship the USS *Olympia*, the year after he had knocked out the Spanish Pacific Fleet in Manila. The nation went wild at the victory but Dewey then had to wait three and a half months in Manila Bay before the American Army arrived.

Right:
A scene on board a US transport headed for Cuba. After the US Navy had locked the Spanish naval units in Santiago harbor, the Army embarked some 16,000 men from Tampa. They were packed into 32 transports and after an uncomfortable journey they were landed 20 miles to the east of Santiago.

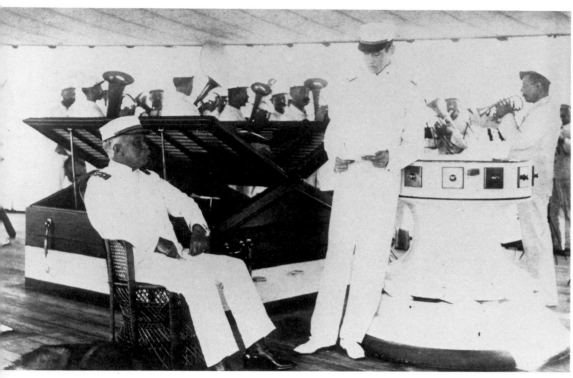

Right:
Transports at Tampa awaiting orders to sail for Cuba.

Below:
Troops climbing aboard the transports in June 1898. The mobilization did not go as smoothly as the War Department had planned.

The War Department in 1898 was a motley conglomeration of ten virtually independent bureaus, relatively efficient individually but with poorly delineated lines of responsibility and authority. The decision-making necessary for the conduct of the war required negotiation among the bureaus and ultimately caused the department to become disjointed. Both Secretary of War Russell Alger and Commanding General Nelson Miles left a certain amount to be desired in character and ability although both had had distinguished careers beginning with exemplary service in the Civil War. Like Polk and Lincoln before him, it was McKinley who really ran the war and determined military strategy to conform to his political goals. From a special 'war room' in the Executive Mansion, the President used telephone and telegraph for ready communication with his officers in the field. Planning and preparations for the war began on 8 March with the passage of the Military Appropriations Bill but McKinley never saw fit to inform the War Department of the nature of his political objectives, hence the Army and Navy had little notion of what kind of war to prepare for. That plus the fact that American strategy took several different turns after war was declared, made army planning in particular a shambles.

The initial American strategy was to use the Navy to blockade Cuba into submission through starvation and in the process draw the Spanish fleet to its destruction trying to relieve the beleaguered island. The Spanish fleet was considered a match for the American and was also known to be faster, thus no military intervention in Cuba was thought possible until the enemy ships had been destroyed or neutralized. Once this had been accomplished the Army was to send supplies and a small force to aid the Cuban insurgents. The Army was adamantly opposed to placing any forces, let alone large forces, in Cuba during the fever season and regarded the war as the proper domain of the Navy. While the Navy efficiently assembled its squadrons during March for the task ahead, the intense war fever caused the appearance of numerous local volunteer companies which wished to participate in the war effort not as part of the Regular Army but in the historic American volunteer pattern. The potent National Guard lobby also rose to the occasion by besting the War Department in a Congressional struggle which gave the National Guard a prominent place in the military system and required that half of the proposed Cuban expeditionary force be State militia.

Although the Army had hoped to get into combat and have the war won before the National Guard could get organized, this political development threw its planned mobilization of the regulars into confusion.

Dewey's unexpected victory at Manila then revealed that the war capabilities of the Spanish had been overestimated while the blockade proved to have little effect on the Spanish position in Cuba. The Spanish squadron under Admiral Cervera first could not be located and then ran into Santiago harbor where it was locked in by the ships of the Atlantic Squadron of Admiral William Sampson. Spain apparently planned not offensives but a period of inactivity during which other European powers might come to her aid. The sudden neutralization of the Spanish fleet made possible immediate intervention in Cuba while the Philippines offered a second front. McKinley thus dispatched General Wesley Merritt to the latter islands with a force which ultimately grew to 20,000 men.

The 2 May then brought a reversal in the roles of Navy and Army as McKinley ordered a major expedition to Cuba. The Army suddenly received the major assignment in the war while the Navy reverted to

its traditional supporting part. Heavily-defended Havana was the object of this campaign until strategy took another twist at the end of the month. With Cervera's squadron in Santiago harbor, that city assumed strategic importance. The President therefore shifted the focus of the expedition to eastern Cuba where he envisaged an extensive land campaign directed against Santiago to force the fleet out. His order of 26 May to the War Department and General William K. Shafter immediately to load 25,000 men along with their equipment and supplies on transports at Tampa Bay threw the whole mobilization effort into total confusion. The expedition finally weighed anchor on 14 June only after Shafter himself descended to the piers to supervise the loading. Shafter had under his command the largest military expedition ever to leave American shores: 819 officers, 15,058 ranks, 30 civilian clerks, 272 teamsters and packers, 107 stevedores, and 2295 horses and mules. The straggling convoy reached its objective after a five-and-a-half-day voyage which was a nightmare for the troops packed into the dank transports.

Shafter elected to land at Daiquiri and Siboney, fifteen miles east of Santiago, while the Cuban insurgents attacked the

Above:
Americans troops relax in a trench during a lull in fighting outside Santiago.

Below:
The premature American attack at Las Guásimas on 24 June forced Linares' forces into a battle even though they had already been ordered to withdraw.

Spanish rear and made feints elsewhere. The Spanish General Arsenio Linares made a number of mistakes, the first of which was to allow his enemy to land unopposed on 22 June when he could have massacred the disorganized Americans. Shafter's strategy was, as he informed an aide, that since 'the country was no longer accustomed to hear of heavy losses in battle (a reference to the Civil War) and would judge us accordingly; that he intended to get his army in position around Santiago and demand a surrender.' The plan was to seize the high ground north and east of the city to trap the garrison against the bay and force the Spanish fleet out to sea with artillery fire. Shafter himself said of his campaign, 'I determined to rush it and I did rush it,' because of the well-founded fear that yellow fever was far more of a threat to his force than the Spanish who numbered about 12,000 with no machine guns and little artillery. By 26 June, two infantry divisions, a dismounted cavalry division, an independent brigade, and cavalry, artillery, and support units were ashore along with 4000

Below:
On 1–2 July General Shafter's troops took the fortified village of El Caney, outside Santiago.

Cubans of García's army. Situated in a mosquito-infested lowland, Siboney became the main American base ashore.

Instead of attacking the exposed and disorganized Americans from the ridges behind Siboney and Daiquiri, Linares committed his second serious mistake by establishing lightly manned defensive positions at Las Guásimas to block the road to Santiago. Las Guásimas could still have been the decisive battle of the war as the Spanish trenches atop a 250-foot high ridge commanded rugged terrain through which the enemy had to pass to get away from the coast and to Santiago. Holding the Americans at that point would have protected the land communications of the city. But Linares compounded his initial mistakes by deciding to abandon Las Guásimas. There would have been no battle had not General Joseph Wheeler, a tough Confederate Civil War veteran, determined to attack the Spanish positions before they could be reinforced and the American be pinned down in the pestilential coastal area. On 24 June 1000 Americans, many of whom were green volunteers, attacked 1500 Spanish armed with Mauser repeating rifles. The heated engagement which ensued cost the attackers sixteen killed and 52 wounded

against ten killed and 25 wounded for the defenders.

Linares withdrew to the outer line of defenses of Santiago, a train of hills about three miles from the city. His men were very short of food and ammunition but the Americans were wrestling with almost insuperable logistic problems in getting supplies and ammunition ashore and up to the front. Due to the daily downpours and lack of roads, lighters and wagons, most of the expedition's equipment did not get ashore until after the fall of the city. The troops fought with only gatling guns and light field pieces for support and lived with a constant shortage of ammunition and food. But by 30 June enough supplies had come up for Shafter, by then suffering from heat exhaustion, to order an attack for the following day. His objective was to press the offensive before the Spanish were reinforced and also to gain the use of Santiago harbor to solve his horrendous supply problem. The task would not be easy, as facing his men were 4000 yards of trenches, two and three deep, punctuated with breastworks, and blockhouses, protected by barbed wire, and manned by 2000 troops, who had long service but many of whom had no experience of battle.

Teddy Roosevelt who in fact led his men up a neighboring hill while the 6th and 16th infantry confronted San Juan Hill proper. The foreign military observers accompanying the expeditionary force were shocked by the frontal assault without artillery preparation. One observed, 'It is very gallant, but very foolish,' while another said simply, 'It is slaughter.' Still fighting doggedly in retreat, the Spanish withdrew to their second line of defenses while the Americans, with over 1100 casualties and no reserves, halted and feared that a counterattack would negate their hard-won gains. The success of the day had in fact been won not by military skill but by superior numbers and foolhardy if valiant tenacity. Not realizing how few Spanish had actually been involved on 1 July, Teddy Roosevelt wrote to Henry Cabot Lodge, 'We have won so far at a heavy cost; but the Spaniards fight very hard and charging these entrenchments against modern rifles is terrible. We are within measurable distance of a terrible military disaster.'

Afflicted with gout and weakened by malaria, Shafter was unable to press his advantage while the Spanish were too weak to do anything but wait. Linares had been wounded, placing José Toral in command.

The attack launched on 1 July was the only full-scale infantry battle of the war and clearly demonstrated the defensive power of entrenched troops with repeating rifles. Shafter sent one regular infantry division against the fortified village of El Caney and two infantry divisions and the dismounted cavalry against San Juan Hill, the two strongpoints of the Spanish defenses. The Americans had thought a few minutes would suffice for El Caney and then its attackers could join the main assault. Outnumbered 560 to 6600, the defenders only broke nine hours later when their ammunition ran low. The attack on San Juan and adjacent hills faltered early under withering rifle fire. Pinned down, the Americans had difficulty spotting targets since, in the words of one trooper, 'The buggers are hidden behind rocks, in weeds, and in underbrush, and we just simply can't locate them; they are shooting our men simply all to pieces.' Linares had so misplaced his men in that area, however, that only 1200 faced 8400 Americans. The American light artillery was indifferently served and Shafter totally ignored the naval fire support available to him in lieu of his own heavy guns, hence the Spanish were not molested in their trenches by other than ineffective rifle fire. He was in fact too ill to direct the battle and thus, as Teddy Roosevelt said, 'The battle simply fought itself.' At about the time Spanish fire began to slacken for lack of ammunition, a battery of four gatling guns forced most of the defenders from their trenches on San Juan Hill. A valiant but costly charge up that and adjacent hills finally cleared the positions. Himself dodging bullets, veteran correspondent Richard Harding Davis described the charge for his readers, 'They had no glittering bayonets, they were not massed in regular array. There were a few men in advance, bunched together, and creeping up a steep, sunny hill, the top of which roared and flashed with flame. . . . Behind these first few, spreading out like a fan, were single lines of men, slipping and scrambling in the smooth grass. . . .'

The charge up San Juan Hill later became romanticized and focused on the role of

Top:
The 9th Infantry prepare for the attack on San Juan Hill on 1 July 1898.

Above:
Infantry in the trenches in front of San Juan Hill. Colonel Roosevelt probably overestimated the importance of this victory.

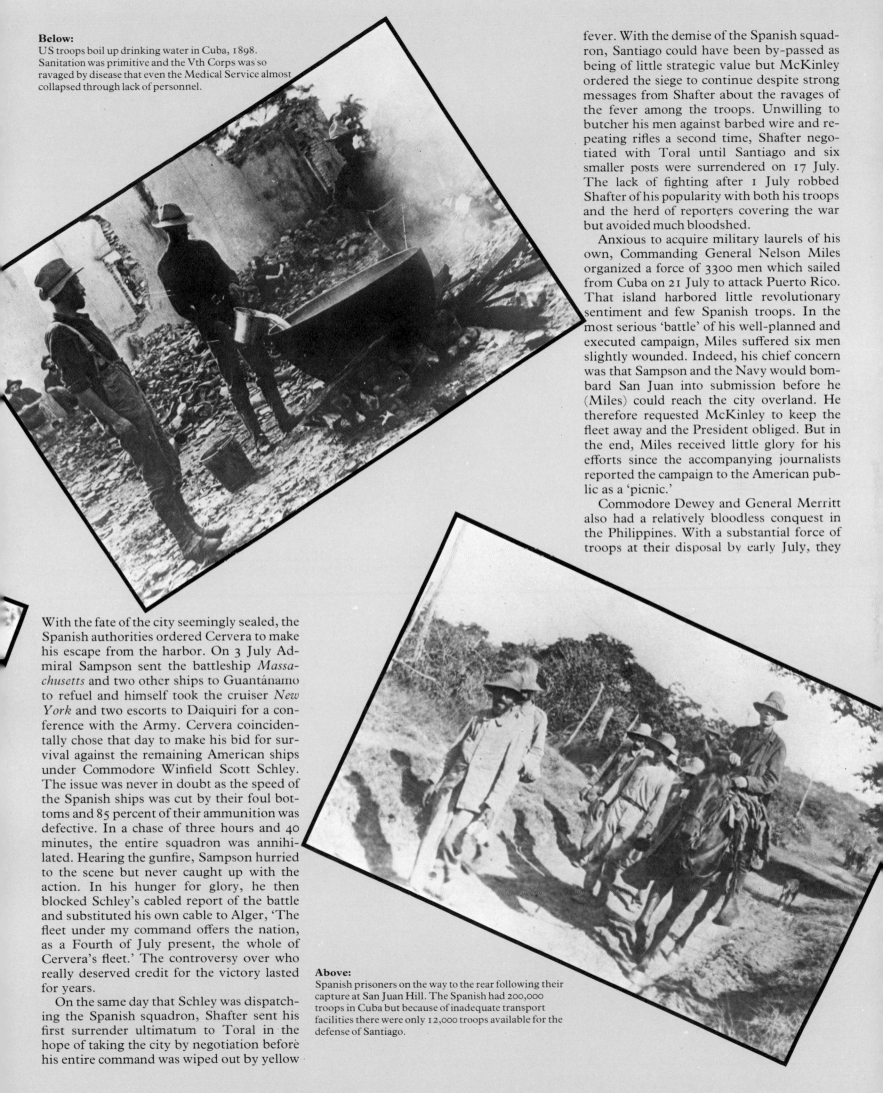

fever. With the demise of the Spanish squadron, Santiago could have been by-passed as being of little strategic value but McKinley ordered the siege to continue despite strong messages from Shafter about the ravages of the fever among the troops. Unwilling to butcher his men against barbed wire and repeating rifles a second time, Shafter negotiated with Toral until Santiago and six smaller posts were surrendered on 17 July. The lack of fighting after 1 July robbed Shafter of his popularity with both his troops and the herd of reporters covering the war but avoided much bloodshed.

Anxious to acquire military laurels of his own, Commanding General Nelson Miles organized a force of 3300 men which sailed from Cuba on 21 July to attack Puerto Rico. That island harbored little revolutionary sentiment and few Spanish troops. In the most serious 'battle' of his well-planned and executed campaign, Miles suffered six men slightly wounded. Indeed, his chief concern was that Sampson and the Navy would bombard San Juan into submission before he (Miles) could reach the city overland. He therefore requested McKinley to keep the fleet away and the President obliged. But in the end, Miles received little glory for his efforts since the accompanying journalists reported the campaign to the American public as a 'picnic.'

Commodore Dewey and General Merritt also had a relatively bloodless conquest in the Philippines. With a substantial force of troops at their disposal by early July, they

With the fate of the city seemingly sealed, the Spanish authorities ordered Cervera to make his escape from the harbor. On 3 July Admiral Sampson sent the battleship *Massachusetts* and two other ships to Guantánamo to refuel and himself took the cruiser *New York* and two escorts to Daiquiri for a conference with the Army. Cervera coincidentally chose that day to make his bid for survival against the remaining American ships under Commodore Winfield Scott Schley. The issue was never in doubt as the speed of the Spanish ships was cut by their foul bottoms and 85 percent of their ammunition was defective. In a chase of three hours and 40 minutes, the entire squadron was annihilated. Hearing the gunfire, Sampson hurried to the scene but never caught up with the action. In his hunger for glory, he then blocked Schley's cabled report of the battle and substituted his own cable to Alger, 'The fleet under my command offers the nation, as a Fourth of July present, the whole of Cervera's fleet.' The controversy over who really deserved credit for the victory lasted for years.

On the same day that Schley was dispatching the Spanish squadron, Shafter sent his first surrender ultimatum to Toral in the hope of taking the city by negotiation before his entire command was wiped out by yellow laid siege to Manila. Their main problem was the large numbers of Filipino insurgents in the field since 1896. After Dewey's triumph at Manila Bay, they quickly overran most of Luzon and loosely enveloped Manila itself. Dewey and the American consuls in Hong Kong and Singapore had led the insurgent leader Emilio Aguinaldo to believe that the United States was as committed to Filipino independence as it was to Cuban when in fact the administration had no policy on the matter. Relations between the insurgents and the growing American expeditionary force became steadily more tense until Dewey and Merritt made a secret agreement with the Spanish general Fermin Jaudenes. The former were to keep the insurgents out of the city if the latter made only a token resistance when the Americans made their attack on 13 August, not knowing that a general armistice had been signed by the United States and Spain the day before.

Some months later, McKinley ordered the occupation of the entire Philippines and thereby touched off a revolt by the insurgents who had expected something more than an exchange of colonial masters. By the time the very dirty war of pacification ended three years later, over 4000 American soldiers and perhaps as many as 200,000 Filipinos had died. The administration finally decided to annex the islands because they were already in American hands and no other suitable alternative was apparent. The business com-

munity, initially opposed to the war, began to see the islands as the gateway to Asian markets while the Protestant community saw the enlargement of its missionary endeavors. Thus the original small band of navalists and imperialists found powerful allies to help it push the administration toward annexation. 'I don't want the Philippine Islands' said McKinley, '. . . but in the end there was no alternative.'

Political pressures had forced the administration to mobilize a total of 275,000 men but between Cuba, the Philippines, and Puerto Rico, fewer than 35,000 ever went overseas. The remainder trained in primitive camps while awaiting the call that never came. The camps were characterized by bad food and poor sanitation while typhoid and measles epidemics soon raged. Poor conditions, prolonged inaction, and news of the armistice talks led to a breakdown in discipline and a number of riots. Shafter's corps before Santiago fared even worse as it was literally destroyed by yellow fever and malaria by the armistice and had to be evacuated to a makeshift convalescent facility called Camp Wyckoff at Montauk Point on the eastern tip of Long Island. With no other war news to print, the plight of Shafter's men and those in the stateside camps was widely publicized in the press. As disease-ravaged soldiers came into public view, outrage mounted and was magnified as other aspects of seeming War Department mismanagement and corruption came to light. The newspapers had a field day with the various scandals while the

public blamed those in command.

Despite the blue ribbon Dodge Commission which investigated the conduct of the war and concluded that the War Department had done its best under very adverse circumstances, the search for scapegoats focused on Alger who was ultimately forced to resign. McKinley had in fact made all military policy and decisions but deftly avoided the political fallout and appointed Elihu Root, a New York corporation lawyer, to succeed Alger. Overall, the War Department had produced quite an amateur effort because it was unprepared for the war it was suddenly called upon to fight and because the war did not last long enough to overcome those problems. But the Army did learn from its unhappy experience in Cuba and ran much better campaigns in Puerto Rico and the Philippines. As in the Civil War and again in World Wars I and II, the response to war had been improvisation, trial and error followed by a gradual mastery of the problems, a process which was perceived by the public as confusion and incompetence. The Navy by contrast emerged from the war relatively free of scandal and an apparent model of efficiency in fulfilling its assigned role. Only in later years did boards of inquiry reveal the poor performance at Santiago where American gunners scored only 122 hits out of 9433 shots fired, a notably poor record for the time. The badly armored American ships had been saved by the defective ammunition of the Spanish and sheer good luck rather than American fighting skill. The media played an important role in the skewed public perception of the war, distorting facts, printing rumor as fact, sensationalizing problems, and vilifying unpopular officers.

The Spanish-American War was small in scale but only the weakness of the Spanish and the incredible luck of the Americans prevented the 'making of a quagmire' and indeed the Philippines did become something of a quagmire after the peace treaty was signed on 10 December 1898. From a military perspective, the Navy won two spectacular victories which the Army was able to exploit at an almost negligible cost. American casualties in the war were 281 killed and 1577 wounded but ten times more men died of disease than of combat. The military lesson which Americans drew from their experience was that modern war was too complex to be fought by disorganized troops regardless of their courage. Root as a result instituted more offices for training and planning in the War Department and developed the staff system and War College.

The war itself was seen as a farce by the public and gave rise to many satires. Only Teddy Roosevelt and Dewey gained any glory and that of the latter was short-lived. The war did, however, reveal the national reconciliation which had occurred in the three decades since the end of the Civil War as many officers who had worn Confederate gray willingly served under the stars and stripes alongside their former adversaries. Indeed, a contingent of Mississippi volunteers marched into Camp Jackson singing, 'Hurrah for the blue! Hurrah for the gray! Hurrah for the sons of them all! Together we come and united we stand to answer humanity's call.'

The fruits of victory were freedom for Cuba and cession to the United States by Spain of Puerto Rico, the Philippines, and Guam in return for 20 million dollars. As the country had entered the war for genuinely altruistic and humanitarian reasons, there was immediate unease about the new territorial acquisitions, especially the Philippines where many army officers resented the military pacification of 'a weak race whose only crime was a badly timed desire for freedom.' The military character of the war – its short duration and brilliant victories with little loss – was taken to exemplify America's

national state of grace and virtue. Events such as Dewey's total victory at Manila Bay without the loss of a single life (one sailor died of heat stroke before the battle) or ship were interpreted as tokens of divine approval. Dewey himself remarked, 'If I were a religious man, and I hope I am, I should say that the hand of God was in it,' while an American general in Cuba, convinced of the righteousness of the war, said, 'This is God Almighty's war, and we are only his agents.' Thus America's reluctant imperialism became the will of God not to be withstood or, as the *Baptist Missionary Review* put it, 'To give to the world the life more abundant both for here and hereafter is the duty of the American people by virtue of the call of God.' Here then was a new statement of the American mission, strikingly different from that of the 1840s, which would lead the country to ever greater involvement on the international scene. Military events had once again strongly reinforced the American legend of success and victory in the popular mind.

Emerging from the formative period of their military experience in 1815, Americans had acquired a distinct set of perceptions of war and their own military tradition. The time between 1815 and the end of the century

forms another rough but discrete period of military evolution. The major external threats to America had been eliminated after the War of 1812 and Americans found themselves enjoying an 'age of free security' with no real external threats. The war with Mexico proved that the southern border was not menaced while the presence of Canada to the north ensured good relations with Britain. To the north and south America was blessed with weak neighbors, said a French ambassador, and to the east and west with nothing but fish. With its energies and attention turned inward and little to fear from abroad, the United States had only an episodic foreign policy and no systematic military policy since it really needed neither.

The prejudice against the professional soldier and standing armies remained deep-seated as evidenced by the fact that the Regular Army remained physically small and geographically exiled to the western periphery. Even in wartime, the primary reliance was on volunteers. The historic legend that the essence of American military prowess lay in the citizen soldier continued despite growing evidence to the contrary. As late as December 1914, President Woodrow Wilson could say 'We must depend in every time of national peril, in the future as in the

Below:
Although Sampson was his superior, Schley was in command at Santiago because Sampson had left to confer with Shafter. It was Schley who therefore engaged and destroyed Cervera's squadron. Sampson, however claimed it as his victory and in a telegram said 'The fleet under my command offers the nation as a Fourth of July present the whole of Cervera's fleet.' This controversy was dwarfed by the Army scandals and did no damage to the Navy's public image.

Bottom:
Although Spain had ceded the Philippines to the US in the treaty at the end of the Spanish-American War, American troops stayed on for three years to fight Filipino insurgents. This painting represents the Battle of Paceo, Manila in 1899.

past, not upon a standing army, nor yet upon a reserve army, but upon a citizenry trained and accustomed to arms.' The Navy continued its traditional exemption from the general distrust of standing forces.

None of the three wars in this period produced events or results to modify the military outlook of Americans and in fact tended to reinforce the existing set. The Mexican and Spanish wars were small spirited adventures in which few participated at a minimal human and material cost. Each war had as its precipitating event barbarous behavior by the enemy so that in the popular imagination Americans took up arms to redress a wrong. The resulting extension of American territory in each case was seen as the justified fruit of superior military skill and national virtue exemplified in the short and victorious course of each conflict. The anomaly of the Civil War should have shaken the American military tradition and legend to their very foundations. The course of the war came to reinforce rather than challenge established belief. In the historic pattern, each side had to improvise a war effort with neither enjoying any initial military advantage. The same military tradition and institutions molded the respective armies. Southern defeat did not call into question the fighting qualities of Americans. The valiant and tenacious struggle waged by the Confederacy against overwhelming odds made defeat honorable. As the inscription on a Confederate monument at Yazoo City, Mississippi reads, 'As at

Thermopylae, the greater glory was to the vanquished.' Southerners were even able to claim a victory of sorts since their social order survived relatively intact with the exception of the formal institution of slavery. The myth that no one lost the war quietly took root and removed the stain of defeat from the American military record. However anomalous, the Civil War, as John Shy has argued, therefore also tended to reinforce historic patterns of thought and action in the military sphere.

The Civil War also failed to shake American faith in the efficacy of military technology. Technology to ensure the national security and victory in war had been a theme in American thought since Benjamin Franklin speculated about airships and Thomas Jefferson espoused the peace-keeping properties of the new torpedoes. The earliest visionary of military technology to defend liberty was Robert Fulton with his submarine *Nautilus* which he thought would bring 'at last peace to the earth, and restore men to their natural industries. . . .' Technology was seen as discouraging the desire to fight and reducing the human cost of war. As Francis Wayland, a leading divine and educator of the pre-Civil War period, argued, 'the more energetic are the means of destruction in war, the less is the loss of life in battle.' Although technology was largely responsible for rendering the Civil War too horrible to remember in its reality, Americans retained their optimism about the benefits of tech-

MT. DAJO FIGHT JOLÓ 1901

Above left:
Emilio Aguinaldo, Filipino revolutionary, led the rising against Spain and the United States (1896–1901). He was captured in 1901 and forced to take an oath of allegiance to America, which meant the collapse of the Philippine Insurrection.

Left:
Colonel Frederick Funston and his 20th Kansas Volunteers march through Caloocan, Luzon during the campaign to pacify the Philippines.

nology in the military domain and thus never developed a realistic picture of their defenses and military needs, a condition which persists to the present. Yet some Americans mourned the loss of romance and glory in battle brought by new weapons, Nathaniel Hawthorne demanding 'How can an admiral condescend to go to sea in a iron pot.'

Until the Civil War, America's enemies had been clearly identifiable and clearly dangerous to the national security. The need to fight the Indians, French, Spanish, and British in the formative period were obvious since hearth, home, and liberty were at stake. The wars were fought largely on American soil with noncombatants often at severe risk. This pattern was broken by the Mexican War, the first to be fought overseas and the first in which American society was not at peril, but here too the enemy had attacked first and was seen to menace American na-

Top:
The guerrilla warfare in the Philippines continued long after the Spanish-American War was over. This photograph shows the result of fighting for Mount Dajo on Jolo in 1901.

Above left:
US troops try to stop Filipino insurgents setting fire to Manila during 22–23 February 1899.

tional interests. The creation of what Thomas Leonard has termed the 'evanescent enemy,' the enemy who is really not an enemy but a friend, after the Civil War introduced an ambivalence into the motivation of the American soldier. How could the cause for which the soldier fought and died be justified if the enemy was in fact a friend? The veterans of the Spanish-American War must have wondered when a clause was inserted into the peace treaty commending the valor of the Spanish Army (but not the American) and the United States paid its passage home from Cuba and Puerto Rico. This ambivalence was characteristic of the aftermath of the Civil War, the subsequent Indian Wars (in which technology was used to compensate for inferior fighting skill), the Spanish-American War and also World War I. The soldier often found himself in sympathy with the foe. Such ambivalence was not a factor in World War II and Korea but reappeared with a vengeance in Vietnam.

As the twentieth century opened, Americans found their age of free security was ending as a result of the changing and increasingly competitive international environment and the rapidly evolving technology of warfare. They came to live with a growing sense of national insecurity and foreign threat while relying ever more on the technology which protected and menaced at the same time. This 'age of insecurity' was formally ushered in by the guns of August 1914.

Chapter 7   America in World War I

Many members of Congress wore or carried tiny American flags, a gesture which did not pass unnoted by the man they had come to hear on the warm and rainy evening of 2 April 1917. A further indicator of the occasion was the clattering troop of cavalry which escorted him to Capitol Hill. When his speech began shortly after 08.30, he described the situation which called for his visit in uncharacteristically simple language. He then asked the Congress 'to accept the status of belligerent which has . . . been thrust' upon the nation and 'to exert all its power and employ all its resources to bring the Government of the German Empire to terms and end the war.' Launching into the rhetoric of idealism for which he was justly renowned, Woodrow Wilson repeated his by then famous statement that 'the world must be made safe for democracy' and then climbed his oratorical peak. 'It is a fearful thing to lead this great people into war . . .' the President said, 'but right is more precious than peace, and we shall fight for the things we have always carried nearest our hearts – for democracy, for the rights and liberties of small nations, for the universal domination of right by such a concert of free people as shall bring peace and safety to all nations and make the world itself at last free. . . . The day has come when America is privileged to spend her blood and her might for the principles that gave her birth and happiness. God helping her,' he concluded, 'she can do no other.'

With this ringing statement placing its historic mission in a new global context, America became the last nation to enter World War I as Congress voted overwhelmingly for war. This act was indeed a deviation from traditional American foreign policy. The country had last been involved in a European war 105 years earlier when it had declared war on Britain to save the 'national honor.' In the intervening century, Americans had fought only one major war and that was against themselves rather than a foreign power. Now the President was calling on Americans to take up arms in a crusade to save democratic societies from the assault of the powers of monarchical autarchy and oppression. By the time Wilson issued the call to arms, the war had been underway for three years and already counted as belligerents most of the European countries and 22 non-European countries, including China, Japan, Siam, and Turkey. Battles and campaigns had taken place off the coasts of Latin America, and in Asia, Africa, and the Middle East as well as various fronts in Europe. What had begun as a European war had quickly become global and at last came to involve a reluctant United States.

Left:
President Woodrow Wilson, the former President of Princeton, was re-elected in 1916 because he promised to keep the United States neutral 'in thought and deed.'

Below:
American troops go into action in 1918. The arrival of American troops in France was an incalculable boost to Allied morale.

Despite its global scope, however, the origins of the war lay in Europe which was the main focus of military conflict. The war resulted from a complex mix of immediate and longer term factors. On one level, Europe was divided into two armed camps composed of Germany, Austria-Hungary, and Italy on one side and France, Russia, and later a reluctant Britain on the other. France and Britain were competing with the newly emergent German state, then only 47 years old, for domination of Western Europe and colonial and maritime supremacy while Austria-Hungary and Russia were in conflict over the remains of the Ottoman Empire in the Balkans. Events in the Balkans brought these monarchies to the brink of war in the summer of 1914 which, when finally declared, immediately involved their primary allies Germany and France. Italy declined to cast her lot with her allies and joined the opposite side the following year while feeble Turkey joined Germany and Austria-Hungary. Britain held back from the war until Germany grossly violated the neutrality of Belgium. The final line-up thus came to be Britain, France, Russia, and Italy, known as the Allies, against the Central Powers of Germany, Austria-Hungary, and Turkey. Two rather distinct conflicts had merged to become an all-encompassing war in Europe.

Greeted with great enthusiasm in Europe, World War I was probably the most popular war in history at its inception. The countries of Europe were in the grip of a time of mass nationalism and chauvinism made possible by widespread popular literacy and the popular press. One of the striking characteristics of the war was the strength of the nationalism which encouraged its onset and sustained its huge moral and material demands for so many years. Europe seemed in fact to be suffering a mass psychological condition perhaps similar to that which had affected

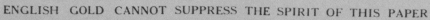

ENGLISH GOLD CANNOT SUPPRESS THE SPIRIT OF THIS PAPER

The Vital Issue

NEW YORK, JANUARY 30, 1915

Vol. II. No. 5   Price 5 Cents SEE PAGE 10

America Keeps 3,000,000 Men at War in Europe.

British Rifle Attachment for Dum-dums.   England's Ecoonomic Crime.

German Chancellor's Reply to Viviani.

Official War Reports

YOUR OBEDIENT SERVANT.

Above:
A German propaganda leaflet aimed at discrediting Great Britain in the eyes of the American public.

Above right:
A US government poster urging the people to give food to help the war effort.

Left:
1917 draftees from New York City on their way to their training camps. War was declared on 6 April 1917 and the first contingent was hurriedly sent out in June of that year.

Americans in the 1890s, a combination of moral weariness and pent-up fears and hatreds easily exploitable by government propagandists. Then serving as First Lord of the Admiralty, Winston Churchill observed of 1914, 'There was a strange temper in the air. Unsatisfied by material prosperity the nations turned restlessly towards strife internal or external.' When the war finally came, there was almost a popular sigh of relief in which even the intellectuals joined.

That none of the Great Powers was anxious to avoid the war while their peoples welcomed it is not surprising. Europeans were accustomed to having international disputes settled by war which was seen as an inevitable part of life. The Austro-Prussian and Franco-Prussian conflicts of 1866 and 1870 had led to an almost universal belief that the next war would be brief and intense.

Yet those encounters were poor indicators of the future because of their short terms and the incompetence of the French and Austrian generalship. Far better harbingers of the nature of the warfare of the future were the American Civil War and the Russo-Japanese War of 1904–1905 and, to a lesser extent, the Russo-Turkish War of 1877–78 and the Boer War of 1899–1902. Here was clear evidence of the primacy which the high-fire power embodied in the breech-loading repeating rifle and especially the machine gun had conferred on the defensive. The Russian trenches and barbed wire entanglements at Port Arthur were the direct ancestors of the trenches of the Western Front a decade later. One American military observer of that hard-fought war wrote 'Modern arms give great defensive power. To get at the enemy with the bayonet may require not minutes and

hours, but days of exposure to fire, coupled with immense exertions and with lack of shelter, food and water . . .,' and then drew this important conclusion for his superiors: 'Battle has become a long-enduring, nerve-racking contest, extending over days and consuming the last minim of mental and physical strength of the participants, inferior forces can no longer be quickly overpowered, an opponent attacking the enemy with equal forces ought to fail. . . .' The weight of the evidence from the wars between 1861 and 1905 was that even against a weak enemy such as Turkey or the Boers, modern wars were difficult to win and required not maneuver but blunt and sustained combat in order to achieve victory.

Yet European opinion both civil and military ignored the evidence. The German Field Marshal von Moltke described the

American Civil War as 'two armed mobs chasing each other around the country, from which nothing could be learned.' Americans were just too unskilled militarily to cope with the problem of rifle firepower. The future French Marshal Ferdinand Foch stated with assurance in 1903 that 'any improvement in firearms is bound to strengthen the offensive' while his future British counterpart Douglas Haig misperceived the nature of the Boer War when he said that 'cavalry will have a larger sphere of action in future wars.' These opinions were widespread in Europe and testified to the continuing grip of Napoleon and his subsequent interpreters on the European military imagination. Whereas Jomini had tended to dominate the formal military thought in Europe and the United States in the first half of the nineteenth century, his Prussian contemporary Karl von Clausewitz was discovered in the second half. His opus *On War*, written in the 1820s while he was director of the Military School in Berlin, was unknown outside of Prussia until an English translation appeared in 1873 and was discovered by the French only in the 1880s.

Below left:
Another call to the American people to finance the war.

Below:
This World War I poster was drawn by F. Strothmann.

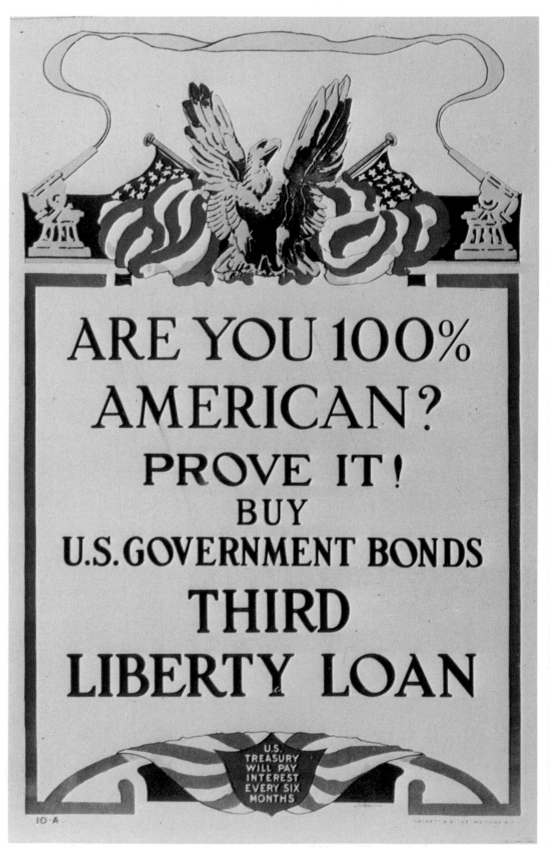

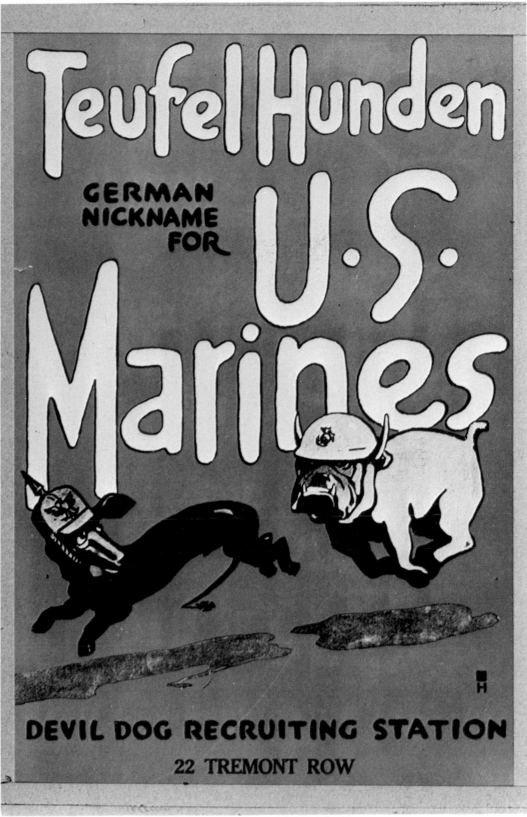

Both Clausewitz and Jomini missed some of the basic features of Napoleonic warfare but the former did identify the crucial relationship between war and politics and produced a more philosophic than practical treatise. His famous but often misunderstood statement that 'War is nothing else than a continuation of political transactions intermingled with different means' sums up his contention that the moral as well as the material resources of a country at war must be completely employed to destroy the desire and ability of the enemy to fight. War inevitably tends to become absolute, said Clausewitz, with extreme violence aimed at total annihilation. The military goal was the destruction of the enemy forces by direct attack, so he placed his stress on battle, mass and concentration but showed that no one strategy or tactical approach could bring certain triumph. His ideas had a powerful impact on the General Staffs of Europe, the United States and Japan. The military, however, read him in narrow perspective and focused on his doctrine of the offensive through continuous attack.

Shaken by its experience of 1870–71, France had prepared for the next inevitable round with Germany by acquiring allies to redress the inherently greater strength of Germany and by a military doctrine stressing the 'nation in arms,' the short war, and especially a strategy of the unrelenting offensive. The latter strategy developed in the late nineteenth century with younger officers as its adherents until Field Marshal Joseph Joffre became a convert. His article of strategic faith was to seize and maintain the offensive with headlong charges in spite of admittedly heavy losses and no concern for flanks. Acknowledging that bloody sacrifice would be required, he argued that 'the most obstinate wins' and dismissed the problem of modern firepower for the attacker with the contention that the superior spirit of the French soldier would triumph. 'We, French,' wrote his colleague and supporter Foch, 'possess a soldier undeniably superior to the one behind the Vosges in his racial qualities, activity, intelligence, spirit, power of exaltation, devotion and patriotism.' The

French General Staff drew up Plan XVII for an offensive defensive against Germany which embraced what the French now referred to as the '*offensive brutale et à l'outrance*' or the savage and relentless offensive. Through prewar staff conversations and coordination, the British accepted and cooperated with this plan which overlooked a number of important factors such as terrain and firepower.

Germany also started from the assumption of a brief war in its planning but had to contend with the probability of a two-front war. France in the west and Russia in the east. Count Alfred von Schlieffen, Chief of Staff from 1891 to 1906, devised a complex plan to deal with the two-front war by means of railroads. Since Russia would require an estimated six weeks to mobilize and present a tangible military threat in the east, his plan called for concentrating maximum force against France in the hope of a swift victory and then shifting the concentration east by railroad to deal with the Russians. In the west, von Schlieffen took the basic strategy

Right:
President Wilson arrives in New York with his wife and mother-in-law to open the Fourth Liberty Loan Campaign. By loans and taxes the government raised some 36 billion dollars.

Below right:
The Willys-Morrow plant in Elmira, New York, a car factory, was converted to airplane production. In spite of these conversions of industrial plant, the US contributed no planes or artillery and only a few tanks. The US Army was essentially armed by its allies.

Below:
Houses were built in Washington, DC for essential war workers.

of envelopment employed by the elder von Moltke in 1870 to produce a plan to roll up the French in a great wheeling movement with the hub nearly stationary by the Swiss border. The right moving wing was to sweep across Belgium and take the French in the left flank to push them toward the Swiss border. The crux of the plan was overwhelming strength on the right wing to keep it in rapid motion. The defeat of France was expected to take less than six weeks.

This plan suffered from three weaknesses. One is that it arrogantly underestimated the French and assumed they would collapse before German troops with overextended lines of communication actually had to fight French soldiers retreating into their main bases. A second is that success required far more army strength than Germany had at that time or at the beginning of the war. And, lastly, it required von Schlieffen to keep it pure. On his retirement in 1906 he was succeeded by Helmuth von Moltke, a nephew of the elder von Moltke, who owed his selection as much to his social position as to his military ability. Far more than other countries,

the Germans had taken the problem of fire-power seriously as a result of 1870 and perfected the use of the machine gun. As a result, they were well aware of its ability to dominate the battlefield, an ability the French and British roundly disparaged. Harboring doubts of his own fitness for command, von Moltke worried about the audacity of the Schlieffen Plan as it was known and the presumed effects of defensive firepower on it. He therefore strengthened the holding aspect of the center at the expense of the moving right wing.

On 3 August 1914 78 German divisions attacked 72 French, six Belgian, and five British. Their initial success and rapid progress had the Germans prematurely toasting victory. But the right wing weakened as its lines of communication lengthened and the advantage of surprise wore off. Far from collapsing, Foch quickly retrieved the situation from the shambles of Plan XVII, shifted much of his strength from the south to the decisive action in the north, and prepared to replace his strategic retreat with a counter-attack on 6 September. Von Moltke further weakened his right wing by withdrawing three divisions against a Russian penetration of East Prussia while the remainder of his troops, footsore and weary from continuous marching, were reaching the limit of physical endurance. At the Marne on 6–12 September, Joffre with the aid of the stalwart British Expeditionary Force defeated the now outnumbered Germans and forced them to retreat to the Aisne. With the failure of both German and French war plans, no options

were left except to try to flank the enemy. The search for open flanks by each side caused the lines to extend until they reached from the English Channel in the north to the Swiss border in the south.

Infantry movement was virtually paralyzed by the machine guns and rifles, so the lines became frozen as each side prepared more and more permanent defenses. The deadlock baffled the military minds of the time so much that it produced no new thinking. Most officers would undoubtedly have

Above:
Village of the Dead: American artillery move through a ruined village. A drawing by George Harding.

Below:
On the trail of the Hun on the St. Mihiel drive by W.J. Aylward.

This kind of warfare had a pronounced effect on the soldiers in the line. Longevity was limited as a soldier in one of the better divisions lasted an average of three months before being killed or wounded, while an officer in an active sector was lucky to survive six weeks. Trench warfare was seen as futile and meaningless since the important qualities of the soldier – bravery, self-sacrifice, professional competence – no longer mattered amid the crashing barrages and deadly machine guns. 'The war seems so damned ridiculous,' says a soldier in Thomas Boyd's 1923 book *Through the Wheatfield*. 'Take our going over the other day. A full battalion starting off and not even a fifth of them coming back. We never even saw a German. . . . That's hell.' The opposing armies were in fact too large to be defeated decisively in one engagement and casualties for both sides were too high for any real advantage. Battle was no longer a sporadic event but a continuous condition which exacted its daily toll morally as well as materially. Yet the troops endured year after year, buried in their 'mausoleums of mud,' becoming steadily more war weary and demoralized as their leaders sent them out to the slaughter.

Since technology had largely created the stalemate, various technological means were tried to break it. On 22 April 1915 the Germans succeeded in making a huge hole in the Allied line with a cloud of chlorine gas but failed to exploit their advantage. Gas came to be employed by both sides but was not decisive because protective masks were quickly issued to the troops. The wind also tended to

agreed with British Secretary of War Lord Kitchener who said simply, 'I don't know what is to be done. *This* isn't war.' The stalemate on the Western Front was the immediate result of the failure of the Schlieffen Plan but its deeper cause was the unassailable position of the defensive as the result of modern firepower. Railroads also contributed because they made possible the rapid movement of masses of men to the front as well as the supplies and munitions to sustain them. Horses and mules were largely supplanted by the new trucks made possible by the internal combustion engine. These moved the mountains of supplies from the railheads to the front.

With no strategy for breaking the impasse, all attention came to be focused on the tactical problems of attack in a given locality. The basic tactic for attack was a concentrated infantry formation, sometimes almost shoulder to shoulder, which advanced after a preparatory barrage by artillery to try to occupy the ground cleared by the guns. Despite the intensity of the barrages, sometimes 5–7000 guns thundering for up to a week, the defense could count on its machine guns to shred the attackers. These attacks entailed high casualties which did not seem to bother the generals who clung to the belief that mass and concentration was the only path to victory. Foch remained the chief propagator of this view, stoutly maintaining that there was 'no victory without fighting' and that it was always correct to attack as he sent his men forward to die in their hundreds of thousands. The callous attitude of the military leadership was exemplified by the British General Douglas Haig who simply referred to casualties as 'wastage.'

Some tactical enterprise did occur. The Germans experimented with the use of small groups of infiltrators and sometimes varied the weight of their attack by moving troops laterally behind the lines by motorbus. Artillery barrages were increased, delivered at un-

expected times, and took such forms as the creeping, box, and saturation barrages. Vast quantities of shells were expended as infantry was tied to artillery support and preparation. Deception was also employed to achieve some local surprise by concealing the build up of troops and supplies. Even if the first line of trenches was captured, the attackers could not exploit the opportunity for lack of artillery and machine-gun support against the second and third lines and enemy counterattacks.

Top:
Street combat at Château Thierry by Henry Dunn.

Above:
A machine gun emplacement by Henry Dunn.

blow west to east and left the Allies with a natural advantage. And Allied propaganda had a field day with the German breach of the Hague Convention. The tank also made its appearance in 1916 in the battle of the Somme. The early tanks were fragile creatures whose use was not really understood. With improvements, however, the tank came to play an important role in 1917 and 1918 but it too was not the solution to the deadlock on the Western Front. Developed in 1903, the airplane had been early adapted to military use. By 1916 virtually every future role of the airplane had been tested operationally. Planes were used for reconnaisance and artillery fire control while specialized fighters came into being to protect the observation craft. Later in the war, tactical bombing and strafing were introduced. Strategic bombing made its appearance as the Germans sent Zeppelins and bombers to raid military bases and cities in Britain and France. Although the damage was slight, the attacks did cause the diversion of precious resources to home defense. The British in turn began to bomb Germany in 1918 and were preparing a raid on Berlin when the war ended. In the end, however, the various new technologies provided no more answer to the problem of the Western Front than did the ideas and tactics of the dogmatic generals.

The war was not confined to the Western Front. Millions of men were mobilized by the Russians to fight and die in a futile war on the Eastern Front. The front itself was so large that it did not become paralyzed like its western counterpart but the German machine guns decimated the mass charges of the Russians as in the west. Early German victories were Tannenberg and the Masurian Lakes where 225,000 Russians were captured. The 1915 offensive of the Central Powers aimed at taking Russia out of the war failed but cost the Tsar two million men while another million were lost the following year. Despite these huge losses, the Russians hung grimly on. Italy entered the war in May 1915 to open a front against Austria-Hungary in return for Allied promises of territory while Winston Churchill persuaded his government to attack the Dardanelles that same year in a foolhardy venture which cost 145,000 casualties before being aborted. The German colonies in Asia and Africa were quickly rolled up by Britain with the assistance of its longtime ally Japan. There was also a sideshow in Egypt and Palestine where Britain, France, and Italy aimed at colonial spoils of war from the decaying Turkish empire.

But the main focus of war remained in France and Belgium where the professional soldiers insisted that the war would be won. General Erich von Falkenhayn, von Moltke's successor after the Marne, was well aware of the advantage of the defensive and preferred to let the Allies expend their manpower on his barbed wire and machine guns. He did not undertake an offensive until 1916 when he tried to draw the French into a meatgrinder at Verdun. In a six-month en-

gagement which both thrilled and horrified the world, he expended 300,000 Germans to inflict 350,000 casualties on the French, not at all the results for which he had hoped. Having wasted 250,000 of their own men in futile frontal attacks in 1915, the Allied generals drew the conclusion that the solution to the problem of breaking the German line was to increase the preparatory barrages. Britain had by now raised an additional 70 divisions through conscription and sent them to France, so the supremely confident Haig determined to use the hundreds of thousands of fresh troops for a grand assault which would succeed through sheer pressure. Before the offensive, notes the official British history of the war, he 'impressed on all, at conferences and other times, that the infantry would only have to walk over and take possession of the enemy trenches.' Thousands of guns pounded a ten-mile sec-

Above left:
The *Mount Vernon* leaves New York harbor in the spring of 1918.

Left:
An official photograph of Generals Foch and Pershing. Foch was the generalissimo of the Allied Armies and Pershing was his subordinate. They came into conflict over the conduct of the St. Mihiel offensive.

Top:
On 4 July 1917 American troops marched down the Champs Elysées. This was no more than a token force and the parade was intended to boost morale.

Above:
US troops on their way to the front in 1918. By October 1918 the American Army in France numbered over 1,750,000.

tor of the German line for a week prior to 1 July when the British went on the attack. The first hours of the battle of the Somme resulted in 60,000 casualties, yet Haig sent his men against the German defenses until November when he finally admitted failure. The price of his defeat was a combined total of one million British, French, and German casualties in the end.

Despite constant proof to the contrary, British and French generals optimistically continued to anticipate the big breakthrough on the Western Front. Unsobered by his monstrous slaughter on the Somme, Haig

persuaded the British Cabinet in 1917 that Germany was on the military brink and so won approval of yet another offensive, this time at Ypres which became what the British historian Liddell Hart called 'the gloomiest drama in British military history.' The campaign has come to be known as Passchendaele, now a synonym for military failure, and was the actualization of Haig's belief that the British alone in Flanders could exhaust German manpower within six months. Once again he ground away at the enemy lines at a cost of hundreds of thousands in exchange for a mile or two of blood-soaked ground.

To the south, a similar but even more pathological confidence on the part of General Robert Nivelle, who had replaced Joffre by promising to break the impasse, thought the German line could be broken 'when we wish' and almost destroyed the French Army as a fighting force. Nivelle had sent his formations forward in a headlong and well-advertised attack in Champagne which resulted in 120,000 casualties. Half of the Army had mutinied in disgust at the callous incompetence of its leadership. Nivelle was replaced by Henri Pétain who by dint of great personal effort finally restored discipline. The crisis had been so severe that France had almost left the war while its Army no longer possessed real offensive capacity. While the British now shouldered the main burden on the Western Front, Pétain could only say, 'I am waiting for the Americans and the tanks.'

And indeed, the Americans were coming. The first division arrived in France in early July 1917. From the point of view of the Allies, it had arrived not a moment too soon. The Italians had suffered a major disaster at Caporetto and had had to be bolstered with a British corps but the major concern of the Allies was the withdrawal of Russia from the war. Its losses had simply been too great for Russian society to bear so in the face of army mutinies, strikes, and riots, the Tsar had abdicated. A liberal democratic government under Alexander Kerensky had tried to continue the war and so fell to the Communist forces of Vladimir Ilyich Lenin. Lenin made peace with Germany, not because he wanted to, but because he now had a civil war to fight. The collapse of Russia freed the large German forces in the east to alter the balance in the west. Believing that they now possessed the wherewithal to break through the demoralized allies, the German generals Paul von Hindenburg and Erich Ludendorff planned a great offensive for the spring of 1918. They were unperturbed by the American declaration of war because the United States could not raise, equip, and train enough soldiers to be a factor before the war was over.

Woodrow Wilson had won re-election in 1916 on the campaign slogan 'He kept us out of war' and yet now he was calling on Americans for a total commitment to the war. American public opinion had undergone some radical changes since 1914, as had the mind of Wilson himself, to permit a dec-

laration of war. The immediate cause of the American decision to fight was the situation in the Atlantic Ocean where American commerce and passengers were caught up in the desperate naval struggle raging between Britain and Germany. The latter had determined that the war would be won by her incomparable Army and so had assigned the Navy the task of attacking British commerce with surface raiders and submarines and preventing a landing on the German coast. The British had quickly established conventional command of the sea and soon eliminated the surface raiding threat. The German fleet remained in harbor by order of the Kaiser himself and only ventured out into a major engagement with the British Grand Fleet on 31 May 1916 when its effort to nibble down the margin of British naval superiority turned into the battle of Jutland which only reinforced the naval status quo.

Blockade, a historic British weapon in continental wars, was again employed in an attempt to close off vital supplies to Germany which in turn proclaimed all the waters around the British Isles as war zones in which ships were subject to attack by submarines. In response the British armed merchant ships and sent out Q or decoy ships to attract and sink the vulnerable submarines on the surface. Rather than the traditional stop and search, the only safe way for submarines to operate was to sink on sight with torpedoes.

Both sides were interfering with American commerce but the British, with control of the surface, were able to adhere to the recognized practices of prize courts and confiscation while Germany was sinking ships with considerable loss of life. To make matters worse, passenger ships such as the *Lusitania* were also sunk because most, like the *Lusitania*, were carrying munitions as well as passengers. Wilson had early announced that he would hold Germany to 'strict accountability' for the actions of the submarines but refused to do the same for Britain despite continuing illegal acts perpetrated in connection with the blockade. His refusal to treat the antagonists equally, in violation of the professed strict American neutrality, finally led to the resignation of Secretary of State William Jennings Bryan. Wilson felt so strongly about the submarine issue that in March 1916 he extracted a pledge from Germany that no ship would be sunk without warning, a fateful act which meant that the United States would have to go to war if Germany violated the pledge. Britain made no concessions on the blockade but did keep a wary eye on the United States lest she declare war over the maritime issue as she had in 1812.

The submarine campaign was highly effective, sinking one in four of the vessels leaving or approaching Britain while the British could replace but one in ten. The situation became so desperate that Prime Minister David Lloyd George predicted the country could not have lasted six more months had not a solution been found in the convoy system which reduced losses to around one percent. Germany was also in increasingly straitened circumstances due to the blockade and continuing military demands of the war. Accordingly in January 1917 Hindenburg and Ludendorff persuaded the government that military victory rested on unrestricted submarine warfare to take Britain out of the war. Soon after that decision several American ships were sunk by mistake and Wilson was forced to make the trip from the White House to Capitol Hill in the rain.

The maritime issues were but one way in which the United States had become increasingly involved with the belligerents. A second way was through the war orders and propaganda of the Allies. The German and Austro-Hungarian war effort was based almost entirely on their own industries and technology which made a speedy transition to war production. In Britain and France, on the other hand, industry was in many respects mid-Victorian in its equipment and techniques while whole ranges of modern manufactures such as chemicals had never been developed. Many of the sophisticated items of the second phase of the industrial revolution such as ball bearings, optics, spark plugs, etc. had been imported from Germany and the United States. The British in particular were not oriented toward mass production and precision light engineering nor was the machine tool industry well developed. Thus American tools and technology were essential to the Allies to build up their own war industries while they depended on American munitions in the interim. One third of the British shells used in 1915–16 were made in the United States and Canada.

Thus long before any official thought was given to industrial preparedness, orders from the Allies had stimulated strong growth in vital war industries. Indeed, the war orders brought prosperity and full employment while the Central Powers were prevented from entering the market by the blockade. American neutrality was thus compromised by supplying war materials to one side and became even more so when, as the Allies ran low on cash, Wilson permitted them to float loans in the United States to pay for their purchases. By the time the United States declared war in April 1917, the Allies owed Americans over two billion dollars in war loans.

British propaganda played a great role in making Americans receptive to the declaration of war. Lacking much popular support for participation in the war, the British government immediately organized a Ministry of Information to conduct an empire-wide campaign to mobilize the forces of good against those of evil. The picture of World War I as a holy crusade originated with British propagandists. As the British journalist-historian Phillip Knightley observed, 'More deliberate lies were told than in any other period of history, and the whole apparatus of the press went into action to suppress the truth.' A similar situation obtained in France and somewhat less so in Germany. The British, French, and German publics never learned the full extent of casualties until after the war because, as Prime Minister David Lloyd George said, 'If the people really knew, the war would be stopped tomorrow.' Some 90 American correspondents went to cover the war and fought a running battle with the British and German (and later American) censors to report the truth of the war as best they could determine it. The American public thus received a somewhat more accurate picture than did the peoples of Europe.

The British had realized early on that American resources would ultimately be necessary and organized an American bureau in their propaganda ministry which operated in the United States as the British Bureau of Information. The function of the Bureau was to sway American opinion and in fulfillment of its mission came to penetrate pervasively every aspect of American life. Over 90 percent of Americans read only newspapers at that time so the campaign exploited the already good relations between the American and British presses. The British almost completely captured the American press and thus ensured that the American public would see the war through British eyes. One London-based American correspondent wrote later that British propaganda efforts 'had much to do with bringing the United States into the war.' The crisis of the Allies in early 1917 caused the British government to heighten the propaganda campaign in a last attempt to lower American resistance to the war. The full details of the British activities in the United States, however, will never be known because the relevant files were prudently destroyed immediately after the war.

Most Americans appear to have been pro-Ally and anti-German from the beginning. No one argued in favor of joining the Central Powers as the options were seen as neutrality or aiding the Allies. A strong minority of pacifists and isolationists were in favor of neutrality but the few pro-German groups gave money to the former, and all became lumped together in the popular mind as pro-German. The vague pro-Ally sympathies of Americans became more and more focused by a succession of events – the German declaration of war on France and England, the violation of Belgian neutrality, the steady diet of atrocity stories produced by the propagandists, and the various incidents arising from the submarine campaign. Americans were also aware of the Prussian tradition of militarism and the pseudo-democratic nature of Germany. War with Britain was unthinkable because of cultural and historical ties. In fact the majority of Americans came to see the war in Europe in simple terms of good versus evil and democracy versus autocracy. Spurred by Wilsonian rhetoric, the war took on the nature of a crusade for Americans, a crusade to deliver France from the barbarous Hun, a crusade to make the world safe for democracy, a crusade to abolish war and iniquity. The main reason that Americans acquiesced to involvement in a European war in defiance of their historical inclinations was their perception that a German victory would threaten their interests and security, their ideals and their institutions. The author Willa Cather captured this feeling with the words, 'Even to those quiet wheat-growing people (of Nebraska) the siege guns before Liège were a menace. . . . Something new, and certainly evil, was at work among mankind.'

But the key to American entry was Woodrow Wilson. A native Virginian descended from Presbyterian ministers of Scottish-Irish origin, he was a man of strong will and strong moral inclinations who viewed life as a struggle between good and evil and thus could never compromise. An academic political scientist, former President of Princeton and former Governor of New Jersey, Wilson had attained the Presidency in 1912 and believed in exercising his official powers to the fullest. His domestic program was quite successful but he was not a good judge of international events and trends. His close adviser, Colonel Edward House, wrote that the President was 'singularly lacking in appreciation of this European crisis.' Wilson thought the war was 'wrong' and should be stopped but, realizing his lack of influence in European affairs, had accepted the European leaders' lack of compunction about plunging into strife in 1914.

As a Southerner, Wilson saw the mission of the United States as preventing Europe from destroying itself in a long war of attrition like the Civil War. He believed a decisive victory by one side followed by a harsh peace would only sow the seeds for another war, consequently, his advocacy of 'peace without victory.' Yet his personal views were strongly pro-British. He said privately in 1914 that 'England is fighting our fight' because a German victory would force the United States to 'give up its present ideals and devote all its energies to defense, which would mean the end of its present system of government.' The rate at which men and resources were being expended on the Western Front made it a virtual certainty that American resources would sooner or later be called on. Given this prospect, Wilson planned to push for a negotiated peace. If Germany refused a reasonable peace, the United States would offer more support to the Allies. If the Allies proved ready for negotiations and Germany refused, then Wilson was prepared to enter the war militarily. But because the United States had so swiftly compromised its neutrality, the Germans profoundly distrusted Wilson. As his plan was frustrated by lack of response from either side, Wilson gradually came around, albeit reluctantly, to the view that the United States would eventually have to support the Allies militarily. His personal revulsion at the submarine campaign seems to have been the particular factor which made him take a stand on an issue from which he could not retreat. Many Europeans were impressed by Wilson's rhetoric and hoped America would be their salvation. 'Tell your President Wilson, he is the man,' said a French soldier to an American correspondent in 1916. 'Tell him that he can stop this. . . . He can make a good peace, so that this will not happen again.'

The United States entered World War I with the least prior preparation of any previous American war and that included the Revolution. Wilson had ignored the practical aspects of preparedness partly from his personal distaste for things military and partly

Left:
French, British, American, Belgian, and Serbian censors reading through articles at the Bureau de la Presse, the Bourse in Paris. Neither side would admit the true extent of the casualty figures.

Top:
A Lewis machine gun with an improvised sling. The Lewis gun was never adopted by the US Army but was used by the US Marines in World War I.

Above:
Truck convoys unload another consignment of American infantry at a troop depot in the Lorraine.

because he thought war preparations would be a provocation to Germany. He also did not want to encourage the substantial body of American opinion which was demanding intervention on the side of the allies. Led by former President Theodore Roosevelt, the living embodiment of popular military ideals, and former Chief of Staff Leonard Wood, various patriotic organizations were advocating an active American role. The Industrial Preparedness Committee, for example, was organized by Howard Coffin, a Vice-President of the Hudson Motor Car Company, to prepare industry for its role in the new warfare. The Committee conducted an intensive survey of the war potential of the industrial scene and followed up with a public relations campaign to acquaint industry with Coffin's belief that 'twentieth century warfare demands that the blood of the soldier must be mingled with from three to five parts of the sweat of the man in the factories, mills and mines.' Leonard Wood had begun a summer camp in 1913 to train college students in the military arts and in 1915 arranged a similar camp for business and professional men at Plattsburg, New York. The purpose of this extremely popular endeavor was to raise enthusiasm for the preparedness movement, ensure that there would be volunteers, and then prepare the way for conscription, a primary objective of the preparedness advocates.

Wilson was fond of referring to preparedness as 'good mental exercise' but even he was moved to order the Secretaries of War and the Navy to begin national security planning in July 1915. Prior to that point, he had refused to allow the General Staff to conduct any contingency planning vis-à-vis the war in Europe. Material and psychological preparedness received an added boost from the Mexican crisis of 1916. Much of the Regular Army plunged into northern Mexico in search of Pancho Villa while Wilson mobilized 158,000 National Guardsmen to protect the border from further Mexican raids. The manifold problems of the mobilization – poor physical quality of many of the men, too little artillery, machine guns and ammunition, poor airplanes, need for motorized transport, and other problems – caused Con-

gress to increase appropriations in some areas such as airplanes and machine guns and paved the way for the National Defense Act of 1916.

This act was the most comprehensive piece of military legislation to that point in American history. It raised the manpower level of the Regular Army in both peace and wartime, multiplied the manpower level fourfold of the National Guard and placed it under stronger federal control, formalized the students' and businessmen's camps through the Officer Reserve Corps and the Reserve Officers Training Corps (ROTC) and created an enlisted man's reserve with veterans to be recruited with the time-honored payment of bounties. The universal military obligation of '. . . all able-bodied male citizens of the United States . . . more than eighteen years of age, . . . not more than 45 years of age . . .' to the nation through the National Guard and the 'unorganized militia' was also affirmed. The act also cast an eye toward economic mobilization with the creation of the Council of National Defense, composed of the Secretaries of War, Navy,

Labor, and other relevant cabinet departments while the President received some coercive powers over the industrial sector. The act was a remarkable accomplishment for the times but the pro-war conservatives were outraged at its weakness, Theodore Roosevelt denouncing it as 'one of the most iniquitous bits of legislation ever placed on the statute books.'

Despite these and other moves toward preparedness, few Americans had much idea what their declaration of war would entail. Wilson at first thought that American participation would continue to be mainly economic and financial supplemented by naval assistance with the submarine problem. That the declaration of war of itself would bring victory was the assumption of some congressmen while Senator Thomas Martin of Virginia, Chairman of the Senate Appropriations Committee, said to a startled War Department official, 'Good Lord! You're not going to send soldiers there, are you?' The realization that the future held hard fighting for large members of American soldiers was indeed slow to grow.

The Allies knew exactly what they wanted from the now-belligerent United States. 'We want men, men, men,' said Marshal Joffre as he headed a French Mission to Washington. The British sent a similar mission under Lord Balfour to co-ordinate. Although the missions were lionized by Americans, Wilson still appeared to have reservations about the war because he insisted on terming the United States an 'associate' rather than an 'allied' power. At their nadir on the Western Front, the Allies wanted a 'show the flag' division immediately but the United States had no unit as large as a division. Five regiments were formed into the 1st Division in May and dispatched to France under Major General John Pershing. Arguing that the United States could not send an adequate field army to Europe in time to be of help, the Allies further suggested that the remainder of the American soldiers be fed into their armies as individuals or small units. Categorically rejecting this suggestion, the Wilson Administration went about mobilizing the economy for war and raising and equipping its army while Pershing's troops went into field training in France in July.

The direction of the war fell largely to Secretary of War Newton Baker, a former pacifist and Mayor of Cleveland, who proved to be one of the most able and effective Secretaries of War in American history. Six committees were set up to supervise production under the general direction of the Committee of National Defense which he chaired. War

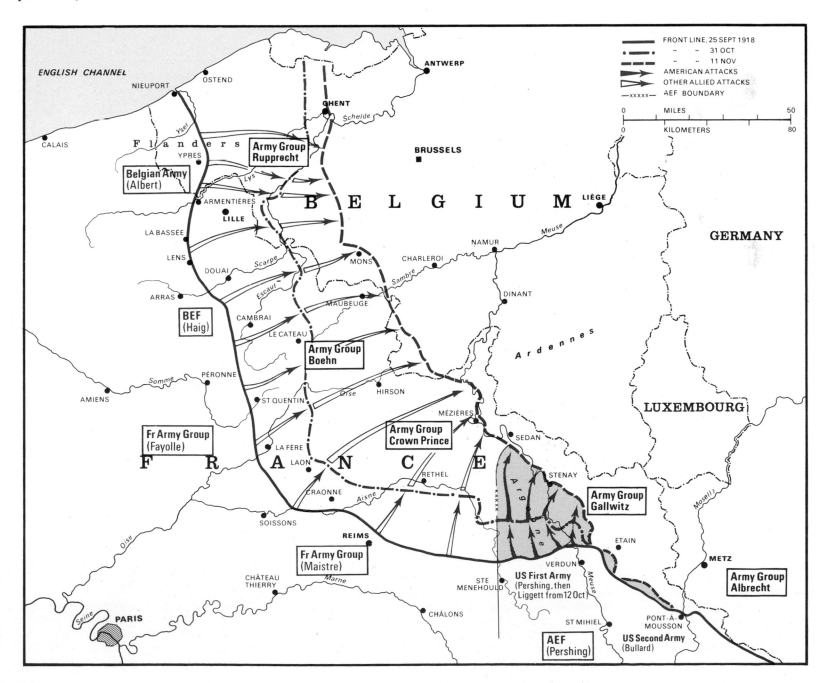

production began poorly because of governmental reluctance to use its newly acquired coercive powers and because authority was too decentralized. The most important of the committees was the War Industries Board which became truly effective only after March 1918 when it came under the direction of the Wall Street financier Bernard Baruch, a man of great executive and administrative abilities. The passage of the Overman Act in May 1918 further changed the situation by granting the administration almost unlimited power over industry. Production took priority over all else as the government entered into partnership with big business and ceased trying to enforce competition. Competitive bidding and negotiating were too time consuming; consequently the cost plus reasonable profit contract was introduced with the expectation that increased taxation would recover the excessive profits made by corporations through pad-

ding their production costs. Production increased by 38 percent between 1913 and 1918 but the increase occurred with less corruption than in any other period of American history. The 32 billion dollars spent by the government on war matters between April 1917 and June 1920 was met, as in the Civil War, one-third through increased taxation and two-thirds added to the national debt. Inflation was the result of the sudden increase in government financed economic activity but no attempt was made to control prices which doubled between 1913 and 1918. The task of economic mobilization was so huge and so complex that it was far beyond the capacities of the military establishment to implement, so the military came to be subordinate to a new class of civilian administrators and planners such as Baruch and Herbert Hoover, the Food Administrator who first introduced Americans to voluntary rationing and the victory garden.

Right:
US troops enjoy German beer and rations in a captured trench. The trench war had been stalemated for three years, but following the failure of the German offensive in August 1918 the decisive contribution made by the Americans came at a time when Allied troops were making a relatively major advance.

Below right:
General Pershing inspects black troops of the 92nd Division.

Below:
A skirmish line of the 103rd Regiment, 216th Division advancing on Toncy on 17 July 1918, following up the attack on Belleau Wood.

Two-thirds of the manpower for the war was provided by the Selective Service Act of May 1917. The many problems of the mobilization of 1916 had made Wilson realize that for the first time in American history a volunteer force would not be adequate to the task at hand. He had directed Baker to have a conscription bill ready in hand should war come. Baker in turn had his staff conduct a careful study of the Civil War draft to avoid its manifest problems. No substitutes, purchased exemptions or bounties were permitted nor did the army conduct the draft itself. Extremely well organized, con-scription was the responsibility of the state governors and local officials who employed strong publicity to bring peer pressure against non-conformists. Some 26 million men were registered but patriotic feeling was strong enough that there were only 337,000 draft dodgers. The draft was probably the most ambitious program yet undertaken by the federal government and created large volumes of paper. At its door can be laid the birth of governmental 'red tape.'

The manpower supplied by the draft and National Guard was organized into 28,000-man divisions composed of two infantry and one artillery brigades, an engineer regiment, machine-gun and signals battalions, and medical and support troops. These divisions were twice as large as their European counterparts on the Western Front, many of which operated at half strength or less. Pershing had opted for the larger formation because he wanted his divisions to be capable of the sustained offensive power to reach their tactical objectives in an attack. The main question was how many of these divisions were required. The American General Staff had not been permitted to study the issue before 1917 and indeed knew little

about the war because its military observers and attachés had not been permitted to visit the front or receive information on weapons' performance. After Pershing arrived in France, his perception that the Allies were at the end of their moral and material resources caused him initially to overestimate the American forces required and, as the Allies lost more and more irreplaceable men, to keep raising his overestimates. He finally asked for three million men in 100 divisions but the War Department would only agree to a program of 80. In the end, 43 divisions with supporting troops, somewhere over two million men, were actually sent to France.

How to officer and equip this force were very difficult problems. The Regular Army consisted of 127,000 men in 1914, including 5791 officers, and approximately 181,000 National Guardsmen. The latter had a few more than 3000 officers to contribute. Most officers were well trained and educated but were generally inexperienced in handling large formations, an historic lack of American officership. Baker, to his credit, firmly ended the long-standing tradition of 'political commissions' even though it meant a long drawn-out public argument with Theodore

Above:
US Marines of the 5th Marines slowly advance through Belleau Wood in the second week of June 1918. The Marines gained control of the wood by 26 June and sent out a message 'Wood now US Marine Corps entirely.' This provoked a feud with the Army who resented the fact that the Marines gained all the credit for taking the wood.

Left:
US troops operate a Stokes trench mortar, which had a range of 800 yards.

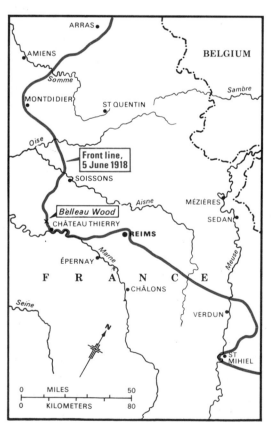

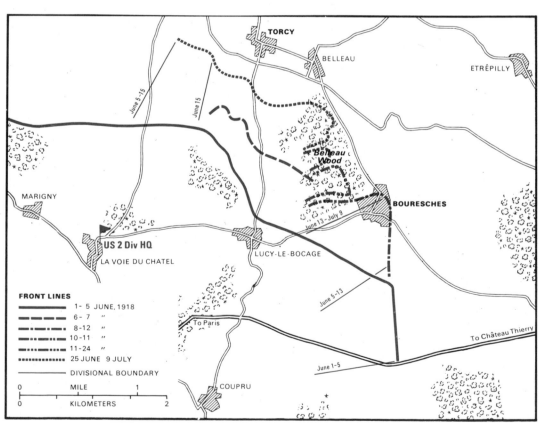

FRONT LINES

———————	1- 5 JUNE, 1918
—·—·—·—·—	6- 7 "
—··—··—··—	8-12 "
▪▪▪▪▪▪▪▪▪▪	10-11 "
▬▬▬▬▬▬	11-24 "
●●●●●●●●	25 JUNE 9 JULY
———————	DIVISIONAL BOUNDARY

Roosevelt and Leonard Wood who wanted to raise and lead divisions in the old Rough Rider tradition. A primary source of new lower-grade officers were the 27,000 civilians and reserve officers commissioned at the end of the summer of 1917 from the sixteen Officers Training Corps camps set up under the National Defense Act of 1916. These were followed by eight General Officers' Training Schools which produced one class per month per school, an aggregate of over 80,000 officers. Most higher command was held by career officers and West Pointers as in the past.

The Army was also in dire straits for weapons and equipment. It had only 285,000 Springfield Model 1903 rifles on hand, so purchased modified Enfields from American contracters producing these for the British. The Army had received its first truck only in 1916, possessed only two field radio sets, and 55 obsolete airplanes. Its artillery and machine guns were also elderly and grossly inadequate in number for the war being fought on the Western Front. It proved simpler to purchase weapons and munitions from Britain and France than to wait for American production, a solution which alleviated shipping problems as well. Thus all of the tanks and most of the artillery, machine guns, trench mortars, automatic rifles, airplanes, and even steel helmets were supplied by Britain and France, a testament to the productivity of their new war industries by 1917. It became Army policy to purchase as much of the other supplies for the American Expeditionary Force (AEF) as possible in France to save precious shipping space. Ten of the eighteen million ship tons of supplies for the American Expeditionary Force were acquired in Europe. The Quarter-Master Corps even set up its own plants in France to process basic foodstuffs for the Army. This supply was made possible through the streamlining and consolidation of the Services of Supply and Procurement carried out by Chief of Staff General Peyton March.

Like the Army, the Navy was taken unaware and unprepared for its role in the war. Roosevelt as President had added substantially to the battleship fleet as did his successor William Howard Taft. The United States thus possessed an excellent fleet of capital ships which were quite useless for the Navy's main mission of transporting and supplying the Army in Europe in the face of the submarine campaign. The Navy was seriously lacking in cruisers and auxiliaries but industry produced over 400 antisubmarine vessels of various types while transports came as much from confiscation of enemy ships interned in American harbors as from new construction. It was in fact the British who shipped the bulk of the American Army to France during the crisis of 1918.

Although a strong President, Wilson was revolted by war and wished to have as little to do as possible with it. He had no intention of running the war in the fashion of McKinley, Lincoln, or Polk but saw his task as the civil and diplomatic side and especially the preparations for peace. Accepting Wilson's leadership almost to the end, Congress was not a factor in the military conduct of the war. So the President delegated military matters to Baker, March, and Pershing and generally made no contribution to strategy

Indeed, with the war already three years old, grand strategy was frozen as the questions of which enemy to attack, where and

how had been settled years before. The main question facing the Americans was more tactical in nature, that of how the AEF was to be used in relation to the armies of the Allies. The Allies did not want an independent American force because it would take time to organize and because they did not believe the Americans had the leadership and staff skills to cope with the Germans. The Allies themselves had never even had a unified command to that point and it was relatively late in the war when creation of the Supreme War Council, based in Versailles, brought unity of high command. Only the crisis brought on by the great German offensive of 1918 forced the Allies to give Marshal Foch supreme field command.

Pershing resisted the arguments for the amalgamation of American troops because he feared for American morale if the soldiers were subsumed in foreign units where they would also absorb the cynicism and war weariness of the British and French troops. Implicit in the amalgamation proposal was the notion that Americans were not skilled enough to conduct operations independently. And without its own Army in the field, the United States would have little influence on the terms of the peace, one important reason Wilson had acquiesced to war.

There was also a strong and well-founded fear that French and British generals would see the Americans simply as more cannon fodder. This fear was amply born out by the Battle of Belleau Wood which came about when four green companies of the 28th Division under French command were not informed of a general withdrawal and left to fight their own way back through German lines. Clearly French generals cared even less about American lives than they did about French lives.

Pershing was determined to have a separate American sector because he believed that the AEF was to play an important role in winning the war. Then 57 years old, he had had a fine military career beginning with his training at West Point and culminating in his command of the Mexican intervention in 1916. He had so impressed Baker that he was appointed to command of the AEF over five senior major generals. His habit of establishing discipline among his troops with his fists as a junior officer had earned him the sobriquet of 'Black Jack.' The front he selected was to the south of the French sector, lying between Pont-à-Mousson and Thiaucourt whence he could menace the iron mines of Briey, the coal fields of the Saar, and the east-west railroad network between Strasbourg and Sedan. His first objective was the St. Mihiel Salient, a wedge driven into the Allied lines remaining since 1914, whence he planned a thrust northward to cut the important German lines of communication. With this accomplished, the Germans would have to withdraw from northern France or surrender. Before all this could happen, however, he had to bring his Army into existence.

Left and above:
After Germany's 'Black Day' on 8 August the heart seemed to have gone out of the Germans' will to fight. When Foch gave his orders to Pershing's First Army to reduce the salient at St. Mihiel he thought the operation would last for a few months. In fact the Germans had already decided on a withdrawal and the American troops advanced with ease, taking 16,000 prisoners.

As the draft and National Guard enlistments brought men into the army camps in the United States, they received four months of basic training but the shortages of weapons and equipment left their experience more than deficient as some troops even had to drill with broomsticks. Such troops could not be sent into combat without further seasoning in weapons and tactics. Pershing thus planned three additional phases of training in France: weapons and tactical exercises up to the division level; a month-long tour of duty in a quiet sector with British and French troops; and combined training with artillery and aviation. Experienced French and British officers were employed to conduct the training which Pershing insisted include techniques of offensive warfare since he believed the way to defeat the Germans was to force them out of their trenches into mobile warfare. He insisted on such thorough training that, to the impatience of the Allies, the first American division did not get into the line until January 1918. Pershing in fact wanted to hold back major American involvement until he had at least four

ments were Belleau Wood and Soissons. In response to the crisis, the British were now delivering 250,000 American soldiers to France each month. By early July, the German offensive had spent itself without achieving its objective and the German armies fell back before the counterattack ordered by Foch on 18 July.

An order of 24 July brought the First American Army into existence. Its three corps contained fourteen divisions comprising 555,000 Americans and 110,000 French. None of its 3000 guns was made in the United States nor were any of its 267 tanks, half of which were manned by French crews. Commanded by Brigadier General William Mitchell, its 1400 planes included British Independent Bombing Squadrons and 600 French-piloted planes. In October the Second American Army was formed which made Pershing an Army Group Commander, co-equal with Haig and Pétain under Foch. Now that Pershing had achieved his own front on which to operate, Foch agreed that the elimination of the St. Mihiel Salient would be valuable but then allowed Haig to

Above:
US tanks move into action in the Argonne forest. This was the last offensive undertaken by the American First Army and by the end of October the forest had been cleared. By this time the US Army in the field was having problems of organization and communication which arose from the sheer number of men they had in action.

Left:
Donkeys were used to transport supplies from rail depots to the front lines during the last American offensive.

Right:
American troops move through the town of Verennes-en-Argonne on 26 September 1918.

divisions ready so that he could open the American Front.

Events overtook his plan in March 1918 when the Germans launched their war-winning offensive. Indeed, the slow pace at which Pershing was proceeding made the German generals think that the American force was not a factor. Over 6000 guns pounded the Allied line before the infantry offensive began. The shock enabled the attackers to push the British and French back 30 and 40 miles, again reaching the Marne only 37 miles from Paris in a repeat of 1914. The crisis was so great that Pershing said to Foch, 'Infantry, artillery, aviation, all that we have are yours.' So American troops came out of their training camps into their first significant action when the 2nd Division engaged the enemy at Château-Thierry. Two American divisions were initially distributed between the various British and French corps. Other important American engage-

divert the remainder of Pershing's planned offensive to the northwest to converge with a British drive to the east. Amid a certain amount of acrimony, Pershing finally acquiesced to the change even though it meant a difficult maneuver to shift direction of his forces after St. Mihiel to attack what was perhaps the most formidable German defenses on the Western Front. The Americans were expected to break through a twelve-mile deep belt of defenses along a rugged ridge lying between the valleys of the Meuse and Aisne Rivers with the Argonne Forest to the left and the Heights of Meuse to the right. Starting their attack on 12 September, Foch thought the Americans would be lucky to break through by Christmas.

St. Mihiel had lost much of its strategic value to the Germans by 1918 and the order to withdraw had been received on 10 September. The American attack thus came at a time when the Germans had already partially

withdrawn and had a considerable amount of troops and artillery out of position. In any event, the combined American-French force was numerically far superior to the defenders. The plan was for simultaneous attacks against the flanks to pinch off the salient and trap as much of the defenders as possible. Only occasionally making a determined stand, the Germans retreated in good order and then dug in at their main defense line known as the Michel Line. They had retreated from a position which they had already been ordered to abandon but nothing more. The entire operation had taken only three days but did a great deal to consolidate the American sense of themselves as an Army. Guns to the number of 450 and 16,000 prisoners were captured at a cost of 8000 American casualties.

The attack on the Meuse-Argonne was scheduled to begin on 26 September as part of a general attack all along the front which

Foch hoped would cause the German defenses to crack in at least one place. The American force of 600,000 shifted direction smoothly through a complex maneuver worked out by Colonel George Marshall, one of the more promising staff officers serving under Pershing. A hard fight was expected because the Germans had no real room to retreat before exposing a vital lateral line of communication. But the terrain favored the defense as it was enfiladed by artillery on the Heights of Meuse and in the Argonne Forest. The Germans did not in fact expect an attack in this strongly defended area but against Pershing's original objective more to the east. The initial advance was generally rapid but the Germans contested every inch of ground with carefully sited machine guns while the rough terrain and lack of roads prevented American field guns from keeping up with the infantry. Heavy rain soon made matters worse while the troops tended to bunch together and straggling became a serious problem. By its third and fourth days, the attack was characterized by widespread confusion. An American general estimated

that ten Americans were falling for every German. By the fourth day, the advance had only made eight miles at its best penetration. With Pershing urging his subordinates on and military police to keep the attacks going from the rear and prevent straggling, the army inched forward until 30 September, when it paused until 4 October.

When it was renewed, 27 German divisions were now in the line and the going was heavy. So hardy was the defense that the combat was likened by some to that of the infamous and bloody Somme two years before. Pershing persevered, however, and despite the fierce resistance actually began to approach his original objectives by mid-October. By this time, a British offensive to the north and a combined French-American drive on Sedan were succeeding while Germany's allies had withdrawn from the war. On 3 October Hindenburg had written to the new Chancellor Prince Max von Baden that 'there is no longer a prospect of forcing peace on the enemy.' Three days later the Swiss government brought Wilson the German request for 'peace negotiations.' The

Americans were by then close to a breakthrough on the Meuse-Argonne Front as the Germans had moved into a fighting retreat. Pershing's plan for a follow-on offensive was overtaken by the armistice of 11 November.

In the course of its 47 days, the offensive in the Meuse-Argonne engaged a quarter of the German forces on the Western Front, a total of 47 divisions. From its original 24 miles, the front came to be over 90. It was not the mobile warfare which Pershing had envisaged but blunt pressure applied as sensitively as possible under the circumstances. The German Army was not broken tactically in the Meuse-Argonne any more than it was on the rest of the Western Front. As Haig said, 'Germany is not broken in a military sense. During the last weeks her armies have withdrawn . . . in excellent order.' The German soldier could still fight but his leaders had decreed that the war finally grind to a halt. The real defeat of Germany lay in the loss of her allies such as they were, the cumulative economic pressure of the blockade, starvation, and especially the despair born of loss of hope of victory. Germany sued for peace as the Kaiser abdicated, revolution broke out, and the Social Democrats assumed power.

One of the factors undermining German morale was the idealism of Woodrow Wilson. At the suggestion of his chief propagandist George Creel, Wilson on 8 January 1918 had summarized his ideas on 'peace without victory' in his famous Fourteen Points. He talked of open covenants openly arrived at, freedom of the seas, removal of international economic barriers, reduction of armaments, impartial settlement of colonial claims, and the principle of national self-determination. His other points dealt with specific territorial changes. Widely publicized, the Fourteen Points made defeat thinkable for Germans even though Wilson did not speak for the Allies. In the peace treaty ultimately signed at Versailles, Britain and France rejected freedom of the seas and insisted that Germany pay immense war reparations for damages done to civilians as evidence of her alleged guilt in starting the war.

Peace without victory was, however, a slogan without reality as the American military goal in World War I was the traditional total victory. The United States had in fact gone to war with Germany over the very limited issue of submarines and could very well have opted to fight a limited war involving only the Navy in the Atlantic. But limited

war was outside the military ethos of Americans and apparently not considered. In pursuit of its total war effort, the United States put 4.8 million men under arms and sent over a million into combat with total casualties of 318,000. Almost 37,000 were killed in action and another 62,000 died of disease, 38,000 of these in the United States. To the extent that the Allied casualties can even be tabulated, it is thought that Germany lost around 1.6 million, France around 1.4 million, and Britain 950,000. American casualties were proportionately higher than those of other combatants because the American forces lacked battle experience and fought with a more aggressive and confident style. World War I was fought and decided by European forces as American troops were engaged in major combat for just two months. The great German offensive of March-July 1918 was defeated by Britain and France with very little American help. In the succeeding Allied

Right:
A soldier of the Occupation Army of the Rhineland.

Below:
Soldiers of the 64th Regiment, 7th Division cheer at the news of the armistice on 11 November 1918.

offensive, it was the British who bore the main burden, advancing the farthest and fastest against the heaviest concentration of German troops.

But Americans did make three distinct contributions to the Allied victory. First, they supplied tools, industrial knowledge, and war materials at the time when the Allies needed to build their own war industries and munitions. Second, they brought a fresh reserve of manpower when the Allies were exhausted and thus helped to tip the balance. Lastly, they brought hope to the Allies and dashed that of the Germans, a very tangible factor in the ultimate outcome.

The war itself had a strong impact on both the military and society in America. One of the most important military results of the war was the destruction of the stereotype of the citizen soldier held by the professional military. The grip of Emory Upton with his disdain for anything but the professional was finally broken by the caliber of the performance of the National Guard and draftees. World War I demonstrated for the first time that a large citizen army could be raised, trained and equipped in a short period and then acquit itself well in combat. This discovery was to have an important influence on postwar military manpower policies. Related was the experience of sending a large army to Europe, a possibility which had never entered previous military thought and planning, although much of American defense planning had traditionally assumed a European invasion of the United States. Following on from the presence of an American Army in Europe was the necessity of Anglo-American control of the Atlantic Ocean. World War I was also the first conflict in which Americans had allies, hence the problems of coalition warfare were a new experience. Because it entered the conflict so late, the United States contributed essentially nothing in the way of planning except

several general principles. One was the insistence on separate American formations rather than amalgamation, a second was unity of command, while a third was that military strategy should emphasize concentrated offensive effort. Pershing's plans to train his troops for offensive operations were in the traditional American mold of focusing resources into a war of mass and concentration. The Americans of 1917 wanted a 'sharp and decisive war' as much as their forbears had in previous conflicts. On a larger scale, the experience of World War I

implanted in American strategic thought the concept that American security was dependent on the balance of power in Europe. The idea that American security might be affected by factors beyond the continental United States and thus require action abroad by the Army was truly revolutionary. World War I, as Maurice Matloff has observed, was thus the harbinger of the future strategic role of the Army as indeed the Spanish-American War had been for the Navy.

The impact on society was also far-reaching. There was another burst of industrialization while agriculture also boomed. But the most important effect of the war was the strong growth of state control over the economic and financial life of the country. Although the legal position of Congress was scrupulously guarded, there was a strong tendency to rule by executive order. Most of the decisions regarding the war and mobilization were taken by men appointed by and responsible to the President. At least as important was the state success at controlling and molding popular opinion. As soon as the United States declared war, Wilson

had formed as an executive agency the Committee on Public Information to give the widest possible publicity to war aims and programs. Under the energetic and able George Creel, this first American venture into state propaganda developed the capacity to give immediate saturation publicity to any event or desire of the government. The success of the Committee at its internal propaganda function was alarming even to many Americans at the time but the success was so impressive that Franklin Delano Roosevelt adopted Creel's methods to publicize the New Deal. Creel's organization was to no little extent responsible for the outburst of chauvinism and anti-German hysteria which followed American entry into the war.

Having entered the war with the highest of motives, Americans emerged from their war experience in a state of deep disillusionment. Because it was so brief and inconclusive, the military experience left the soldiers frustrated and alienated. The majority of the people had shared Wilson's view of the war as a crusade for higher ideals. As in the Spanish-American War, many people thought that participation in the war would be regenerative for an America steeped in decadent commercialism. To restore America's national virtue meant national and personal sacrifice in pursuit of the American mission to save Europe. 'We have prospered with a sort of heedless and irresponsible prosperity' said Wilson. 'Now we are going

to lay all our wealth, if necessary, and spend all our blood, if need be . . . I am thankful for the privilege of self-sacrifice.' The war thus represented national chastisement, a testing and purification not unlike that of the Civil War, through which America might fulfill her historic mission and regain her state of divine grace.

The crusade of Woodrow Wilson and his fellow Americans had failed. There was no peace without victory nor was war abolished. Wilson himself, now locked into 'self-righteous obstinacy' prior to a stroke, had been unable to compromise with the Senate over qualifications to American participation in the League of Nations, so that promised covenant for peaceful international relations had turned to ashes for Americans as well. Suffering a revulsion against war and things military, Americans quickly dismantled their military apparatus and tried to pretend that all was well in Europe. Military means had failed to realize their international goals, so they now turned to other means in the postwar period – legislation to prevent the country from going to war, international agreements to limit navies and outlaw war, and diplomatic and economic sanctions to discourage aggression. This attitude caused the military establishment to shrink to a point where two decades later Chief of Staff General George Marshall could say with truth that his country possessed the military forces of 'a third-rate power.'

Chapter 8   America in World War II

The 'war to end all wars' was how World War I had been billed, but little more than a decade after the guns fell silent on the Western Front conflicts began to break out in Asia and Africa which culminated in the greatest struggle the world has yet seen. World War II was truly the epitome of total war fought on a global scale. Nothing appeared inviolate as the contenders struggled for victory. Neutral states were felled without warning while conquered territories were pillaged and depopulated by the conquerors. The price of defeat was political alteration and even oblivion as historic states were disposed of in accord with the whims of the victors or simply disappeared as political entities. Far more than World War I, this war was a fight to the death as the stakes were national survival. Politico-military objectives were total domination to remove permanently military and political threat or to harness the defeated to the will of the victor. Not only the economic infrastructure of the enemy came under attack but civilian populations as well. In this all-encompassing conflict, an estimated 80 million men bore arms with perhaps 15–20 million killed in combat. How many civilians died cannot be known with any certainty but surely numbered in the tens of millions at a minimum. Millions more were forcibly taken from their homes while more millions migrated voluntarily to escape the path of military operations or foreign political domination and exploitation they found obnoxious.

Radical changes in the configuration of world power arose from the war as the former powers of Europe lay physically and morally exhausted while the Asian giants China and Japan were also prostrate. There were only two first-class powers in the world at the end of the war. Both the United States and the Soviet Union had harnessed their vast resources in people and industrial capacity to win the war for the United Nations. While the United States became the 'arsenal of democracy' to equip and sustain much of the Allied war effort, the Soviet Union made a herculean effort to focus its industry on war production and gained the wherewithal for its mass armies to grind down and overwhelm the enemy. In some respects, World War II represents a culmination of some of the main trends in American history in that it was pre-eminently a war of mass and concentration militarily, industrial capacity (the first of the so-called 'gross national product wars'), and organizational and managerial necessity, all the things at which Americans had historically come to excel. So great were the resources and managerial capacity of the United States that it could fight two major but separate wars and still raise its standard of living appreciably. Built with the sweat

and blood of its people, the Soviet war effort was cruder but still resulted in the emergence of a true nation-state possessing military power second only to that of the United States, coupled with the confidence born of having beaten in open battle the world's most modern and impressive war machine.

World War II was in fact two different wars on opposite sides of the globe with the United States and to a lesser extent Britain as the connecting link. In Europe, Germany and Italy with some puppet allies fought the Soviet Union, Britain, the United States, and the Free French; in Asia, Japan and the United States grappled, with the latter supported by Britain and China. The war in Asia originated with the imperial ambitions of Japan which dreamed of a 'Greater East Asia Co-Prosperity Sphere' under Japanese hegemony, a hegemony which had no place for the Asian interests of such Western colonial powers as Britain, the United States, France, and the Netherlands. The war was thus fundamentally an attack on the established Western colonial systems by the rival Japanese system. The Japanese seizure of Manchuria from disunified and strife-ridden China in 1931 opened the attack which became a major war between China and Japan in 1937. The war in Europe grew out of the aftermath of World War I as the first totalitarian states in modern history appeared in Communist Russia, Fascist Italy, and Nazi Germany. Social and economic upheaval, defeat, unemployment, and unfulfilled national aspirations combined in various ways to allow the Fascists of Benito Mussolini, the Nazis of Adolf Hitler, and the Communists of first Vladimir Ilyich Lenin and then Joseph Stalin to seize power and establish one-party states maintained by military force and propaganda. All three regimes were warfare states, the Soviets obsessed with the struggle against its capitalist enemies and the Nazis and Fascists, glorifying war, using military regimentation and rearmament to solve economic ills and consolidate state control of people and economy. Italy invaded Ethiopia in 1935 while Hitler defied the Versailles Treaty with rearmament in 1935 and remilitarization of the Rhineland the following year.

The Western democracies, absorbed in their own problems with the social and economic turmoil resulting from World War I, tried to ignore the emergence of the warfare states in their midst. While Mussolini remained bogged down in Ethiopia where the locals resisted fiercely, they tried to rationalize Hitler's 1938 seizure of Austria and the Sudetenland region of Czechoslovakia, only to be forced to abandon this policy of 'appeasement' by public outrage at Hitler's absorption of the rest of Czechoslovakia the following year. Both Britain and France tried to guarantee the integrity of Poland, Hitler's obvious next target, with the threat of war. After less than two decades of Communist rule, the Soviet Union of Joseph Stalin was militarily and industrially unprepared for war and, its overtures for a collective security arrangement with Britain and France rebuffed, gained the two years between 1939 and 1941 for further preparations through a treaty with Germany which each saw as only a temporary expedient.

Invaded on 1 September 1939, Poland fell within three weeks to the Germans from the west and the Russians from the east, the latter also taking Latvia, Lithuania, and Estonia and attacking Finland in the process. Britain and France made good on their threat by declaring war on 3 September but took no real action against Germany in a period termed the 'Phony War.' It was Hitler who again took the offensive, sweeping through the Netherlands, Belgium, Norway, and Denmark in the spring of 1940 and then overrunning most of France in a six-week period in May and June. On 25 June the new French government at Vichy under Marshal Henri Pétain, hero of World War I, signed an armistice permitting the German occupation

of much of France. Three days earlier, Mussolini also declared war on France, then invaded Greece and soon challenged the British in Egypt.

With the exception of Switzerland in the middle and several other small neutrals on the peripheries, Hitler was now master of continental Europe outside of Soviet-occupied territories. The remarkable aspects of the military operations which had carried him to such a position was their speed and employment of a limited mode of warfare in stark contrast to the total war of World War I. Surprise aerial bombing had destroyed the Polish air force before it got off the ground, the vaunted Polish cavalry was winnowed by machine guns and Warsaw suffered a terror bombardment from the air to demoralize its citizens, all while a mere seven armored divisions including motorized infantry rolled up the country in three weeks. Mobility and

Below:
Marlene Dietrich left Nazi Germany and pursued her career in Hollywood. She actively supported the American war effort against her native country. On a nationwide tour to promote the sale of war bonds she is greeted by a crowd in Cleveland, Ohio on 19 June 1942.

decisiveness had been returned to warfare in what the Germans called 'Blitzkrieg' or lightning war. Mechanized armored columns with close tactical air support knifed through the opposing forces to surround points of resistance and engulf the civilian population.

The same tactics were employed on Denmark, Holland, Norway, Belgium, and France where the impact of the assault was heightened by the sabotage and subversion of 'fifth columnists' (a term originating in the Spanish Civil War), the use of paratroops to clear obstacles in advance, and the strafing of refugee-jammed highways. The speedy collapse of France at the hands of a relatively few armored divisions amazed even the Germans but especially astounded Americans who had thought France had the finest army in the world. France and Britain had both been caught unprepared and with poor strategy. The defensive lines were static and linear while the supposedly impregnable Maginot Line had never been extended to the English Channel, so the Germans flanked it to the north. A German thrust through the Ardennes, thought by the French to be unsuitable tank terrain, found the French armor spread thinly along the entire front and

no match for the concentrated weight of the Panzer columns. The Luftwaffe quickly dominated the air while the Royal Air Force (RAF) prudently and correctly withheld its strength for home defense.

After the fall of France, Britain stood alone, her Army stripped of most of its equipment in the debacle culminating at Dunkirk, defended mainly by her Navy and Air Force, and sustaining her morale with the inspiring rhetoric of Winston Churchill. The German Luftwaffe had been designed for tactical rather than strategic operations, and as a result the RAF was able to defeat Hitler's strategic air bombardment campaign in what is known as the Battle of Britain. Unable to cross the channel because of British naval and air superiority, Hitler like Napoleon before him turned in the direction of his real ambition, the march area of Eastern Europe which he saw as a pastoral hinterland for the industrial German heartland. His implacable rival in this area was the Soviet Union, so on 22 June 1941 Hitler took the fateful step of invading his adversary and thus unleashed the greatest struggle of the war. The Soviets were still not prepared to fight, their industry not yet adequately mobilized for war production and the armed forces still in

some disarray managerially, especially the armor, after the great purges of the Army in the late 1930s. Yet Stalin possessed a huge Army with strong armor. The mobile armored columns of Hitler encircled vast pockets of Russian resistance as the battle ranged over a front extending thousands of miles. When the Soviets had recovered from their initial defeats and defects, the Germans found themselves locked in combat with a foe possessing armor and ground formations rivalling their own. Soviet tanks and anti-tank weapons, not before encountered by the Germans, foiled German attempts at armored breakthroughs and forced them to give their tanks infantry screens and improved artillery support. The Blitzkrieg was a short-lived phenomenon as the Eastern Front gradually became a war of attrition in which its superior population and the rapid mobilization of its war production potential

Below:
Black Marines on leave in Harlem. Over a million blacks were drafted into segregated service units in the Army in World War II. An acute shortage of infantry replacements in Europe led the US Army to drop its traditional discrimination and allow 4500 black volunteers to serve in the infantry.

made the odds increasingly favor the Soviet Union.

Germany thus remained at loggerheads with both Britain and the Soviet Union. With the whole of the German economy and society harnessed for war by the Nazi state, forced labor and resources were drawn from the conquered areas to increase greatly the Nazi war potential. The 5.6 million Germans under arms in May 1940 increased to a peak of 9.5 million in May 1943. Britain and the Soviet Union also conscripted huge numbers of men into their armed forces, registered and directed labor, requisitioned private property, controlled industrial and agricultural production, and rationed consumer goods. Britain imposed its customary blockade of Germany which worked well through black lists of neutral firms trading with the enemy and control of contraband at ports of lading rather than on the high seas. Germany in turn launched a submarine campaign against Britain in the hope of destroying her enemy economically, a goal it had come so close to achieving in World War I. Yet all of these aspects of total war had their precedents in World War I and thus expanded an existing pattern. The United States remained a concerned but ostensibly neutral spectator.

The war between China and Japan had unfolded to the mounting unease of Americans as well. Pushing the Nationalist government of Chiang Kai-shek out of North China and the coastal areas, the Japanese had turned their attention next to French Indo-China, in limbo due to the fall of France, and prepared to add the remainder of Southeast Asia to their sphere of dominance. With its Pacific interests increasingly threatened, the United States attempted to control Japanese expansion with mounting diplomatic and economic pressure, culminating in a trade embargo which left the military clique ruling Japan no choice but war or capitulation. To assure the continued supply of resources and especially oil needed by Japan's economy, it was decided to seize Southeast Asia in tandem with a surprise strike against the United States. The strategy was to destroy American and British power in Asia and then await negotiations behind strong rings of inner and outer defenses which, it was thought, would be impregnable.

In a war to be fought by an island empire in the vast expanses of the Pacific ocean, the primary target had to be the American fleet based at Pearl Harbor in Hawaii. A brilliant surprise attack was devised and executed by Japan's leading proponent of naval air power, Admiral Isoroku Yamamoto, as the prelude to the grand advance throughout Southeast Asia which carried the Japanese flag to the peripheries of India and Australia. It was thus Japan which finally brought a reluctant United States into the war and sent President Franklin Roosevelt to Capitol Hill

to tell Congress, 'Yesterday, 7 December, 1941 – a date which will live in infamy – the United States of America was suddenly and deliberately attacked by naval and air forces of the Empire of Japan. . . . I ask the Congress to declare that since the unprovoked and dastardly attack . . . a state of war has existed. . . .'

Although Japan had attacked them, the road to war for Americans had not been so different from that which led them into World War I. The anti-military mood of the 1920s was strengthened in the following decade by preoccupation with the depression and domestic affairs. The growing spector of war in Europe and Asia made the Americans uneasy all the same. The prospect of involvement in another war was not popular as evidenced by the various 'neutrality' acts passed by Congress between 1934 and 1937. This was also the time when a growing suspicion held that the United States had been tricked into entering World War I by the 'merchants of death' as the arms manufacturers were known, and British propaganda. So current were these charges that a congressional committee spent two years investigating them.

While Americans viewed Germany and Japan with increasing suspicion, they remained uncertain of the significance of the disturbing trends in the world or what action could or should be taken. Anti-German and anti-Japanese sentiment grew as these states came to be seen as internally oppressive, externally aggressive, and economically domineering. The anti-Semitic program in Germany strongly offended many Amer-

icans but feeling ran far deeper against Japan whose actions were threatening American interests in the Pacific and severely hurting China, a country to which many Americans had strong sentimental ties. At the same time, the majority of Americans instinctively leaned toward Britain and France, their allies of the last war, rather than Germany and Italy. While Congress tried to legislate Americans out of any involvement in the disturbing trends in the world, Roosevelt had no European policy because he feared to rouse the ire of the domestic isolationists and still hoped to minimize any American involvement. He himself was less sanguine about the American position, saying in a

Below:
Gasoline rationing had to be introduced to ensure that
the armed forces had adequate supplies.

Right:
Cramped quarters aboard a transport leaving New York
in 1944.

speech in Chicago in October 1937, 'There is a solidarity and interdependence about the modern world, both technically and morally, which makes it impossible for any nation completely to isolate itself from economic and political upheavals in the rest of the world.' And indeed, Roosevelt devised and Americans supported a policy of 'aid short of war' to beleaguered China.

This policy soon became extended to Britain and France as Roosevelt increasingly came to believe that the coming war would inevitably involve the United States. He had been relieved when the Munich Agreement of 1938 had forestalled war in Europe in 1938 but was shocked by Hitler's subsequent actions in defiance of that agreement.

Roosevelt's desire to remain uninvolved, however, led Hitler to discount the United States as a factor in the situation. It took the fall of France to convince Roosevelt and many Americans that they could not allow the defeat of Britain. For the first time, Americans saw a tangible threat to themselves emerging from the loss of the French fleet combined with German and Italian naval power possibly incorporating the former French fleet. Congress had been passing larger and larger military appropriations for several years before the fall of France and indeed had already revised the neutrality legislation in November 1939 to allow the belligerents to buy American arms on a cash and carry basis.

While the United States was thus embarking on a modest rearmament in the late 1930s, Roosevelt attempted through his 'fireside chats' over the radio to tell the public that the United States was under de facto attack to prepare it for the eventuality of war. He promised repeatedly not to send American troops abroad 'except in case of attack.' One of the two main reasons for his unprecedented decision to run for a third term in 1940 was the probability of war and the need for a strong and experienced President in the White House. His other consideration was the lack of acceptable liberal democrats on the scene to preserve the domestic programs of the New Deal. Few believed the 'campaign oratory' of the President and his Republican

opponent Wendell Willkie about the avoidance of war because both in reality held the
same position. The voters apparently agreed
with Roosevelt that the times demanded an
experienced leader and he interpreted his
substantial victory as a mandate for the total
support of Britain, saying in a speech of
December 1940 that 'the Axis powers are not
going to win this war' and that the United

States 'must be the great arsenal of democracy.' As a result, the Lend-Lease Act
was passed on 11 March 1941. British Prime
Minister Winston Churchill called it 'the
most altruistic act in history' because it enabled arms and supplies to be lent or leased to
any country 'whose defense the President
deems vital to the United States.' Repay-
ment was to be made in kind or in any other

way satisfactory because the British were understandably hard pressed for cash. Canada co-ordinated its war production with that of the United States through the Hyde Park Agreement of April 1941 and extended a billion dollar credit to Britain. The United States had earlier exchanged 50-year-old destroyers for control of British bases in North American waters.

The United States also moved to assist Britain with the submarine problem in the Atlantic as losses had reached 600,000 tons of shipping per month by April 1941. American Marines occupied Iceland in July 1941 to relieve British troops sorely needed elsewhere and thus involved the Navy in ongoing operations in a combat zone. British shipping was allowed to join American supply convoys while the Navy and the German submarines fought a clandestine war of which Congress and the public remained unaware. Roosevelt and Churchill had the first of their wartime meetings in August at Placentia Bay, Newfoundland where Americans were further prepared morally for war by the war aims of the Atlantic Charter drawn up there. This eight-point statement declared that Britain and the United States sought no territorial gains for themselves, did not wish any territorial changes contrary to the desires of the populations involved, would respect the right of peoples to choose their own form of government, promised free access to trade and raw materials for all nations, and called for the disarmament of aggressor nations in tandem with a peace to give all peoples security and freedom.

When Roosevelt went before Congress on 8 December, he asked only for war with Japan. Yet three days later, Hitler declared war on the United States in what has been called 'one of the most astounding acts of the war.' Even though the US was in fact in a state of 'passive belligerency' through its active support of Britain and the Soviet Union, Hitler had genuinely tried to avoid provoking Roosevelt through naval incidents in the Atlantic and ignored the many American provocations of him. Indeed, he had never even wanted war with Britain or the United States, having tried first to negotiate, then to defeat and subsequently to ignore the former. What he had done was to encourage Japan to attack Britain and the United States in Asia in the hope of destroying British power and support in that region and distracting the United States from Europe. So in November 1941 he had promised Japan that Germany would declare war on the United States when Japan did. But his strategy failed because the Japanese, despite their early success, proved unable to destroy the British position completely while the United States surprised all by its ability to fight on all fronts concurrently. Hitler had in fact badly misjudged the American factor partly because he failed to consider how the march of events would alter American public opinion from the rampant isolationism of the early and mid-1930s and partly due to his distorted conception of the nature of American society. He apparently believed that Americans would be receptive to Nazi dogma because they lived in a demoralized and corrupt society and were near revolt against a predominantly Jewish ruling class. These ideas and the lack of any American policy toward Europe in the 1930s led him to see the United States as a weak variable in the equation despite its undeniable material power. His

declaration of war on the United States took him from a European war which he could conceivably have won to a world war in which he lacked the resources to compete. Thus two distinctly separate wars in Europe and Asia became merged into a global conflict.

Although Roosevelt worried about preparing Americans psychologically for the coming war, public opinion polls of the late 1930s show that he was overestimating by far the strength of popular resistance to the idea of war. The majority of Americans supported 'aid short of war' as a necessary defense of their interests and came rapidly to see the Nazis as evil and the Japanese as perfidious. They thus supported the rearmament of the later 1930s while the peacetime conscription of 1940 was unilaterally enacted by Congress on the strength of public feeling. A historically strong trend in American society encouraged Americans to think of politics and foreign policy not in terms of national expediency and advantage but of right and wrong. Most notably expressed in the American dedication to democracy and freedom as war aims in World War I, this trend made impossible the professed desire for neutrality in the late 1930s because Americans saw the issues as important – fascism versus democracy and the barbarism of Nazism versus the values of Western Civilization. Pearl Harbor and the subsequent German declaration of war united most Americans behind the Declaration of the United Nations signed on 1 January 1942 by the US, Britain, the Soviet Union, China and 22 other nations. The principles of the Atlantic Charter were formally adopted as war aims and there was to be no peace until the enemy was defeated.

This policy of no peace until victory accorded well with historic American concepts of total victory through strategies of annihilation. If the enemy was a dangerous threat to the peace and values of Americans, he had to be rendered harmless through total victory in total war. The immense effort put forth by the American people in the war testifies to their acceptance of these ideas. Yet the war did not turn into a popular crusade as had World War I. Roosevelt in fact tried to avoid Wilson's errors such as the exalted rhetoric and crusading fervor, the arousal of unrealistic expectations, and hatred of everything German by official propaganda, all of which contributed to the later reinterpretations of the 1930s arguing that American involvement had been a mistake.

The people whom Roosevelt had to lead in war were very different from the Americans of 1917 who had celebrated the onset of their war as a cleansing and sacrificial national experience. The social and economic difficulties of the depression years had left Americans with no need for adventure or relief from boredom, for they had grown up amid breadlines, strikes, riots, the Sino-Japanese War, revolutions in South America, and the Italian adventure in Ethiopia for starters. Their traditional American sense of idealism had been dulled by the national experience of the depression which, as Malcolm Cowley said, had left them 'tougher and more sophisticated than their fathers in 1918.' 'Glum resignation' might well describe the mood for Americans who saw the war as yet another onerous obligation enforced by conscription. For many men, military service was only the most recent problem in lives beset with a succession of problems. The war was viewed pragmatically as a job, however unpleasant, to be done. The sooner it was completed, the sooner they could get on with their lives.

In addition to their lack of idealism, the majority of Americans by their own admission could not explain 'what the war is all about' but did not question the need to fight. 'In World War II, everybody went into the service' said a social commentator in 1978. 'I don't recall having any reservations about it, nor the question even being raised.' A 1944 debriefing report on attitudes of returning airmen stated 'there is very little idealism. Most regard the war as a job to be done and

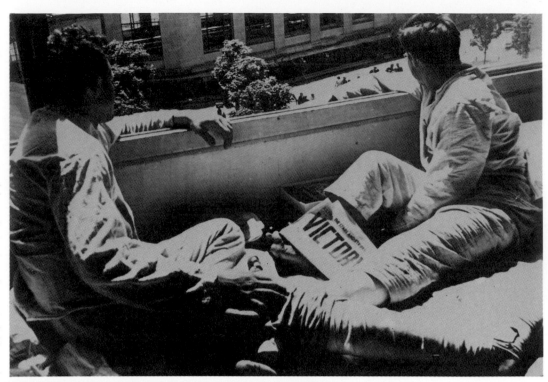

there is not much willingness to discuss what we are fighting for.' Serving as a war correspondent on Guadalcanal in 1942, John Hersey one day asked a group of Marines about to go into action what they were fighting for. After a silence, 'one of them spoke. . . . He whispered, "Jesus, what I'd give for a piece of blueberry pie" . . . Fighting for pie . . . they mean they are fighting "to get the goddam thing over and get home". . . . Home is where the good things are – the generosity, the good pay, the comforts, the democracy, the pie.' Reporting from Tunisia, Ernie Pyle also wrote of the growing acceptance by the soldiers 'of the bitter fact that we must win the war or else. . . . The immediate goal used to be the Statue of Liberty; more and more it is becoming Unter den Linden.' Men thus fought not from idealism or patriotism as much as from necessity and with the fairly realistic goal of peace as soon as possible.

Although the United States had been preparing for war for several years before the conflict finally involved it, the military establishment was in no way ready for the demands made on it. Several million Americans had been under arms in 1918 but two years later scarcely a tenth of these remained in uniform. The armed forces reached their nadir in the interwar period as Congress reduced the budgets of the War and Navy Departments with each passing year. Fiscal austerity and hostility to all things military caused the Army in particular to lose any real combat capacity and become 'hardly more than a small school for soldiers' in the words of Russell Weigley. Former Chief of Staff General Peyton March was moved to write in his memoirs that 'by its own hand' the US had become weaker than Germany as limited by the Versailles Treaty.

Even so, important changes were occurring in military doctrine and organization. General John Pershing had returned in triumph from France to become Chief of Staff in 1921 and set in train various developments. Command and control was centralized by adoption of the General Headquarters (GHQ) concept which meant that a future war would be directed largely from Washington rather than an independent field command as in World War I. As it evolved, GHQ came to be organized into five separate areas: G-1 (Personnel), G-2 (Military Intelligence), G-3 (Operations and Training), G-4 (Supply and Procurement), and the War mobilization rather than strategic issues and emphasize manpower over logistics in its plans. As Chief of Staff from 1930 to 1935, General Douglas MacArthur made important contributions to improving and balancing the planning process.

Despite the best efforts of MacArthur, the Army remained in a woefully low state of combat readiness throughout the 1930s. Congress forced the Army to use World War I equipment until it was no longer serviceable through wear. There were, for example, only twelve post-World War I tanks in service in 1934 while the Army could not afford to equip its meager formations with the new semi-automatic Garand rifle (later called the M-1) invented by a government ordnance worker. Because it was so strapped for funds

Left:
Despite the dislocation of war the mail got through to troops with some regularity. Corporal Albert Franczaki hands out letters to GIs in an old barn west of St Lô. Unit officers censored the outgoing letters of their enlisted men but their own letters were only subject to random checks by the postal service.

Above left:
Two GIs recuperating on the day the war ended. American casualties did not compare with German, Japanese, Soviet, British, or French numbers. The total of 290,000 casualties would have been considerably higher if the Americans had not had the best medical services among combatants.

Above:
Chow time at the camp near Bizerta in November 1943. Most front-line units managed to feed their soldiers at least one hot meal a day. Otherwise the men carried their own rations which contained enough food for a few days.

for equipment, neither MacArthur nor his successor General Malin Craig ever put much more than one percent of their budget into weapons research and development. The Army and National Guard were still basically armed with the weapons of World War I in 1939. It was only in that year that Congress began raising the manpower quotas of the Army and National Guard substantially without the urging of Roosevelt while the Army suddenly found itself with a doubled budget and peacetime conscription in 1940.

The Army had emerged from World War I firmly committed to a Clausewitzian strategy of mass and concentration to destroy the enemy armed forces through offensive action.

army of strength enough to defeat a major European power. This principle was formalized in the National Defense Act of 1920 which legislated a small regular army of skeletonized formations as the framework for a mass citizen army, hence the emphasis on manpower mobilization plans in the War Plans Division.

But the Army was little influenced by the doctrinal developments which occurred in Europe during the interwar period, principally in the writings of Basil Liddell Hart and John Frederick Charles Fuller in England. Appalled at the bloody stalemate of the Western Front, these theorists tried to reintroduce maneuver into warfare through the use of highly mobile formations of tanks

One of the important changes in the Army after World War I was the emancipation of the Air Service from the Signal Corps. Realization of the potential of air power was one of the important developments arising from World War I. The concept of strategic bombing had seized the imagination of many. The Germans had sent 103 raids against Britain and France delivering 270 tons of bombs and causing less damage than that done annually by rats. Wilson had been predictably opposed to strategic bombing, saying 'I desire no sort of participation by the Air Service of the United States in a plan . . . which has as its object promiscuous bombing upon industry, commerce or populations in enemy countries disassociated from obvious mili-

'Clausewitz's book on war . . .' wrote one officer in 1928, 'occupies about the same relation to the study of the military profession as does the Bible to all religious studies.' Army doctrine thus held that the offensive was necessary to maintain freedom of action and obtain decisive results. The defensive was relegated to a temporary phase to be employed only until the initiative could again be seized. Direct combat with the enemy's main forces was the means to annihilation of his ability to fight and thus victory in the best tradition of Ulysses Grant whose campaigns young officers carefully studied at West Point and the advanced service schools. Its experience in World War I had converted the Army to a force structure envisioning a mass

and motorized infantry. Such ideas were also espoused by Charles de Gaulle in France and Marshal Mikhail Tukhachevsky in the Soviet Union and actualized by Heinz Guderian in the Blitzkrieg campaigns of 1939–40. Possibly because the Army's experience in World War I had been too brief for it to suffer the ultimate frustration of the static war in western Europe, the American Army kept such tanks as it had tied to the infantry while MacArthur only encouraged mechanization of the cavalry. For this reason, the army developed durable long range light tanks for reconnaissance, useless for battle. Only the experience of the Spanish Civil War forced a hasty development of the General Sherman M-4 in 1941.

tary needs to be served by such action.' Yet the United States quickly produced its own champion of strategic bombing. General William Mitchell, like so many others, was revolted and disillusioned by the tactical impasse on the Western Front where he served as air commander for Pershing. His original espousal of the value of tactical air operations soon moved into an extreme advocacy of strategic air power as the ultimate arbiter in warfare. At his most extreme, Mitchell wrote 'The result of warfare by air will be to bring about quick decisions. Superior air power will cause such havoc or the threat of such havoc in the opposing country that a long-drawn out campaign will be impossible.' Influenced by the Italian Giulio Douhet and

Left below:
M-3 tanks move up to strengthen positions in the battle for control of the Kasserine Pass, Tunisia in February 1943. The M-3 'General Lee' was a medium tank which was mainly supplied to the British to fight in North Africa. It went into production in July 1941 but already its replacement the M-4 Sherman tank was in prototype form. The M-3 proved vulnerable to the German 88-mm anti-tank gun but it was employed in the field until 1944.

Right:
These M-4 tanks, armed with a new type of rocket gun were part of the 752nd Tank Battalion of the Fifth Army, which served in Italy, 1944.

Below:
Outside St. Vith M-4 Sherman tanks of the 40th Tank Battalion wait to go into action during the Battle of the Bulge. The M-4 made a decisive contribution in the war against Germany. At first the M-4 was equipped with a 75-mm gun but in February 1944 it was replaced by a 76-mm high velocity gun which had a much higher rate of fire. During the war 48,347 tanks were built which was the greatest production total of any single tank ever achieved.

Bottom:
A mine-roller M-4 of the US Sixth Army moves down to take part in the crossing of the Moselle.

Britain's Hugh Trenchard, Mitchell advocated strategic bombing of the 'vital centers' of the enemy to disrupt his economy and demoralize his population through terror. The ongoing horror of the Western Front had apparently so compromised morality that it was no longer considered immoral to attack the general civilian population if in so doing a speedy decision in war was achieved by breaking the morale of the enemy.

The resistance to his ideas led Mitchell to make a most insubordinate verbal assault on the management of the War Department in public in 1925, which was followed by his court-martial and resignation from the service the following year. He did not sacrifice his career in vain, however, as the Air Force

in its natural pursuit of autonomy from the Army built on his ideas to formulate an independent strategic mission for itself. At the Air Corps Tactical School at Maxwell Field, Alabama in the 1930s, air force strategists developed a doctrine of total war through attack by a strategic air arm of the whole national structure of the enemy and especially of his industry. This doctrine caused the Air Force to ask contractors to develop a long-range bomber which would not need fighter protection. The year 1936 saw the creation of GHQ Air Force which gave the air force at least operational autonomy from GHQ and represented the beginnings of a strategic strike force. That same year, the air force began to place orders for the B-17 Flying Fortress (so named to emphasize its defensive mission to a still anti-military Congress!) developed by Boeing in response to the Air Force request. So a few years later General Henry Arnold of the Air Force could say that 'America's air doctrine has for years been based solidly on the principle of long-range bombardment. . . . Strategic air power is a war-winning weapon in its own right. . . .' The Air Force thus entered the war equipped with a long-range bomber and the doctrine for use of that weapon but so

committed to its strategic mission that development of other types of aircraft had been neglected.

Other than convoy escort and anti-submarine duty, the Navy had played no combat role in World War I. The naval construction program of 1916 had emphasized battleships reaching a size of 43,000 tons and carrying twelve 16-inch guns as armament. With war over before the new capital ship program was far advanced, the economy-minded Republicans of the Harding administration began to curtail it while the Washington Naval Conference of 1921–22 involving the United States, Britain, France, Italy, and Japan placed a ten-year moratorium on capital-ship construction and limitations on total tonnage. The United States as a result scrapped fifteen capital ships, and only three battleships of the original 1916 program – the *Colorado, Maryland*, and *West Virginia* – came to join the fleet. Naval limitation remained in effect until 1936 when the Japanese unilaterally abrogated the extended treaty. All the powers resumed construction, the United States of the 45,000 ton *Iowa* class of battleships.

The Navy was committed to the battleship as its main offensive weapon but did contain

would be lost in the beginning, that the Navy would have to fight its way across the vast expanse of the Pacific through the successive groups of islands until meeting the Japanese Fleet in a climactic Jutland-style engagement which would largely decide the war. The Japanese saw a similar scenario and from 1936 began building battleships like the 72,000-ton *Yamato* with batteries of 18-inch guns in preparation for the ultimate confrontation at sea. With its thinking early fixated on this sort of campaign in the Pacific and 20 years in which to prepare, the Navy was able to perfect the necessary tactics, equipment, and doctrine. Submarines and their tactics were improved, techniques for refueling the fleet at sea were devised, and the concept of the fast carrier task force began to take shape. The anticipated island-hopping campaign across the Pacific spurred the development of landing craft while the Marines, with no clearly defined combat role since their formation in 1775, developed highly sophisticated ship-to-shore assault tactics. The Marine doctrine and techniques of amphibious warfare were among the most radical tactical innovations of the war. Navy preparations for war were thus quite advanced in equipment, concepts, and practice.

an active group of aviation and carrier enthusiasts who believed that the aerial torpedo and bomb would transform naval tactics through the bombing of enemy warships and bases. 'Any fleet which has a number of aircraft squadrons will have a tremendous advantage over one which is not so equipped' wrote one officer in 1919. 'We must get carriers in our fleet and aircraft bases at strategical points or we will invite disaster when the next crisis comes.' And the Navy did obtain its first carrier, the *Langley*, in 1922. By 1941 the US had seven carriers and well-developed carrier doctrine and already had under development a new class of fast carriers. The struggle in the Pacific, the greatest naval war in history, thus found the US relatively well prepared from the outset.

The Navy had indeed been preparing for war with Japan for two decades. And Japan was the most probable enemy in the eyes of both the Army and the Navy. The War and Navy Departments embodied their strategic planning in the 'color' plans, each color denoting a particular contingency or country. War Plan Orange was a scenario for the Far East which envisaged that the outlying American positions such as the Philippines

Top:
General Patton, commander of the Western Task Force in Operation Torch, goes ashore at Fedala on 9 November 1942. One of Patton's famous sayings was 'I am a soldier, I fight where I am told and I win where I fight.'

Left:
On 9 September 1943 the Allies launched an amphibious assault on Salerno, Italy. General Mark Clark's Fifth Army (the British X Corps and US VI Corps) participated in this operation, code-named Avalanche. In this photograph British and American troops come ashore.

Above:
Black troops of the 92nd Division, Fifth Army wade across the Arno in the Pontedera area in September 1944. The American and British armies made very slow progress in the Italian theater. The German General Kesselring fought a defensive battle moving from one fortified line to take up another. Having abandoned the Gustav Line he was able to hold up the Allies long enough at the Gothic Line for the autumn rains to come to his assistance.

Below:
'A little poker, en route to Noumea, Pacific' by David Fredenthal.

Above:
'Carolina Bivouac' by Oliver Baker.

Above:
'The Beach' by Tom Lea.

Below:
'Forward camp near Anzio' by Tom Craig.

The manpower to fight the war came largely from the conscription which Congress enacted in August 1940, the first peacetime draft in American history. In effect for only one year, the act limited the employment of conscripts to the Western Hemisphere and American possessions. Subsequently extended, the draft claimed around eleven million Americans, including over a million blacks. Initially passed over in favor of whites, blacks were given equality in the draft by an executive order of 1943 due to the crucial manpower shortage and the political pressure brought to bear on Roosevelt by black leaders. The Army itself remained rigidly and completely segregated until later in the war when some integration began to occur in response to various circumstances. The draftees received thirteen weeks of basic training, followed by small unit training, combined training in the weapons of the regiment and division, and finally large unit maneuvers. The emphasis in training was on general proficiency as evidenced by testing, free as opposed to rigidly structured maneuvers, simulation of battle conditions, and the integrity of tactical units after they had been formed. The training process was designed to turn the sometimes reluctant and often bewildered draftee into a competent and aggressive combatant thoroughly identified with his unit and its team spirit. Even Private Eddie Slovik, that most reluctant of soldiers, 'found himself unwilling to let the side down' in the words of Peter Aichinger.

Congress brought the draft into being with no concern for the problems which would be visited on the Army in particular. World War I experience was not that relevant because most of its training had taken place abroad, so the extensive camps necessary for the inductees in 1940 and 1941 were not ready. This simple fact early forced a curtailment of the induction of draftees and National Guard units. The prewar skeletonized Army had been severely short of equipment while much of United States arms production was shipped directly to Britain and the Soviet Union. The diversion of bombers to Britain, for example, forced the Air Force to cut its 1940 training program in half while all medium tank production was shipped out as Lend-Lease that year. There was also the problem of producing large numbers of officers quickly. The ROTC provided 106,000 officers of remarkably high quality and new Officers Candidate Schools began to function in July 1941 to the ease the situation at the lower levels.

By the time of Pearl Harbor, the Army

Right:
Members of the 325th Glider Infantry clean up small pockets of resistance in Germany.

Below right:
Lieutenant Vernon Richards at the controls of his North American P–51 Mustang. The P–51 B served mainly with the UK-based US 8th Air Force as a long-range escort fighter. The USAAF finally had an aircraft which could cover the B-17s on their bombing missions over Germany. By 1944 there were sufficient numbers of Mustangs in service to have made a drastic reduction in USAAF losses.

alone had 1.638 million men and 36 divisions but only one of these divisions was considered combat ready. War Department plans called for 71 divisions by the end of 1942 and 213 by June 1944. After 37 new divisions were created in 1942, the remainder of the program was deferred because of lack of equipment and competing demands for manpower from the other services and industrial sector. Since much of the German Army was committed to the Eastern Front, the need for American divisions in Europe was also correspondingly reduced. After 1942, therefore, the Army concerned itself with improving the support and maintaining the manpower of its existing formations as three months of heavy combat meant an average of 100 percent casualties for an infantry regiment. The ground combat forces contained 1.9 million men at the beginning of

1943, a figure which only increased to two million by the end of the war. The number of divisions climbed to just 89 which meant that American ground combat forces were stretched extremely thinly. The last of the combat reserves were thrown into the line in Europe in the crisis created by the German drive in the Ardennes in late 1944. The thinness of the ground forces probably resulted in a higher casualty and battle fatigue rate from the heavier stress on the soldiers who were left in the line too long and felt they had to fight on until they became casualties.

In contrast to the 89 American divisions, the Soviet Union, Germany, and Japan had 400, 300, and 100 respectively. This disparity is partly explained by the fact that the US held more men in its industrial workforce because it was producing much of the war material for its allies as well as itself, partly due to increased mechanization (there were only about 300,000 more American combat troops in World War II than in World War I), partly due to the 2.35 million men in the Air Force which was still part of the Army and the millions more in the Navy and Marines, and partly due to the standard of living of the troops. Even in combat zones, the Army made a strenuous effort to approximate the standard of living to which the troops were accustomed in civilian life. The Army Services of Supply under General Brehon Somervell was responsible for all support and logistic functions in the United States and ultimately absorbed around 1.6 million of the men available to the Army. This huge enterprise was a reflection of the sheer size and complexity of global logistics. The Air Force had achieved operational autonomy in March 1942 under General Henry Arnold and soon developed its own parallel system of logistics as part of its constant quest for autonomy. One of the outstanding characteristics of the Army in World War II was this incredible diversion of manpower into support functions. The official history of the Army notes of this phenomenon, '. . . some commanders . . . fought to keep the army lean and simple. In World War II they lost this fight.'

The organization of the American division in World War II was changed from the large four regiment 'square' division developed by Pershing for the AEF. General Lesley MacNair created a 'lean and simple' theory of army organization which became the three regiment or 'triangular' division. MacNair argued that the purpose of the division was to attack and advance, and it should have only such weapons and organization as were necessary to move forward against average resistance. Heavy or specialized equipment and support units were pooled while infantry companies possessed their own anti-tank weapons and communications gear, drove their own trucks, and hauled their own supplies. Specialty units and equipment such as anti-aircraft, tank destroyers, bridging, engineers, and many others were available for flexible assignment from non-divisional pools. The savings in manpower from this

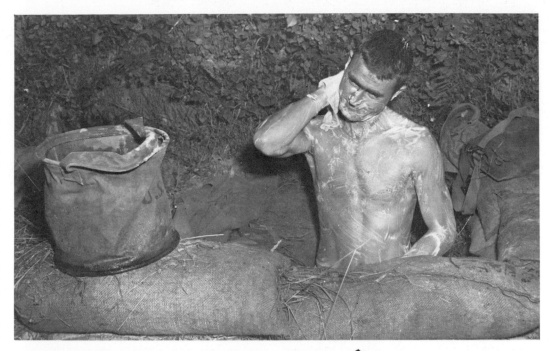

Far left:
The first colored artillery unit man their 105-mm howitzers in action against the Germans across the Arno River.

Top:
Sergeant Pete Staton, in service in France, washes himself in a foxhole, August 1944.

Above:
The US promised the Philippines independence which was granted in 1946. The US retained bases on the islands. The photograph shows GIs enjoying the Kay Kyeser USO Show on Luzon on 12 August 1945.

Left:
Winter 1944 of the Western Front: Thomas O'Brien tries to eat his frozen rations.

streamlining of the divisional organization was enough for an additional six divisions at a time when the Army was strapped for divisions.

Totaling 14,250 men, each division contained 27 rifle companies with each company comprising three rifle platoons and a weapons platoon. Three rifle squads of twelve men each armed with a Browning Automatic Rifle and Garand M-1 rifles made up the platoon. The next level of organization was the battalion of three rifle companies and a heavy weapons company. Above the battalion was the regiment of three infantry battalions, a headquarters company with anti-tank guns, machine guns, and bazookas, an anti-tank company with twelve 57-mm guns and machine guns, and a service company. Three infantry regiments and three artillery

battalions with twelve 155-mm and 36 105-mm guns made up the fighting components of the infantry division. With the exception of the 82nd Airborne Division, the only specialized divisions were sixteen armored formations with three armored, three infantry, and three artillery battalions. Divisions and other units were purposely kept flexible and mission-oriented and were organized into corps and task forces for specific circumstances or missions. The principle in all cases was not to tie up resources in permanent formations but to assign units as circumstances and strategy dictated.

The fire power of the infantry was greatly increased over World War I as a result of the semi-automatic Garand and increased concentrations of machine guns, anti-tank guns, and other weapons. Able to fire thirteen

Right:
Infantrymen on the alert as they move up in the jungles of Dutch New Guinea. Because of the rapid building up of units the men of the first American division to fight in New Guinea were very inexperienced, especially for fighting in the jungle. For many 'green' Americans the experience of fighting a hidden enemy who could strike unpredictably was nerve-racking. The troops were also vulnerable to disease: malaria, dengue fever, dysentery, and jungle rot.

Below:
Tanks of a US Armored Division cross a bridge in China. General Joseph Stillwell served as Chiang Kai-shek's Chief of Staff and as Commander of US forces in China from 1942–44. Stilwell's US and Chinese units fought to open up the land route from Burma to China, the Burma Road. All equipment for units in China had to be airlifted from India 'over the Hump.'

different kinds of shell at 20 rounds per minute, the 105-mm field gun was the 'workhorse of the army' and was supplemented by 155-mm MI Long Toms and the 8-inch howitzer. American artillery tactics were characterized by an aggressive forward employment of the guns aided by ground and aircraft spotting. Continuing the tradition of artillery excellence which had been a feature of the army since the revolution, gunners were highly skilled in laying down massive barrages on targets which infantry, tanks, self-propelled guns, and tactical aircraft then overwhelmed. 'We believe that our use of massed heavy artillery fire was far more effective than the German techniques and clearly outclassed the Japanese . . .' later wrote Chief of Staff George Marshall, '. . . our method of employment of these weapons had been one of the decisive factors of our grand campaigns throughout the world.' Closely related was the use of the self-propelled gun, one of the important tactical innovations of the war. Although originally intended as tank destroyers, 76-mm, 3-inch and 90-mm guns were mounted on tracked firing platforms and provided immediate support for the advance of infantry and armor, thus greatly increasing the ability to exploit breakthroughs rapidly which had been one of the major problems of World War I. The final assault on Germany's last lines of defense in 1945 saw the 155-mm guns and 8-inch howitzers mounted on tank chassis, being used to bombard and demolish enemy positions.

The main American tank was the General Sherman M-4 mounting a 75- and later a 76-mm gun. Save only for its endurance, this tank was notably inferior in weapons and armor to the German Panthers and Tigers. Only in the fall of 1944 was the M-4 equipped with hypervelocity armor-piercing shells which could penetrate German armor except in front. As a result many M-4s were expended as American tank commanders maneuvered to gain the flanks of the enemy. The General Pershing M-26 heavy tank with its 90-mm gun only went into mass production at the end of the war and never appeared on the battlefield. Over 250,000 tanks were produced for World War II as compared to 10,000 for World War I.

The Russians soon demonstrated on the Eastern Front that the blitzkrieg mode of warfare did not fare well against improved anti-tank weapons and defenses. Infantry thus remained the basic ingredient in combat and, as in World War I, offensive tactics revolved around infantry-artillery combinations. It was quickly recognized that tanks alone could not force a breakthrough nor operate without infantry support; therefore one armored division was usually assigned to two infantry divisions to exploit breakthroughs and prevent the enemy from immediately reforming his lines. Tanks and motorized infantry could thus keep the enemy under sustained pressure until fuel was exhausted. Tanks also provided support needed by infantry formations as from three to seven usually accompanied an infantry

237

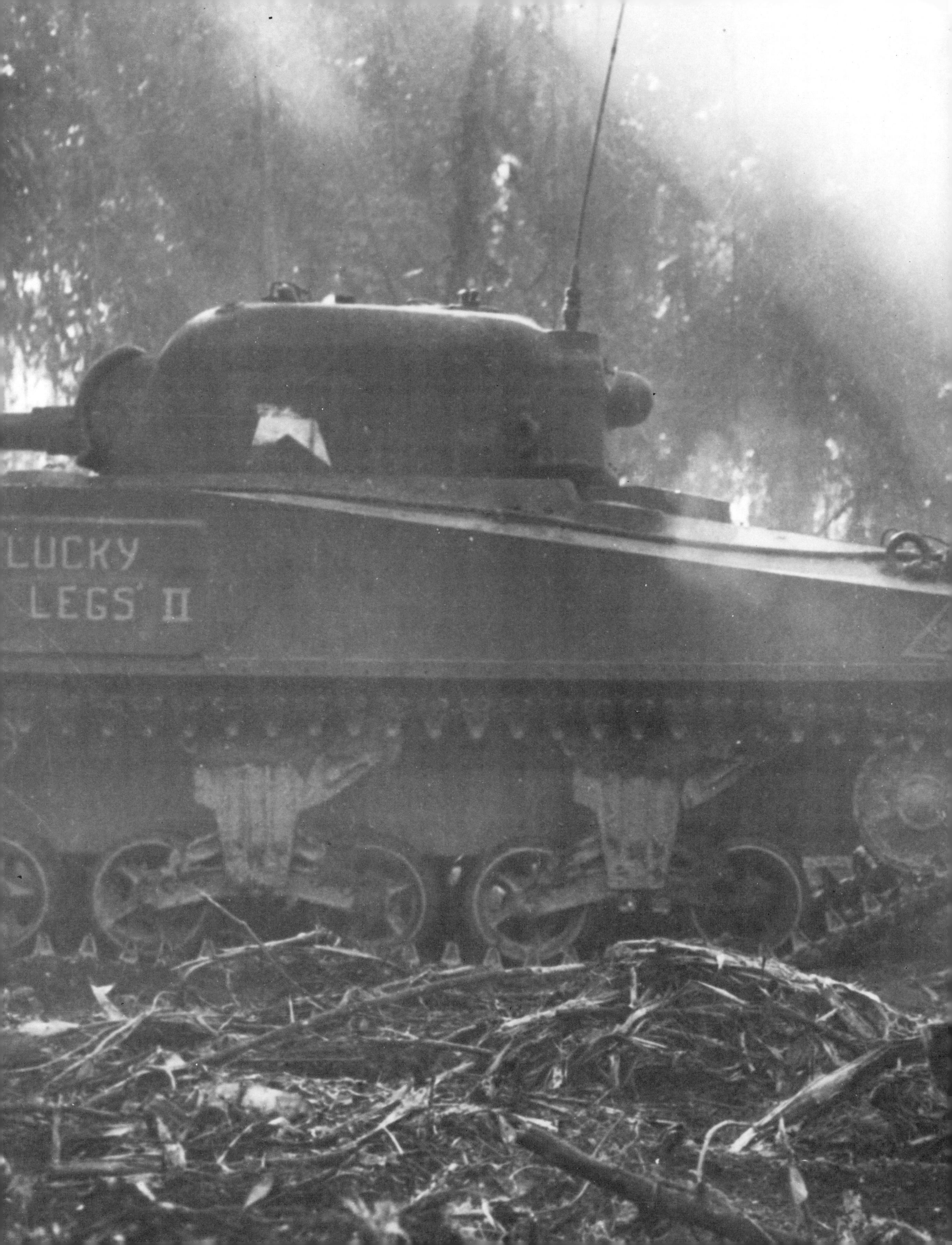
LUCKY
LEGS II

company on the attack. Anti-tank weapons were the job of the foot soldiers while the tanks attacked the main points of resistance. Depending on the circumstances, the tanks spearheaded the attack or advanced with the infantry in a skirmish line. General George Patton, an enthusiastic advocate of armored warfare, developed another tactic which he called the 'marching fire offensive' in which the attack consisted of a dense skirmish line with close tank, machine gun, and BAR support supplemented by all the supporting artillery fire that could be mustered. The density and high firepower of this tactic was a psychological and physical shock to the defenders while the attackers drew moral support from their own mass. Patton achieved good results with this approach but paid for them with higher casualties. The battle tactics of World War II thus avoided the slaughter of World War I while proving capable of achieving decisive results. The individual soldier could identify himself as a member of a team and gain some sense of personal accomplishment and significance through performance of his specific task.

Cut in the mold of Polk and Lincoln as a Commander in Chief, Roosevelt was undoubtedly the greatest American war President. Already 59 and confined to a wheelchair from polio, he was intimately involved in all aspects of strategy and administration and insisted that the basic command decisions be his. Victory as soon as possible was the sole focus of Roosevelt's wartime policies. He planned to use the wartime coalition not just to prosecute the war but for political purposes in organizing the postwar world but his insistence on unconditional surrender tended to keep foreign and strategic policy divorced.

American political and strategic policies never came to be related in a coherent pattern either before or during the war. The reason for this divorce lay not so much with Roosevelt but with the American military leadership which, in the apolitical military tradition of the United States, insisted that no direct connection existed between the military campaigns and positions and the subsequent political settlement. The notion that political as well as military factors must be

taken into account in the planning and execution of military operations was firmly resisted by the generals who wished to be left unfettered in their traditional job of beating the enemy into submission in the shortest and most direct fashion possible. Supporting Roosevelt at the cabinet level were Secretary of War Henry Stimson and Secretary of the Navy Frank Knox, both able Republicans who shared the President's single-minded fixation on victory above all else. General George Marshall had succeeded Malin Craig as Chief of Staff in 1939 to become one of America's finest military minds and military executives.

Because of its sheer size and global nature, the war for the Allies had to be one of organization, corporate leadership, and big planning and liaison staffs, sometimes likened to a large corporation. Roosevelt, Churchill, and Stalin were the joint chairmen of the board in this analogy, hearing recommendations from the numerous supporting committees and making the executive decisions. The resulting strategy was usually the result of compromise among the competing viewpoints and

Left:
Mopping up on Bougainville: the Japanese often held out in the jungles of the Solomon Islands for years.

concerns of the three major powers. The United States was at a particular disadvantage in this situation vis-à-vis Britain because the Americans had virtually no tradition of interservice planning and co-ordination, an area in which the British performed extremely well. Indeed, the initial Anglo-American strategic planning was dominated by Churchill's men from the early ABC staff conversations in 1941 until the Cairo and Teheran Conferences of 1943 largely on the basis of superior staff work. For the first time in its history, the United States was forced to adopt a high-level unified command to cope with coalition warfare. The American war effort was directed by the Joint Chiefs of Staff comprising Marshall of the Army, Arnold of the Air Force, and Admiral Ernest King of the Navy with Admiral William Leahy, Roosevelt's personal Chief of Staff, as chairman. The overall Anglo-American effort was controlled by the Combined Chiefs of Staff consisting of the respective American and British Joint Chiefs supported by a vast array of committees to supervise the various aspects of planning, operations and logistics. The division of responsibility left the Americans in charge of the Pacific Theater and China, the British the Middle and Far East except China, and the Combined Chiefs in direct control over the European-Atlantic area. Apart from participation in the strategy conferences between Roosevelt and Churchill, the Soviet Union and China largely fought their own wars with some material aid from the United States.

Certainly one of the most important aspects of the Anglo-American collaboration was the close partnership between Roosevelt and Churchill who found each other congenial and were in constant communication. Like Roosevelt, Churchill also insisted on directing strategy and policy. Strongly influenced by the British experience in World War I and Britain's situation as an island with limited manpower and resources, Churchill wanted to adopt a very different strategy from that of the American Joint Chiefs and Stimson who kept a close watch to ensure that Roosevelt was not swayed too far from primary American concerns by the persuasive Churchill. Although Britain and the United States agreed on the need to defeat Germany first, the best way to effect that end remained a constant source of contention for most of the war. Churchill as arbiter of the British position above all did not want major operations against Germany in Europe proper too soon to conserve British resources. He preferred to weaken the German will to resist through strategic bombing, blockade, subversion, and propaganda while probing the peripheries of German power with highly mobile strike forces, attacking Germany itself only when it had been sufficiently weakened. Such a war of attrition and opportunity was very much in accord with the British historical experience and suited his desire to influence the political outcome through military dispositions, especially in Eastern Europe where he hoped to curb the Soviets.

Churchill therefore did not want to face the full power of the German Army in grand combat too early in the war, preferring a Mediterranean strategy of clearing North Africa and Italy, historic concerns of British policy, and a thrust into what he was fond of calling the 'soft underbelly of Europe.' This would not only give the Allies a position in Southeast Europe to counter Stalin but vindicate his disastrous Dardanelles strategy of World War I. But his American ally insisted on a cross-channel invasion to confront Hitler in Northwest Europe and destroy the German Army as soon as possible. Firmly rooted in the tradition of Ulysses Grant and with Clausewitz as its bible, the American Army argued for a strategy of mass and concentration because the only way to defeat Germany was to destroy her armed forces in battle. Advocacy of this direct approach reflected many aspects of the American military tradition – confidence in American military prowess and skill, belief in the ability to field a large and well-trained citizen army quickly, optimism about American industrial capacities, dislike of long wars, and desire for quick and decisive results. Basic army doctrine held that a strategy of annihilation was the best choice if the resources were available to carry it to fruition. Americans believed that they possessed the requisite resources. Major (later Major General) Albert Wedemeyer, one of the chief planners in the War Plans Division, later said that 'We counted on our advanced weapons systems, technical prowess, and stupendous production capabilities to enable us to win the war. . . .' While a War Department study in the summer of 1941 stated 'We must prepare to fight Germany by actually coming to grips with and defeating her ground forces and definitely breaking her will to combat.'

Marshall and Stimson were absolutely committed to the strategy of annihilation while Stalin also pushed Churchill and Roosevelt on the matter to relieve German pressure on the Eastern Front. Churchill remained completely opposed while Roosevelt supported the idea out of concern for Russian survival. The question however was academic because the Allies simply lacked the resources in all areas to undertake such a major operation against the Fortress Europe which Hitler was creating. The Pacific War was claiming American resources, the United States was still a long way from full industrial and military mobilization, neither the British nor Americans possessed the necessary specialized equipment for such a huge amphibious operation, and the Battle of the Atlantic against the German submarines was still to be won. The improved U-Boat of World War II was a far more formidable threat than its World War I predecessor as it had greater speed and range, improved acoustic torpedoes, the schnorkel tube, and hunted in 'wolf packs' aided by aerial reconnaissance. Sinkings reached their peak in 1942 and then were gradually brought under control by the convoy system, aerial escort, asdic (sonar) detection, radar and hunter-killer squadrons of surface anti-submarine vessels. By August 1943 more submarines were being sunk than merchant ships, so it became possible for the first time to transport large American forces to Europe and maintain them there.

Marshall from the outset argued for the earliest possible cross-channel attack and was supported by the chief planner for that operation in the War Plans Division, General Dwight Eisenhower, who was soon detailed to London to take charge of the American side of the proposed operation. When it became apparent even to Marshall that no such operation was possible in 1942, he bowed to Roosevelt's 'immediate objective of the United States ground forces fighting against Germans in 1942' and agreed to a plan for the invasion of French North Africa as preferable to the other peripheral objectives proposed by the British. The plan finally emerged as a pincer movement – an Anglo-American force under Eisenhower from the west and the British Eighth Army of General Bernard Montgomery from Egypt where it had been engaging the Afrika Korps of General Erwin Rommel in a fiercely fought campaign – to expel the Axis from North Africa. On 8 November 1942 Eisenhower's forces landed at Oran, Casablanca and Algiers with minimal opposition from the French, the majority of whom soon joined the allied side. After ten days of hard fighting at El Alamein, one of the epic land battles of the war, Montgomery finally broke through the Axis line and forced Rommel into a fighting retreat westward. But in the meantime, Hitler moved troops into Tunisia where they quickly and efficiently established a line in the mountains west of the Tunisian plains. Rommel took up a new position in the east known as the Mareth Line to block Montgomery and then took part of his force westward where, combined with the 100,000 Germans in Tunisia, he nearly succeeded in destroying Eisenhower's positions. This first major test of Allied operations revealed more than a few problems. The training and experience of the troops was clearly inferior to that of the Germans, while the French refused to take orders from the British and even Anglo-American co-operation was not that good. Yet Eisenhower and Montgomery persevered and finally succeeded in driving the Axis from Tunisia in May 1943, capturing 240,000 Germans and Italians and mountains of equipment.

The victory in North Africa simply reopened the debate over strategy. The next stage in the European war was decided at the Casablanca Conference in January 1943 where 'unconditional surrender' was publicly stated as the Allied war aim. Sicily became the next objective over American protests but the fact that shipping losses in the Atlantic in 1942 had been nearly six million tons left Marshall little choice. That plus a severe shortage of landing craft made the choice between Sicily and no action until 1944 an option which neither Roosevelt nor Churchill could accept politically. Such an operation might also take shaky Italy out of the war. The rapid conquest of Sicily in the summer of 1943 so undermined the Fascist government of Mussolini that he fell from power on 25 July and even Marshall agreed that much of Italy could be taken quickly and cheaply. But by the time landings were made at Salerno on 9 September, the new Italian government of Marshal Pietro Badoglio had already surrendered and the Germans had occupied the country. The landing at Salerno was almost thrown back by the German defenders and the Allies had a long and painful ascent of the Italian boot ahead, reaching Rome only in June of the following year. The Allies had a superiority of two to one in manpower but they would not take advantage of this or of their new superiority in armor and trucks for mobility because of the terrain. That theater gradually began to be stripped of its equipment as preparations for the cross-channel attack increased. The German commander Albert von Kesselring dug into a new defensive position, the formidable Gothic Line, just to the north of Pisa, Florence, and Ravenna. From this position, he stalemated the American Fifth Army of General Mark Clark and the British Eighth Army of General Harold Alexander until April 1945. As a result, the Soviets marched into Vienna rather than the British and Americans. The Allies had made an expensive investment in pursuit of Churchill's dream in Eastern Europe and gained little in return.

At the Teheran Conference in November 1943 Roosevelt and Stalin turned aside more Churchillian schemes for operations in the Eastern Mediterranean and Balkans. The Soviet leader desperately wanted the Allies to engage Hitler in Northern Europe to relieve pressure on his beleaguered country. The tenets of Soviet strategy were also similar to the American in that each stressed a war of mass and concentration against the enemy's main forces. Lacking the mass armies of his Allies, Churchill preferred smaller more controlled operations in which British forces could play central roles as they had in North Africa and Italy. But he was now forced to bow to the inevitable when Stalin added his voice to that of Roosevelt. The operation against Europe was codenamed Overlord with a target date of 1 May 1944 and Eisenhower as its supreme commander. Another operation named Anvil was simultaneously to use American and re-armed French troops in an invasion of southern

France to protect the southern flank of Overlord once it broke out of its projected beachheads in Normandy and later link up with the advance against the Rhine from the south. But a shortage of landing craft and the Churchill-inspired disaster at Anzio in Italy caused Anvil to be delayed until 15 August 1944 when it took place under the name of Dragoon, allegedly because Churchill had been 'dragooned' into it.

Since Overlord was delayed for two years, the United States found another way to attack Germany directly. The Air Force was allowed to test its theory of strategic bombing through use of the B-17. Air Force planners had in fact drawn up a plan for strategic bombardment in the summer of 1941. They believed the plan would defeat Germany without need for an invasion by destroying its 'vital centers' in the best tradition of Douhet who had argued that unescorted bombers would always get through to their targets. In a brief flirtation with daylight bombing, the RAF had already discovered that the two-engined Wellington bombers were highly vulnerable to interceptors and thus shifted to night-time bombing with

four-engined Lancasters, Halifaxes, and Stirlings. Flying large and even mammoth raids of up to a thousand planes, the RAF saturated its targets with two- and four-thousand pound bombs with accuracy so poor that the British had to admit their target was civilian morale rather than specific military and industrial targets.

The American approach was the daylight precision bombing of carefully selected economic targets with the emphasis on oil, transportation, and electric power facilities. The evidence accruing from China, the Spanish Civil War, the Battle of Britain, and the RAF bombing of German cities already indicated that civilian morale was not nearly as fragile as the interwar theorists had supposed. The Air Force had had since 1933 the Norden bombsight for precision bombing and planned to use massed formations of bombers at high altitude with sufficient armor and armament for intensive raids on Germany from as many points as possible. The purpose was, in the words of Arnold, to knock out 'the most vital parts of Germany's war machine, such as the power plants and machine shops of particular factories . . .'

Left:
Generals Patton and Eisenhower discuss the campaign in Tunisia, 16 March 1943.

Far left:
Soldiers of the 2nd Battalion, 16 Infantry march through Kasserine Pass en route to Kasserine and Feriana. By 26 February 1943 advance units had cleared the way and the US II Corps could resume its advance in Tunisia. In early May British and American troops overran Tunis and the Afrika Korps' resistance had come to an end.

Below:
A Ranger Battalion marches rapidly over the hilly terrain during a maneuvering operation in Tunisia, January 1943.

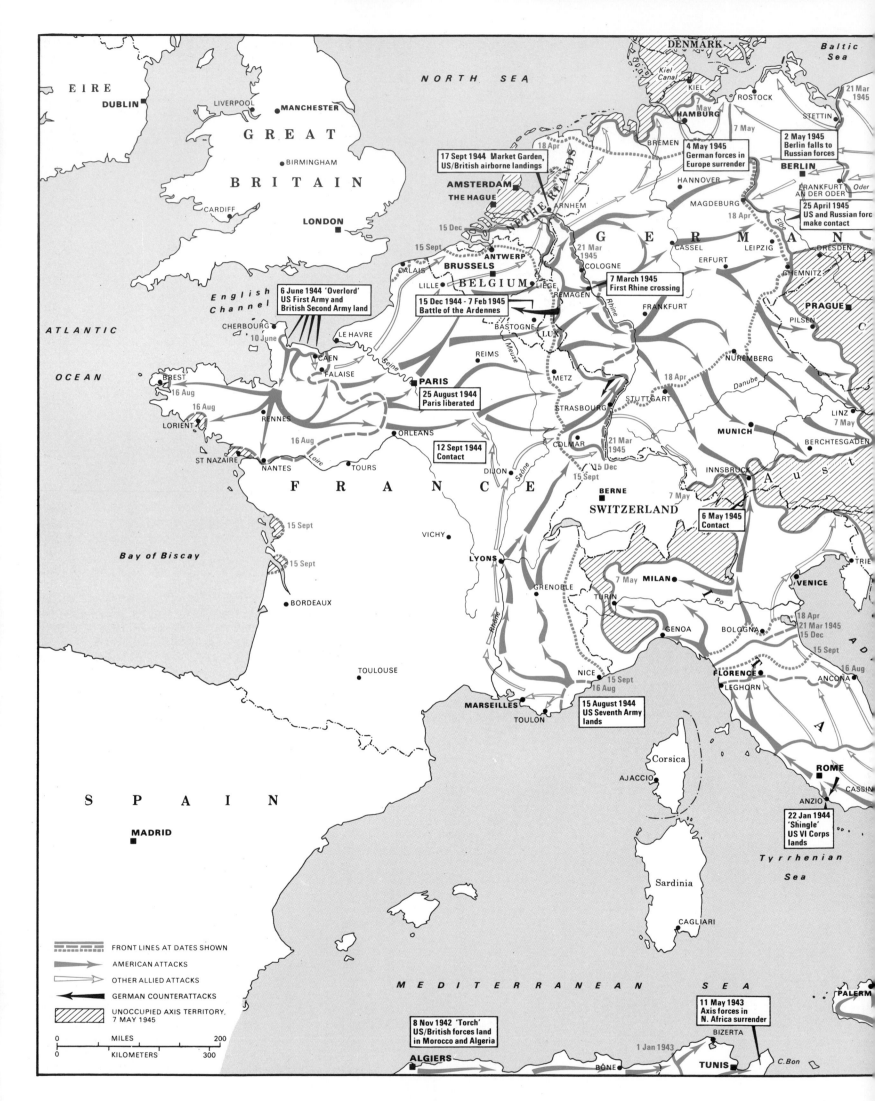

EIRE

DUBLIN

GREAT BRITAIN

LIVERPOOL
MANCHESTER
BIRMINGHAM
CARDIFF
LONDON

NORTH SEA

DENMARK
Baltic Sea

KIEL
Kiel Canal
HAMBURG
BREMEN
HANNOVER
ROSTOCK
STETTIN

21 Mar 1945

7 May

4 May 1945
German forces in
Europe surrender

2 May 1945
Berlin falls to
Russian forces

BERLIN

FRANKFURT
AN DER ODER *Oder*

25 April 1945
US and Russian forc
make contact

18 Apr

17 Sept 1944 Market Garden,
US/British airborne landings

AMSTERDAM
THE HAGUE
ARNHEM

NETHERLANDS

MAGDEBURG
CASSEL
ERFURT
LEIPZIG
DRESDEN
CHEMNITZ

18 Apr

G E R M A N

PRAGUE

15 Sept

BRUSSELS
BELGIUM
CALAIS
LILLE
ANTWERP
LIEGE
REMAGEN

21 Mar
1945
COLOGNE

7 March 1945
First Rhine crossing

FRANKFURT

Rhine

NUREMBERG

PILSEN

LINZ
7 May

6 June 1944 'Overlord'
US First Army and
British Second Army land

English Channel

CHERBOURG
10 June
LE HAVRE
CAEN
FALAISE

15 Dec 1944 - 7 Feb 1945
Battle of the Ardennes

BASTOGNE
LUX

Meuse

METZ

STRASBOURG

18 Apr

STUTTGART

Danube

MUNICH

BERCHTESGADEN

ATLANTIC OCEAN

BREST
16 Aug
16 Aug
LORIENT
ST NAZAIRE

Seine
RENNES

PARIS

25 August 1944
Paris liberated

12 Sept 1944
Contact

16 Aug

ORLEANS

NANTES
TOURS
Loire

DIJON
Saône

BERNE

SWITZERLAND

COLMAR

21 Mar
1945
15 Dec
15 Sept

INNSBRUCK

Au

6 May 1945
Contact

7 May

15 Sept
15 Sept

Bay of Biscay

VICHY

LYONS

Rhône

GRENOBLE

7 May

MILAN

TURIN

VENICE

TRIE

BORDEAUX

GENOA
BOLOGNA

18 Apr
21 Mar 1945
15 Dec
15 Sept

Po

S P A I N

MADRID

TOULOUSE

MARSEILLES
TOULON

NICE

15 Sept
16 Aug

15 August 1944
US Seventh Army
lands

FLORENCE
LEGHORN

16 Aug

ANCONA

Corsica

AJACCIO

ROME

CASSIN

ANZIO

22 Jan 1944
'Shingle'
US VI Corps
lands

Tyrrhenian Sea

Sardinia

CAGLIARI

FRONT LINES AT DATES SHOWN

AMERICAN ATTACKS

OTHER ALLIED ATTACKS

GERMAN COUNTERATTACKS

UNOCCUPIED AXIS TERRITORY,
7 MAY 1945

0   MILES   200

0   KILOMETERS   300

M E D I T E R R A N E A N   S E A

8 Nov 1942 'Torch'
US/British forces land
in Morocco and Algeria

ALGIERS

BÔNE

1 Jan 1943

11 May 1943
Axis forces in
N. Africa surrender

BIZERTA

TUNIS

C. Bon

PALERM

244

Above:
A motorcycle dispatch rider takes a few precious moments of sleep during the defensive action fought by MacArthur's army in Bataan, January–April 1942.

which would defeat Germany within six months and obviate the necessity of assaulting Fortress Europe. The first B-17 raid, a modest affair of only twelve planes, occurred on 17 August against Rouen. Germany itself was struck by the first major American raid on 27 January 1943 when 91 planes, 53 of which reached the target, attacked the submarine yards at Wilhelmshaven. Increasingly heavy swarms of German interceptors soon greeted each daylight raid and losses passed the tolerable point in terms of planes and crews. The emphasis then shifted to bombing the German aircraft industry which responded by being dispersed and continued to increase production of interceptors. Night interceptors were now raising British losses as well.

Allied commanders believed that control of the air was an absolute requisite for the success of Overlord and Anvil; consequently the order went out on 27 December 1943 – 'Destroy the Enemy Air Force wherever you find them, in the air, on the ground and in the factories.' The instrument which made possible the realization of this order had only arrived in Europe that very month. The North American P-51 Mustang was a long-range fighter which was superior to any German counterpart except the few jets then flown by the Germans. Large numbers of P-51s were in action by March 1944, the same month that escorted raids began against Berlin. The battle of the air was decided not by German losses of planes – fighter production

continued to increase despite the bombing campaign – but because the P-51s downed too many irreplaceable pilots. Later air attacks on German petroleum production left too little gasoline for the adequate functioning of the Luftwaffe. German armies essentially had to fight without air cover during the Allied invasion. Thus the more standard strategy of confronting and destroying the enemy in battle succeeded while the new theories of strategic air power, ignoring the fighter as a factor, were demonstrably failing. With hindsight, it is clear that the essential elements of industry attacked were far more resistant to damage and the accuracies of delivery under combat conditions were far less than the theoretical calculations of prewar planners using data from training exercises. World War II therefore did not render a clearcut answer to the question of whether air power alone can defeat an enemy.

D-Day came to be 6 June rather than 1 May to give Allied air power the chance to isolate the landing beaches from the interior by completely wrecking the transportation network of northern France. The beaches of Normandy were the scene of the largest and most ambitious amphibious operation in history. The beach-heads were quickly established against the German defenses, incomplete except for Omaha Beach in the American sector, but then the Germans hemmed in the Allies for seven weeks. It was only after General Montgomery's British troops had sufficiently weakened the concentration of

German armor confronting the beach-heads that the First Army of General Omar Bradley broke out and turned the war toward highly mobile operations. Hitler ordered that no ground was to be yielded, and as a result Field Marshal Günther von Kluge threw away what chance remained to the Germans to halt the Allies in France in futile counter-attacks. As a result, the German forces were nearly encircled and destroyed by the Third Army of General Patton moving toward a junction with Montgomery through a sweep to the Loire and then east toward Paris. Postponed to 15 August, Dragoon resulted in a hasty collapse of the German position in Southern France while Hitler's men in the north fell back all along the line. The rapid Allied drives across France had been possible because the bulk of German ground forces were still locked in heavy combat with the Soviets while the forces in France received virtually no air cover or support. Allied air and tank superiority, coupled with Hitler's inappropriate dicta on defensive strategy, overcame the German superiority in manpower. The German Army however could tie up the Allies in static warfare in the west.

Left:
Just before D-Day General Eisenhower visited E Company, 502nd Parachute Brigade as they were about to board their aircraft.

Far left:
Landing Ships carrying the US V Corps head for the beach codenamed Omaha, 6 June 1944.

Far left below:
The landings in Normandy were facilitated by the use of special 'gooseberries' (known to the English as 'mulberries'). These were artificial harbors with an outer breakwater composed of partly sunken blockships and partly concrete 'caissons.' After the first week of the invasion 6500 vehicles and nearly 40,000 tons of stores had been landed.

Below:
US troops landing on Utah beach.

Below:
US troops were welcomed enthusiastically by Parisians who had suffered German occupation for four years.

Only when the Allies had entered Holland, Belgium, and parts of Germany itself in September did German resistance again coalesce along the Rhine and force a return to static warfare. Here the Allies had another strategic debate as Montgomery requested that all the gasoline and supplies available be directed to his 21st Army Group for a thrust across the northern European plain to Berlin. Supply was, however, extremely tight as only a few ports were then operational and the Allies had outrun their lines of communication. Apart from the supply problem, Eisenhower saw problems with this strategy and opted for a general, less spectacular push all along the front after supply had eased. Montgomery did receive as much extra supply as possible but failed to sustain a foothold across the Rhine in September in the famous Market Garden Operation. While the Allies paused because of logistic shortages, Hitler tried a last desperate gamble by sending his best remaining armored strength against a thinly defended portion of the Allied lines in the Ardennes, a sector where he could muster a three to one superiority. The Germans penetrated over 50 miles under cover of bad weather which grounded aerial reconnaissance and support but then the American First and Third Armies to the north and south respectively cut into the flanks of the bulge created by the German drive. In what came to be known as the 'Battle of the Bulge,' Hitler simply wasted men and armor which he could not afford to lose.

Although the German Army fought on doggedly, it was already exhausted when the final Allied drive into Germany began in February 1945. By this time a Russian army was crossing the Oder to threaten Berlin while another was advancing on Vienna through Hungary. Adolf Hitler, the primary architect of the war in Europe, died in his beleaguered command bunker in Berlin, supposedly by his own hand, toward the end of April. On the 12th of that month, President Franklin Roosevelt also died, to be succeeded by Vice-President Harry Truman, a little-known politician from Missouri. The smoldering remains of Germany were surrendered by Hitler's successor, Admiral Karl Doenitz, on 7 May. The close of the war in Europe also brought to an end the Anglo-American debate over strategy which the Americans had dominated since Overlord as threequarters of the military strength in Europe was theirs.

The consistent American objective had been to get into Northern France and come to grips with the German Army while the Air Force attacked the war-making capacity of the enemy. This strategy of annihilation through mass and concentration ultimately led to victory in Western Europe. In the Pacific as well, the United States followed a similar strategy in a maritime situation. Since the war was fought against an island empire protected by the immense spaces of the ocean, the object of strategy was not the Japanese Army but the Japanese Fleet. In its

Left:
Operation Market Garden: American paratroopers run
through a field under heavy fire from German 88-mm
guns. The Allies planned an ambitious airborne
operation to secure a bridgehead over the Rhine in
September 1944. The American 101st and 82nd
Airborne Divisions were to capture the bridges at
Eindhoven and Nijmegen. The American landings were
successful but the British ran into trouble and did not
secure the bridge at Arnhem.

Below left:
Although Allied troops liberated Paris from 19–25
August 1944, small groups of snipers held out. Parisians
celebrating the Allied entry into Paris in the Place de la
Concorde come under fire.

Bottom left:
Infantrymen of I Company, 331st Infantry Regiment
carefully advance through the streets of St. Malo,
August 1944.

Below:
US men and equipment pour over the bridge over the
Rhine at Remagen on 11 March 1945.

practical applications, this meant repeatedly
challenging the enemy to battle through bold
attacks on his bases in the hope of drawing
his fleet into a major confrontation. In pursuit of this strategy, almost a textbook application of Alfred Thayer Mahan within the
context of the historic American preference
for strategies of annihilation, the United
States did not have to contend with the conflicts inherent in the coalition war of the
European Theater. The war in the Pacific
was almost completely an American war with
an important supporting role played by Australia. This did not mean, however, that the
Pacific was free of strategic controversies as
the Army and Navy had strongly differing
views on how best to defeat Japan.

The attack on Pearl Harbor altered the
Europe First Strategy, first agreed in the
summer of 1941 and reaffirmed in early 1942.
The tide of the Japanese opening offensive
was so great – from Burma almost to Australia – that even Churchill agreed that Japan

could not be left to consolidate its conquests
nor could Europe have priority until the Indian, Australian, and trans-Pacific lines of
communication were secure. For over a year,
equipment originally intended for Europe
was diverted to the Pacific where such Allied
forces as there were could not remain idle
once the Japanese offensive wound down in
the spring of 1942. Another problem was the
lack of an American doctrine for fighting a
limited war. Although the Navy had lost its
Pacific battleship strength at Pearl Harbor, it
still had four carriers and supporting ships
and was ready for offensive operations. A
decision was also made to support China
materially in its war with Japan, already five
years old. Thus the war in the Pacific would
not stay limited in the face of these factors.
Reviving the old War Plan Orange, the Navy
pressed hard for resources for what it considered to be 'its war.'

The Army found it difficult to resist the
Navy's demands for the Pacific because one
of its most prestigious generals, Douglas
MacArthur, was totally committed to vigorous prosecution of the war against Japan. A
former Chief of Staff, MacArthur had been
in command of the Philippines when those
islands fell to the Japanese onslaught. He
believed that the Western colonial powers,
having been so disastrously defeated by
Asians, must prove their superiority militarily, a factor he felt a folly not to take into
consideration when planning strategy for the
defeat of Japan. The only road to Tokyo
which took account of American political
interests lay through the Philippines in
his view; he was an exception to the
apolitical nature of the American military
leadership. The naval commander in the
Pacific, Admiral Chester Nimitz, and the
naval Chief of Staff, Admiral Ernest King,
did not want large naval forces under Army
command and proceeded to implement War
Plan Orange strategy for a drive across the
Central Pacific. Thus MacArthur's Southwest Pacific Command and Nimitz's Central
Pacific Command were autonomous in violation of the principle of unity of theater command. Roosevelt approved this arrangement
partly because of MacArthur's prestige and
domestic political support and partly because he hoped the natural rivalry between
Army and Navy would produce faster results. King and MacArthur were successful
in diverting increasing amounts of resources
to the Pacific with the argument that it was
vital not to allow Japan to regain the initiative
or dig in. So successful were they that the 26
available army divisions were split evenly
between Europe and the Pacific as late as
September 1943. Europe never got clear
priority until Overlord was near its target
date.

The overall strategy in the Pacific required
sustained pressure on the enemy to prevent
him from digging in so deeply that it would
require huge resources and some years to
blast him out. Committed to total victory
through unconditional surrender, Roosevelt
feared that a long and indecisive war would

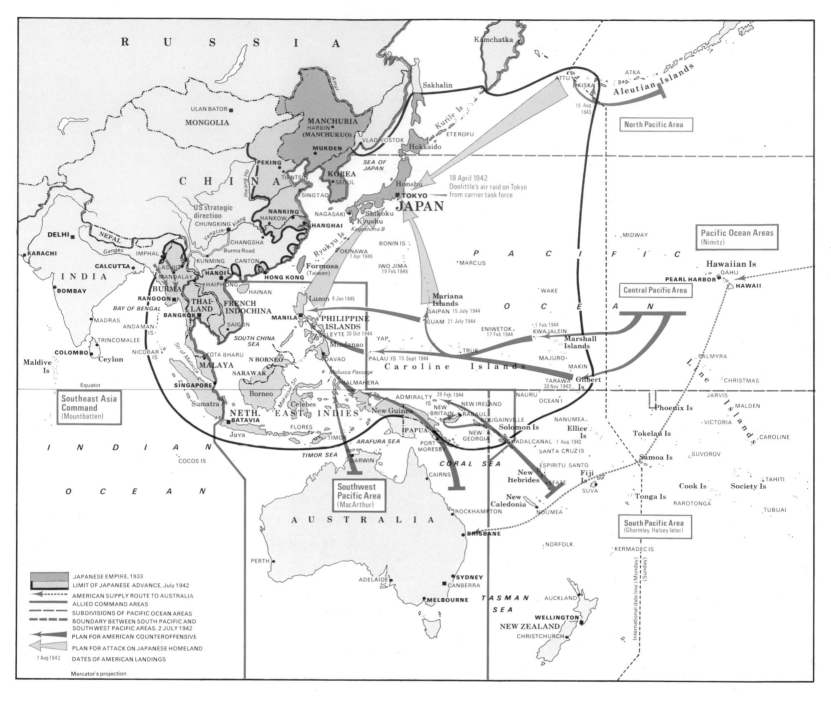

Map legend:

JAPANESE EMPIRE, 1933
LIMIT OF JAPANESE ADVANCE, July 1942
AMERICAN SUPPLY ROUTE TO AUSTRALIA
ALLIED COMMAND AREAS
SUBDIVISIONS OF PACIFIC OCEAN AREAS
BOUNDARY BETWEEN SOUTH PACIFIC AND
SOUTHWEST PACIFIC AREAS, 2 JULY 1942
PLAN FOR AMERICAN COUNTEROFFENSIVE
PLAN FOR ATTACK ON JAPANESE HOMELAND
7 Aug 1942   DATES OF AMERICAN LANDINGS

Mercator's projection

make this traditional American war aim impossible to attain because public opinion would turn against the war. At first he entertained high hopes that China would prove to be a valuable ally in the vigorous prosecution of the war but internal factors prevented the government of Chiang Kai-shek from much more than passive resistance. China's real contribution to the war was to tie down over a million Japanese troops until 1945.

So the main strategy came to be the MacArthur campaign north from Australia through New Guinea to the Philippines and the Nimitz push west from Hawaii through the Gilbert, Marshall, Caroline, and Mariana Island groups with the intent that the two would converge either on Luzon or Formosa. MacArthur had cleared New Guinea and some of the adjacent islands with a series of flanking attacks by July 1944. His tactics were, as he described them, 'to avoid the frontal attack with its terrible loss of life, to by-pass Japanese strongpoints and neutral-ize them by cutting their lines of supply; to thus isolate their armies and starve them on the battlefield; as Willie Keeler used to say, to "hit 'em where they ain't."' These tactics were dictated partly by personal inclination and partly by the lack of resources to do anything else.

The Central Pacific campaign began in November 1943 with the assaults on Tarawa and Makin Islands in the Gilberts and progressed atoll by atoll to Saipan in the Marianas by June 1944. Off the Marianas occurred the third great naval battle of the Pacific war – the Battle of the Philippine Sea in which the Japanese lost heavily in planes and pilots. Nimitz's forces had fought and held off the Japanese in the Coral Sea in May 1942 and then inflicted a crushing defeat on a major Japanese naval thrust eastward toward Hawaii at Midway the following month. The Navy was now organized into task forces and fleets which could remain at sea indefinitely because seaborne logistics bases consisting of oilers, supply and ammunition ships, repair ships and even floating drydocks sailed along with the fleets. Improved radar enabled the combat formations to operate at high speed day or night while the new fast *Essex* class carriers and the lighter *Independence* class auxiliary carriers (sometimes called 'jeep' or 'Woolworth' carriers) gave Nimitz a formidable weapon with which to strike sudden blows against enemy bases.

Nimitz repeatedly challenged the Japanese Fleet after Saipan but, desperately short of fuel and airplane pilots, the Japanese admirals did not offer battle again until the combined forces of MacArthur and Nimitz landed on Leyte Island in the Philippines on 20 October 1944. In the climactic Battle of Leyte Gulf which took place on 22–26 October, the Japanese High Command gambled all in a last desperate bid to inflict a major defeat on the Americans and thus stall their drive toward Japan. The greatest naval battle in history shattered the Japanese Imperial Navy and it ceased to exist as a fighting force, capable of affecting the outcome of the war.

Above:
Admiral Chester Nimitz, Commander in Chief
of the Pacific Fleet during World War II.

Right:
The United States flag is lowered on Corregidor after
the island fell to the Japanese on 6 May 1942. US troops
under General Jonathan Wainwright had held out for a
month under intense bombardment from Bataan.

Below:
Four wounded American soldiers have to walk from the
front to reach a hospital on 22 November 1942.

Even before the disaster of Leyte Gulf, Japan was in dire straits. American submarines and airplanes had been exacting an increasing toll on the shipping on which her survival depended. By late 1944 most of her merchant shipping capacity had been destroyed and she lacked the industrial capacity to replace much of it. The home islands also came under concentrated strategic attack. The Japanese population was more concentrated in urban areas than that of Germany while her industries were smaller scale and mixed in with residential areas. Japan was thus more vulnerable to the bombing raids directed at her from Saipan some 1500 miles away by B-24 Liberators and the new B-29 Super Fortresses. The XXI Bomber Command of General Curtis LeMay at first tried high-altitude precision attacks against industry with disappointing results, so the raids were switched to low-level incendiary attacks. These were so successful that they were directed at urban areas to break Japanese morale. The most destructive air attack

253

in history occurred on 9 March 1945 when 334 B-29s dropped 2000 tons of incendiaries on Tokyo, killing 83,000, wounding 41,000, and leaving one million homeless. In the hope of forcing a Japanese surrender without an invasion of the home islands, eight and a half million Japanese were made refugees in a bombing offensive far heavier than that inflicted on Germany.

A strong debate within the American High Command had been taking place over the best means to bring Japan to unconditional surrender. The army was firm in its Clausewitzian belief that invasion was necessary to destroy the Japanese armed forces for victory while the Navy believed Japan could be starved into submission through blockade and bombardment alone. The Air Force remained true to its doctrine of strategic bombing as a war-winning strategy of itself. A weapon on which the United States had spent two billion dollars from fear that Germany would develop it first made the debate academic. In a logical extension of the strategic bombing offensive, President Truman ordered the atomic bomb dropped on Hiroshima on 6 August, killing between 70 and 80,000 people, and a second delivered to Nagasaki at a cost of 35,000 dead. Although it has since been argued strongly that the use of the atomic bomb was unnecessary because Japan was already beaten, Truman and his advisers acted in the

belief that the bombs would shorten the war by making an invasion of the Japanese home islands unnecessary. Intelligence reports of the time show clearly that the Japanese not only had the resources but the determination to resist to the bitter end. Only the personal intervention of the Emperor pushed the government into suing for peace while the surrender on 14 August was threatened virtually to the last moment by the specter of revolt by the Japanese military.

Left:
Supported by tanks, American infantry move forward on Kwajalein, part of the Marshall Islands, 31 January 1944.

Top:
Three Marines blow up a Japanese dug-out during the bitter fighting on Saipan in June 1944. The Japanese had a 32,000-strong garrison on the island who had orders to fight until death. Of the garrison only 1000 survived. US casualties were also high: 10,347 Marines and 3647 soldiers.

Above:
Covered by tanks of the 7th Division and machine gunners infantry men move from the beaches on Kwajalein atoll, February 1944.

Left:
The commanding officers and visiting dignitaries inspect the battlefield at Namur, left to right: Admiral Raymond Spruance; unknown; James Forrestal, Secretary of the Navy; Major General Schmidt; Major General Holland Smith; Admiral Connolly; Colonel Evans Carlson; Admiral Pownall.

Right:
Members of the 1st Marine Division participate in the last amphibious operation in the Pacific on Okinawa.

Below right:
Accurate shelling by naval forces hit a Japanese gas and oil dump on Leyte Island, October 1944.

Below left:
American paratroops of the 503rd Parachute Brigade drop onto Noemfoor island, part of the Marshalls in July 1944.

Winston Churchill called it 'an achievement which the soldiers of every other country will always study with admiration and envy.' And indeed it was. The American armed forces had fought the war in accord with the best in their military tradition – the armed citizenry, technological know-how, managerial skills, and a bold strategy of attack through mass and concentration. In less than four years, the United States had emerged as the world's premier power economically, politically and militarily. The military had had to cope with all kinds of new problems and approaches to warfare and national defense, including submarines, amphibious operations, fast carriers, armored task forces, and long-range bombing. The Navy had developed its strategy, tactics, and techniques for these new situations to a high level. Never producing a strategic doctrine on a par with that of the Navy, the Army took the lessons of theater warfare which its leaders Marshall, Eisenhower, MacArthur, Bradley, and others had learned in France in World War I and applied them on a global basis. The Air Force came to balance its doctrine of strategic bombing with a greater appreciation of tactical and ground-support operations.

The strategic concepts with which the United States entered the war stemmed from American experience and European theories but the American military leaders emphasized those which were congruent with their own military tradition. Since war, as Maurice Matloff observes, had always been 'an aberration from normality' for Americans and thus to be ended in the most expeditious manner possible, the United States always argued for the most rapid, direct, and total approaches in strategy. The more American power came to determine the war in Europe, the more Americans came to direct the course of Allied strategy. Its newly-emergent military power enabled the United States to assert its strategic independence from Europe.

Grand strategy, the relation of warfare to politics and diplomacy, was the least successful aspect of the American war effort. Here again the American military tradition came to the fore. Historically the military have been relatively apolitical and considered their mission to obtain the objectives set by the political leadership. Even today, the civilian sector of the community does the primary thinking about grand strategy for the United States. The most successful aspect of the American war effort was solving the production, organizational, and managerial problems of such a huge war of material on a global scale. Americans were also the most successful in relating the revolution in military technology and tactics arising out of World War I to the war of mass and mobility that World War II came to be.

World War II was undoubtedly the greatest military challenge and trial yet faced by Americans, a challenge from which they emerged as the superpower of the world. During and after the war, Americans firmly believed in the 'special virtue' of their nation and their experiment. The final and crushing defeat of the enemy reinforced yet again this historic belief in divine favor and, in contrast to World War I, gave people renewed faith in warfare as an agent of progress in human affairs, a faith Americans had not really had since the Civil War brought about the rebirth of their foundering experiment. It was easy for Americans to contrast their strength and good fortune with the squalor and rubble of Asia and Europe. Once again, the United States had made a selfless and unimperialistic foray into a troubled world to set it aright. The immense military and economic strength of the nation was a reflection of its national virtue and made it unnecessary to bow to the wishes of any other power. American principles of democracy were now being extended to the defeated nations of Germany, Italy, and Japan and to the international order in general through the new United Nations for a future to be dominated by an 'era of goodwill' so that, as Secretary of State Cordell Hull said, 'There will no longer be need for spheres of influence, for alliances, balance of power, or any other of the special arrangements through which, in its unhappy past, the nations strove to safeguard their security or promote their interests.'

Americans had fought for two goals in the war. They had wanted victory and they had wanted security. Security meant freedom from the threat of war and thus from the foreign situations that bred war. The United Nations as an embryonic world government offered one hope while military invulnerability seemed to offer another. Security also meant jobs and material comfort. Even during the prosperity engendered by

the war, Americans had worried about a resumption of the depression, which they did not understand, in the postwar period. The public mood was dominated by this fear in 1944–45 as both soldiers and civilians hoped for a better postwar life on one hand and feared unemployment on the other. In the event, victory was coupled with continued prosperity, so the fears of depression proved to be unfounded. But the security from war and foreign threat which Americans so desired proved to be elusive. Indeed, Americans after 1945 came to live in an increasingly perilous and complex world.

The source of American insecurity was the emergence of the Soviet Union as the second-ranking power in the world, a situation foreseen as early as the 1830s by the Frenchman Alexis de Tocqueville who wrote, 'There are, at the present time, two great nations in the world. . . . I allude to the Russians and the Americans . . . each of them seems to be marked out by the will of Heaven to sway the destinies of half the globe.' Because of its distaste for Communism, the United States had been reluctant to take on the Soviet Union as an ally but accepted the situation because of Roosevelt's and Churchill's fixation with employing every possible means to defeat Germany. Without the Soviet Union to tie up much of the German ground and air strength, the Allies would have found themselves in a far more difficult situation and could not have defeated Hitler in continental Europe. The cornerstone of Allied policy toward the Soviet Union was the fear of a separate peace between Hitler and Stalin.

There were indeed many problems in the wartime alliance with Stalin. The Soviet leader early on spelled out his territorial desires in Eastern Europe which were offensive but not necessarily unacceptable to Britain and the United States. Stalin was convinced that his allies were delaying the second front so that Germany and the Soviet Union would exhaust each other. The United States and Britain would then be left to dictate the peace with both Germany and the Soviet Union destroyed. While Churchill was far less sanguine, Roosevelt firmly believed that Soviet suspicions and hostility could be overcome to bring about postwar cooperation between the 'Big Three.' This illusion was quickly shattered by Soviet expansion in Eastern Europe and Communist pressure in Greece, Turkey, and Iran. Churchill in fact coined the term 'iron curtain' to describe the postwar Soviet hegemony over East Europe in a speech in early 1946. The wartime alliance had quickly been transformed into strong hostility and the perception of threat on both sides led to a state of high tension. What soon came to be known as the 'cold war' thus had some of its roots deep in the wartime relationship between the Allies and the Soviet Union and has dominated American foreign and military policy ever since. Thus Americans failed to realize one of their two wartime dreams and came to live in a world of permanent military threat.

Chapter 9   Korea—The First Limited War

The 24th of June 1950 was a beautiful Saturday and President Harry Truman was enjoying a family reunion in Independence, Missouri. He had just finished dinner that evening when summoned to the telephone. Secretary of State Dean Acheson was on the line with word of troubling developments in Korea. Cables were coming in from Seoul that the North Koreans were moving across the boundary of the 38th parallel. Whether this was an invasion or merely another raid in force was not clear. The President considered and then rejected the thought of returning to Washington immediately and instead ordered Acheson to alert the United Nations, then located at Lake Success in Long Island. The United Nations had been trying for several years to arrange elections for a unified Korean government and claimed legal authority over all of that country. 'My God, this is war against the United Nations,' exclaimed Secretary General Trygve Lie on hearing of the news. At the Security Council meeting he called for the next afternoon, a resolution was adopted demanding an immediate cease-fire and withdrawal by the North Koreans. Two days later, a second resolution was adopted urging full-scale UN military support to beleaguered South Korea which by then was clearly the victim of an all-out invasion. These momentous resolutions were adopted in the absence of the Soviet delegate Jacob Malik who had been boycotting the Security Council for five months in protest against its refusal to give the seat of Nationalist China to Red China.

The United Nations found that the Korean situation was the first time its resolutions had to be backed up with action. If it could do nothing but pass these resolutions, it was doomed to the same ignominious fate as its predecessor, the League of Nations. And the key lay in the response of the United States which alone had sufficient power to determine the issue. After two days of secret intensive discussions with his Cabinet, Truman announced that the United States would defend South Korea under the auspices of the United Nations. Even as he spoke, he had already committed United States air and naval power. His decision was influenced by the threat to the integrity of the United Nations, by the perceived danger to American security interests in Asia, and by the large body of postwar expert opinion which held that World War II could have been forestalled had a firm stand been taken against aggression. To a tense country already obsessed by the Communist threat to Europe, the Middle East, and Asia, the President's announcement was greeted with relief and jubilation. Public opinion fully supported the stand taken by Truman and the support was fully bipartisan. The man he had bested in the 1948 presidential election, Thomas Dewey, sent a wire saying 'I whole-

Left:
General Ridgway and five UN senior officers at the
time of the abortive July 1951 peace negotiations. Left to
right: Rear Admiral Arleigh Burke, Major General
Laurence Craigie, Major General Paik Sun Yup, Vice-
Admiral Turner Joy, General Matthew Ridgway, and
Major General Henry Hodes.

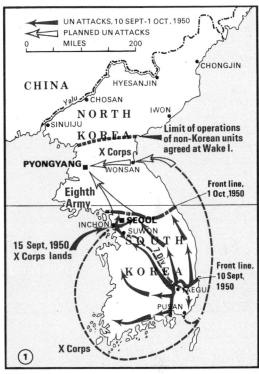

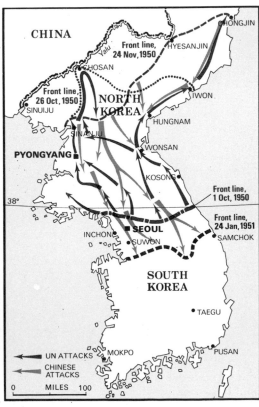

261

Above:
General MacArthur inspects territory along the Yalu River, Korea, which lay in the path of the huge offensive movement by UN forces on 24 November 1950, the eve of his disastrous attempt to 'liberate' North Korea. Truman and MacArthur had assumed that the Chinese would not intervene: they did, and drove the American Army out of North Korea in two weeks.

Opposite:
MacArthur at Inchon, 16 September 1950, at the beginning of the week in which he cleared the North Koreans out of the South. MacArthur, the charismatic if not messianic hero of the Pacific War, was ostensibly acting as a United Nations Commander of United Nations troops. However he took his orders from the American Joint Chiefs of Staff and was never in direct contact with the UN at any time during the Korean conflict.

heartedly agree with and support the difficult decision you have made,' while even the arch-conservative Senator Robert Taft of Ohio, son of President William Howard Taft, said the country should go 'all out.' Strong support came from Europe where it was felt that Truman had saved the United Nations and relieved a little of the Soviet military pressure on Europe. 'A few days ago I was filled with despair,' said a high French official. 'I saw as in a nightmare all the horrors repeated that followed the first surrender to Hitler in 1936. Now there is a burst of sun.'

The burst of sun came not a moment too soon, for early on the morning of 30 June came a cable from General Douglas MacArthur, American commander in Japan, that 'The South Korean forces are in confusion, have not seriously fought, and lack leadership. . . . It is essential that the enemy advance be held or its impetus will threaten the over-running of all Korea.' MacArthur added, the immediate commitment of United States forces was the only way to retrieve the situation. Faced with the desperation of the situation, Truman authorized MacArthur to send a regimental combat team to the battle zone and later that day permitted MacArthur to commit all of his forces as well as ordering a naval blockade of North Korea. Not even five years after the

defeat of Japan, Americans were again involved in a serious shooting war. Korea was to be unlike any previous American war and certainly bore no relation to the titanic and heroic effort of World War II. For the first time, Americans would not be fighting a total war with total victory as their goal. Despite its initial popularity, the limited war that Korea was to become aroused intense opposition on the home front.

Like the United Nations itself, the situation which led to the North Korean invasion was part of the political fall-out of World War II. A peninsula pointed from Manchuria at Japan, Korea had passed from Chinese control to annexation by Japan in 1910 and had become a formal part of that country during World War II. The Allies at the Cairo Conference of December 1943 decreed eventual unity and independence for Korea. As the war in the Pacific came to a close, American planners decided that United States troops would occupy Korea south of the 38th parallel, an arbitrarily chosen line of no political or geographic significance, and Soviet forces the area to the north. Entering the war only six days ahead of Japan's surrender, the Soviets learned of their assignment at the last moment. The transformation of the 38th parallel from temporary line of demarcation to permanent barrier began almost immediately. Korean

nationalism focused on the followers of tough old Syngman Rhee, who had first protested at the Japanese annexation in 1910 and later formed a Provisional Korean Government in Shanghai, and those of Kim Il-sung, a Soviet-trained guerrilla leader whose real name was Kin Sung-chu. Numerous People's Committees sprang up to govern the Soviet zone and the indigenous Communists soon gave way to Soviet-trained cadres. Then Kim, in Soviet uniform, took control of the governing apparatus. The Soviet-oriented Communists in July 1946 merged with the many thousands of Korean Communists then returning from service with Mao Tse-tung to form the North Korean Workers' Party.

Koreans both north and south wanted immediate independence but the north of Kim Il-sung and the south under a right-wing coalition government headed by Syngman Rhee were completely at odds ideologically and had no intention of co-existing within the same state. With the situation in a complete stalemate, the United States delivered the issue to the United Nations which set up a temporary commission to supervise elections for a central government. The stalemate continued, however, as the commission was barred from North Korea by the Soviets who proclaimed the Korean People's Republic in 1947 with Kim as premier. Lethal politicking had eliminated his rivals and subordinated the Chinese-oriented faction, sizeable though it was. The United Nations did hold elections in the south which resulted in the formation of the Republic of Korea in August 1948 with Syngman Rhee as President. A few months later, this government was recognized by the United Nations as the legitimate authority for the whole country. Each declaring the other illegal, both north and south laid claim to be the rightful government of the entire peninsula. Soviet troops withdrew in late 1948 and the American occupation force some six months later.

North Korea began immediately to prepare for armed conquest of the south. A Soviet military mission 3000-strong took up residence and 10,000 North Koreans were sent to the Soviet Union for advanced training. The Korean People's Army (KPA) envisioned by Kim and his Soviet mentors was a small, highly mobile Soviet-style force as opposed to the huge infantry and militia army for which the Chinese faction had argued. Conscription appeared in July 1948 to give the armed forces around 135,000 men two years later. This force received modern Soviet equipment as fast as it could absorb it, so that by June 1950 seven full-strength divisions of around 11,000 men each, three under-strength divisions, several regiments and an armored brigade could muster nearly 240 T-34 tanks and over 2000 pieces of artillery. Over one-third of the men were combat veterans of Mao's campaigns against the Japanese and the Chinese Nationalists. The Air Force was less formidable with around 210 planes while the Navy consisted of less than two dozen patrol boats and light coastal craft.

The Republic of Korea (ROK) began life with a gendarmerie of 5000 men intended only for internal security duty but the obvious military build up and bellicose intentions across the 38th parallel led to the creation of the ROK Army in August 1948 with a United States military mission of 500 advisers. It was purposely allowed no heavy equipment to insure that its employment would be purely defensive because, like his rival to the north, Rhee made no secret of his intention to reunify Korea by force at the first opportunity. The ROK thus had no tanks, only a few 105-mm guns, few experienced officers, and less than one-third of its troops with completed basic training. The Air Force possessed 22 planes, not one of which was a combat ship. But the ROK did possess a formal defense agreement with the United States. The authoritarian nature of the rule of Syngman Rhee disturbed the United States and its allies but since no other leader of stature was available Rhee received support for lack of alternatives.

Opposite:
American and Korean MPs check Korean refugees on the road to Taegu for possible smuggled weapons, August 1950, after the ROK had been routed and MacArthur held only the insecure bridgehead at Pusan.

Below:
ROK (Republic of Korea) troops marching past the Diamond Mountains on their way to Wonsan, 5 October 1950.

Early on the morning of 25 June, 90,000 KPA troops and 100 tanks rolled over the border to achieve complete tactical surprise in a five-pronged attack conceived by a Soviet general. A few hours later came an official North Korean radio broadcast announcing its declaration of war. MacArthur began to send small amounts of equipment from Japan while Truman ordered the Seventh Fleet to the Straits of Formosa to protect Taiwan in case the Korean attack was to be accompanied by a Chinese Communist invasion of that island. The North Korean drive was spearheaded by T-34s, a 35-ton tank mounting an 85-mm gun, which smashed through the surprised South Koreans because the latter had no anti-tank weapons of any sort. North Koreans in civilian clothes penetrated South Korean positions by mingling with the hordes of refugees and disrupted rear echelon areas and lines of communications. Aircraft dropped leaflets urging surrender which further demoralized the confused ROK troops. Over a third of the weapons and equipment of the ROK army was lost in the hasty withdrawal from Seoul. With over 40,000 killed or missing, only a few divisions maintained any discipline.

After MacArthur had personally visited Korea to ascertain the gravity of the situation and Truman had authorized the use of the forces in Japan, American troops began to arrive on 1 July. The problem was that MacArthur's Eighth Army in Japan comprised only four under-strength divisions possessing few tanks. Less than 20 percent of the soldiers had seen combat in World War II. These were occupation rather than combat troops and used to being, as General William Dean said, 'fat and happy in occupation billets, complete with Japanese girl friends, plenty of beer, and servants to shine their boots.' With little artillery and only World War II bazookas whose projectiles bounced off the T-34s, the Americans fared little better than the South Koreans as the tanks crashed through their blocking positions and forced them to scatter into the hills. General Dean was captured while trying to rally his broken men against the tanks. The Americans became caught up in the momentum of the rout. 'All day and night we ran like antelopes' recalled one soldier. 'We didn't know our officers. They didn't know us. We lost everything we had. . . . My feet are cut to pieces. I saw guys running barefooted. . . .

Oh my God, what it did to me.' To make matters worse, authenticated stories of atrocities began to appear, Americans found in ditches shot in the back of the head, hands tied behind the back. 'Ever-retreating, outmanned, outattacked, outsupplied, outflanked, and outyelled' as Eric Goldman said, the troops were bitter and bewildered. Suddenly yanked out of their billets in comfortable Japan with no preparation psychologically or physically, they had little idea of why they were now in a shooting war.

The first break in the war came when the KPA outran its supply lines and ground to a halt for ten days to resupply and redeploy across the girth of the peninsula. American forces and equipment poured into Korea during this time and enabled stiffer resistance to be mounted against the renewed North Korean advance. The pause in fact probably prevented the complete conquest of South Korea. By 10 July the North Korean Air Force had been annihilated as had its Navy. Other United Nations members such as Britain, Australia, New Zealand,

and Canada were now sending forces as well. MacArthur was made Commander in Chief of the United Nations command with General Walton Walker as commander of all ground forces including the ROK troops. The ROK forces, recovered from the initial shock, were now fighting well but neither Koreans nor Americans could halt the T-34s when the KPA resumed its offensive. The retreat continued under heavy pressure until early August when 47,000 Americans and 45,000 ROKs – all that were left – were compacted within the Pusan perimeter, a heavily defended bridgehead at the extreme end of the peninsula. Despite the confused withdrawal, American and ROK forces had fought well when the odds were not too desperate, costing the North Koreans almost 60,000 casualties. For several weeks, there was fierce fighting as the North Koreans pressed the perimeter but already heavy bombers were flying saturation raids on their assembly areas and beginning to attack economic and military targets in North Korea while tactical aircraft were giving close

ground support and interdicting supply lines. The first week of September saw the KPA expend its remaining offensive energy against the perimeter. Dangling at the end of a long and vulnerable supply line, they had to face the failure of their plan for a swift two-month campaign. The balance of strength was now tilted against them as their 98,000 men and 100 tanks – all they had left – confronted 180,000 United Nations troops and 500 tanks.

Although the United Nations force was hemmed into a relatively small space, it had complete control of the air and maritime aspects of the war while its ground forces were rapidly increasing. MacArthur was already beginning to lay plans to seize the initiative on a sweeping scale. But Secretary of Defense Louis Johnson had embarked on what he thought was the politically opportune policy of scaling down the American military establishment and cutting the military budget while Secretary of State Acheson feared a more aggressive conduct of the war would stoke up the Chinese civil war again

Left:
American and ROK soldiers wounded while on patrol near Kumhwa, February 1952. By this time the front had stabilized at the 38th parallel again, but there was total diplomatic deadlock.

Right:
Wonsan oil refinery under attack by aircraft of the American 7th fleet in July 1950. In these early days, Truman thought only American air support for the Korean was neccessary to turn back the North Koreans. The total collapse of the ROK changed their minds and led to the transfer of 47,000 American ground soldiers to Pusan by August.

Below:
UN forces spread out as Chinese mortars zero in on one of their tanks. The paratroopers were rushed to the east-central front to help close a trap on retreating North Koreans in the Inje area in May 1951.

and thus bring widespread conflict. Indeed, the war was already presenting some hard problems for the United States. American national strategy was geared toward the strategic threat perceived to be emanating from the Soviet Union, particularly where Europe was concerned, and the Army in particular was quite unprepared for a small conventional war. The grand plans and demands of MacArthur were evaluated by the administration from a far broader perspective than the narrow Asian focus held by the general.

The Communist attack in Korea seemed to Americans to fit into the larger picture of Postwar Communist aggression and expansion. Eastern Europe was under de facto Soviet rule through Communist puppet governments imprisoned behind the 'iron curtain.' Indigenous Communists had created a serious civil war in Greece while Turkey and Iran were also under Soviet pressure. Most traumatic of all for Americans had been the fall of China to the Communist forces of Mao Tse-tung and the withdrawal of the defeated Nationalist leader Chiang Kai-shek to Taiwan. The Soviet Union had never demobilized at the end of World War II and glared menacingly at defenseless Western Europe with huge conventional armies

Far left:
An American soldier hurls a grenade at a North Korean sniper hidden in a village 20 miles north of Taegu, 29 August 1950.

Far left below:
Pershing M-26 tanks firing at a North Korean observation post across the Naktong River, August 1950. Pershing tanks were developed after World War II but were superseded by the famous Patton M–46, M–47, and M–48 tanks.

Left:
Two American artillery men rest in the rain between firing missions against North Korean positions at the end of July 1950.

Below:
Private Prentiss Thrower of H Company, 27th Infantry Regimental Combat Team, 25th Infantry Regiment mans a .30-caliber machine gun on the defensive perimeter around the Pusan bridgehead at the end of August 1950. Two weeks later the Americans broke out of their positions.

from Eastern Europe. Perhaps worst of all, the Soviets had exploded in 1947 their first atomic bomb, thus ending the American monopoly of that ultimate weapon. Overall the Soviet Union was seen as following a vigorous policy of expansion which, if left unchecked, would gobble up so much of the world as to imperil the United States and its close allies in Europe. The North Atlantic Treaty Organization (NATO) had been formed in response to the perceived Soviet threat only four months before the outbreak of war in Korea while three days after the outbreak, the American Air Defense Command had inaugurated a 24-hour airborne alert with strategic bombers. Anti-Communist paranoia and witch hunts had already begun on the domestic scene led by Senator Joe McCarthy with then Congressman Richard Nixon in a supporting role.

A very real and pervasive fear of Soviet Communism, seen as relentlessly aggressive with world domination as its goal, gripped the United States and Western Europe. Only eighteen months after the surrender of

Left:
Tired out from 43 straight days of front-line fighting a GI takes a rest in September 1950.

Below:
Hwachon Dam in South Korea is demolished by Navy Skyraiders using aerial torpedoes, shortly after the UN intervention in Korea.

Japan, Truman had announced a strategy of containment known as the Truman Doctrine. Since the Soviet Union had unilaterally ended the wartime co-operation, Truman argued before Congress that the United States could only survive in a world of freedom, therefore it had to be willing to help free people maintain their integrity and institutions in the face of aggressive movements. 'This is no more than a frank recognition that totalitarian regimes imposed on free peoples, by direct or indirect aggression, undermine the foundations of international peace and hence the security of the United States' said the President. 'I believe it must be the policy of the United

States to support free peoples who are resisting attempted subjugation by armed minorities or by outside pressure.' Here was a direct and forceful articulation of one of the great lessons that Americans had learned from World War II, namely that American security is directly affected by foreign events and developments. Thus the United States must become involved politically and militarily to forestall serious military threats to the nation. This policy of containment was really forced upon Truman by the bipolar distribution of power between the United States and the Soviet Union in the postwar period. Soviet gains in the international arena were seen as American losses in power and vice versa. Anti-Communism was not the motive behind this unfortunate reality but did provide the moral basis for the new policy which required the United States to assert its power in the postwar world. Anti-Communism was what enabled Americans to maintain their historic perception of the distinction between their peaceful and democratic society and despotic and warlike Europe now represented by the Soviet Union.

Out of the Truman Doctrine came the Marshall Plan for the recovery of Europe and the aid which enabled Greece to withstand a Communist takeover. Foreign and military aid became a standard part of American foreign policy from that time and was gradually expanded beyond Europe to Asia, Africa and Latin America. For the first time in its history, the United States was pursuing a systematic and sustained foreign policy which was a great departure for Americans. This new look in foreign relations had its basis in the exercise of United States economic and military power in the world and required a

later wrote, 'we added the atomic bomb to our arsenal without integrating the implications into our thinking.'

The other advantage of reliance on the bomb was that it suited the postwar mood of the nation. The idea of a large permanent military was still not accepted by the public which raised an overwhelming demand for a speedy return to peacetime conditions. A rapid demobilization followed as the Army had shrunk by 1947 to little over a million men, 400,000 of whom were Air Force. In the face of heavy pressures from the Republican-dominated Congress, Truman

compatible military policy. Containment, especially in the face of the Soviet military threat, meant reliance on the United States military but not for combat purposes. The deterrent provided by these forces but mostly by the atomic bomb was to support American policies without recourse to war and at the same time dissuade the Soviets from war. Historically American forces had always been intended for combat with just hints of deterrence in the coastal forts and the small navy intended for the attack of enemy commerce. The atomic bomb was considered the 'master card' of American diplomacy even though, as Henry Kissinger

cut the military budget by several billion dollars each year. The military was shrinking but even so, a most important development came about through the National Defense Act of 1947. The Army, Navy, and newly independent Air Force became departments within the Department of Defense headed by the Secretary of Defense. A unified administration was finally imposed on the services and the modern Pentagon began to take shape. The same act also created the Central Intelligence Agency and the National Security Council.

Thus the military establishment atrophied because most Americans thought 'the bomb'

was the ultimate weapon of annihilation and rendered large conventional forces unnecessary to carry out their traditional strategy of annihilation in war. The only arm of the military honed to a high state of combat readiness were the eighteen wings of the Strategic Air Command, equipped with both nuclear and conventional capability. The remainder of the military consisted of 48 air force wings, 671 navy ships, two understrength marine divisions, ten understrength army divisions, and eleven regimental combat terms. Most of these forces were thinly deployed around the globe. This de-emphasis of the conventional military in

Truman, in common with most other Americans, believed that the invasion had been Soviet-inspired and thus failure to halt and punish the North Koreans would verge on appeasement in the Munich sense. Yet he had pursued a cautious policy in Asia, leaving the new Communist government in China strictly alone, tendering only limited economic assistance to the defeated Nationalist regime in Taiwan, and generally seeking the goodwill of other Asian nations through economic assistance. The administration throughout kept its eyes firmly fixed on the Soviet Union as the real enemy. It was

good but not the latest Soviet equipment. The World War II bazooka was replaced with a 3.5-inch model which was able to penetrate the T-34. Some M-26 heavy tanks went into action but the old M-4 medium proved to be best adapted to the hilly terrain and style of fighting in Korea. Other weapons of World War II were also employed: the M-1 rifle, the BAR, .30 and .50 caliber machine guns, mortars, and 105-mm howitzers. The division at the outbreak of the war was still basically the World War II triangular formation with a tank and anti-aircraft battalion added. But the divisions were skele-

favor of the primacy of SAC and the bomb is a clear reflection of the prevailing attitude of both the public and government that the Communist military threat represented the specter of World War III, a cataclysm in which the United States would fight with the A-bomb and the strategic bomber force. The surprise of the North Korean attack and its rapid success forced a decision to intervene on the Truman administration in the space of only a few days, far too short a time to think through the military nature and goals of that intervention. How to respond to this situation touched off a debate within the administration and armed forces.

thus reluctant to use up any of its small store of atom bombs on Korea when the Soviet Union might start a general war at any moment but the atom bomb seemed quite out of proportion to the situation in Korea in any case. The main focus of American military strategy thus could not be utilized and the United States was forced to employ the conventional military forces it had thought no longer necessary.

Providing the conventional forces needed to fight the war was another matter. Equipment was no real problem since there were copious stocks of World War II material available and the North Koreans were using

tonized with the regiments having only two and not three battalions and artillery battalions two rather than three batteries. All were short of weapons and ammunition when the war began. Partial mobilization brought forth ample quantities of material and imposed no strain on the healthy American economy to which the war soon brought boom conditions. War-related production removed the few remaining slow areas and brought a record high of 62 million employed. Times were so good that the State of New York had to lay off 500 workers in its unemployment compensation division for lack of claims to be processed.

There was also a steady levelling of the social scene during the war. Civil rights made progress as, in the words of the *Cleveland Plain Dealer*, 'it is high time we stopped this business. We can't do it as decent human beings and we can't do it as a nation trying to sell democracy to a world full of non-white peoples.' Some progress in the desegregation of the armed forces had been made during World War II but 1950 found the Army, Navy, and Marine Corps generally segregated. Only the Air Force was largely integrated even though Truman had ordered the desegregation of the armed forces in 1948. The practical circumstances of the war in Korea had brought about much integration but the armed forces really did not win this battle until 1954 and later.

The four divisions of the Occupation Army in Japan were the first American forces committed to Korea but it was soon all too obvious that more manpower was necessary. The Selective Service Act had been reinstated in 1948 and was extended by Congress just before the war. The early disasters of the war caused the Army to federalize a total of eight National Guard divisions and fill out their structures with draftees. Two went to Korea and two to Germany while the others became 'personnel and training stations' through which draftees and reserves were processed. Some 34 percent of the Army National Guard, over 138,000 officers and men, were called up, along with 287,000 reserve officers and ranks. Eight army and one marine divisions served in Korea while twelve more army divisions constituted the strategic reserve in case of general war. One of the great preoccupations of the administration was that the Soviet Union was planning moves elsewhere while its adversary was tied down in Korea.

The main problem with the mobilization for the war was that it involved a total of less than three million men. Some citizen soldiers were needed but the question was who should serve. The draft law allowed deferments and exemptions for various reasons or disabilities, thus many men avoided the draft and service while some National Guardsmen and reserves were called and others not. The armed forces simply did not need enough men to distribute the burden of service with even a semblance of equity. The reintroduction of the draft so soon after World War II was received by the public rather passively, perhaps because of the conditioning of that war and the widespread fear of the Soviet Union. But the small number of civilians who were drafted often bitterly resented the fact and sometimes questioned the purpose and meaning of the war. That combined with the Army's attempt to alleviate the manifest inequities through the rotation system tended to lower the combat qualities of front-line units. It soon became apparent that the war would last longer than originally thought, so in 1951 draftees, reservists, and National Guardsmen were given short tours of duty in Korea, then rotated into non-combat duty and finally to reserve duty. Rotation out of Korea stemmed from the accumulation of 36 points, four per month being received for battle duty, three for duty in a combat zone, and two simply for being in Korea. Thus a front-line soldier could expect rotation out after nine months. The advantages were that the individual soldier was

Below:
Men of the Heavy Mortar Company, 7th Infantry Regiment try to vary their diet by cooking local rice in their foxholes in the Kangdong area of North Korea, December 1950.

not forced into indefinite service in Korea and that the Army was blooding large numbers of troops who were viewed as a valuable asset in a time of anticipated general war. The main disadvantage was that units never developed the cohesion and teamwork characteristic of the World War II Army and were considered by the enemy to be low in 'aggressiveness and stamina.' The Army also suffered from one of its major problems in World War II in that it called up nearly three million men to put a tenth of that number into its 20 combat divisions. Logistic support was even more full-blown than in World War II, partly because of the problems of supporting a large force in the mountainous terrain of a country so far from the United States but also partly to maintain morale through an almost lavish standard of living for the men.

Morale was a problem after the first eight months when the war entered its static phase. The troops had little spirit in a war whose purpose was not clear, which they were not supposed to win, and which just seemed to go on and on. 'The idea of this war as an endless one is almost universally accepted here' wrote journalist E. J. Kahn from Korea. Al-

Above:
Members of the US 3rd Division display a Communist sign which plays on the idea that GI wives were having a good time while their husbands were away fighting.

Below:
The US Army has kept troops in South Korea to the present day. Private Hans Hirsch of the US 2nd Division stationed in Korea takes a bath in a gasoline drum on 24 May 1953.

though the military had overcome its long-standing Uptonian dislike of citizen soldiers as a result of their performance in World Wars I and II and thus was enthusiastic about making soldiers out of draftees and National Guardsmen, Korea marked a historic turning point in the attitudes of American civilians toward military service. Americans were becoming more cautious because the war was not directly linked to national peril but to difficult to understand political objectives. 'I'll fight for my country' said one corporal, 'but I'll be damned if I see why I'm fighting to save this hell hole,' a sentiment which many of his comrades would heartily have seconded. There was thus little ebullience and elan among the troops, no spirited 'Kilroy was here' but rather a resigned 'Well, that's the way the ball bounces' to explain why they in particular had been singled out to serve and perhaps die.

Douglas MacArthur was very much a creature of the Far East. By the start of the war, he had been away from the United States for fourteen years, first as Commander in Chief of the Philippines, then as Commander of the Southwest Pacific Theater in the war, and later as head of the American occupation government and forces in Japan. He was, not surprisingly, very much out of touch with the moods and currents of the American scene, but was still a man whom the Democratic Presidents Roosevelt and Truman treated with respect for he had often

been promoted as a potential Republican Presidential candidate by the far right. He was also a captive of his own success in World War II. His tactics of the flank attack and leap-frogging had made his campaign from Australia through the Philippines one seemingly unbroken string of fast-moving successes. Korea seemed to offer an ideal situation to exploit the same tactics as the main enemy forces were concentrated at the bottom of the peninsula against the United Nations perimeter at Pusan. It thus would be vulnerable to the sudden amphibious flanking assaults and sealing off by air power by which MacArthur had worked his way up the New Guinea coast in 1943–44, 'amphibious end runs' as Russell Weigley has termed them. MacArthur had a complex of reasons for choosing Inchon, the port of Seoul on the western coast, as his first target for amphibious operations. The sudden recapture of the Korean capital would be a psychological blow to the enemy and a great boost to the still uncertain United Nations cause. The north-south highways in Korea tended to be routed through Seoul, so here was a golden opportunity to cut the enemy lines of communication. But uppermost in his thinking was that a strong force cutting across the waist of the peninsula would trap the main enemy force between it and the Eighth Army breaking out of the Pusan perimeter in a sort of 'hammer and anvil' situation. If all went well, the KPA should be

277

Below:
On 27 September MacArthur was authorized to carry
out military operations north of the 38th parallel. He
decided on another amphibious operation to take
Wonsan on 26 October 1950. Landing craft stream onto
the beach at Wonsan.

annihilated, leaving the United Nations to
occupy North Korea virtually without opposition. The problem was that the United
Nations had no firm war objectives beyond
saving South Korea. Were United Nations
forces to halt at the 38th parallel or were they
to liberate all or part of North Korea? The
Joint Chiefs of Staff raised objections to the
Inchon plan because they thought Inchon
was too far north to receive adequate support
from Pusan and also recognized that

Inchon's tides, tortuous channels and lack of
a beach presented formidable problems for
an amphibious operation.

In the event, MacArthur had his way,
arguing that 'the deep envelopement, based
upon surprise, which severs the enemy's
supply lines, is and always has been the most
decisive maneuver of war.' And he was right.
Resistance proved to be negligible on 15 September, despite the fact that North Korean
intelligence had gotten wind of the operation, because they had failed to get the information to Pyongyang in time. The Marine
Division, 7th Infantry Division and ROK
units, known collectively as X Corps and
totalling about 70,000 men, stormed ashore
and had seized Seoul by the 26th. The Pusan

30,000 KPA troops escaped over the 38th parallel. Over 135,000 were taken prisoner. It was estimated that the KPA had taken 150,000 casualties to that point. As a fighting force it was essentially destroyed, leaving North Korea defenseless before the powerful United Nations forces.

MacArthur urged that the military situation required an advance into North Korea to complete the destruction of the enemy and indeed such an idea had strong attraction as punishment for the perfidious attack on South Korea. But the Joint Chiefs had reservations as did Truman and eventually ordered MacArthur to make the decision, enjoining him to complete the destruction of the KPA and to cross the parallel if necessary to complete this task. Rhee had already ordered ROK units into the north, so there was no need for MacArthur to hold back the rest

break out had begun on the 16th. North Korean resistance began to collapse on the 22nd as a general retreat was ordered to save as much of the KPA as possible. As the whole of South Korea was occupied, American and European criticism of the Syngman Rhee regime was silenced when the remains of an estimated 26,000 Koreans liquidated by North Korean security forces were found, in mass graves in the Taejon area alone yielding a grisly 6000 bodies. Perhaps 25,000 to

Above:
The bridges over the Yalu at Sinuiju, were attacked by aircraft from the USS *Leyte Gulf* in November 1950 to cut communications between China and North Korea. Note that the highway bridge has lost three spans but the railroad bridge is intact. US aircraft failed to destroy the bridges.

of the United Nations force. Another resolution was passed by the United Nations that its objective was to restore 'conditions of tranquility throughout the country' so elections could be held, in essence a revival of the original United Nations plan. Still concerned with the possibility of Chinese or Russian intervention to save Kim's Communist regime, the administration cautioned MacArthur that his men should not cross the parallel if there was any indication of intervention. In early October, China made known her intention to enter the war if American troops crossed the parallel, causing Truman to fly to Wake Island for a conference with MacArthur on this possibility. The general insisted that there was 'very little' chance of such an intervention. 'If the Chinese tried to get down to Pyongyang,' he said, 'there would be the greatest slaughter.' North Korean resistance would be ended by Thanksgiving and he hoped to 'withdraw the Eighth Army to Japan by Christmas.' Based on MacArthur's success to date, Truman stifled his doubts and returned to Washington as elements of the 1st Cavalry Division crossed the 38th parallel on 9 October. The advance became a race between units trying to be first to reach the Yalu River boundary between Korea and Manchuria. Based on this success, the United Nations created the Interim Committee of the UN Commission for the Unification and Rehabilitation of Korea. MacArthur issued a surrender decree to the surviving KPA forces and prepared to take over civil governance of North Korea in accord with United Nations instructions.

MacArthur was truly the man of the hour as the war appeared to be over. In the space of three short weeks, he had transformed the military disaster of South Korea into spectacular victory and now seemed about to restore a unified Korea to the western fold. Such a feat was indeed heady after the long string of Communist successes in Europe and Asia. Still close to the victorious experiences of World War II, Americans of all ilks were excited to see their country flexing its military muscles again and confirming their belief in the special military prowess of Americans. But the euphoria was short-lived as on 25 October American and South Korean units near the Yalu River were badly mauled by large formations of Chinese troops covered by MiG-15 jets from Manchurian bases. Having already won one war by outgeneraling and annihilating the enemy, MacArthur suddenly was confronted with a complete new war and by a different enemy.

Right:
On 1 November 1950 the Chinese Army crossed the Yalu River and entered North Korea. By December the US were retreating from the positions they had achieved in October 1950. Seen here troops and equipment are evacuated from Hungnam in December 1950.

The KPA had been a tough and well-trained foe which very nearly had succeeded in destroying the ROK in spite of the United Nations intervention. The Chinese, on the other hand, were not a modern force well-equipped with armor and artillery and thus fought a different kind of war. The Chinese Army in 1950 was about one-third former Nationalist troops, one-third hastily drafted peasants, while only the remaining third was composed of reliable and loyal troops. The Army was still engaged in mopping up the remnants of the Nationalists and occupying the Chinese peripheries; having just emerged from a long and hard war, the Communist government of Mao Tse-tung was not a party to the North Korean invasion and certainly did not want a war with the United States. No preparatory moves for assistance or intervention in Korea were made while China kept a low political profile. When United Nations forces moved into North Korea, however, it appears in retrospect that the Soviet Union persuaded Mao to intervene to save the Soviet client state. The specific ar-rangement seems to have been that the Soviets would supply equipment and munitions while the Chinese supplied the manpower necessary to salvage the situation. Whatever its motivation, China communicated its decision to the West through various public speeches and intermediaries. MacArthur's headquarters discounted the warnings even though large formations of troops were massing just north of the Yalu River. The Soviets however, clouded the issue by making the first suggestion of truce negotiations while the diplomatic world also doubted that China would intervene. The doubts were aided by strong pressures within the United Nations and the United States for the unification of Korea by military means.

Even when Chinese troops appeared in strength, MacArthur still believed that they were a token force of 60,000 sent to act as a screen behind which the KPA could be resuscitated. The military intelligence assessments of these developments have been a source of some controversy and may well have been a significant factor in MacArthur's failure to appreciate the new situation. He planned to complete his mission of occupying all of North Korea and launched an offensive on 24 November but the 200,000 Chinese then in North Korea badly mauled the surprised United Nations forces and forced a general retreat. Again drawing on his World War II tactics, MacArthur tried to seal North Korea off from China with his air power, in effect trying to make an island which could be totally isolated, and failed here as well. The Joint Chiefs forbade him from bombing Manchuria and only permitted the attempt to bomb the extreme Korean ends of the bridges over the Yalu, a near impossible task for the air force and navy planes which tried. The river soon froze, rendering the attack on the bridges pointless.

The momentum of the Chinese attack pushed the discouraged United Nations troops back over the 38th parallel and well south of Seoul before halting. The earlier confidant optimism of MacArthur was now changed to pessimism which argued that none of South Korea could be saved unless

Above:
A Navy Chance Vought F4UF Corsair comes in to attack a North Korean railroad bridge in September 1951. Although this plane had been designed during World War II it was still operational during the Korean War because of its good flight endurance. Also it was capable of taking off from the shorter runways typical of Korean airfields.

Left:
US troops raced to reach the Yalu River in October 1950. Three corporals enjoy a Thanksgiving dinner on the banks of the Yalu on 23 November. Shortly afterwards the momentum of the Chinese advance pushed the UN troops back behind the 38th parallel.

heavy reinforcements were sent, a naval blockade of China instituted, and bombing attacks, including use of the atomic bomb, destroyed its sources of military power. To win in Korea, said MacArthur, China must be the object of the same kind of all-out strategic attack directed at Germany and Japan in World War II. Such proposals were completely out of proportion to the situation in Korea and bluntly rejected by the Truman Administration which continued to see the Soviet Union as the real threat. Enlargement of the war in Asia would require much more of the conventional and strategic strength of the United States, thus adding to the danger to Europe and generally weakening the United States in its dealings with the Soviet Union. Indeed, the Joint Chiefs at that precise time were seriously concerned that the Soviet Union was about to launch a military effort elsewhere and had even raised the question of requesting a ceasefire with the administration. Relatively unindustrialized, China did not offer decisive military or industrial targets for the atom bomb or stra-

tegic conventional bombing but did have vast expanses of territory and what MacArthur himself called the 'bottomless well of Chinese manpower.' Coupled with the problems of formulating any decisive and war-winning strategy against China was the fact that the Allies of the United States were firmly opposed to any widening of the war. There was thus serious conflict over strategy between the Administration and its Commander in the field, a situation that was bound to bring a serious political crisis.

Yet MacArthur's proposals were entirely consonant with those aspects of the United States military experience which emphasized direct and overwhelming action against the heart of the enemy's power to force a quick decision. Unless the war was carried to China on a large scale, the outcome clearly would be stalemate and MacArthur and many other Americans could not accept that. When MacArthur said 'War's very object is victory,' he was articulating the essence of the American military tradition as it had been evolving from the colonial period. His superiors both military and political felt that the risks were too great in his calls for a strategy of annihilation and he was ordered not only to keep the war limited but to clear all his public statements on the war through Washington. His increasingly outspoken advocacy of his position in public was politically intolerable to the Administration and he was relieved of his command on 11 April 1951 after a particularly flagrant violation of the gag order from his Commander in Chief, Truman.

The immense public uproar over the firing of a man so associated in the popular mind with victory in World War II caused Truman's popularity to hit its nadir. As MacArthur closed an emotional speech to Congress with the now famous words, '. . . I now close my military career and just fade away, an old soldier who tried to do his duty as God gave him the light to see that duty, Goodby.' Truman became the butt of wisecracks such as 'This wouldn't have happened if Truman were alive' and 'Have a Truman beer, it's just like any other beer except it hasn't got a head.' The Administration rode out the storm and then launched a carefully planned counterattack which culminated

with Chief of Staff Jo Lawton Collins testifying to Congress that MacArthur had advocated 'the wrong war, at the wrong place, at the wrong time, and with the wrong enemy.' Exposure to MacArthur's 1930ish views on social and economic issues also served to cool considerably the public's enthusiasm for him and within six months the old warrior really did just fade away into obscurity.

General Walton Walker was killed in a jeep accident in December 1950 and replaced as commander of all ground forces by General Matthew Ridgway on 25 January. The latter, the tough commander of the 82nd Airborne Division in World War II, did not agree with MacArthur's gloomy prognostications which was the main reason for his appointment by the Joint Chiefs. He further recognized that much of the United Nations military problem was due to deficiencies in tactics, training, unit cohesion, and mental toughness. Schooled in the guerrilla warfare of Mao, the Chinese used fluid tactics such as the night infiltration of United Nations lines by small units of specially trained and armed troops to gather intelligence, disrupt supply lines and destroy artillery positions. The Chinese always attacked at night and pre-

ferred 'human sea' assaults in which thousands of massed infantry accompanied by bugles and cymbals attempted to overwhelm United Nations positions. Moving across the rugged hills, the Chinese liked to attack from several directions at once. The United Nations forces, fighting with the tactics of World War II, depended on artillery and tank support which often was not available in the mountainous terrain where the radio and telephone communications so vital to American tactics often did not function well either. The United Nations had subdued a KPA already worn down by superior numbers and material but the United Nations collapse against the Chinese showed that its toughness and determination did not match that of the enemy. This factor was reflected in the collaboration with the enemy of a number of American soldiers who proved unable to bear up mentally and physically under the strain of the harsh Chinese and North Korean prison camps.

Ridgway found the Eighth Army defeated and 'reluctant even to make contact with the enemy.' Through his personal confidence and example, he reinvigorated his subordinate commanders and imbued the troops

Right:
A helicopter of the EUSAK Aviation Section in Taegu is prepared for take-off on 13 January 1951. The helicopter did not play such an important role in Korea as it was to play in Vietnam but it did save countless pilots downed deep in enemy territory.

Below left:
Men of the GHQ Raider Company of the X Corps fight a defensive action against the Communist forces near Yechon in January 1951.

Below:
Elements of A and K Company, 35th Infantry Regiment, 28th Division, scrutinize a Communist position as aircraft pinpoint the area with white phosphorus in February 1951.

with a new fighting spirit, no mean feat in the circumstances. He accomplished this transformation by high standards of discipline and tactical changes. An obvious and simple change was better patrolling and tighter security but more importantly, he took his men away from the main valleys which his predecessor had preferred because they were suitable tank terrain. He instead sent his own men into the mountains and made them learn how to fight the enemy on his own terrain, thus robbing the Chinese of the ability to make the deep penetrations which had contributed so much to their success. Abandoning the mobile armored strike columns of Walker, Ridgway preferred to hammer the enemy with systematic application of his vastly superior artillery and air power. His men called this tactic the 'meatgrinder,' the chewing up of enemy manpower at a rate which even the 'bottomless well' could not sustain.

Left:
Men of the 27th Infantry Regiment, 25th Infantry Division pass a burning house as UN forces launch 'Punch' operation against Chinese Communist forces eight miles southwest of Seoul in February 1951.

Once the United Nations forces had made these adjustments, the military deficiencies of the Chinese became all too apparent. They could still penetrate United Nations lines and make mass charges at a huge cost in casualties but could not exploit such tactical gains as they made for lack of mobility and supply capability. Their tactical communications consisted of bugles and flares and simply were not adequate for quick exploitation of battlefield opportunities. Their tactics tended to be 'mechanical and repetitive' and thus predictable. Whatever the Chinese did, it was always at a high cost in men because of United Nations fire power. Ridgway indeed thought the United Nations

strong enough to launch an offensive of its own as early as mid-February. As the troops moved forward, they found, in the words of Robert Leckie, 'evidence of how cruelly the winter and American firepower had treated the armies of Red China. The hills were littered with their dead; shallow mass graves were uncovered everywhere. . . . The People's Volunteers who had been fresh and aggressive . . . had not been able to withstand the climate and the failures of a supply line running back 260 miles to the Yalu.' By the end of March, the Eighth Army was again crossing the 38th parallel but now the war objective was no longer the unification of Korea but to keep the Chinese on the defensive and force them to negotiate. When Ridgway had arrived on the scene, MacArthur had said, 'The Eighth Army is yours, Matt. Do what you think best' and Ridgway had certainly done just that.

The Eighth Army was driving steadily northward when Ridgway was made MacArthur's successor and the Korean command was turned over to General James van Fleet. One last Chinese grasp at total victory came in April and May when masses of men

were eaten up in futile assaults on the United Nations line. The effort left the Chinese exhausted and virtually at the mercy of the United Nations forces. Van Fleet launched his own offensive on 23 May supported by airpower and naval gunfire on both flanks of the peninsula. The Chinese by now had lost over half a million men, the KPA had essentially ceased to exist, and North Korea was a ruin. Van Fleet himself later wrote '. . . in June 1951 we had the Chinese whipped. They were definitely gone' and yet Ridgway and the Joint Chiefs did not give him permission for the bold offensive operations he proposed to wrap up the victory. At the time, the High Command, including van Fleet himself, apparently did not appreciate just how desperate the enemy situation was. Van Fleet did not press his views hard and the Administration ordered the Eighth Army to halt more or less where it was. Van Fleet could conduct local operations to seize better ground but he was basically restricted to an 'active defense' while the United Nations awaited a Chinese request for a cease-fire. This possibility had been raised by the Soviets at the United Nations as early as March.

Right:
Members of the 5th ROK Division move north to support the 187th Airborne RCT, X Corps in an attack on the Communists, north of Hamnhung, February 1951.

Below:
A 40-mm gun of the USS *Missouri* trained on targets in the Chongjin area tries to disrupt North Korean communications in October 1950.

Above:
Back in Washington DC in December 1950 officers relax in a room of the Soldiers, Sailors, Marines and Airmen's Club.

Right:
Members of B Battery, 937th Field Artillery Battalion US Eighth Army, supporting the US 25th Infantry Division fire Long Toms as they blast Communist-held positions during a night-fire mission in Munemi, Korea.

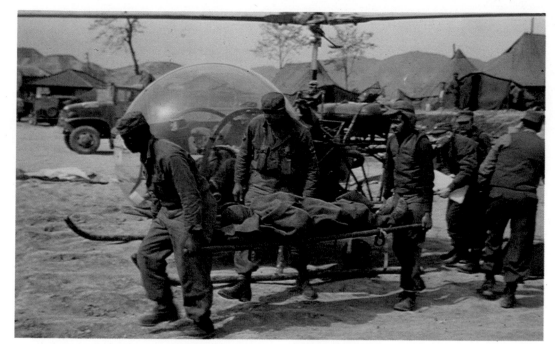

Below:
Members of the crew of Number 2 gun, B Battery, 780th Field Artillery Battalion, US Eighth Army, cover their ears as an 8-inch howitzer gun fires at Communist-held positions on Hill 983.

Above:
An anti-Communist poster issued by the ROK which was displayed in Chunju in March 1951.

Right:
Soldiers of L Company, 3rd Battalion, 27th Infantry Regiment, 25th Division guard the UN Advanced Peace Base Camp at Musan-ni in July 1951.

The Chinese were in a completely desperate situation. Their two best armies had been destroyed, the logistic situation was tenuous and the sea and air dominance of the United Nations was complete. The United Nations ground offensive made their immediate problem simple survival of the forces already in Korea and the larger problem provision of enough reinforcements to hold a line somewhere north of the 38th parallel. But the solution to these problems miraculously came about when the United Nations ordered van Fleet to halt the offensive. Here was the great strategic blunder of the war because the best means to extract the speedy armistice which the United Nations wanted from China would have been to maintain the pressure through the offensive. The war objective of the United Nations had now become to end the war as soon as possible and restore a rough approximation of the *status quo ante bellum*. By applying only minimal military pressure at the first sign of Chinese willingness to discuss a cease-fire, the United Nations allowed the Chinese to recover, prolonging the war for two more years.

Right:
A tank of C Company, 6th Tank Battalion, 24th Infantry, fires on Communist positions.

Below:
A Navy F4U Corsair napalms enemy positions in the Inijin section of the front in close support of the ground troops.

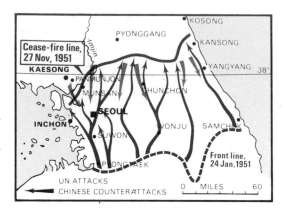

Armistice negotiations began at Kaesong on 10 July 1951 and later moved to Panmunjom. Relieved of pressure, the Chinese reinforced and dug in with the almost certain knowledge that they would not again be subject to a major United Nations offensive such as the one which had come so near to breaking them. They thus had little incentive to come to terms and adopted the tactics of procrastination, the studied insult and outrageous demands as they tested the will of the United Nations negotiators and probed for every possible advantage. Having lost the war on the battlefield, the negotiations offered a forum through which they could recoup their prestige and international stature. As the negotiations dragged on, both sides settled down in a Western Front situation, secure in elaborate complexes of trenches, bunkers and barbed wire separated by a no-man's land. Artillery became the primary weapon for each side because of the defensive strength of the respective positions. More shells were fired in Korea than in all of World War II since the Chinese brought up even more guns than the United Nations. Artil-

lery and air power on the United Nations side could not break the enemy positions, so the infantry had to keep on fighting because the Truman Administration believed that the local struggles for nameless hills had to be won to keep the Chinese negotiating.

The futility of the ground fighting was immensely frustrating to both American soldiers and civilians. 'I have never seen anything like it in all my 74 years . . .' said journalist George Creel in a lecture in San Francisco. '. . . Those damned hills of Korea. You march up them but there's always the sinking feeling you are going to have to march right back down again.' As the war became more and more unpopular during this protracted stationary phase, Truman's Gallup Poll rating fell to 26 percent and he suffered such vituperative personal attacks that the *New York Post* pleaded 'After all, the President of the United States is a member of the human race.' Critics began to call Korea 'Truman's war' while Senator Robert Taft, a conservative power in the land, became increasingly less controlled in his attacks on

what he called 'an utterly useless war . . . begun by President Truman without the slightest authority from the Congress or the people.' The chauvinist crusade headed by Senator Joe McCarthy of Wisconsin attracted strong public support by charging that the military stalemate had been caused by Communists in the government and especially in the State Department.

The election contest of 1952 between the Republican candidate General Dwight Eisenhower, a man whose entire career as a senior officer had been intimately associated with the Roosevelt and Truman foreign policies, and Adlai Stevenson for the Democrats had as its two major issues Korea and corruption and Communism in the government. Probably the key factor in Stevenson's loss was popular frustration and misgivings over the war and the hope that the immensely popular Eisenhower, the general who had led the Allies to victory in Europe, would resolve the maddening stalemate. Indeed, one of Eisenhower's most effective campaign statements was 'I will go to Korea.' Once in office,

Eisenhower determined to end the war to rid the nation of that incubus. After a visit to Korea, he made known through his Secretary of State John Foster Dulles, a strong supporter of complete containment, to China and the Soviet Union that an armistice would be signed soon or the United Nations would resume the offensive with air attacks beyond the Yalu and use atomic weapons on North Korea. Eisenhower's 'peace or else' policy was followed by the armistice signed on 27 July 1953 after 37 months and two days of war and the expenditure of 33,629 American lives, 103,284 other American casualties and 22 billion dollars. And even at the time, the armistice was seen as shaky. The President himself observed that the United Nations had achieved 'an armistice on a single battle ground, not peace in the world. We may not now relax our guard nor cease our quest.'

Korea came to be called a 'limited war,' a genre of conflict which received serious study and debate in military and academic circles from about 1954. Even so, important lessons were overlooked as Bernard Brodie has suggested. What was limited war to Americans was total war to their opponents whose will and moral commitment were accordingly superior. Limited war was also expensive in terms of blood and treasure and thus represented more of a moral and economic commitment than Americans had bargained for. Since limited war had been undertaken for threats to national security which were decidedly peripheral, the casualties and cost eroded its popular support as it dragged on. Significantly, the war retained broad popular support as long as the public could see direction and movement, even if adverse. Anti-war feeling surged only when the war entered its static phase and the military operations were seen as pointless. By accepting limits on its military operations, the United States denied itself the use of much of its vast military power. The military arena was so small and the political constraints so great in military terms that a far weaker power was able to stalemate the situation. Only when the United States threatened to abandon limited warfare was the impasse broken, however unsatisfactorily.

War was never legally declared by the United States, so Korea was not even technically a war. The United States theoretically was assisting a legitimately recognized government with a civil war under the authority of the United Nations. Neither the North Korean nor the Chinese Communist states legally existed in the eyes of the United

Above:
Infantrymen of K Company, 38th Infantry Regiment, 2nd Division dig trenches and bunker positions near 'Old Baldy,' near Chorwon.

Below:
Infantrymen of the 1st Platoon, C Company, 27th Infantry Regiment, 25th Infantry Division, near Heartbreak Ridge take advantage of cover and concealment afforded by the tunnel positions.

Above:
Men of the Heavy Mortar Company, 1st Platoon, 35th Infantry Division, fire the 4.2-inch heavy mortar gun on a Communist-held hill in the Mung Dung-ni Valley.

executive to embark on such action. Despite the eventual unpopularity of Truman and the war, the constitutional issue was not seriously raised by Congress, probably because of the feeling that the welfare of the troops in Korea would thereby be imperiled as would the attempts to end the conflict. The war consequently ran its course in the absence of any formal Congressional authorization or hindrance.

There were other aspects to the war as well. Air power did not seriously impede Chinese troop or logistic movements but tactical air support had won a permanent place in ground operations. The Air Force thus proceeded to develop this aspect of its operations more fully for the first time in its history. Also for the first time, political considerations were allowed to dictate military strategy and operations with sometimes questionable results. The unpopularity of the war and the war President almost certainly lost the election of 1952 for the Democrats. But as the years passed after 1953, what the American public and government came to remember above all else was that a firm application of American military might had halted Communist aggression in Korea and turned that country into a showcase of economic if not political development. This rather than all the problems and frustrations was the memory that most influenced Americans at the beginning of their next venture into limited war.

Nations or the United States. In the course of its history, the United States has committed itself to many undeclared wars by executive action of the President, notably the numerous Indian campaigns, the naval actions against early nineteenth-century France and Barbary, and Lincoln's Civil War blockade. The longer the conflict, the more tenuous is the constitutional authority of the chief

Above:
Private Harry Langar of K Company, 35th Infantry Regiment, 25th Infantry Division has a cigarette after being relieved from guard duty on a heavy .30-caliber machine gun near Kumhwa.

Above:
Lieutenant Chung Won (right) of the 9th ROK Division briefs a platoon sergeant prior to his going on a mission.

Chapter 10

Vietnam–The Second Limited War

Far from disillusioning Americans with the policy of containment articulated by President Truman, Korea strengthened their resolve as an example of the repulse of Communist aggression. President Dwight Eisenhower also adopted containment as a central aspect of his foreign policy, which remains an issue in the debate over American foreign policy to this time. American foreign policy in the 1950s and 1960s came to incorporate programs of foreign aid involving large transfers of capital, technol-

Right:
Ho Chi Minh, Vietnamese nationalist and communist. He was leader of the Viet Minh throughout the postwar years and Premier of North Vietnam until his death in 1969. His personality and prestige played a major role in the Vietnam War.

Below:
President Eisenhower, the French General Paul Ely and Admiral Arthur Radford (right) discussing Indo-China 19–27 March, in the middle of the Dien Bien Phu debacle.

World War II had given the nationalists in Vietnam the opportunity to gain the arms and organization to launch their postwar struggle for independence. In all cases save Vietnam, the Communist factions within the nationalist movements either immediately or ultimately lost out to the non-Communists, although in the cases of Malaya and the Philippines long and difficult guerrilla wars had to be won first. The Viet Minh led by the long-time Communist Ho Chi Minh was different in that it controlled seven provinces of North Vietnam and seized the capital of Hanoi as soon as the Japanese surrendered in 1945. A nationalist movement also controlled most of the south but was far more diverse in composition than the Viet Minh. Unlike the British in Burma and India and the United States in the Philippines, postwar France refused to relinquish sovereignty over Indo-China. French hostilities with the nationalists began in 1947 and soon came to involve 100,000 French troops. In January 1950 the new state of Communist China recognized the Viet Minh as the legal government of Vietnam and began to provide sanctuary, arms, and training. The Soviet Union and the East European states soon followed suit. The United States disapproved of the French policy and had tried to persuade the French to adopt a policy of independence. But the onset of hostilities in Korea caused the Truman Administration to see Vietnam as another battlefield in the same war. When Truman said on 27 June 1950 that 'The attack on Korea make it plain beyond all doubt that Communism has passed beyond the use of subversion and will now use armed invasion and war,' he added 'I have similarly directed acceleration in the furnishing of military assistance to the forces of France and the Associated States in Indo-China and the dispatch of a military mission to provide close working relations with those forces.' China was the connecting link between the two wars because she was the main source of support for the Viet Minh in addition to her central role in Korea, and thus aid to the French in Indo-China was thought to weaken the Chinese position in Korea.

The Eisenhower Administration continued the Truman policy of support to France, the President himself propounding the famous 'domino' theory: 'You have a row of dominoes set up and you knock over the first one and what will happen to the last one is the certainty that it will go over very quickly. So you have the beginning of a disintegration that would have the most profound influences.' General James Gavin, then Chief of Plans in the Pentagon, wrote that 'We assumed Peking was a pawn of Moscow, that Russia, thwarted in Europe by NATO

ology, and human skills to assist the new and not so new states of Asia, Africa, and Latin America with their quest for economic and social development. These programs were the outgrowth of the Marshall Plan which played an important role in the economic rebuilding of Western Europe after World War II. Unprecedented in human history, this exercise in international philanthropy was the ultimate expression of the historic American mission in that it was intended to extend the fruits of the American experience in terms of national wealth and the special American ingenuity in technologic, economic, and military matters to the less fortunate nations of the earth. By assisting them to become more socially and economically viable entities, the United States was also favorably altering the environment in terms of its own national security. With Europe

stabilized and Eisenhower threatening 'massive nuclear retaliation' against any Soviet military moves, the contest between the two super powers largely shifted to the so-called 'less developed' areas where American aid programs competed with Soviet and Chinese backed 'wars of national liberation.' In this contest, American aid, influence, and citizens flooded the world as the United States reached the apex of its global military and economic power. And from that apex Americans again decided to take a military stand against a case of naked Communist aggression in Asia.

The roots of United States involvement in Vietnam go back to the administration of President Harry Truman. Vietnam was part of French Indo-China along with Laos and Cambodia. As had been the case in Burma, Indonesia, Malaya, and the Philippines,

Right:
ARVN soldiers with their American Advisers distributing propaganda supporting the Diem regime to civilians near an ARVN training area, 20 February 1963. Diem's repressive and corrupt government had thoroughly alienated the population and proved itself incapable of defending itself. It was to be toppled by an American-supported coup within six months. Throughout the long years of war, the massive American and South Vietnamese propaganda campains were to prove possibly even less effective than their military ones.

Below:
A member of the 1st Special Forces group atop a bunker, the South Vietnamese flag behind him, in 1964. The 'Green Berets' were an elite corps formed largely under the impetus of John F. Kennedy and trained in 'unconventional' warfare.

and the Marshall Plan, was on the march in Asia. The Communist world was assumed to be an integrated monolithic block.' The crisis in Vietnam for the French came when General Henri Navarre and the Viet Minh General Vo Nguyen Giap, each in search of a decisive military victory, contested the fate of the French fortress at Dien Bien Phu. By that time, the United States was spending over a billion dollars annually (78 percent of French war costs) in Vietnam and only American intervention could save the French position. As the plight of Dien Bien Phu became increasingly desperate, debate within the administration over intervention was resolved by opposition from Congress and Britain. Eisenhower then rejected the proposition and the French hold on Vietnam collapsed with the fall of Dien Bien Phu on 7 May 1954.

The fate of Vietnam thus came to be on the agenda of an international conference at Geneva in 1954. Ho Chi Minh was forced by his Chinese and Soviet patrons to compromise on his demand for the withdrawal of all foreign troops and immediate elections and to settle for partition at the 17th parallel and elections in two years. There was little consensus at the conference and only the cease-fire signed by the military commands of each side had any formal status. In a situation similar to that of Korea, the Communist north under Ho and the non-Communist south under a new government headed by Ngo Dinh Diem were so completely at odds politically and ideologically that the ambiguity and haphazard nature of the so-called 'accords' were, as Hans Morgenthau has written, devices 'to hide the incompatibility of the Communist and Western positions . . . to disguise the fact that the line of military demarcation was bound to be a line of political division as well.' The final declaration never came to a final vote and was never signed while both the United States and South Vietnam explicitly disassociated themselves from it. South Vietnam was recognized by France, the United States, and over 30 other states as a legal entity. The partition of Vietnam with the two halves separated by a demilitarized zone (DMZ) thus left Ho with his dream of a unified Communist country only partially fulfilled.

Within a year of Geneva, France had ceased to be involved in South Vietnam, leaving the United States to provide economic assistance and the supplies and training for a South Vietnamese Army. Concerned over Communist subversion in Southeast Asia, Secretary of State John Foster Dulles persuaded Britain, France, Pakistan, Australia, New Zealand, Thailand, and the Philippines to join the United States in the Southeast Asia Treaty Organization to maintain the independence and collective resistance to subversion and aggression as well as that of Laos, Cambodia, and South Vietnam. With increasing American aid, Diem, a

Left:
Vietnamese troops being reviewed by President Ngo Dinh Diem, late 1950s. Diem's anti-Viet Cong strategy was purely military and yet his army was poorly trained, inexperienced, demoralized and faced superb fighting units.

Above left:
Vice-President Nixon, American Ambassador Donald Heath, and Vietnamese President Nguyen Van Tam at the tomb of the unknown soldier in Saigon, 2 November 1953, at the beginning of the Dien Bien Phu crisis. Nixon, an outspoken anti-Communist, favored giving military aid to the French. His suggestion in April 1954 that the US should put 'our boys' in provoked outrage and furore in Washington.

Above:
A US destroyer squadron rendering honors to the HMS *Alert* while en route to Saigon, October 1953. American policing of affairs in Indo-China and its naval presence in the area were legitimized a year later in the SEATO alliance.

tough and capable leader, began to build his new state. Over a million refugees from the North were settled, agricultural production increased, new industries started, and modest stability appeared. Yet Diem was unwilling to implement serious economic and political reforms and soon alienated much of the population by his authoritarian rule and corrupt administration. Indeed, his strict rule and the excesses of his anti-terrorist campaign provoked some armed struggle against his highly personalized administration. As a result, South Vietnam did not develop modern governmental institutions as its political framework but operated on the network of political patronage relationships which Diem and his family created. The country thus lacked the ability to mobilize itself for economic development or defense. The growing gulf between the formal government and the population was an ideal situation for the intrusion of an outside force.

North Vietnam by contrast was a far more modern state, highly organized and controlled by the Communist Party apparatus. Itself a new country with many problems, North Vietnam embarked on a policy of waiting until its own house was in order before exploiting the situation in the South. Between 1956 and 1959, Communist cadres in South Vietnam helped prepare the way with a program of systematic executions of local officials, school teachers, and social workers to provoke the Diem regime into an even more heavy-handed reaction. 'We had to make the people suffer, suffer until they could no longer endure it' said one defector. January 1959 saw the beginning of the in-

Top:
Operation Oregon, a search and destroy mission carried out near Duc Pho, April 1967. An armored helicopter prepares to land troops to attack a suspected Viet Cong outpost.

Above:
Troops of 1st Cavalry Division (Airmobile) advance on Viet Cong bunker near Bong Son during Operation Masher, January 1966.

Right:
American squad leader Sergeant Ronald Payne crawls through a tunnel in search of Viet Cong and their equipment during Operation Cedar Falls in the HoBo Woods, 25 miles north of Saigon, January 1967.

Right:
Viet Minh troops attack French forces. There was a long tradition of Vietnamese resistance to French colonialism and the Allied decision to allow French landowners to reoccupy the country after the war in the face of fierce nationalist sentiment and a militarily highly competent guerrilla force quickly brought matters to a violent head.

Below:
South Vietnamese await the arrival of the 100,000th refugee from the North, September 1954. After a military cease-fire was signed by the French and Vietminh commands at the 1954 Geneva Conference (the only document pertaining to Vietnam with any validity in international law to result from the conference), over a million people moved from North to South Vietnam.

Bottom:
Operation Lorraine: French troops radio their position during a halt in a village in North Vietnam, January 1953. By this time, the French public was already war-weary. Their army's defeat at Dien Bien Phu and the election of Mendes-France in 1954 facilitated their final withdrawal.

filtration of an estimated 4000 armed cadres into the South as the North Vietnamese Central Committee adopted an official policy of conquest. The Third Congress of the Vietnamese Worker's Party, meeting in Hanoi in 1960, resolved that 'to ensure the complete success of the revoltuionary struggle in south Vietnam, our people there must strive to . . . bring into being a broad National United Front directed against the United States and Diem and based upon the worker-peasant alliance.' Thus was born the National Liberation Front. The North Vietnamese aim was to mask its involvement because, learning from the experience of Korea, it wished to deny the United States any excuse to expand the conflict to the north. An 'elaborate world-wide propaganda effort' was also undertaken to convince international opinion that the National Liberation Front was of southern origin and pursued an independent policy. A number of Vietminh in the South supported Ho.

Left:
American troops of the 101st Airborne Division fire from a former Viet Cong trench during Operation Hawthorne, June 1966. Vietnam was a very mobile war with constantly shifting positions.

Below:
American troops searching for snipers after being fired upon on Hill 822, November 1967.

Diem's response to the new threat was to
increase suppression of all political dissent
and insist that the social and political reforms
urged on him by the United States must be
deferred until the Communist challenge had
been defeated. Diem would thus only tolerate a strictly military approach to the problem as the southern Communist insurgents,
known as Viet Cong or VC, dominated increasingly large areas of the countryside. The
military approach adopted by Diem did not
work because his demoralized troops were
poorly trained and inexperienced and had
neither the will nor the skill to cope with their
formidable enemy. When John Kennedy
took the oath of office as President in January
1961, therefore, he was confronted with a
rapidly declining military situation and an
increasingly unacceptable Diem Administration.

As a Democratic senator, Kennedy had
shown a keen interest in the Vietnam problem and supported the policy of United
States involvement. As a presidential candidate, he had made national defense policy
a major issue in his campaign through the
'missile gap' controversy. As President, he
and his Secretary of Defense Robert
McNamara set out to revamp United States
military policy and strategy. In one of his
first major speeches, Kennedy stated that
'Our defense posture must be both flexible
and determined. Any potential aggressor
contemplating an attack on any part of the
free world with any kind of weapons, conventional or nuclear, must know that our
response will be suitable, selective, swift,
and effective.' He further emphasized that
military power must be usable in that 'Diplomacy and defense . . . must complement
each other.' This meant a much stronger
emphasis on conventional forces, although
Kennedy and McNamara launched the
United States on a vigorous strategic program
as well. They also refined American military

Top:
Male and female members of the Civil Defense Guard stand at attention during drill practice at Hao Cain, South Vietnam, June 1962. Vietnamese women were closely and actively involved in combat and the war effort.

Above:
A member of the Vietnam Junk Force searches a native fishing vessel for Viet Cong shipments and infiltration, May 1962. A characteristic of this war was the ability of the VC to move men and materiel almost anywhere in Vietnam under the noses of the Americans and the ARVN, as was exemplified during the Tet offensive. Supply routes like the famous Ho Chi Minh trail were only one way into the south.

The drafting of a resolution to be presented to Congress to support the President if he decided on military action against North Vietnam was well underway when an incident occurred in the Gulf of Tonkin. The destroyer *Maddox* on an electronics intelligence-gathering mission was attacked by three North Vietnamese torpedo boats 28 miles off the coast of North Vietnam, apparently because it was mistakenly thought to be connected with a South Vietnamese covert operation taking place on that part of the coast. The *Maddox*, reinforced by the *Turner Joy*, was again attacked two days later about 60 miles off the coast. On 5 August the President ordered an air attack on North Vietnamese naval bases in retaliation and asked Congress for a statement supporting his policy. The resulting Gulf of Tonkin Resolution passed the House unanimously but went through the Senate under the tutelage of Senator William Fulbright only after eight hours of serious questioning. The resolution stated that 'the Congress approve and support the determination of the President, as

Commander in Chief, to take all necessary measures to repel any armed attack against the forces of the United States and to prevent further aggression.' When one senator asked if the resolution would authorize the landing of large American armies in Vietnam or China, its chief spokesman Fulbright responded 'the language of the resolution would not prevent it. It would authorize whatever the Commander in Chief thinks is necessary. . . .' This support for Johnson was nearly unanimous in the Congress, Senator Frank Church remarking 'There is a time to question the route of the flag, and there is a time to rally around it, lest it be routed. This is the time for the latter course, and . . . a time for all of us to unify.'

Although Johnson was now equipped with the Congressional mandate which Truman had lacked, he still refused to change his policy although he was under strong pressure from the military and his national security advisers for major military moves. Having spent virtually his entire career in Congress, he was a master of domestic issues and poli-

Left:
A sergeant writing home during rest after ten days on the line in Operation Masher, 1966.

Right:
American soldier surveys the terrain before crossing open area during Operation Masher, January 1966.

Below:
American POL dump at Cam Ranh Bay, January 1966.

tics and wanted to build his Presidency on the 'Great Society,' his monumental program of social reform and uplift. He feared that a major commitment to the war in South Vietnam would doom his program just as World War I had doomed Woodrow Wilson's New Freedom and World War II the New Deal of Franklin Roosevelt. 'Yet everything I knew about history told me that if I got out of Vietnam and let Ho Chi Minh run through the streets of Saigon, then I'd be doing exactly what Chamberlain did in World War II' said Johnson. 'And I knew that if we let Communist aggression succeed in taking over South Vietnam, there would follow in this country an endless national debate . . . that would shatter my Presidency, kill my Administration, and damage our democracy.' Despite Johnson's idiosyncratic expression, his view was widely held by the many who drew the same lessons from history recent and not so recent. Johnson was not, however, comfortable with foreign affairs or the men who advised him on foreign policy, 'insecure, fearful, his touch unsure' in the words of his biographer Doris Kearns. He was also worried by the fear that the 'loss' of Vietnam to Communism would be blamed on his administration's 'softness' on Communism and thus sink him as Democratic President before the salvoes of his political foes. He found himself as a result caught between his dream of the Great Society and his fear of blame for losing Vietnam to Communism.

Right:
American Long Range Patrol move through undergrowth on their way to an ambush site, 30 January 1968.

Below right:
ARVN operation in downtown Saigon after VC attack on American Embassy during Tet, 1 February 1968.

Below:
House-to-house search for Viet Cong snipers at Bien Hoa during Tet offensive, 2 February 1968.

It was only at the end of January 1965 after he had been inaugurated as President in his own right that his advisers convinced him that South Vietnam would be lost within a matter of months without a change in United States policy. In early February, a large number of American advisers were killed and wounded in VC attacks on Pleiku. Within a month the several retaliatory air raids he ordered on the North had become a sustained bombing offensive codenamed Rolling Thunder. The United States was in open warfare with North Vietnam as Johnson had come to the sudden realization that 'doing nothing was more dangerous than doing something.' The bombing campaign had three main goals. The most important was to demonstrate to North Vietnam the American determination to defend South Vietnam from northern aggression. From this demonstration was to follow improved South Vietnamese morale. Lastly, the bombing was intended to raise the cost of the North's activities in the South to an intolerable level.

The President opted for a limited campaign which would gradually escalate. 'By keeping a lid on all the designated targets' Johnson said, 'I knew I could keep control of the war in my own hands. . . . I saw our bombs as my political resources for negotiating a peace.' Johnson thus thought he could force Ho to bargain with him. In return for the ending of the northern aggression, the President had ready a billion dollar project for the social and economic development of both South and North. 'I want to leave the footprints of America in Vietnam' he said in 1966. 'We're going to turn the Mekong into a Tennessee Valley.'

The Rolling Thunder campaign was punctuated by various halts, sometimes lasting over a month, as a series of peace feelers surfaced through the Soviets at the United Nations. Between 1965 and 1968 the Johnson administration maintained almost continuous contact with North Vietnam through intermediaries or directly. While the military became frustrated at what they viewed as the Administration's failure to use force in an effective manner, the North Vietnamese finally agreed to negotiate in 1968 while still under air attack. The targeting of the bombing focused on interdicting the flow of men and supplies to the South, a compromise between those who wanted military results and those who viewed the bombing as primarily political in function. As the bombing failed to alter the North's strategy of increased pressure in the South, the campaign was in-

Above:
A mortar crew of 1st Cavalry Division (Airmobile) during a fire mission against the Viet Cong in the Bong Son District during Operation White Wing, February 1966.

Top:
A soldier prepares a 105-mm howitzer for a fire mission against the Viet Cong in the Vinh Thanh Valley, near An Khe, 1966.

Far right:
US Navy aircraft destroying the Hai Duong Highway Bridge in North Vietnam, January 1967.

tensified and expanded in targeting coverage to convince the American public and the Congressional believers in air power that this means had been employed to the maximum before American ground troops were committed. The peak was reached in 1966 but by the following year analyses revealed that no major component of North Vietnam's military or economy had been destroyed. One such analysis concluded 'The available evidence does not suggest that Rolling Thunder to date has contributed materially to the achievement of the two primary objectives of air attack – reduction of the flow of supplies to VC/NVA forces in the South or weakening the will of North Vietnam to continue the insurgency.' McNamara had also reached the conclusion that limited bombing was a failure. Despite strong pressures from the military and such 'hawkish' Congressional power centers as the Senate Preparedness Subcommittee, the President gradually de-escalated the bombing through 1968.

American troops were introduced into the South Vietnamese situation almost concurrently with the start of Rolling Thunder when several Marine battalions were landed to protect United States bases and installations from VC attack. They were specifically enjoined from engaging in 'day-to-day actions against the VC.' While the Administration continued to see the solution to the war in the air campaign, Westmoreland had already decided that the ARVN was incapable of victory on its own, and that American combat forces in strength would be necessary. Army Chief of Staff Harold Johnson held a similar view of the situation. Westmoreland requested two divisions and planned an offensive strategy to seek and destroy enemy concentrations in the central highlands, envisioning what was in essence the traditional attack mission of the infantry. The Chairman of the Joint Chiefs of Staff, General Taylor, doubted the effectiveness of American troops in a counter-insurgency role and proposed instead a series of strategic enclaves along the coast to protect vital centers. Johnson also shared Taylor's doubts but in one of the pivotal decisions of the war did approve a limited offensive role for the troops operating from the enclaves. His intention was to evaluate the performance of the troops and withdraw them if necessary. As with the air campaign, he thus hoped to maintain his control over American participation in the ground war.

The Joint Chiefs and Westmoreland took the early and gradually increasing commitments of troops as the necessary preparation for a larger American role and argued forcefully for higher troop levels in the face of resistance from McNamara and the President. Once again, however, events in the field forced Johnson's hand. The VC began a major offensive in May with regiment-sized attacks which decimated ARVN units. Most Americans on the scene concluded that the complete collapse of the ARVN was imminent. The enclave strategy was simply inadequate to save the situation and yet

another military coup occurred in Saigon to leave the South Vietnamese generals in formal command of the government. While state Department official William Bundy warned the President and his top advisers in an official memo that the growing United States role 'would appear to be turning the conflict into a white man's war with the United States in the shoes of the French,' the United States forces in Vietnam, together with newly arrived Australian units, began to engage in major combat operations. Having continually reiterated the complete United States commitment to South Vietnam, Johnson recognized the great loss of prestige that the United States would suffer if he withdrew the by-then 75,000 American soldiers. If he did not make a major commitment at that point, all the signs said that South Vietnam would go under. He thus approved a total of 175,000 men for Vietnam in July but added in his briefing to Congressional leaders, 'Additional forces will be needed later, and they will be sent as requested.' The military commitment made by Johnson was thus open-ended.

Johnson was able to send large American forces to Vietnam on short notice because he had inherited the Army built by his predecessor. Comprising sixteen combat-ready divisions, American forces were deployed abroad in the Seventh Army in Germany and the Eighth Army in Korea, the former with

six divisions and the latter with two, while the remainder were in the United States as the strategic reserve. The Regular Army was supported by the Ready, Standby, and Retired Reserves as well as the National Guard. As the build up in Vietnam proceeded in 1965–66, the strategic reserve was seriously weakened by the commitment of five army and two Marine divisions to Vietnam. The Army depended on the reserves in an operation as large as Vietnam was becoming, to serve as training centers and to provide specialist and support units. The main source of manpower continued to be selective service, and those regular divisions in the United States were simultaneously swamped with draftees for training and stripped of their support and specialist units. To avoid sending draftees to the combat zone, they were at first used to replace regulars in units from around the world to release the latter for duty in Vietnam but the demand for manpower had become such by 1966 that draftees were sent to Vietnam in substantial numbers as well.

The Army had to make do with this situation, however, because Johnson refused McNamara's request to call up reserve divisions. This refusal was rooted in Johnson's desire to give the appearance of business as usual because to do otherwise would have threatened his Great Society programs. For this same reason he refused to increase taxation to pay for the mounting cost of the war. Coupled with the high cost of the Great Society programs, war-related expenditures raised the rate of inflation from about one percent in 1963 to 4.6 percent in 1968. To prevent an open national debate on the Vietnamese commitment and its potential effect on the Great Society, Johnson insisted that the United States was not at war and in so doing created a 'credibility gap' as the magnitude of American activity in Vietnam increasingly belied his assertions. Although Johnson's policies were intended to preserve a domestic political consensus, they had the opposite result. The failure to mobilize the reserves brought the selective service system under stronger and stronger attack as the inequities associated with the Korean War draft reappeared in an accentuated manner. The growing number of domestic opponents of the war found in the draft a potent weapon with which to attack the administration and its policy while substantial amounts of draft avoidance and resistance appeared, primarily among college students.

Above:
A rocket is launched from a US ship off the coast of
South Vietnam. The picture is of a dawn attack
supporting ARVN troops engaged in combat against the
VC, May 1966.

Memory of the defeat of the French Army in Vietnam a decade earlier was a strong factor in Pentagon thinking concerning the commitment of conventional troops to the unconventional environment of Vietnam. Intensive training programs to prepare the soldiers for the unusual conditions of combat in Vietnam were set up, one of the best known being the 'ambush academy' of the 25th Division. The American plan was to use the vast modern capabilities of the military to defeat the VC through excellent intelligence, rapid mobility, and overwhelming firepower. Systematic aerial and ground reconnaissance with extensive use of electronic paraphernalia was to be used to locate the enemy, mobility through helicopters to prevent his escape and the high firepower of new infantry and tactical weapons to annihilate him. Firepower was seen as the key, so the old M-1 rifle, for example, was replaced by the M-14, a light rapid-fire piece using a 7.62-mm cartridge. Because the performance of the M-14 was somewhat erratic, the M-16 came into use with its .223 caliber bullet and 120 round clip. Soldiers were no longer taught to fire single aimed shots but to spray the target with a stream of bullets. The Army thus hoped to wear down its adversary by maintaining the offensive and clearly still conceived of its mission as the destruction of the enemy forces in battle.

The basic American tactic in this strategy of attrition soon became the search and destroy mission. The United States units

Left:
ARVN soldiers on field training exercise, 1963. John Kennedy's policy then was for America to provide the skills and equipment and for South Vietnam to provide the men.

Below:
Members of the 5th ARVN Cavalry return the fire of NVA snipers hidden in the buildings on the outskirts of Bien Hoa, just north of Saigon.

Above:
An American soldier takes cover as armored personnel carriers open fire on NVA snipers during the attack on Bien Hoa, February 1969.

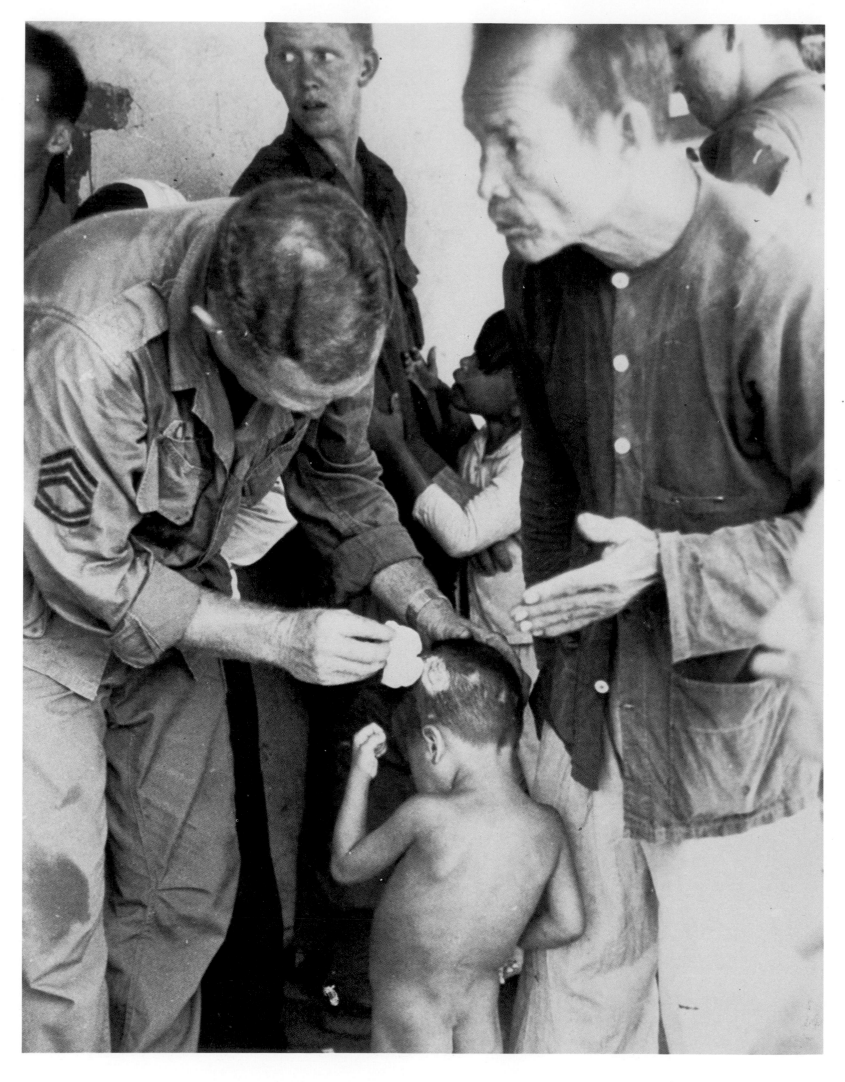

would search suspected VC positions and then attack and destroy the enemy and his logistic support. Westmoreland's plan was for the United States and other allied forces – Korean, Thai, Australian – to use these operations against larger enemy units while ARVN forces attacked the local guerrillas and VC infrastructure and provided security for the civilian population. The first problem with this approach was the inability of the ARVN to carry out its mission while the second was that United States units had to mount repeated operations against the same areas because the VC simply returned once the operation was over. VC tactics were also to place their positions in villages and thus to involve the civilian population in the war. It was often difficult to differentiate between active combatants, civilian sympathizers, and civilian 'friendlies.' Large numbers of civilians were killed, large amounts of property destroyed, and large numbers of refugees created. The VC tactics thus exposed the civilian population to the massive application of firepower favored by the Americans. The aggressive-offensive strategy manifested in the search and destroy mission in retrospect failed also to consider possible enemy responses. One response was a VC/NVA build up by the end of 1965. Westmoreland himself reported that the enemy was escalating twice as fast as the United States was. 'Whereas we will add an average of seven maneuver battalions per quarter,' he wrote, 'the enemy will add fifteen.' To keep its strategy from failing, therefore, the United States was required to keep raising its troop level.

At the end of 1966, 95 percent of American combat troops were committed to the search and destroy tactic as Westmoreland continued to try to annihilate enemy main force

Left:
An American applies ointment to the head of a Vietnamese child during a MEDCAP operation, May 1967. The scale of civilian casualties was horrific during this war, due to a combination of the VC policy of involving the civilian population in the war and to the American policy of massive application of fire-power, napalming and search and destroy missions.

Below:
A South Vietnamese administrator gives an indoctrination class to Viet Cong defectors to the South. Desertion rates were very high in both directions.

Bottom:
An American soldier laundering his clothes between combat patrols near An Khe, 1967. The American army in Vietnam was in fact the most well-serviced army in history.

units and prevent them from operating in heavily populated areas. The rationale was that these operations were creating a 'shield' behind which the pacification of the countryside could take place. Yet most American attention and resources were focused on the larger military operations and pacification made little progress. While the American Commander believed that his strategy of attrition was working, his force projections kept rising as did his casualties, almost 5000 in the first half of 1967 alone. There was increasing criticism of the conduct of the war both within and without the government. 'Political and social repercussions, not strategies or tactical military considerations in Vietnam, were to dictate American war policy from that time on' observes the *Pentagon Papers*, the classified official history of the war which was leaked to the public by a disgruntled Pentagon employee. Already under fire, the Administration soon was to find itself in a completely untenable position.

The turning point in the war came at the end of January 1968 when the NVA and the remnants of the by-then heavily decimated VC executed a large and well-planned attack on the major urban centers of South Vietnam in the expectation of provoking a general

uprising of the people against the military government of General Nguyen Van Thieu. Coming at Tet, the Vietnamese New Year, the offensive scored spectacular early successes as half of the ARVN was on leave for the holiday. The American and Vietnamese response was rapid and overwhelming however, and the attackers and VC infrastructure were so badly hurt that no large enemy offensives could be mounted for over four years. Indeed, Tet was what the American military had been longing for as the NVA/VC came out of the hills and jungles to fight openly. But for the first time, the American public saw the enemy and saw him in the compound of the American Embassy in Saigon. The shock was tremendous. 'What the hell is going on here?' Walter Cronkite is alleged to have exclaimed when the news came over the teletype. 'I thought we were supposed to be winning this war,' a reaction surely shared by many of his countrymen.

Left:
An ARVN soldier checks the area around his bunker, October 1968.

Above:
A LRRP Team moves out into the landing zone to be air lifted out of Bein Hoa, May 1969.

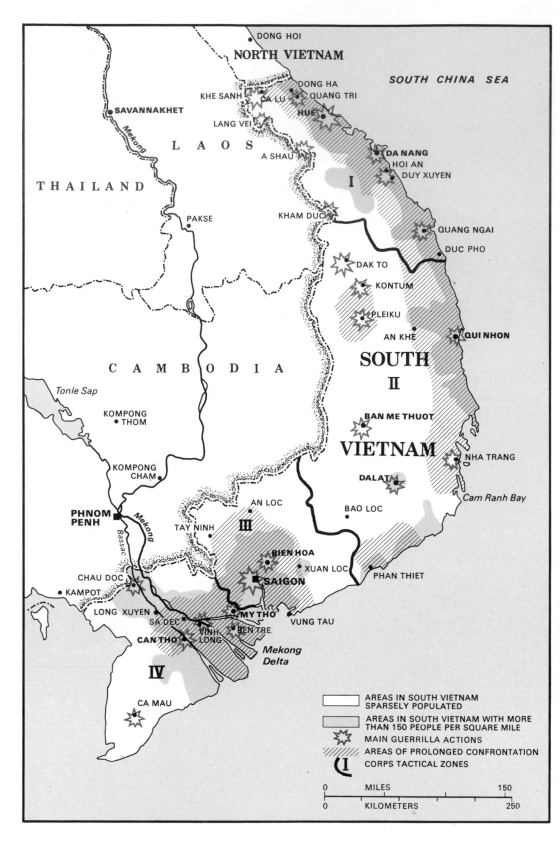

The press played an important role in the public perception of Tet as a military disaster. For weeks the nightly news on television showed footage of the dogged fight put up by the enemy in Saigon and Hue. Stunned by the initial attacks, many of which occurred in downtown Saigon where the press corps stayed, the press emphasized the early success of the enemy, put out much erroneous factual material which remained uncorrected, and mixed a high degree of interpretation with its reporting. In sum, Tet was an extreme case of crisis reporting, says Peter Braestrup in his monumental study of the press and Tet, which resulted in a 'portrait of defeat' because 'the special circumstances of Tet impacted to a rare degree on modern American journalism's special susceptibilities and limitations.'

Tet had a profound political impact on the domestic American political scene as the contrast between the continual optimism of the Administration and the reality of the news was starkly displayed. The presidential primary elections quickly revealed the depth of public disenchantment with Johnson. The major media each in its own way came out against the war and by extension the Admin-istration, while the President's Gallup poll rating fell to 36 percent. Johnson was under siege by both the 'doves' who wanted de-escalation and the 'hawks' who wanted more military force applied in Vietnam. The majority of Americans still supported the domestic and foreign policy of the Administration but no longer trusted Johnson the man from a belief that he had regularly lied to them about the war. Challenged first by Senator Eugene McCarthy and then by Robert Kennedy for the Democratic presidential nomination and having lost his personal credibility with the electorate, Johnson stunned the world on 31 March with the announcement that he was both de-escalating the war and withdrawing from politics. Negotiations with the Vietnamese began in May in Paris while Vice-President Hubert Humphrey, carrying the albatross of his association with Johnson's Vietnam policy around his neck, lost narrowly to Richard Nixon in the election.

Nixon had campaigned with the promise that he had a plan to end the war honorably.

Above:
Two Viet Cong soldiers in a Viet Cong base camp in the Rung Sat Special Zone. The Zone was overrrun by Southern forces in June 1967. The photo was made from film discovered in the camp.

Right:
An American rifleman cleans his M-16 rifle before going out on patrol during Operation Wheeler, November 1967, near Chu Lai.

Taking office as President of a troubled and turbulent country in January 1969, Nixon knew that at the least American involvement in Vietnam had to be minimized to deal with the domestic issues and restore some national consensus. His plan was therefore for a cease-fire, a phased withdrawal of American troops to minimize casualties, a change in battle strategy from 'maximum pressure' on the enemy to 'protective reaction,' and a crash program to Vietnamize the war. If he could maintain domestic support through re-

Vietnamese remained intransigent at the negotiating table. President Thieu in Saigon also became more rather than less intransigent concerning internal reforms and the creation of a broader political base. The war also began to spill over into neighboring Laos and Cambodia as the United States responded to the growing NVA use of these countries as sanctuary and training bases. But the response in turn provoked further domestic pressure to end the war.

One benefit of the Tet offensive was that it

duced draft calls and withdrawal of troops, the Vietnamization program might improve the South Vietnamese conduct of the war enough to persuade the North Vietnamese that they faced an increasingly more capable and strong South Vietnamese regime and thus bring them to serious negotiations. But opposition to the war increased in intensity in the United States and spread far beyond the bounds of the college campuses. Hundreds of thousands of demonstrators converged on Washington to 'March for Peace' and 'Out Now.' Even after the death of Ho Chi Minh in September 1969, the North

had delivered the coup de grace to the VC. From that point, the war was entirely fought by the NVA. The guerrilla war thus became a minor factor militarily which enabled the pacification program to proceed in a relatively secure environment for the first time. The United States and ARVN shifted from high technology warfare to an emphasis on population protection, local organization building, economic development, and local participation in district administration. After 1968, pacification and development began to record some success and the rural economy began to grow.

Vietnamization also achieved some success in military terms as government control over the countryside increased notably. As one United States adviser noted, 'The GVN (Government of Vietnam) by 1971 occupied roughly the position that the VC had in 1967.' Much of this reversal of trend was undoubtedly due to the low level of NVA military activity but some is attributable to the improving fighting capacity of the ARVN. Prior to 1968, the ARVN and related Popular Defense Forces had been armed with the old M-1 rifle, and enjoyed relatively little artillery, air or armored support compared to the US troops. After being almost a spectator as the United States aggressively fought the war between 1965 and 1967, the ARVN was re-equipped with modern weapons such as the M-16, tanks, Armored Personnel carriers, helicopters, and communications gear to allow it to compete with the well-equipped NVA. More men were drafted into the Army, leadership improved, and the regional militia and local self-defense forces also re-equipped and reorganized. South Vietnamese commitment was also higher now as a result of the Tet attacks and the apparent United States determination to reduce its involvement.

The timing is not known for certain but probably in early 1971 the government of North Vietnam decided to abandon guerrilla warfare and invade South Vietnam openly with conventional forces. The heavy offensive weapons such as trucks, tanks and 130-

Below:
Members of Company D, 151st (Ranger) Infantry, Long Range Patrol, open fire against the enemy, September 1969.

Right:
The colors pass in review during a departure ceremony at Da Nang for the 3rd Marine Division, August 1969.

mm artillery were supplied by the Soviet Union. It was probably thought that United States ground forces would be so reduced by that time the ARVN would have to fight on its own. A major military defeat of the United States/South Vietnamese might bring benefits similar to those unexpectedly reaped from Tet in terms of United States domestic politics since the 1972 presidential election was nearing. On 30 March 1972, what has become known as the 'Easter Offensive' began with a two-pronged assault from Cambodia and from across the DMZ by a total of six divisions supported by 200 Soviet T-54 tanks. Several provinces were quickly overrun as the attack threatened to cut the country in two. But the ARVN regrouped and held after the initial NVA thrust slowed and, supported by massive United States air attacks, began a counteroffensive. By the time the operations wound down in September, the ARVN had captured most of the territory lost and inflicted 100,000 casualties on the

Above:
Sergeant Curtis Hester of a Long Range Patrol Team takes his position and listens for enemy movement in September 1969.

Left:
Aerial view of the fortified firing position for American 105-mm howitzers at Camp Gorvad.

Right:
Meeting of the Military Armistice Commission at Panmunjom, Korea, addressed by Air Force MG Felix Rogers, United Nations chief spokesman, 16 December 1970.

NVA. The turmoil had unsettled the pacification program and created nearly a million new refugees, however, and allowed the NVA to regain some lost ground in population control. The failure of the offensive did lead to a breakthrough in the diplomatic stalemate in Paris where a cease-fire agreement was signed on 27 January 1973. The terms left much to be desired because they implicitly legitimized the presence of NVA troops in South Vietnam. President Thieu accepted the cease-fire only after he received a letter from Nixon stating 'You have my absolute assurance that if Hanoi fails to abide by the terms of this agreement it is my intention to take swift and severe retaliatory action.' North Vietnam immediately began to violate the agreement by openly infiltrating men and heavy equipment into the South. On 29 March the last American troops left South Vietnam and the last American POWs were released by North Vietnam.

Left:
MK-3 helicopter mounted-weapons system composed of 24 tube rocket pods mounted on each side.

Far left:
A crew chief aboard a helicopter surveys a Delta village with his M-60 ready.

Bottom left:
A Hanoi gasoline dump goes up in flames on 29 June 1966.

Below:
Smoke pours from a Viet Cong camp in the Mekong Delta which has been hit by automatic weapon and rocket fire from two helicopters.

Bottom:
M-60 machine guns mounted on the sides of a UH–1B helicopter gunship.

Bottom center:
Seven tube pod for two 75-inch ten-pound rockets mounted on the side of a helicopter.

The American disengagement was now complete. By then, however, Nixon was under growing attack domestically because of the widening Watergate scandal. Congress took advantage of the weakening position of the President to adopt a proposal by Senator Church to cut off all funds for United States military activity in Southeast Asia effective 15 August.

North Vietnam in the meantime had been resupplied by the Soviet Union with the latest modern weaponry. Totally dependent on the United States for its war supplies and funds to purchase gasoline, South Vietnam found its aid allotments cut regularly by a war-weary Congress anxious to liquidate the remaining United States involvement in Southeast Asia in spite of the urgent pleas of Secretary of State Henry Kissinger. When seventeen North Vietnamese divisions again crashed across the DMZ in the spring of 1975, the ARVN was severely short of gasoline for its trucks, tanks and planes and of ammunition and spare parts, causing the NVA commander General Van Tien Dung to remark that 'Nguyen Van Thieu was then forced to fight a poor man's war. Enemy firepower had decreased by nearly 60 percent because of bomb and ammunition shortages.' The course of the campaign was swift. Some ARVN units fought until their ammunition ran out while others collapsed in confusion at the outset. Hordes of refugees and leaderless ARVN soldiers clogged the roads in flight from the advancing armored columns of the NVA. The war and the existence of the Republic of Vietnam both came to an end on 30 April when NVA tanks rolled into Saigon.

The United States and its South Vietnamese client had lost not a guerrilla war but a conventional war. The guerrilla conflict originally waged by Hanoi had proved incapable of producing a decision, thus a conscious choice was made to switch to con-

Right:
American troops interrogate South Vietnamese farmers about VC and NVA activities in the area during a search and destroy mission in January 1968. Such missions were the basis of American strategy at the time, but proved of very limited effect.

Below:
The battle for Hue, the ancient capital of Vietnam, after its capture by the VC during Tet, proved to be one of the fiercest encounters of the war, lasting 25 days and resulting in the total destruction of the city.

Bottom right:
American soldiers receive their first mail call after arriving on Hill 680, near Khe Sanh, April 1968. Khe Sanh was besieged for months and threatened to become another Dien Bien Phu, with the American Army surrounded and airlifts very difficult.

Map Labels

SAVANNAKHET

THAILAND

LAOS

PAKSE

Mekong

Demilitarized Zone

QUANG TRI

KHE SANH

HUÉ

DA NANG
30 Mar

26 March 1975
Hué falls to Communist forces

TAM KY
23 Mar

SOUTH CHINA SEA

QUANG NGAI

Central
KONTUM

PLEIKU
Highlands

Ho Chi Minh trail

Highway 1

QUI NHON
1 Apr

SOUTH

TUY HOA
1 Apr

CAMBODIA

BATTAMBANG

Tonle Sap

BAN ME THUOT

VIETNAM

NHA TRANG

'FISHHOOK'

DALAT

Cam Ranh Bay

PHUOC BINH

PHNOM PENH
17 Apr

AN LOC

Mekong

TAY NINH

NEAK LUONG

3 Apr

KOMPONG SOM

BIEN HOA

XUAN LOC

PHAN THIET

'PARROT'S BEAK'

SAIGON

30 April 1975
Communist forces enter Saigon

VUNG TAU

CAN THO

Mekong Delta

COMMUNIST CONTROLLED AREAS
(APPROX), MID-JAN 1975
AND BY 25 MARCH

| 0 | MILES | 200 |
| 0 | KILOMETERS | 300 |

ventional attack with equipment supplied by the Soviet Union. This strategy was only possible because of the emergence of a rough strategic parity between the United States and the Soviet Union during the late 1960s, a time when the latter had more Inter-Continental Ballistic Missiles (ICBMs) deployed than did the former. With this major shift in the world balance of power, the United States had lost its military leverage over the Soviet Union which enabled the Soviets to place constraints on United States options while widening its own. The United States therefore operated under far greater constraints in Vietnam than it had in Korea where the limits were largely self-imposed.

From the outset, it had been clear that America's second venture into limited war would not render a clear-cut decision but the many problems which beset the United States had not been foreseen at all. One of the major problems was the United States military itself and its historic strategy of annihilation and emphasis on the offensive. John Kennedy had made a tentative commitment to Vietnam while calling for a 'whole new kind of strategy' but he was not at all in accord with the notions of the military.

These were stated quite bluntly by General Earle Wheeler when he succeeded Taylor as Chairman of the Joint Chiefs in 1964: 'It is fashionable in some quarters to say that the problems in Southeast Asia are primarily political and economic rather than military. I do not agree. The essence of the problem is military.' The conduct of limited war to achieve limited political objectives was simply counter to the historic tradition of the military which wanted to destroy the enemy through attack. Under Westmoreland between 1965 and 1967, the military essentially took over the war from the South Vietnamese in the belief that it could win swiftly and efficiently. The search and destroy tactic was the embodiment of this belief which Westmoreland clung to in rejection of any other tactical approach. Only when the enemy came out into the open during Tet was the high technology war of the Americans able to be employed to good effect. Tet marked the end of the guerrilla war in South Vietnam as the North Vietnamese turned to conventional attack to wring a decision from the long stalemate. The resulting Easter Offensive of 1972 failed partly due to serious tactical errors by the North Vietnamese

Above:
A scout dog 'Duke' responds as VC move through the underbrush during patrol operations, June 1970.

Far left:
Members of the Vietnamese Mobile Strike Force conduct operations in an airboat on the Mekong River, April 1970.

Left:
American soldier sets a trip flare outside the perimeter of his company night defensive position, early 1970.

Above:
American soldiers fire their Quad 50 machine guns to check their operation at Fire Support Base Nancy.

Bottom left:
Crew members at a fire base four miles south of the DMZ firing a 105-mm howitzer, March 1971.

Below:
A soldier throws a grenade at a Viet Cong bunker as his comrade kneels with his M-16 rifle.

Below right:
American soldiers returning home to the US board a National Airlines aircraft at Bien Hoa Air Terminal in February 1970. From a peak of over 500,000 American troops in Vietnam, most American ground troops had been withdrawn by 1972.

Below:
Three US prisoners released by the North Vietnamese are shown to reporters after their arrival in Vientiane, Laos. The transfer of prisoners was a relatively smooth operation.

Bottom:
An American B–52 bomber pilot captured after his plane had been shot down over North Vietnam is shown to the press in Hanoi.

General Giap, partly due to the ability of the ARVN to recover and counterattack, and partly due to the heavy United States air attack on the highly vulnerable North Vietnamese conventional forces and lines of communication. The March 1975 offensive succeeded primarily because the South Vietnamese lacked the ammunition and gasoline to sustain their resistance at the outset. The other important factor in the collapse of the South was the unique situation in American domestic politics which made it impossible for Nixon to fulfill American commitments to South Vietnam in regard to the Paris cease-fire.

Although the debacle of Vietnam is mainly associated with Johnson and Nixon, it grew out of the policy of six presidents from Harry Truman to Gerald Ford and was endorsed by no less than nine Congresses. Approximately 2.8 million soldiers served in Vietnam out of the approximately 9.4 million Americans called into uniform during that period. American casualties were 47,000 killed in action and 62,000 dead 'from other causes.' As in other wars, the majority of the troops apparently had little notion of why they were there. One veteran wrote to the *Washington Post* in 1978 that 'I never knew what to think of the war, I never knew, even while I was there, whether committing United States forces to Vietnam was the right decision.' The American soldier in Vietnam faced a difficult dilemma in that he was fighting to save a government that was clearly corrupt and unpopular in a land whose people seemed not to appreciate his sacrifice. Often downright hostile, the natives seemed

to feel that defending their country was his own rather than their affair. Once truce negotiations and troop withdrawals began, severe discipline and morale problems appeared as the soldiers were understandably reluctant to die in a no-win war that was almost over. The problem was accentuated when many college and professional school deferments for selective service came to an end in 1970, causing the Army to take in a large number of draftees better educated and more politically aware than their officers in Vietnam.

The American public no less than the American soldier was uncertain about the meaning of the war. A Gallup poll in 1967 reported that half of all Americans had no idea what the war was about while even the Chairman of a Senate Committee can be found at that time inquiring of the Army Chief of Staff just who the enemy was. Yet popular opposition to the war came considerably later than in Korea, possibly because of Johnson's persistent denial that the country was at war but more likely because only after Tet did the war become linked in the public mind with the socio-political issues of the domestic scene. Vietnam gave the radical young and not so young a concrete issue on which to focus their disquiet with the values of American society but it is questionable to what extent any really understood the issues of the war. None appear to have been close enough to the enemy to learn any disillusioning truths and thus compromised their legitimate opposition to the war by becoming vocal partisans of one side. When the war finally ended for all Vietnamese in 1975, the majority of Americans would probably have agreed with the suburbanite who said 'We have seen that war on dinner-time television for years. . . . We don't want to hear about Vietnam anymore. We shouldn't have gotten into Vietnam in the first place. Now, what's happening there is none of our business.'

In retrospect, the problem of Vietnam for Americans may be that the war did not result in a justifying accomplishment. Had South Vietnam survived as an independent country, the huge cost in money, lives, devastation, and domestic discord would have seemed justified by the outcome and the American public probably could have begun to assimilate the Vietnamese experience as they had assimilated the Korean experience a decade before.

Left:
Two of the 3000 South Vietnamese refugees evacuated
from Saigon to the USS *Hancock*, April 1975.

Conclusion

When the first colonists arrived in North America early in the seventeenth century, they carried with them the fundamentals of the European military system and experience. The hostile conditions they immediately encountered began to mold a new military experience and conceptions of requirements for security as they faced the fluid warfare of the Indians. The need to destroy permanently the ability of the elusive enemy to make war made their military goals total victory through a strategy of annihilation. Obsessed with their military vulnerability during the horrors of the seventeenth-century Indian wars, the colonists came to see military security as an absolute value. The subsequent threat presented by the French, Spanish and British was perceived to require the complete elimination of these alien powers from North America to guarantee American security. The colonial and early post-Revolutionary periods were a time of high military threat and physical insecurity, hence the early American conceptions of war and security arose out of crisis and mortal peril. The genesis of the historic American desire for quick and decisive wars through the application of overwhelming force can be traced to these early conceptions.

Thus arose what came to be the typical American belief that national security problems require and are amenable to definitive military solutions. In terms of strategy and tactics, this belief resulted in what Russell Weigley has termed the 'American way of war' in which the objective has been victory defined as the complete destruction of the military capability and will to fight of the enemy rather than the achievement of limited goals or specific gains. The notion of war as other than victory has tended to be alien to the American mind. Americans have seen their wars as total and waged them with corresponding strategies of annihilation.

With the conclusion of its second war with Britain, the United States emerged from an age of insecurity to face no immediate external threat or mortal peril in military terms until the early twentieth century. During this long period of 'free security,' the wars waged were justified not on the grounds of national security but on the universal moral principles on which Americans believed their country was built. War waged with this moral justification must have as its goal the destruction of the enemy threatening the principles. There could be no room for compromise. The exercise of righteous power protected not only national survival but also the survival and existence of the principles which rendered America uniquely successful and blessed with divine favor as a nation. From the time of World War I, Americans began to perceive foreign threats to their security which became added to the principles as a motivating factor in war. The major

American wars of the nineteenth and twentieth centuries have tended to be ideological crusades to defend the Union, to defend the Southern way of life built on slavery, to make the world safe for democracy, to end all wars, or to contain Communism. Even though World War II was not blown up into a moral crusade, Americans clearly understood that their special way of life and values were under attack by the alien ideologies of Fascism and Nazism. Even the minor conflicts such as the Mexican and Spanish-American Wars were partially justified by the Manifest Destiny element in American ideology.

When in the early twentieth century Americans began to perceive the existence of threats to their security in foreign developments, they ended their century-long isolation through their first experiments with an active foreign and military policy. In a radical departure from American tradition, a mass army was committed to a coalition war in Europe in World War I and again in World War II. Since the end of the latter war in 1945, the United States has maintained a large military deployment abroad in the light of perceived security needs and twice has made major military efforts in Asia. The United States has also built an immense standing military establishment supported by an extensive research and development and intelligence apparatus which presently absorbs around 50 percent of the national budget. This recent development is directly counter to the traditional American aversion to the standing military and peacetime military expenditure. It is, however, accepted by the majority of Americans in the face of the military and ideological threat they perceive emanating from the Communist world. This acceptance is certainly consonant with the historic American justification of military activity in terms of physical threat and moral principles.

Americans have also seen a fairly consistent pattern in their wars. Because they have historically tended to agree with Congressman Fisher who said in 1821 that 'the best feature of our government is its unfitness for war,' they have generally been caught unprepared for war. Indeed, military preparedness has long been equated with political tyranny. It was not until Vietnam that Americans were able to undertake war without undue travail. Prior to that time, early adversity, sometimes encompassing invasion or defeat, was followed by perseverance, recovery and final victory. Exceptions here are the Mexican, Spanish-American and First World Wars. The short and totally victorious courses of the first two were highly reinforcing to popular notions of American military prowess while World War I also bred a confidence born of military accomplishment. In the case of Vietnam, the expanded and revamped army of John Kennedy allowed his successor to make a major

military commitment with no prior period of build up. Contemporary circumstances suggest that a future war will allow no time for preparation whether the conflict be minor or major. The military thus attempts to exist in a high state of 'combat readiness.' In this new age of electronic and high technology warfare, the traditional confidence of Americans in their military prowess now rests less on their perception of themselves as skillful warriors and more on their well-founded belief in themselves as the world's best managers and technicians.

Since the industrial revolution of the nineteenth century, there has been a persistent belief in America that a mechanical device could be invented to eliminate bloodshed and personal contact from warfare. Like coal mining or manufacturing, war was a problem that could be solved in terms of 'cost accounting, time and motion studies, and the avoidance of loss due to employee fatalities,' in the words of Peter Aichinger. Yet even small advances in technology such as the rifle and subsequently the machine gun served to lessen the ability of the offense to force a decision from battle with the result that antagonists were forced to adopt strategies of attrition at huge cost. After World War I, air power was probably the major factor returning decision to war. During World War II, it revolutionized strategy and tactics and made possible a warfare more total then ever before as the enemy infrastructure could be bombed into rubble. Air power was a major cause for the advantage returning to the offensive in that war.

From the time of World War I, the trend in battle was toward staggering amounts of firepower expended with a very low kill probability. It has been estimated that 300,000 small arms rounds were necessary to kill a single soldier in World War II. The trend reached its peak in Vietnam where millions of relatively simple and inexpensive bombs and projectiles were fired with an extremely low kill probability. And yet Vietnam also saw the beginning of a new trend in the technology of warfare pioneered by Americans. After years of effort and loss of eighteen planes attempting to destroy the heavily defended Thanh Hoa bridge in Hanoi, a single sortie utilizing a Hobo homing glide bomb succeeded. This weapon was among the first of the new 'smart' or 'precision guided munitions,' using a TV camera to view its target and reaching it via a laser beam. The combination of many small and very sensitive sensors, effective computation, and guidance, and new explosives now means that one or several soldiers can destroy a plane, tank or ship with one shot. Smart weapons fire a few sophisticated and expensive projectiles with a kill probability of between 80 and 90 percent. Such weapons now promise to return to the defense the battlefield advantage heretofore enjoyed by

Above:
The Vietnam War saw the first operational use of the 'precision guided weapons' which are revolutionizing the warfare of the future. This post-strike photograph shows the destruction of the Ninh Binh Railroad and Highway Bridge near Thanh Hoa, North Vietnam, by American guided bombs.

the offense as a result of air power and fire-power. But the advantage may be short-lived as counter-developments are already on the horizon. Their mastery of this kind of technological innovation and development is the strongest military advantage Americans now possess.

The increasing domination of warfare by technology in the twentieth century has been but one of several factors in the changing position of the military in American society. The professional has traditionally lived in isolation and suspicion from the historic American fear of standing armies and traditional belief that regular soldiers existed parasitically on the productive members of society. 'Part of this country's historic schizophrenia toward war and armies . . . is the conviction, often justified, that "joining up" was prima facie evidence of failure in responsible citizenship' Stanley Cooperman has written. 'Before World War I a man became a "regular" soldier – especially an infantry soldier – because there was nothing else he could do, or because he had been involved in legal, economic or social difficulties.' But the advent of the mass army composed of citizen soldiers and citizen officers in World Wars I and II changed that conception of the military. After 1939, even the traditional military garb intended to set the soldier apart was abandoned in favor of

such relatively civilized apparel as the Eisenhower jacket modeled on standard golfing dress while battle dress became a simple variation of the lumberjack shirt.

While the military began to look more like civilians, the changing nature of war and technology has tended to civilize the role of the soldier in some respects. Coalition warfare, global warfare, and high technology warfare require soldiers who are diplomats, managers, engineers, and technocrats as much as they are fighters and commanders. Now requirements for level of knowledge and training and the need for men with primarily scientific training dilute the importance of military ritual and tradition as well as the values and motivations imputed to the professional soldier as large numbers of officers are drawn from the civilian sector through the draft, the ROTC or enlistment. Apart from the requirements of the high level of

technology now involved, this civilianizing tendency probably results from the need of the military to adopt modern management techniques and organization and to liaise closely with industry, other government agencies, and the political organs of the federal government. A further factor is that the problems of warfare have become so complex and challenging as to attract the energies of a substantial group of the country's better intellects in the postwar period. The military has tended to defer on issues of strategy, military policy and even tactics to this primarily civilian group whose best known member is undoubtedly Henry Kissinger.

The job of the soldier is often interchangeable with that of the civilian in this new world of military technology and technicians. By virtue of these factors, then, the military has become more integrated into American society than ever before in American history. Yet the United States has had a professional standing army since 1973, an event unique in American history which has paradoxically served to perpetuate the historic function of the regular military as the repository for the social and economically less viable members of society. Beneath its layer of well-educated and highly specialized officers, the All-Volunteer Army continues to attract a high percentage of recruits whose educational and vocational skills are so limited that they

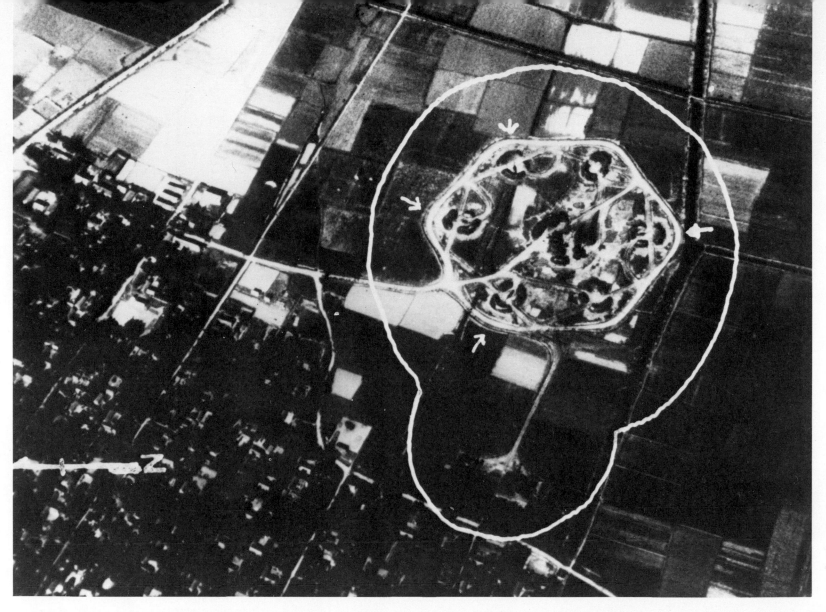

cannot find employment in civilian life. Yet these are the recruits the services need to train to run the complex equipment of modern warfare.

An important part of the historic American legend of success and victory has been the martial tradition. The belief in divine favor has been consistently reinforced by the course of military events. The Mexican and Spanish-American Wars have been important in this respect because of their unbroken sequences of often spectacular victories at low cost were easily interpreted as divine blessing for the endeavors. The two most significant wars from this point of view have been the Civil War and World War II, the two greatest military challenges America has yet faced. Doubting their special state of grace at the outset, Americans of both sides saw the Civil War as a regenerative national experience whose outcome allowed even the defeated to retain their belief in their uniqueness as Americans. World War II was proof on an even greater scale as Americans achieved the crushing defeat of all their enemies through a monumental military and economic effort. The supreme position of American political, military, and economic power at the end of the war was proof positive that the American mission was to extend the American way to the rest of mankind. The special mission of the United States was to

protect and help rebuild the war-ravaged and the threatened. This is the ideological impulse which made the Korean and Vietnamese endeavors initially acceptable to the American public. Popular opposition to the Korean War mounted when the static military situation and ambiguous political goals of the United Nations made it difficult for Americans to see visible signs of divine favor to legitimize their participation in the war.

Vietnam was a more complex example of the same phenomenon. Opposition originally grew in the intellectual and religious communities which saw the contradiction between the high technology destruction being visited upon South Vietnam and the professed American mission of bringing protection and a better life to the South Vietnamese people. The nature of counterguerrilla war and the relatively small and indecisive scale of the military operations

made it difficult for Americans to discern any visible indications of divine approval. Indeed, the lack of military progress, the perceived disaster of Tet, the discord caused by the war at home and abroad, and its seemingly deleterious effect on the integrity of American governmental institutions seemed to point in the opposite direction. For the first time in American history, there occurred a serious questioning of the nature of the historic American sense of destiny and mission and their relation to the American military as military events failed to reinforce Americans in their beliefs. As Morris Dickstein has written, 'In Vietnam we lost not only a war and subcontinent, we also lost our pervasive confidence that American arms and American aims were linked somehow to justice and morality, not merely to the quest for power. America was defeated militarily, but the "idea" of America, the cherished myth of America, received an even more shattering blow.' Vietnam was certainly not the first time Americans had questioned their special state of grace and all that flowed from it, but Vietnam was the first time military events did not reaffirm Americans in their historic beliefs in divine favor and associated military prowess. It remains to be seen whether Americans will rationalize their first defeat in war or begin to alter the belief structure of almost two centuries.

Index

Numbers in *italic* indicate illustrations